Advanced C++ Metaprogramming

Revised on 2011-05-15

I hope Tibet will find this book
As interesting as all the others he reads

Template meta-programming and expression templates are not techniques for novice programmers, but an advanced practitioner can use them to good effect

Technical Report on C++ Performance, ISO/IEC TR 18015:2006(E)

Nothing described in this report involves magic

Technical Report on C++ Performance, ISO/IEC TR 18015:2006(E)

People should not be asked to do things "just because we say so."
At least we can try to explain the reasons behind the rules.

An Interview with Bjarne Stroustrup - Dr. Dobb's Journal

1. Preface

Template Metaprogramming, TMP from here on, is a new way of using C++:
* *it has a scope: a known set of problems where it proves useful*
* *it has a philosophy: a peculiar way of thinking about problems*
* *it has a language: idioms and patterns.*

This book, according to the 80-20 law, aims to be an introduction to the first 20% of metaprogramming - philosophy, scope and language - that can improve 80% of daily activities.
All chapters will be driven by some simple ideas:
* *With modern compilers, most practical benefits come from simple techniques, if correctly applied.*
* *TMP indeed produces better software; "better" is simply a placeholder for faster, safer, more maintainable, more expressive or a convex combination of these features.*
* *State-of-the-art TMP libraries usually offer a huge set of features and unfortunately, documentation is either too large or too small; while reuse is a long-term winning strategy, mastering the basic principles may suffice*
* *Getting gradually accustomed to elementary techniques, the reader will develop a deeper comprehension of the problems and eventually, if necessary, look for more advanced tools.*

The reader is assumed at ease with classic C++ programming, including STL concepts and conventions.
A systematic study of TMP exceeds the capacity (in C++ sense) of any single book. For a comprehensive and robust training, the interested reader may wish to see the bibliography.

1.1. Source code

This book is not focused on results, but on the path, the steps and motivations that lead to an implementation.
Many examples derive from production code: however, in a book, problems must look as easy and evident as possible, sometimes even more; in practice, they are never.
So for illustration purposes, source code is unquestionably sub-optimal and oversimplified.
Oversimplification means partial or full omission of implementation details, special cases, namespaces, system headers, compiler bugs... The most advanced programming technique is hardly an advantage if it crashes the company official compiler.

In short, these details are important, as they make the difference between a curious prototype and a useful implementation.
In addition, code has been streamlined to satisfy visual constraints, in particular: indentation is systematically inconsistent, some function bodies have been removed, names may be shorter than necessary and macros have been introduced for the sole purpose of shortening the text.
Readers are asked to be patient and review section 1.3 below.

Finally, we admit results are rarely supported with experimental data: TMP techniques give a compiler the opportunity to create optimized code, and as a rule, we don't verify it is indeed the case.

The C++ Standard is being updated with lots of new features. The first edition of the document in 1998 had less than 800 pages. A 200-page Technical Report was published in 2003 and revised in 2006, and in March 2010 the Committee released the FCD, a milestone draft more than 1300 pages long.
Even if the FCD is not official, most of the improvements will be confirmed; some of the new language additions have already been implemented in compilers.
In this book we will deal with a very small part of "C++0x", as the new Standard is called; more precisely, we'll discuss what has a serious impact on TMP code and is also available in the major compilers.

1.2. Book structure

Chapters are divided in three parts, and the reader should not arbitrarily skip sections. Each chapter starts with its own rationale, or a summary of the motivations of the previous arguments.
The first part deals with the basics, and in particular chapter 3 is a prerequisite for most of the source code contained in the book; it contains a description of the basic class templates that will be constantly and silently reused without further comments.
In the second part, we develop some techniques for writing software, in an approximate order of increasing complexity.
The third part contains some practical advice for real world issues, so it has been pretentiously labeled "applications".

We will refer to some compilers with an abbreviation, followed by a version number: MSVC for Microsoft Visual C++ and GCC for GNU G++.
From time to time, we show the output of a compiler, without mentioning explicitly which, to emphasize what a "generic" compiler would emit.

This is a note: the page below contains a sample of the typographic conventions in use in the rest of the book.

```
filename.cpp
this->is(source*code);
```

```
this is the resulting compiler output.
```

```
The same format denotes also an algorithm description in pseudo-code
```

```
int i = [[double square brackets denote
          a piece of pseudo-code inside valid code]];
```

Odd for a book that puts emphasis on readability, fragments of source code have no syntax highlighting, so they will look scarier than they actually are.

1.3. Errata

This book obviously contains plenty of errors, for which the author himself is entirely responsible. Readers are encouraged to send their feedback to psion.s5@gmail.com *and as a reward for cooperation and debugging, they will receive an updated electronic copy of the book.*

1.4. Acknowledgements

Learning C++ is a process that never ends: as someone wrote, C++ is the only language whose features get discovered, as through an unexplored land.
While a book may be the work of a single person, discovery always comes from teamwork.
The author would like to thank all the teams that made possible his journey through C++, they all had something to teach, and their contributions - direct or indirect - led to this book: his family, Carla, Alberto, Tibet and Asia; the people at Logikos, especially Max; the Natam core team: Alberto L., Alberto T., Bibo, Fabio, Graziano, Marco, Roberto, Rocco; the friends at Brainpower, in particular Alberto, Andrea, Davide, Fabio, Giacomo, Giancarlo, Luca, Marco D., Marco M., Matteo, Paolo, Pino, Vincenzo, and all the others.

Many Googlers kindly reviewed the draft and actively provided lots of suggestions, fixes, constructive criticism, exercises, or simply appreciation.

A very special thank goes to Attilio Meucci, who proved that writing a book is not impossible, and it's always worthwhile.

#include <prerequisites>

#include <techniques>

#include <applications>

2. Templates

"C++ supports a variety of styles"
Bjarne Stroustrup, A Perspective on ISO C++

Programming may be thought as teaching something to a computer, talking to the machine in one of the common languages. The closer to the machine idiom we go, the less natural will be the words.
Each language carries its own expressive power: for any given concept, there is a language where its description is simpler, or more concise, or more detailed.
In Assembler we have to give an extremely rich and precise description for any (possibly simple) algorithm, and this makes it very hard to read back.
On the opposite, the beauty of C++ is that, while being close enough to the machine, the language carries enough instruments to enrich itself.
C++ allows expressing the same concept with different ***styles*** and good C++ looks more natural.

First we are going to see the connection between templates and style, and then we will dig into the details of the C++ template system.

Given the C++ fragment:

```
double x = sq(3.14);
```

Can we guess what is `sq`? It could be at least
A macro:

```
#define sq(x) ((x)*(x))
```

A function:

```
double sq(double x)
{
   return x*x;
}
```

A function template:

```
template <typename scalar_t>
inline scalar_t sq(const scalar_t& x)
{
   return x*x;
}
```

A type (i.e. an unnamed instance of a class that decays to a double)

```
class sq
{
   double s_;

public:

   sq(double x)
   : s_(x*x)
   {}

   operator double() const
   { return s_; }
};
```

A global object:

```
class sq_t
{
public:
   typedef double value_type;

   value_type operator()(double x) const
   {
      return x*x;
   }
};
```

```
const sq_t sq = sq_t();
```

Regardless of how it's implemented, most humans will guess what `sq(3.14)` does, just looking at it; but *visual equivalence* does not imply *interchangeableness*: if `sq` is a class, for example, passing a square to a function template will trigger an unexpected argument deduction:

```
template <typename T> void f(T x);
```

```
f(cos(3.14)); // instantiates f<double>
f(sq(3.14));  // instantiates f<sq>... counterintuitive?
```

Furthermore, we expect every possible numeric type to be squared as efficiently as possible; but implementations may perform differently in different situations:

```
std::transform(begin, end, begin, sq);
```

If we need to transform a sequence, most compilers will get a performance boost from the last implementation (and an error if `sq` is a macro).

The purpose of TMP is to write code:

- visually clear to human users, so that nobody will need to look underneath.
- efficient in most/all situations, from the point of view of the compiler
- self-adapting to the rest of the program[1]

Self-adapting means both "portable", i.e. independent of any particular compiler, but also "not imposing constraints"; an implementation of `sq` that requires its argument to derive from some abstract base class, would not qualify as self-adapting.

The true power of C++ templates is ***style***.

```
double x1 = (-b + sqrt(b*b-4*a*c))/(2*a);
double x2 = (-b + sqrt(sq(b)-4*a*c))/(2*a);
```

All template argument computation and deductions are performed at compile time, so they impose no runtime overhead; if the function `sq` is properly written, line 2 is at least as efficient as line 1, and easier to read at the same time.
Using `sq` is elegant:

- it makes code readable or self-evident
- it carries no speed penalty
- it lets the program open to future optimizations

In fact, after the concept of squaring has been isolated from plain multiplication, specializations are easily plugged in:

```
template <typename scalar_t>
inline scalar_t sq(const scalar_t& x)
{
   return x*x;
}

template <>
inline double sq(const double& x)
{
   // here, use any special algorithm you have!
}
```

2.1. C++ templates

The C++ language admits two types of templates, ***function templates*** and ***class templates***:

[1] Loosely speaking, that's the reason for the prefix "meta" in "metaprogramming"

```
template <typename scalar_t>
scalar_t sq(const scalar_t& x)
{
   return x*x;
}
```

```
template
<
   typename scalar_t,                     // type parameter
   bool EXTRA_PRECISION = false,          // bool parameter with default value
   typename promotion_t = scalar_t        // type parameter with default value
>
class sum
{
public:

   // ...

};
```

Remarking that they are totally different, the most important issue from the TMP viewpoint is that:

- Class templates can perform computations at compile time
- Function templates can auto-deduce their parameters from arguments

Both kinds of template entities start declaring a *parameter list* in angle brackets; parameters may include *types* (declared with the keyword `typename` or `class`), and non-types: integers and pointers.[2]

Note that, when the parameter list is long, or simply when we want to comment each parameter separately, we may want to indent it as if it was a block of code within curly brackets.

Parameters can in fact have a default value:

```
template
<
   typename scalar_t,                     // type parameter
   bool EXTRA_PRECISION = false,          // bool parameter with default value
   typename promotion_t = scalar_t        // type parameter with default value
>
class sum;

sum<double> S1;                           // template argument is 'double'
sum<double, true> S2;
```

[2] Usually any integer type is accepted, including named/anonymous `enum`, `bool`, typedefs (like `ptrdiff_t` and `size_t`) and even compiler-specific types (for example, `__int64` in MSVC). Pointers to member/global functions are allowed with no restriction; a pointer to a variable (having external linkage) is legal, but it cannot be dereferenced, so this has very limited use in practice.

A template can be seen as a metafunction that maps a tuple of parameters to a function or a class; for example, the square template

```
template <typename scalar_t>
scalar_t sq(const scalar_t& x)
```

maps a type T to a function:

`T → T (*)(const T&)`

In other words, `sq<double>` is a function with signature `double (*)(const double&)`.
Note that `double` is the value of the parameter `scalar_t`.
The class template

```
template <typename char_t = char>
class basic_string;
```

maps a type T to a class:

`T → basic_string<T>`

With classes, *explicit specialization* can limit the domain of the metafunction: we have a general template, then some specializations; each of these may or may not have a body.

```
// the following template can be instantiated
// only on char and wchar_t

template <typename char_t = char>
class basic_string;
// note: no body

template < >
class basic_string<char>
{ ... };

template < >
class basic_string<wchar_t>
{ ... };
```

`char_t` and `scalar_t` above are called ***template parameters*** and when `basic_string<char>` and `sq<double>` are used, `char` and `double` are called ***template arguments***, even if there may be some confusion between `double` (the template argument of `sq`) and `x` (the argument of the function `sq<double>`).
When we supply template arguments (both types and non-types) to the template, seen as a metafunction, the template is *instantiated*, so if necessary the compiler produces machine code for it.

Note that different arguments yield different instances, even when instances themselves are identical: `sq<double>` and `sq<const double>` are two unrelated functions.[3]

When using function templates, the compiler will usually figure out the parameters, we say that an argument *binds* to a template parameter.

```
template <typename scalar_t>
scalar_t sq(const scalar_t& x);

double pi = 3.14;
sq(pi);                    // the compiler "binds" double to scalar_t
```

```
double x = sq(3.14);       // ok: do *not* explicitly write sq<double>(3.14)
```

All template arguments must be compile-time constants.

- type parameters will accept everything which is known to be a type (see also page 16)
- non-type parameters work according to most automatic casting/promotion rule[4]

Here are some typical errors:

```
template <int N>
class SomeClass
{
};

int main()
{
   int A = rand();
   SomeClass<A> s;       // error: A is not a compile time constant
}
```

```
   const int A = rand();
   SomeClass<A> s;       // error: A is not a compile time constant
```

The best syntax for a compile-time constant is `static const [[integer type]] name = value;`

```
   static const int A = 2;
   SomeClass<A> s;
```

[3] The linker may eventually collapse them, as they will likely produce identical machine code, but from a language perspective they are different.

[4] An exception being that literal 0 may not be a valid pointer

The static prefix could be omitted if the constant is local, in the body of a function, as above; however it's usually harmless and clear (you can find all the compile time constants in a project searching for "static const", rather than "const" alone).[5]

The arguments passed to the template can be the result of a (compile-time) computation: every valid integer operation can be evaluated on compile-time constants:

- division by 0 causes a compiler error;
- function calls are forbidden;[6]
- you cannot (portably) produce an intermediate object of non-integer/non-pointer type, except inside `sizeof`: `(int)(N*1.2)` is illegal, instead use `(N+N/5)`. `static_cast<void*>(0)` is fine too.[7]

```
SomeClass<(27+56*5) % 4> s1;
SomeClass<sizeof(void*)*CHAR_BIT> s1;
```

Division by zero will cause a compiler error only if the computation is entirely static: to perceive the difference, note that this program compiles (but it won't run).

```
template <int N>
struct tricky
{
   int f(int i = 0)
   {
      return i/N;              // i/N is not a constant
   }
};

int main()
{
   tricky<0> t;
   return t.f();
}
```

```
test.cpp(5) : warning C4723: potential divide by 0
```

On the opposite, compare with:

```
   int f()
   {
      return N/N;              // N/N is a constant
   }
```

[5] See also section 2.3.5 and 12.2.2 for a more complete discussion

[6] This will likely change in the next C++ standard. See the note on page 40

[7] You can cast a floating point literal to integer, so strictly speaking `(int)(1.2)` is allowed. Modern compilers, such as MSVC9, are not rigorous in this rule.

```
test.cpp(5) : error C2124: divide or mod by zero
        .\test.cpp(5) : while compiling class template member function 'int tricky<N>::f(void)'
        with
        [
            N=0
        ]
```

And with:

```
tricky<0/0> t;
```

```
test.cpp(12) : error C2975: 'N' : invalid template argument for 'tricky', expected compile-time
constant expression
```

More precisely, compile-time constants can be:

- integer literals, e.g. `27`, `CHAR_BIT` and `0x05`
- `sizeof` and similar non-standard language operators with integer result (for example, `__alignof__` where present)
- non-type template parameters (in the context of an "outer" template)

```
template <int N>
class AnotherClass
{
   SomeClass<N> myMember_;
};
```

- static constants of integer type

```
template <int N, int K>
struct MyTemplate
{
   static const int PRODUCT = N*K;
};

SomeClass< MyTemplate<10,12>::PRODUCT > s1;
```

- some standard macros, such as `__LINE__` (there is actually some degree of freedom: as a rule they are constants with type `long`, except in implementation-dependent "edit and continue" debug builds, where the compiler must use references)

```
   SomeClass<__LINE__> s1;   // usually works…
```

The use of __LINE__ as a parameter in practice occurs rarely; it's popular in automatic type enumerations (see section 8.6) and in some implementation of custom assertions.

A parameter can depend on a previous parameter:

```
template
<
   typename T,
   int (*FUNC)(T)      // pointer to function taking T and returning int
>
class X
{
};
```

```
template
<
   typename T,         // here the compiler learns that 'T' is a type
   T VALUE             // may be ok or not… the compiler assumes the best
>
class Y
{
};

Y<int, 7> y1;           // fine
Y<double, 3> y2;        // error: the constant '3' cannot have type 'double'
```

Classes (and class templates) may also have ***template member functions***:

```
// normal class with template member function

struct mathematics
{
   template <typename scalar_t>
      scalar_t sq(scalar_t x) const
   {
      return x*x;
   }
};
```

```
// class template with template member function

template <typename scalar_t>
struct more_mathematics
{
   template <typename other_t>[8]
      static scalar_t product(scalar_t x, other_t y)
   {
      return x*y;
   }
};
```

2.1.1. Typename

The keyword ***typename*** is used:

[8] We have to choose a different name, to avoid shadowing the outer template parameter `scalar_t`

- As a synonym of class, when declaring a type template parameter
- Whenever it's not evident to the compiler that an identifier is a type name

For an example of "not evident", think about `MyClass<T>::Y` in the following fragment:

```
template <typename T>
struct MyClass
{
   typedef double Y;
};

template < >
struct MyClass<int>
{
   static const int Y = 314;
};
```

```
int Q = 8;

template <typename T>
void SomeFunc()
{
   MyClass<T>::Y * Q; // what is this line? it may be:
                      // (a) declaration of local pointer-to-double named Q;
                      // (b) product 314*(global variable Q)
};
```

`Y` is a ***dependent name***, since its meaning depends on X, which is an unknown parameter.
Everything that depends directly or indirectly on unknown template parameters is a dependent name. If a dependent name refers to a type, then it must be introduced with the `typename` keyword.

```
template <typename X>
class AnotherClass
{
   MyClass<X>::Type t1_;              // error: 'Type' is a dependent name
   typename MyClass<X>::Type t2_;     // ok

   MyClass<double>::Type t3_;         // ok: 'Type' is independent of X
};
```

Note that `typename` is required in the first case and forbidden in the last:

```
template <typename X>
class AnotherClass
{
   typename MyClass<X>::Y member1_;      // ok.
                                         // if X is 'int' it won't compile

   typename MyClass<double>::Y member2_; // error
};
```

`typename` may introduce a dependent type when declaring a... non-type template parameter:

```
template <typename T, typename T::type N>
struct SomeClass
{
};

struct S1
{
   typedef int type;
};

SomeClass<S1, 3> x;   // ok: N=3 has type 'int'
```

As a curiosity, the classic C++ standard specifies that if the syntax "`typename T1::T2`" yields a non-type during instantiation, then the program is ill-formed. However, it doesn't specify the converse: if "`T1::T2`" has a valid meaning as a non-type, then it could be re-interpreted later as a type, if necessary. For example:

```
template <typename T>
struct B
{
   static const int N = sizeof(A<T>::X); // note 'typename' missing here
};
```

Until instantiation, B "thinks" it's going to call `sizeof` on a non-type; in particular, `sizeof` is a valid operator on non-types, so the code is legal. However X could later resolve to a type, and the code would be legal anyway, e.g.:

```
template <typename T>
struct A
{
   static const int X = 7;
};

template <>
struct A<char>
{
   typedef double X;
};
```

Although the intent of `typename` is to forbid all such ambiguities, it may not cover all corner cases.[9]

2.1.2. Angle brackets

Even if all parameters have a default value, we cannot omit entirely the angle brackets:

---

[9] See also http://www.open-std.org/jtc1/sc22/wg21/docs/cwg_defects.html#666

```
template <typename T = double>
class sum;

sum<> S1;      // ok, using double
sum S2;        // error
```

Template parameters may carry different meanings:

- sometimes they are really meant to be generic, e.g. `std::vector<T>` or `std::set<T>`; there may be some conceptual assumptions on T - say constructible, comparable... - that do not compromise the generality
- sometimes instead parameters are assumed to belong to a fixed set; in this case the class template is simply the common implementation for two or more similar classes.[10]

In the latter case, we may feel like angle brackets should be omitted: either derive from a template base or just typedef:[11]

```
template <typename char_t = char>
class basic_string;

class my_string : public basic_string<>
{
   // empty or minimal body
   // note: no virtual destructor!
};

typedef basic_string<> your_string;
```

A popular compiler extension, which became official in C++0x, is that two or more adjacent "close angle brackets" will be parsed as "end of template", not as an "extraction operator": anyway, it's good practice to put extra spaces:

```
std::vector<std::list<double>> v1;
//                          ^^
// may be parsed as "operator>>"

std::vector<std::list<double> > v2;
//                          ^^^
// always ok
```

[10] Even if it's not a correct example, an open-minded reader may want to consider the relation between `std::string`, `std::wstring` and `std::basic_string<T>`,

[11] Cfr. 2.4.9

2.1.3. Universal constructors

Template copy constructor and assignment are not called when dealing with two objects of the very same kind:

```
template <typename T>
class something
{
public:

   // not called when S == T

   template <typename S>
   something(const something<S>& that)
   {
   }

   // not called when S == T

   template <typename S>
   something& operator=(const something<S>& that)
   {
      return *this;
   }
};
```

```
   something<int> s0;
   something<double> s1, s2;

   s0 = s1;    // calls user defined operator=
   s1 = s2;    // calls the compiler generated assignment
```

The user-defined template members are sometimes called ***universal copy constructor*** and ***universal assignment***. Note that universal operators take `something<X>`, not X.

The C++ Standard 12.8 says:

- "Because a template constructor is never a copy constructor, the presence of such a template does not suppress the implicit declaration of a copy constructor"
- "Template constructors participate in overload resolution with other constructors, including copy constructors, and a template constructor may be used to copy an object if it provides a better match than other constructors"

In fact, too generic template operators in base classes can introduce bugs, as this example shows:

```
struct base
{
   base()
   {
   }

   template <typename T>
   base(T x)
   {
   }
};

struct derived : base
{
   derived()
   {
   }

   derived(const derived& that)
      : base(that)
   {
   }
};
```

```
   derived d1;
   derived d2 = d1;
```

The assignment `d2 = d1` causes a stack overflow.

An implicit copy constructor must invoke the copy constructor of the base class, so by 12.8 above it can never call the universal constructor: had the compiler generated a copy constructor for `derived`, then it would have called `base` copy constructor (which is implicit); unfortunately a copy constructor for `derived` is given, and it contains an explicit function call, namely `base(that)`. Hence following the usual overload resolution rules, it matches the universal constructor with `T=derived`; since this function takes x by value, it needs to perform a copy of `that`, and hence the call is recursive.

2.1.4. Function types and function pointers

Mind the difference between a function type and a pointer-to-function type:

```
template <double F(int)>
struct A
{
};

template <double (*F)(int)>
struct B
{
};
```

They are mostly equivalent:

```
double f(int)
{
   return 3.14;
}
```

```
   A<f> t1;    // ok
   B<f> t2;    // ok
```

Usually a function decays to a function pointer, exactly as an array decays to a pointer.
But a function type cannot be constructed, so it will cause failures in code that looks harmless:

```
template <typename T>
struct X
{
   T member_;

   X(T value)
   : member_(value)
   {
   }
};
```

```
X<double (int)> t1(f);          // error: cannot construct 'member_'
X<double (*)(int)> t2(f);       // ok: 'member_' is a pointer
```

This problem is mostly evident in functions that return a functor (the reader can think about `std::not1` or see chapter 5.3.4); in C++ function templates that get parameters by reference prevent the decay:

```
template <typename T>
X<T> identify_by_val(T x)
{
   return X<T>(x);
}

template <typename T>
X<T> identify_by_ref(const T& x)
{
   return X<T>(x);
}
```

```
double f(int)
{
   return 3.14;
}
```

```
identify_by_val(f);   // function decays to pointer-to-function:
                      // the template is instantiated with T = double (*)(int)

identify_by_ref(f);   // no decay:
                      // the template is instantiated with T = double (int)
```

For what concerns pointers, function templates with explicit parameters behave like ordinary functions:

```
double f(double x)
{
   return x+1;
}

template <typename T>
T g(T x)
{
   return x+1;
}
```

```
typedef double (*FUNC_T)(double);

FUNC_T f1 = f;
FUNC_T f2 = g<double>;
```

However if they are member of class templates and their context depends on a yet unspecified parameter, they require an extra `template` keyword before their name:[12]

```
template <typename X>
struct outer
{
   template <typename T>
   static T g(T x)
   {
      return x+1;
   }
};

template <typename X>
void do_it()
{
   FUNC_T f1 = outer<X>::g<double>;              // error!
   FUNC_T f2 = outer<X>::template g<double>;     // correct
}
```

Both `typename` and `template` are required for inner template classes:

[12] Compare with the usage of typename described in paragraph 2.1.1

```
template <typename X>
struct outer
{
   template <typename T>
   struct inner {};
};

template <typename X>
void do_it()
{
   typename outer<X>::template inner<double> I;
}
```

Some compilers are not rigorous at this.

2.1.5. Non-template base class

If a class template has members that do not depend on its parameters, it may be convenient to move them to a plain class:

```
template <typename T>
class MyClass
{
   double value_;
   std::string name_;
   std::vector<T> data_;

public:
   std::string getName() const
   {
```

Should become:

```
class MyBaseClass
{
protected:
   ~MyBaseClass() {}

   double value_;
   std::string name_;

public:

   std::string getName() const
   {
```

```
template <typename T>
class MyClass : MyBaseClass
{
   std::vector<T> data_;

public:

   using MyBaseClass::getName;
```

The derivation may be public, private or even protected.[13]
This will reduce the compilation complexity and the size of binary code.
Of course, this optimization is most effective if the template is instantiated many times.

2.1.6. Template position

The body of a class/function template must be available to the compiler at every point of instantiation, so the usual header/cpp file separation does not hold, and everything is packaged in a single file, with extension hpp.
If only a declaration is available, the compiler will use it, but the linker will return errors:

```
sq.h

template <typename T>
T sq(const T& x);
```

```
sq.cpp

template <typename T>
T sq(const T& x)
{
   return x*x;
}
```

```
main.cpp

#include "sq.h"                // note: function body not visible

int main()
{
   double x = sq(3.14);       // compiles but does not link
```

A separate header file is useful if we want to publish only some instantiations of the template; for example, the author of `sq` might want to distribute binary files with the code for `sq<int>` and `sq<double>`, so that they are the only valid types.
In C++ it's possible to explicitly force the instantiation of a template entity in a translation unit without ever using it. This is accomplished with the special syntax:

```
template class X<double>;
```

```
template double sq<double>(const double&);
```

[13] Cfr. the "brittle base class problem" mentioned by Bjarne Stroustrup in his "C++ Style and Technique FAQ", http://www.research.att.com/~bs/

Adding the line above to sq.cpp will "export" `sq<double>`, as if it were an ordinary function, and the plain inclusion of sq.h will suffice to build the program.
This feature is often used with algorithm tags: suppose we have a function template, say `encrypt` or `compress`, whose algorithmic details must be kept confidential, and template parameter T represents an option from a small set (say `T=fast, normal, best`); obviously, users of the algorithm are not supposed to add their own options, so we may force the instantiation of a small number of instances, `encrypt<fast>`, `encrypt<normal>` and `encrypt<best>` and distribute just an header and a binary file.

> A feature of the upcoming C++ standard that is already available in most compilers is the external instantiation of templates: if the keyword `extern` is used before `template`, the compiler will skip instantiation and the linker will borrow the template body from another translation unit.
>
> This will appear in the next C++ standard (around paragraph 14.7.2).

See also section 2.6.1 below.

2.2. Specialization and argument deduction

By definition, we say that a name is *at namespace level*, at *class level* or *at body level*, if the name appears between the curly brackets of a namespace, class or function body, as the following example shows:

```
class X                           // here, X is at namespace level
{
public:

   typedef double value_type;     // value_type is at class level

   X(const X& y)                  // both X and y are at class level
   {
   }

   void f()                       // f is at class level
   {
      int z = 0;                  //   body level
      struct LOCAL {};            //   LOCAL is a local class
   }
};
```

Function templates – member or non-member – can automatically deduce the template argument looking at their argument list: roughly speaking[14], the compiler will pick the most specialized function that matches the arguments; an exact match, if feasible, is always preferred, but a conversion can occur.

[14] The exact rules are documented and explained in [2]. The reader is invited to refer to this book for a detailed explanation of what's summarized here in a few paragraphs.

A function F is more specialized than G if we can replace any call to F with a call to G (on the same arguments), but not vice versa. In addition, a non-template function is considered more specialized than a template with the same name.

Sometimes *overload* and *specialization* look very similar:

```
template <typename scalar_t>
inline scalar_t sq(const scalar_t& x);    // (1) function template

inline double sq(const double& x);        // (2) overload

template <>
inline int sq(const int& x);              // (3) specialization of 1
```

But they are not identical; consider the following counterexample:

```
inline double sq(float x);                // ok, overloaded sq may
                                          // have different signature

template <>                               // error: invalid specialization
inline int sq(const int x);               // it must have the same signature
```

The basic difference between overload and specialization is that a function template acts as a single entity, regardless of how many specializations it has. For example, the call `sq(y)` just after (3) would force the compiler to select between entities (1) and (2). If y is `double`, then (2) is preferred, because it's a normal function, otherwise (1) is instantiated on the type of y: only at this point, if y happens to be `int`, the compiler notices that `sq` has a specialization and picks (3).

Note that two different templates may overload:

```
template <typename T>
void f(const T& x)
{
   std::cout << "I am f(reference)";
}

template <typename T>
void f(const T* x)
{
   std::cout << "I am f(pointer)";
}
```

Remember that template specialization is legal only at namespace level (even if most compilers will tolerate it anyway):

```
class mathematics
{
   template <typename scalar_t>
   inline scalar_t sq(const scalar_t& x);      // template member function

   template <>
   inline int sq(const int& x);                // illegal specialization!
};
```

The standard way is to call a global function template from inside the class:

```
template <typename scalar_t>
inline scalar_t gsq(const scalar_t& x);     // global function template…
outside

template <>
inline int gsq(const int& x);               // specialization… outside

class mathematics
{
   template <typename scalar_t>
   inline scalar_t sq(const scalar_t& x)    // template member function
   {
      return gsq(x);
   }
};
```

Sometimes we may need to specify explicitly the template parameters, because they are unrelated to function arguments (in fact they are called *non-deducible*):

```
class crc32 {  … };
class adler { … };

template <typename algorithm_t>
size_t hash_using(const char* x)
{
   // …
}

size_t j = hash_using<crc32>("this is the string to be hashed");
```

In this case, we put non-deducible types and arguments first, so the compiler can work out all the remaining:

```
template <typename algorithm_t, typename string_t>
int hash_using(const string_t& x);

std::string arg("hash me, please");
int j = hash_using<crc32>(arg);          // ok: algorithm_t is crc32
                                         // and string_t is std::string
```

Argument deduction obviously holds only for function templates, not class templates.

It's generally a bad idea to supply argument explicitly, instead of relying on deduction, except in some special cases.

- when necessary for disambiguation:

```
template <typename T>
T max(const T& a, const T& b)
{ ... }
```

```
int a = 7;
long b = 6;

long m1 = max(a, b);            // error: ambiguous, T can be 'int' or 'long'
long m2 = max<long>(a, b);      // ok: T is 'long'
```

- when a type is non-deducible:[15]

```
template <typename T>
T get_random()
{ ... }
```

```
double r = get_random<double>();
```

- when we want a function template to look similar to a built-in C++ cast operator:

```
template <typename X, typename T>
X sabotage_cast(T* p)
{
    return reinterpret_cast<X>(p+1);
}
```

```
std::string s = "don't try this at home";
double* p = sabotage_cast<double*>(&s);
```

- to perform simultaneously a cast and a function template invocation:

```
double y = sq<int>(6.28)    // casts 6.28 to int, then squares
```

- when an algorithm has an argument, whose default value is template-dependent (usually a functor)[16]

[15] See also the next section.
[16] This example is taken from [2]

```
template <typename LESS_T>
void nonstd_sort (..., LESS_T cmp = LESS_T())
{
   // ...
}

// call function with functor passed as template argument
nonstd_sort< std::less<...> > (...);

// call function with functor passed as value argument
nonstd_sort (..., std::less<...>());
```

A template name (e.g. `std::vector`) is different from the name of the class it generates (e.g. `std::vector<int>`); only at class level, they are equivalent:

```
template <typename T>
class something
{
   public:

      something()                // ok: don't write something<T>
      {
         // at local level, 'something' alone is illegal
      }

      something(const something& that);       // ok: 'something&' stands for
                                              // 'something<T>&'

      template <typename other_t>
      something(const something<other_t>& that)
      {
      }
};
```

As a rule, the word `something` alone, without angle brackets, represents a template, which is a well-defined entity of its own: in C++ there exist in fact ***template-template parameters***:

```
template <template <typename T> class X>
class example
{
   X<int> x1_;
   X<double> x2_;
};

typedef example<something> some_example;        // ok: 'something' matches
```

Note that `class` and `typename` are not equivalent here:

```
template <template <typename T> typename X>     // error
```

Class templates can be fully or partially ***specialized***: after the general template, we list specialized versions

```
template <typename T>
struct is_a_pointer_type
{
   static const int value = 1;    // in general T is not a pointer type
};

template <>
struct is_a_pointer_type<void*>
{
   static const int value = 2;    // 2: full specialization for void*
};

template <typename X>
struct is_a_pointer_type<X*>
{
   static const int value = 3;    // 3: partial specialization for all
pointers
};
```

```
int b1 = is_a_pointer_type<int*>::value;      // uses 3 with X=int
int b2 = is_a_pointer_type<void*>::value;     // uses 2
int b3 = is_a_pointer_type<float>::value;     // uses the general template
```

Partial specialization can be recursive:

```
template <typename X>
struct is_a_pointer_type<const X>
{
   static const int value = is_a_pointer_type<X>::value;
 };
```

The following example is known as ***the pointer paradox***:

```
#include <iostream>


template <typename T>
void f(const T& x)
{
   std::cout << "My arg is a reference";
}

template <typename T>
void f(const T* x)
{
   std::cout << " My arg is a pointer";
}
```

In fact, the following code:

```
const char* s = "text";
f(s);
f(3.14);
```

prints as expected:

```
My arg is a pointer
My arg is a reference
```

Now write instead:

```
    double p = 0;
    f(&p);
```

We would expect to read `pointer`, instead we get a call to the *first* overload: the compiler is correct, since type `double*` matches `const T*` with one trivial implicit conversion (namely, adding const-ness), but it matches `const T&` perfectly, setting `T=double*`.

2.2.1. Deduction

Function templates can deduce their parameters, matching argument types with their signature:

```
template <typename T>
struct arg;

template <typename T>
void f(arg<T>);

template <typename X>
void g(arg<const X>);
```

```
arg<int*> a;
f(a);             // will deduce T = int*

arg<const int> b;
f(b);             // will deduce T = const int
g(b);             // will deduce X = int
```

On the opposite, if a type is contained in a class template, then its context (i.e. the parameters of the outer class) cannot be deduced:

```
template <typename T>
void f(typename std::vector<T>::iterator);

std::vector<double> v;
f(v.begin());                // error: cannot deduce T
```

Note that the above error does *not* depend on the particular invocation: this kind of deduction is logically not possible: T may not be unique.

```
template <typename T>
struct A
{ typedef double type; };

// if A<X>::type is double, X could be anything
```

A dummy argument can be added to enforce consistency:

```
template <typename T>
void f(std::vector<T>&, typename std::vector<T>::iterator);
```

The compiler will deduce T from the first argument, and then verify that the second argument has the correct type.
We can also supply explicitly a value for T when calling the function:

```
template <typename T>
void f(typename std::vector<T>::iterator);

std::vector<double> w;
f<double>(w.begin());
```

Experience shows that we'd better minimize the usage of function templates with non-deduced parameters. Automatic deduction usually gives better error messages and easier function lookup.

First, when a function is invoked with template syntax, the compiler does not necessarily look for a template: this can produce obscure error messages.

```
struct base
{
   template <int I, typename X>      // template, where I is non-deduced
   void foo(X, X)
   {
   }
};

struct derived : public base
{
   void foo(int i)                   // not a template
   {
      foo<314>(i, i);                // line #13
   }
};
```

```
1>test.cpp(13) : error C3867: 'derived::foo': function call missing argument list; use '&derived::foo'
to create a pointer to member
1>test.cpp(13) : error C2446: '<' : no conversion from 'int' to 'void (__cdecl derived::* )(int)'
1>        There are no conversions from integral values to pointer-to-member values
1>test.cpp(13) : error C2296: '<' : illegal, left operand has type 'void (__cdecl derived::* )(int)'
1>test.cpp(13) : warning C4804: '>' : unsafe use of type 'bool' in operation
1>test.cpp(13) : warning C4552: '>' : operator has no effect; expected operator with side-effect
```

When the compiler meets `foo<314>`, it looks for any `foo`; the first match within `derived`, is `void foo(int)`, and lookup stops; hence, `foo<314>` is misinterpreted as (ordinary function name) (less) (314) (greater). The code should explicitly specify `base::foo`.

Second, if name lookup succeeds with multiple results, then the explicit parameters constrain the overload resolution:

```
template <typename T>
void f();

template <int N>
void f();

f<double>();    // invokes the first f, since "double" does not match "int N"
f<7>();         // invokes the second f
```

However this can cause unexpected trouble, because some overloads[17] may be silently ignored:

```
template <typename T>
void g(T x);

double pi = 3.14;
g<double>(pi);      // ok, calls g<double>
```

```
template <typename T>
void h(T x);

void h(double x);

double pi = 3.14;
h<double>(pi);      // unexpected: still calls the first h
```

Here's another example:

[17] Template functions cannot be partially specialized, but only overloaded.

```
template <int I>
class X {};

template <int I, typename T>
void g(X<I>, T x);

template <typename T>          // a special 'g' for X<0>
void g(X<0>, T x);             // however, this is g<T>, not g<0,T>
```

```
double pi = 3.14;
X<0> x;

g<0>(x, pi);                   // calls the first g
g(x, pi);                      // calls the second g
```

Last but not least, old compilers used to introduce subtle linker errors (such as calling the wrong function).

2.2.2. Specializations

Template specializations are valid only at namespace level:[18]

```
struct X
{
   template <typename T>
   class Y
   {};

   template <>                 // illegal, but usually tolerated by compilers
   class Y<double>
   {};
};

template <>                    // legal
class X::Y<double>
{
};
```

The compiler will start using the specialized version only after it has compiled it:

[18] Unfortunately, this is tolerated by popular compilers.

```
template <typename scalar_t>
scalar_t sq(const scalar_t& x)
{ ... }

struct A
{
   A(int i = 3)
   {
      int j = sq(i);       // the compiler will pick the generic template
   }
};

template <>
int sq(const int& x)       // this specialization comes too late
{ ... }
```

However the compiler will give an error in such a situation (stating that *specialization comes after instantiation*). Incidentally, it can happen that a generic class template explicitly "mentions" a special case, as a parameter in some member function: the following code in fact causes the compiler error mentioned above.

```
template <typename T>
struct C
{
   C(C<void>)
   {
   }
};

template <>
struct C<void>
{
};
```

The correct version uses a *forward declaration*:

```
template <typename T>
struct C;

template <>
struct C<void>
{
};

template <typename T>
struct C
{
   C(C<void>)
   {
   }
};
```

Note that we can partially specialize (and we'll do it often) using integer template parameters:

```
template <typename T, int N>
class MyClass                   // general template
{ ... };

template <typename T>
class MyClass<T, 0>             // partial specialization (1) for any T with N=0
{ ... };

template <typename T, int N>
class MyClass<T*, N>            // partial specialization (2) for pointers, any N
{ ... };
```

However this may introduce ambiguities:

```
MyClass<void*, 0> m;            // compiler error:
                                // should it use specialization (1) or (2)?
```

Usually we must explicitly list all the "combinations": if we specialize X<T1, T2> for all T1∈A and for all T2∈B, then we must also specialize explicitly <T1,T2>∈A×B.

```
template <typename T>
class MyClass<T*, 0>            // partial specialization (3) for pointers with N=0
{ ... };
```

It's illegal to write a *partial* specialization when there are dependencies between template parameters in the general template.

```
// parameters (1) and (2) are dependent in the general template

template <typename int_t, int_t N>
class MyClass
{};

template <typename T>
class MyClass<T, 0>
{};
```

```
error: type 'int_t' of template argument '0' depends on template parameter(s)
```

Only a full specialization is allowed:

```
template <>
class MyClass<int, 0>
{};
```

A class template specialization may be completely unrelated to the general template: it need not have the same members, and member functions can have different signatures.
While a gratuitous interface change would be a symptom of bad style (as it inhibits any generic manipulation of the objects), the freedom can be usually exploited:

```
template <typename T, int N>
struct base_with_array
{
   T data_[N];

   void fill(const T& x)
   {
      std::fill_n(data_, N, x);
   }
};

template <typename T>
struct base_with_array<T, 0>
{
   void fill(const T& x)
   {
   }
};
```

```
template <typename T, size_t N>
class cached_vector : private base_with_array<T, N>
{
   // ...

public:

   cached_vector()
   {
      this->fill(T());
   }
```

2.2.3. Inner class templates

A class template can be a member of another template; one of the key points is syntax: the inner class has its own set of parameters, but it knows all the parameters of the outer class

```
template <typename T>
class outer
{
   template <typename X>
   class inner
   {
      // use freely both X and T
   };
};
```

The syntax for accessing inner is `outer<T>::inner<X>` if T is a well-defined type; if T is a template parameter, then we'll have to write `outer<T>::template inner<X>`:

```
outer<int>::inner<double> a;                   // correct
```

```
template <typename Y>
void f()
{
   outer<Y>::inner<double> x1;                  // error
   outer<Y>::template inner<double> x1;         // correct
}
```

It's usually difficult or impossible to specialize inner class templates: specializations should be listed outside of outer, so as a rule they require two `template <...>` clauses, the former for T, the latter for X.

Primary template: it defines an `inner<X>` which we'll call `"inner_1"`

```
template <typename T>
class outer
{
    template <typename X>
    class inner
    {
    };
};
```

Full specializations of outer may contain an `"inner<X>"`, which to the compiler is completely unrelated to `"inner_1"`; we'll call this `"inner_2"`

```
template <>
class outer<int>
{
    template <typename X>
    class inner
    {
        // ok
    };
};
```

`"inner_2"` can be specialized:

```
template <>
class outer<int>::inner<float>
{
    // ok
};
```

specialization of `"inner_1"` for fixed T (=`double`) and X generic

```
template <>
template <typename X>
class outer<double>::inner
{
    // ok
};
```

specialization of `"inner_1"` for fixed T (=`double`) and fixed X (=`char`)

```
template <>
template <>
class
outer<double>::inner<char>
{
    // ok
};
```

It's *illegal* to specialize `"inner_1"` for fixed X, with any T

```
template <typename T>
template <>
class outer<T>::inner<float>
{
    // error!
};
```

Note that, even if X is the same, `inner_1<X>` and `inner_2<X>` are completely different types:

```
template <typename T>
struct outer
{
   template <typename X> struct inner {};
};

template <>
struct outer<int>
{
   template <typename X> struct inner {};
};
```

```
   outer<double>::inner<void> I1;
   outer<int>::inner<void> I2;

   I1 = I2;
```

```
error C2679: binary '=' : no operator found which takes a right-hand operand of type
'outer<int>::inner<X>' (or there is no acceptable conversion)
```

It's impossible to write a function that, say, tests any two `"inner"` for equality, because given an instance of `"inner<X>"` the compiler will not deduce its `outer<T>`

```
template <typename T, typename X>
bool f(outer<T>::inner<X>);     // error: T cannot be deduced?
```

The actual type of I1 is not simply `inner<void>`, but `outer<double>::inner<void>`, so if for any X, all `inner<X>` should have the same type, then `inner` must be promoted to a global template: if it were a plain class, it would yield simply

```
struct basic_inner
{
};

template <typename T>
struct outer
{
   typedef basic_inner inner;
};

template <>
struct outer<int>
{
   typedef basic_inner inner;
};
```

If `inner` does not depend on T, we could write:[19]

[19] Consider the simpler case when `outer<T>` is a container, `inner1` is "iterator" and `inner2` is "const_iterator", and they both derive from an external common base `basic_outer_iterator`

```
template <typename X>
struct basic_inner
{
};

template <typename T>
struct outer
{
   template <typename X>
   struct inner : public basic_inner<X>
   {
      inner& operator=(const basic_inner<X>& that)
      {
         static_cast<basic_inner<X>&>(*this) = that;
         return *this;
      }
   };
};

template <>
struct outer<int>
{
   template <typename X>
   struct inner : public basic_inner<X>
   {
      inner& operator=(const basic_inner<X>& that)
      {
         static_cast<basic_inner<X>&>(*this) = that;
         return *this;
      }
   };
};
```

Otherwise, we have to design `basic_inner`'s template operators that support mixed operations:

```
template <typename X, typename T>
struct basic_inner
{
   template <typename T2>
   basic_inner& operator=(const basic_inner<X, T2>&)
   { /* ... */ }
};

template <typename T>
struct outer
{
   template <typename X>
   struct inner : public basic_inner<X, T>
   {
      inner& operator=(const basic_inner<X, T>& that)
      {
         static_cast<basic_inner<X, T>&>(*this) = that;
         return *this;
      }
   };
};

template <>
struct outer<int>
{
   template <typename X>
   struct inner : public basic_inner<X, int>
   {
      inner& operator=(const basic_inner<X, int>& that)
      {
         static_cast<basic_inner<X, int>&>(*this) = that;
         return *this;
      }
   };
};
```

```
outer<double>::inner<void> I1;
outer<int>::inner<void> I2;

I1 = I2;    // ok: it ends up calling basic_inner::operator=
```

This is known in the C++ community as the S.C.A.R.Y initialization.[20] S.C.A.R.Y. stands for *"Seemingly erroneous (Constrained by conflicting template parameters), but Actually work with the Right implementation"*; put simply, two inner types that should be different (specifically, `outer<T1>::inner` and `outer<T2>::inner`), actually share the implementation, so that it's possible to treat them uniformly as "two `inner`-s"

As seen for function templates, we should never instantiate the master template before the compiler has met all the specializations: if we use only full specializations,

[20] The Y is little more than poetic license. Refer to the excellent article from Danny Kalev http://www.informit.com/guides/content.aspx?g=cplusplus&seqNum=454

the compiler will recognize a problem and stop, however *partial* specializations that come too late will be just ignored:

```
struct A
{
   template <typename X, typename Y>
   struct B
   {
      void do_it() {}   // line #1
   };

   void f()
   {
      B<int, int> b;    // line #2: the compiler instantiates B with <int,int>
      b.do_it();
   }
};

template <typename X>
struct A::B<X, X>      // this should be a specialization of B<X,X>
                       // but it comes too late for B<int,int>

{
   void do_it() {}     // line #3
};
```

```
A a;
a.f();       // calls do_it on line #1
```

Furthermore, adding a full specialization of B will trigger a compiler error:

```
template <>
struct A::B<int, int>
{
   void do_it() {}
};
```

```
test.cpp(41) : error C2908: explicit specialization; 'A::B<X,Y>' has already been instantiated
        with
        [
            X=int,
            Y=int
        ]
```

The obvious solution is to move the function bodies after the specializations of `A::B`.

2.3. Style conventions

Style is the way code is written; this definition is so vague that it includes many different aspects of programming, from language techniques to position of curly braces.

All the C++ objects in namespace `std` exhibit a common style, and this makes the library more coherent.
For example, all names are lowercase[21], multi-word names use underscores; containers have a member function `bool T::empty() const` that tests if the object is empty and a `void T::clear()` that makes the container empty. These are elements of style.
A fictional STL written in pure C would possibly have a global function `clear`, overloaded for all possible containers: writing code as `cont.clear()` or `clear(&cont)` has the same net effect on `cont`, might even generate the same binary file, but granted, it has a very different style.

All these aspects are important during code reviews: if style agrees with the reader forma mentis, then code will look natural and clear, and maintenance will be easier. Some aspects of style are indeed less important, because they can be easily adjusted (for example, using beautifiers: each worker in a team might have a pre-configured beautifier on his machine, integrated with code editor, which reformats braces, spaces, and newlines at a glance)

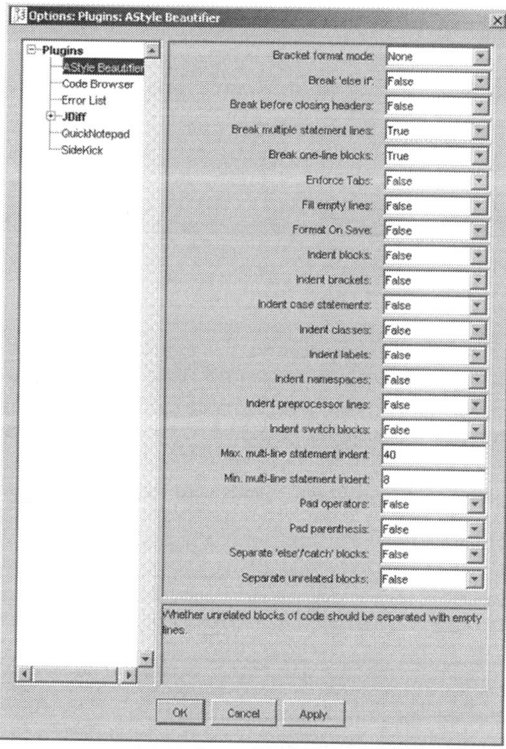

Figure 2-1: The AStyle plug-in for JEdit

21 Except `std::numeric_limits<T>::quiet_NaN()`

JEdit (see http://www.jedit.org) is a free multiplatform code editor which supports plugins.

AStyle (Artistic Style) is a command-line open source code beautifier (see http://astyle.sourceforge.net) whose preferences include the most common formatting option.

Most reasonable style conventions are equivalent: it's important to pick one and try to be coherent for some time[22].

Ideally, if code is written according to some ***common behaviour conventions***, a reader may deduce how it works, without looking into the details, basing only on the style.
For example:

```
void unknown_f(multidimensional_vector<double, 3, 4>& M)
{
   if (!M.empty())
      throw std::runtime_error("failure");
}
```

Most readers will describe the above fragment as: "if the multidimensional vector is not empty, then throw an exception"; however, nothing in the code states that this is the intended behavior, except style.
In fact, `multidimensional_vector::empty` could in principle make the container empty, and return a non-zero error code if it does not succeed.[23]

The naming convention is a big component of style.
The following sections list some ideas, as an example of how to convey extra meaning when building the name of an object. It is not intended as a set of axioms, and in particular no item is worse/better than its opposite, but it's a detailed example of how to assemble a style that is able to help diagnosing and solving problems.

Remember that the C++ standard prescribes that some identifiers are "reserved to the implementation for any use" and some are reserved for names in the global or `std` namespace, so user names should never:

- begin with underscore (in particular, followed by a capital letter)
- contain a double underscore
- contain a dollar sign (it's tolerated by some compilers, but it's not portable)

---

[22] Even source code has a life cycle and eventually it's going to "die", i.e. it will be rewritten from scratch: however the more robust the design, the longer its life will be, and somehow style is part of the design. See also [5]

[23] As discussed in [5], usually member function names should be actions, thus `empty` should be a synonym for `make_empty` and not for `is_empty`; however STL convention is established and universally understood. When in doubt, do as `std::vector` does.

2.3.1. Macros

Macros play a special role in TMP. While some programmers consider them a necessary evil, indeed they are necessary, but it's not obvious they are also evil.

The main issue with macros is
- allow the reader to recognize them
- prevent name collisions

The easiest way to satisfy both requirements is to choose a unique and sufficiently ugly common prefix for all macros, and play with lower/uppercase to give extra meaning to the name.
As an example, we could agree that all macros begin with `MXT_`.
If the macro is persistent, i.e. never undefined, the prefix will be MXT; if the macro scope is limited (i.e. it's defined and undefined later in the same file), the prefix will be `mXT_`.

```
#ifndef MXT_filename_
#define MXT_filename_                // this is "exported" - let's name it MXT_*

#define mXT_MYVALUE 3                // this macro has limited "scope"
const int VALUE = mXT_MYVALUE;       // let's name it mXT_*
#undef mXT_MYVALUE                   //

#endif //MXT_filename_
```

A lowercase prefix `mxt` is reserved to remap standard/system function names in different platforms:

```
#ifdef _WIN32
#define mxt_native_dbl_isfinite        _finite
#else
#define mxt_native_dbl_isfinite        isfinite
#endif
```

For better code appearance, we may decide to replace some keywords with a macro:

```
#define MXT_NAMESPACE_BEGIN(x)         namespace x {
#define MXT_NAMESPACE_END(x)           }

#define MXT_NAMESPACE_NULL_BEGIN()      namespace {
#define MXT_NAMESPACE_NULL_END()        }
```

And/or enclose the namespace directives in a comment box:

```
///////////////////////////////////////////////////////////////////////////////
MXT_NAMESPACE_BEGIN(XT)
///////////////////////////////////////////////////////////////////////////////
```

It's useful to have some (integer) functions as a set of macros:

```
#define MXT_M_MAX(a,b)        ((a)<(b) ? (b) : (a))
#define MXT_M_MIN(a,b)        ((a)<(b) ? (a) : (b))
#define MXT_M_ABS(a)          ((a)<0 ? -(a) : (a))
#define MXT_M_SQ(a)           ((a)*(a))
```

The infix _M_ stands for "macro" and these will be useful when working with templates:

```
template <int N>
struct SomeClass
{
   static const int value = MXT_M_SQ(N)/MXT_M_MAX(N, 1);
};
```

The next C++ Standard will introduce a new keyword: `constexpr`.
A function declared `constexpr` always produces the same result if given the same arguments, and has no side effects; in particular they can be called in constant expressions:

```
constexpr int sq(int n) { return n*n; }
constexpr int max(int a, int b) { return a<b ? b : a; }

template <int N>
struct SomeClass
{
   static const int value = sq(N)/max(N, 1);
```

Finally, we consider a special class of macros: a ***macro directive*** is a macro whose usage logically takes an entire line of code.
In other words, the difference between an ordinary macro and a directive is that the latter cannot coexist with anything on the same line (except possibly its arguments):

```
// this is not a directive:
#define MXT_PI        3.1415926535897932384626433832795029

MXT_NULL_NAMESPACE_BEGIN()              // directive

const double x = std::cos(MXT_PI);     // MXT_PI does not take the whole line

MXT_NULL_NAMESPACE_END()                // directive
```

The definition of a macro directive, in general, should not end with semicolon, so the user is forced to close the line manually (when appropriate), as if it were a standard function call.

```
// note: no trailing ';'
#define MXT_INT_I(k)        int i = (k)

int main()
{
   MXT_INT_I(0);        // put ';' here
   return 0;
}
```

Here is a more complex example: note that the trailing semicolon is a very strong style point, so it's used even in places where, in ordinary code, a semicolon would be unnatural.

```
#define mXT_C(NAME,VALUE)                                    \
static scalar_t NAME()                                       \
{                                                            \
   static const scalar_t NAME##_ = (VALUE);                  \
   return NAME##_;                                           \
}

template <typename scalar_t>
struct constant
{
   mXT_C(Pi, acos(scalar_t(-1)));          // note ';' at class level
   mXT_C(TwoPi, 2*acos(scalar_t(-1)));     // this is legal but quite uncommon
   mXT_C(PiHalf, acos(scalar_t(0)));
   mXT_C(PiQrtr, atan(scalar_t(1)));
   mXT_C(Log2, log(scalar_t(2)));
};

#undef mXT_C
```

```
double x = constant<double>::TwoPi();
```

However, special care is required when invoking macro directives, which expand to a sequence of instructions:

```
#define MXT_SORT2(a,b)    if ((b)<(a)) swap((a),(b))

#define MXT_SORT3(a,b,c) \
   MXT_SORT2((a),(b)); MXT_SORT2((a),(c)); MXT_SORT2((b),(c))

int a = 5, b = 2, c = 3;
MXT_SORT3(a,b,c);              // apparently ok: now a=2, b=3, c=5
```

Nevertheless, this code is broken:

```
int a = 5, b = 2, c = 3;

if (a>10)
   MXT_SORT3(a,b,c);           // problem here!
```

Since it expands to:

```
if (a>10)
   MXT_SORT2(a,b);

MXT_SORT2(a,c);
MXT_SORT2(b,c);
```

More surprising is that the following fragment is clear, but incorrect:

```
if (a>10)
   MXT_SORT2(a,b);
else
   MXT_SORT2(c,d);
```

Because of the way if-then-else associate in C++, the macro expands as

```
if (a>10)
   if (a<b)
      swap(a,b);
else
   if (c<d)
      swap(c,d);
```

The indentation does not resemble the way code is executed: the block actually groups as

```
if (a>10)
{
   if (a<b)
      swap(a,b);
   else if (c<d)
      swap(c,d);
}
```

To solve the problem, we can use the `do {...} while (false)` idiom:

```
#define MXT_SORT3(a,b,c)    \
  do { MXT_SORT2((a),(b)); MXT_SORT2((a),(c)); MXT_SORT2((b),(c)); } \
  while (false)
```

This allows both to put "local code" inside a block and to terminate the directive with a semicolon.
Remember that this will not save from an error like:

```
MXT_SORT3(a, b++, c); // error: b will be incremented more than once
```

This is why we insist that macros are immediately recognizable by a "sufficiently ugly" prefix.
To tackle the "if" macro problem, write a do-nothing `else` branch:

```
#define MXT_SORT2(a,b)   if ((b)<(a)) swap((a),(b)); else
```

Now `SORT2(a,b);` expands to `if (…) swap(…); else;` where the last semicolon is the empty statement. Even better:[24]

```
#define MXT_SORT2(a,b)   if (!((b)<(a))) {} else swap((a),(b))
```

2.3.2. Symbols

Most C++ projects contain several kinds of symbols (classes, functions, constants...): a rough division line can be drawn between system/framework utilities, which are completely abstract and generic, and project specific entities, which contain specific logic and are not expected to be reused elsewhere.
This simple classification may turn out important for (human) debuggers: if any piece of code is considered a "system utility", then it's implicitly trusted, and it may usually be "stepped over" during debug; vice versa, project-specific code is possibly less tested and should be "stepped in".

We can agree that stable symbols should follow the STL naming conventions (lowercase, underscores, such as `stable_sort`, `hash_map`, etc.); this will be often the case for class templates.
The rest should be mixed-case (the Java convention is fine).

```
(framework header) sq.hpp

template <typename scalar_t>
scalar_t sq(const scalar_t& x);    // 'system-level' function - lowercase
```

```
(project file) custom_scalar.h

struct MySpecialScalarType          // 'project-level' class - mixed case
{
   // ...
};
```

[24] The difference between the last two implementations is largely how they react to an invalid syntax: as an exercise, consider some malicious code like: `MXT_SORT2(x, y) if (true) throw an_exception;`

```
(project file) main.cpp

int main()
{
   MySpecialScalarType x = 3.14;
   MySpecialScalarType y = sq(x);

   return 0;
}
```

A ***functor*** is an instance of an object that implements at least one `operator()`, so the name of the instance behaves like a function.[25]
A functor is said ***modifying*** if it takes arguments by non-const references.
A ***predicate*** is a non-modifying functor that takes all arguments of the same type and returns a boolean: for example, "less" is a binary predicate

```
template <typename T>
struct less
{
   bool operator()(const T&, const T&) const;
};
```

Most functors contain a typedef for the return type of `operator()`, usually named `result_type` or `value_type`.[26]

Functors are usually stateless or they carry few data members, so they are built on the fly; occasionally we may need a meaningful name for an instance, and this may not be so easy, because if the functor has a limited "scope", the only meaningful name has already been given to the class.

```
   calendar myCal;
   std::find_if(year.begin(), year.end(), is_holiday(myCal));

// is_holiday is a class
// how do we name an instance?
```

We may use one of the following:

- use a lowercase functor name and convert it to uppercase for the instance:

```
   calendar myCal;
   is_holiday IS_HOLIDAY(myCal);
   std::find_if(year.begin(), year.end(), IS_HOLIDAY);
```

- use a lowercase functor name with a prefix/postfix and remove it in the instance:

```
   calendar myCal;
   is_holiday_t is_holiday(myCal);
   std::find_if(year.begin(), year.end(), is_holiday);
```

[25] The reader might want to review the simple example at page 8.
[26] See section 7.2.1

2.3.3. Generality

The best way to improve generality is to reuse standard classes, such as `std::pair`.

This brings in well-tested code and increases interoperability; however it may often hide some specific logic, for example the meaning of `pair::first` and `pair::second` may not be obvious at first sight. See the following paradigmatic example:

```
struct id_value
{
   int id;
   double value;
};

id_value FindIDAndValue(...);
```

This may be replaced by:

```
std::pair<int, double> FindIDAndValue(...)
```

However the caller of the first function can write `p.id` and `p.value`, which is easier to read than `p.first` and `p.second`; we may want to provide a *less generic* way to access `pair` members:

- macros

```
#define id              first         // bad idea?
#define value           second        // bad idea?
```

```
#define id(P)           P.first       // slightly better
#define value(P)        P.second      // slightly better
```

- global functions (these are called ***accessors***, see section 7.2.1)

```
inline int& id(std::pair<int, double>& P)
{ return P.first; }

inline int id(const std::pair<int, double>& P)
{ return P.first; }
```

- global pointer-to-members

```
typedef std::pair<int, double> id_value;

int id_value::*ID = &id_value::first;
double id_value::*VALUE = &id_value::second;


// later
std::pair<int, double> p;
p.*ID = -5;
p.*VALUE = 3.14;
```

To make `ID` and `VALUE` constants, the syntax is:

```
int id_value::* const ID = &id_value::first;
```

2.3.4. Template parameters

A fairly universally accepted convention is to reserve `UPPERCASE` names for non-type template parameters; it's not always necessary to give names to template parameters (as with function arguments), so if something is not intended to be referenced, and the compiler allows it, you'd better remove entirely its name:

```
// the following line is likely to give strange errors
// since some compilers define BIGENDIAN as a macro!

template <typename T, bool BIGENDIAN = false>
class SomeClass
{
};

template <typename T>
class SomeClass<T, true>
{
};
```

A safer declaration would be:[27]

```
template <typename T, bool = false>
class SomeClass
```

Type parameters are usually denoted by a single uppercase letter, usually `T` (or `T1`, `T2`...) if type can be indeed anything[28]; `A` and `R` are also traditionally used for parameters that match arguments and results:

---

[27] Some compilers, such as MSVC71, used to have problems with unnamed parameters; refer to paragraph 12.3.3 for a detailed example.

[28] Some authors reserve the keyword `typename` for this purpose; in other words they declare `template <typename T>` to mean that T is "any type" and `template <class T>` to suggest that T is indeed a class, as opposite to a native type, however this distinction is rather artificial.

```
template <typename R, typename A>
inline R apply(R (*F)(A), A arg)
{
   return F(arg);
}

template <typename R, typename A1, typename A2>
inline R apply(R (*F)(A1, A2), A1 arg1, A2 arg2)
{
   return F(arg1, arg2);
}
```

```
double x = apply(std::cos, 3.14);
```

Otherwise we may wish to use a (meaningful) lowercase name ending with `_t` (e.g. `int_t`, `scalar_t`, `object_t`, `any_t`, `that_t`).

```
template <typename T, int N>
class do_nothing
{
};

template <typename int_t>   // int_t should behave as an integer type29
struct is_unsigned
{
   static const bool value = ...;
};
```

The suffix "`_t`", which in C originally means "typedef", is also widely used for (private) typedefs standing for template instances:

```
template <typename scalar_t>
class SomeContainer
{
   // informally means:
   // within this class, a pair always denotes a pair of scalars

   private:
      typedef std::pair<scalar_t, scalar_t> pair_t;
};
```

On the opposite, a public typedef name usually is composed by lower case regular English words (e.g. `iterator_category`), so in that case `_type` is preferred:

```
template <typename scalar_t>
class SomeContainer
{
   public:
      typedef scalar_t result_type;
};
```

[29] Note that this is not a formal requirement: it's just a name! The name reflects how we think the type should be; later we will enforce this, if necessary

2.3.5. Metafunctions

We often meet stateless class templates, whose members are only enumerations (as a rule, anonymous), static constants, types (typedefs or nested classes) and static member functions.

Generalizing paragraph 2.1, we consider this template a ***metafunction*** that maps its tuple of parameters to a class, which is seen as a *set of results* (namely, its members).

```
template <typename T, int N>
struct F
{
   typedef T* pointer_type;
   typedef T& reference_type;

   static const size_t value = sizeof(T)*N;
};
```

The metafunction F above maps a pair of arguments to a triple of results:

```
(T,N)              →   (pointer_type, reference_type, value)
{type}×{int}  →   {type}×{type}×{size_t}
```

Most metafunctions return either a single type, conventionally named `type` or a single numeric constant (an integer or an enumeration), conventionally named `value`.[30]

```
template <typename T>
struct largest_precision_type;

template <>
struct largest_precision_type<float>
{
   typedef double type;
};

template <>
struct largest_precision_type<double>
{
   typedef double type;
};

template <>
struct largest_precision_type<int>
{
   typedef long type;
};
```

[30] The mathematically inclined reader should consider the latter as a special case of the former: the constant '5' can be replaced by a type named `five` or `static_value<int, 5>`. This leads to greater generality. See [3] for more information.

Similarly:

```
template <unsigned int N>
struct two_to
{
   static const unsigned int value = (1<<N);
};

template <unsigned int N>
struct another_two_to
{
   enum   { value = (1<<N) };
};
```

```
   unsigned int i = two_to<5>::value;             // invoke the metafunction
   largest_precision<int>::type j = i + 100;      // invoke the metafunction
```

Historically, the first metafunctions were written using enums:

```
   template <size_t A>
   struct is_prime
   {
      enum { value = 0 };
   };

   template <>
   struct is_prime<2>
   {
      enum { value = 1 };
   };

   template <>
   struct is_prime<3>
   {
      enum { value = 1 };
   };

   // ...
```

The main reason was that compilers were unable to deal with static const integers (including bool). The advantage of using an enum over a static constant is that the compiler will *never* reserve storage space for the constant, as the computation is either static or it fails.
Vice versa, a static constant integer could be "misused" as a normal integer: for example, taking its address (operation which the compiler would not allow on enums).

> According to the 2003 C++ standard, the use of a static constant as a normal integer is illegal (unless the constant is re-declared in the .cpp file, as any other static data member of a class); however most compilers already allow it, and the requirement will be removed in C++0x.
>
> Specifically, http://www.open-std.org/jtc1/sc22/wg21/docs/cwg_defects.html#454 reads:

> "the current C++ standard is not in sync with existing practice and with user expectations as far as definitions of static data members having const integral or const enumeration type are concerned. Basically what current implementations do is to require a definition only if the address of the constant is taken."

Furthermore, the language allows declaring a static integer constant (at function scope, not at class scope) that is *dynamically* initialized, and so *not* a compile-time constant:

```
int main()
{
   static const int x = INT_MAX;                          // ok
   static const int y = std::numeric_limits<int>::max();  // dynamic
   static const int z = rand();                           // dynamic

   double data[y];                                        // error
}
```

In practice an enum is usually equivalent to a *small* integer: enums are in general implemented as `signed int`, unless their value is too large. The most important difference is that you cannot bind an unnamed enum to a template parameter without an explicit cast:

```
   double data[10];
   std::fill_n(data, is_prime<3>::value, 3.14);    // may give error!
```

The code above is non-portable, because `std::fill_n` may be defined

```
   template <..., typename integer_t, ...>
   void fill_n(..., integer_t I, ...)
   {
      ++I; // whatever...
      --I; // whatever...
   }
```

```
C:\Program Files (x86)\Microsoft Visual Studio 9.0\VC\include\xutility(3197) :
error C2675: unary '--' : '' does not define this operator or a conversion to a type acceptable to the
predefined operator
see reference to function template instantiation
'void std::_Fill_n<double*,_Diff,_Ty>(_OutIt,_Diff,const _Ty &,std::_Range_checked_iterator_tag)' being
compiled
        with
        [
            _Diff=,
            _Ty=double *,
            _OutIt=double **
        ]
```

In practice, an enum is fine to store a small integer (for example, the logarithm of an integer in base 2); as its type is not explicit, it should be avoided when dealing with potentially large or unsigned constants. As a workaround for the `std::fill_n` call, just cast the enumeration to an appropriate integer:

```
std::fill_n(…, int(is_prime<3>::value), …);    // now ok!
```

Frequently, metafunctions invoke helper classes (we'll see less trivial examples later):

```
template <int N>
struct ttnp1_helper
{
   static const int value = (1<<N);
};

template <int N>
struct two_to_plus_one
{
   static const int value = ttnp1_helper<N>::value + 1;
};
```

The moral equivalent of auxiliary variables are private members; from a TMP perspective, a numeric constant and a type(def) are equivalent compile-time entities.

```
template <int N>
struct two_to_plus_one
{
private:
   static const int aux = (1<<N);

public:
   static const int value = aux + 1;
};
```

The helper class is not private and not hidden[31], but it should not be used, so its name is "uglified" with `_helper` or `_t` (or both).

2.3.6. Namespaces and using declarations

Usually all "public" framework objects are grouped in a common namespace and "private" objects reside in special nested namespaces.

[31] It should reside in an anonymous namespace, but this does not make it inaccessible

```
namespace framework
{
   namespace undocumented_private
   {
      void handle_with_care()
      {
         // ...
      };
   }

   inline void public_documented_function()
   {
      undocumented_private::handle_with_care();
   }
}
```

It's not a good idea to multiply the number of namespaces unnecessarily, since Koenig lookup is not fully supported in all compilers, and friend declarations between objects in different namespaces are problematic or even impossible.

Usually the core of a general-purpose metaprogramming framework is a set of headers (the extension *.hpp is in fact used for pure C++ headers). ***Using-namespace declarations*** in header files are generally considered bad practice:

```
my_framework.hpp

using namespace std;
```

```
main.cpp
#include "my_framework.hpp"

// main.cpp doesn't know, but it's using namespace std
```

However, ***using-function declarations*** in header files are usually ok and even desirable (see the `do_something` example later in the paragraph).

A special usage for using-namespace declaration is header versioning.[32]
This is a very short example:

[32] The advantages are described extensively in Apple Technical Note TN2185, refer to the following page: http://developer.apple.com/technotes/tn2007/tn2185.html

```
namespace X
{
   namespace version_1_0
   {
      void func1();
      void func2();
   }

   namespace version_2_0
   {
      void func1();
      void func2();
   }

#ifdef USE_1_0
   using namespace version_1_0;
#else
   using namespace version_2_0;
#endif
}
```

Thus the clients using the header always refer to `X::func1`.

Here's another case to remark the importance of using-function declarations. Function templates are often used to provide an "external interface", i.e. a set of global functions that allow algorithms to perform generic manipulations of objects:[33]
The author of `framework1` provides a function `is_empty` that works on a broad class of containers, and also on C-strings:

```
framework1.hpp
MXT_NAMESPACE_BEGIN(framework1)

template <typename T>
inline bool is_empty(T const& x)
{
   return x.empty();                        // line #1
}

template <>
inline bool is_empty(const char* const& x)
{
   return x==0 || *x==0;
}

MXT_NAMESPACE_END(framework1)
```

One of the good properties of this approach is the ease of extensibility: for any new type X, we can provide a specialized `is_empty` that will have priority over the default implementation.
However, consider what happens if the function is explicitly qualified:

[33] Such functions are denoted shims in [5].

```
framework2.hpp
#include "framework1.hpp"

MXT_NAMESPACE_BEGIN(framework2)

template <typename string_t>
void do_something(string_t const& x)
{
   if (!framework1::is_empty(x))          // line #2
   {
      // ...
   }
}

MXT_NAMESPACE_END(framework2)
```

```
#include "framework2.hpp"

namespace framework3
{
   class EmptyString
   {
   };

   bool is_empty(const EmptyString& x)
   {
      return true;
   }
}

int main()
{
   framework3::EmptyString s;
   framework2::do_something(s);          // compiler error in line #1
}
```

The user-supplied `is_empty` is ignored in line #2, since `do_something` explicitly takes `is_empty` from namespace `framework1`; to fix, we can either reopen namespace `framework1` and specialize `is_empty` there, or modify `do_something` like this:

```
framework2.hpp
MXT_NAMESPACE_BEGIN(framework2)

using framework1::is_empty;

template <typename string_t>
void do_something(string_t const& x)
{
   if (!is_empty(x))
   {
```

Thus we let Koenig lookup to pick an available `is_empty` but we ensure that `framework1` can always supply a default candidate (see also the discussion in 2.4.2 below).

2.4. Classic patterns

When coding a framework/library, it's typical to use and reuse a small set of names; for example, containers can be expected to have a member function `[[integer type]] size() const`, returning the number of elements.
Adopting a uniform style increases interoperability of objects: for more details, see section 6.

2.4.1. size_t and ptrdiff_t

In C++ there's no unique standard and portable way to name large integers.
Modern compilers will in general pick the largest integers available for `long long` and `unsigned long long`. When one needs quickly a large and fast integer, the preferred choices are `size_t` (unsigned) and `ptrdiff_t` (signed).
The former, being the result of `sizeof` and the argument of `operator new`, is large enough to store any amount of memory; the latter represents the difference of two pointers, so, since the length of an array of chars is end-begin, as a rule of thumb they will have the same size.
Furthermore, in the flat C++ memory model, `sizeof(size_t)` will be also the size of pointers, and these integers will likely have the natural size in an architecture - say, 32 bits on a 32-bit processor and 64 bits on a 64-bit processor - so they will also be fast (the processor bus will perform atomic transport from registers to memory).
Given this class:

```
template <int N>
struct A
{
   char data[N];
};
```

`sizeof(A<N>)` is at least `N`, so it also follows that `size_t` is not smaller than `int`.[34]

2.4.2. void T::swap(T&)

This function is expected to swap `*this` and the argument in constant time, without throwing any exception; a practical definition of "constant" is: an amount of time depending only on `T`.[35]

---

[34] If `a` is an array of `T` of length 2, then `(char*)(&a[1])-(char*)(&a[0])` is a `ptrdiff_t` which is at least as large as `sizeof(T)`; so in particular, also `ptrdiff_t` is at least as large as `int`. This argument actually shows that every result of `sizeof` can be stored in a `ptrdiff_t`; a generic `size_t` may not be stored in a `ptrdiff_t`, because `sizeof` is not necessarily surjective: there may be a `size_t` value that is larger than every possible `sizeof`.

[35] For example, to create a copy of `std::string` takes time proportional to the length of the string itself, so this depends not only on the type, but also on the *instance*; vice versa, copying a double is a constant-time operation. Mathematically speaking, the notion of "constant time" is not well defined in C++; the issue is too complex for a footnote, but we'll sketch the idea. An algorithm is O(1)

If T has a swap member function, the user expects it to be not worse than the traditional three-copy swap (i.e. X=A; A=B; B=X).
Indeed, this is always possible, because a member function can invoke each member's own swap:

```
class TheClass
{
   std::vector<double> theVector_;
   std::string theString_;
   double theDouble_;
   // ...

public:

   void swap(TheClass& that);
   {
      theString_.swap(that.theString_);
      theVector_.swap(that.theVector_);
      std::swap(theDouble_, that.theDouble_);
      // ...
```

The only step that could take non-fixed time is swapping dynamic arrays element by element, but this can be avoided swapping the arrays as a whole.

The class std::tr1::array<T,N> has a swap that calls std::swap_range on an array of length N, thus taking time proportional to N and depending on T; however N is part of the type, so according to our definition, it is constant time. Furthermore, if T is a swappable type (e.g. std::string), swap_range will perform much better than the three copy procedure, so the member swap is definitely an advantage.

The first problem to address is how to swap objects of unspecified type T:

```
template <typename T>
class TheClass
{
   T theObj_;       // how do you swap two objects of type T?
```

```
   void swap(TheClass<T>& that)
   {
      std::swap(theObj_, that.theObj_);
   }
```

if its execution time is bounded by a constant K, for any possible input; if the number of possible inputs is finite, even if huge, the algorithm is automatically O(1). For example, in C++ the sum of two int is O(1). In general, the C++ memory model has a finite addressable space (because all objects have a fixed size, and an "address" is an object) and this implies that the number of possible inputs to some algorithms is finite. Quicksort complexity is O(N*log(N)), but std::sort may be formally considered O(1), where - loosely speaking - the constant K is the time required to sort the largest possible array.

The explicit qualification `std::` is an unnecessary constraint: we'd better introduce a using declaration, as seen in section 2.3.6

```
using std::swap;

template <typename T>
class TheClass
{
   T theObj_;

public:

   void swap(TheClass<T>& that)          // line #1
   {
      swap(theObj_, that.theObj_);       // line #2
   }
```

However this results in a compiler error, because by the usual C++ name resolution rules, `swap` in line 2 is the `swap` defined in line 1, which does not take two arguments.

The solution, an idiom known as ***swap with ADL***, is to introduce a global function with a different name:

```
using std::swap;

template <typename T>
inline void swap_with_ADL(T& a, T& b)
{
   swap(a, b);
}
```

```
template <typename T>
class TheClass
{
   T theObj_;

public:
   void swap(TheClass<T>& that)
   {
      swap_with_ADL(theObj_, that.theObj_);
   }
```

Due to Koenig lookup rules, `swap_with_ADL` forwards the call to either a `swap` function defined in the same namespace as `T` (which hopefully is `T`'s own version), or to `std::swap` if nothing else exists; since there's no local member function with a similar name, lookup escapes class level.

The traditional argument for `swap` is `T&`, however it may make sense to provide more overloads: if an object internally holds its data in a standard container of type `X`, it might be useful to provide also `void swap(X&)`, with relaxed time-complexity expectations:

```
template <typename T>
class sorted_vector
{
   std::vector<T> data_;

public:

   void swap(sorted_vector<T>& that)
   {
      data_.swap(that.data_);
   }

   void swap(std::vector<T>& that)
   {
      data_.swap(that);
      std::sort(data_.begin(), data_.end();
   }
```

And even more:[36]

```
struct unchecked_type_t {};
inline unchecked_type_t unchecked() { return unchecked_type_t(); }

template <typename T>
class sorted_vector
{
   // ...

   void swap(std::vector<T>& that, unchecked_type_t (*)())
   {
      assert(is_sorted(that.begin(), that.end()));
      data_.swap(that);
   }
```

```
sorted_vector<double> x;
std::vector<double> t;

load_numbers_into(x);
x.swap(t);

// now x is empty and t is sorted
// later...

x.swap(t, unchecked);   // very fast
```

To sum up:

- explicitly qualify `std::swap` with parameters of fixed native type (integers, pointers…) and standard containers (including string)
- write a using declaration for `std::swap` and call an unqualified `swap` when parameters have undefined type `T` in global functions
- call `swap_with_ADL` inside classes having a `swap` member function.

`std::swap` grants the best implementation for swapping both native and `std` types.

[36] Compare with section 3.3.1.

`swap` is used in algorithms with move semantics:

```
void doSomething(X& result)
{
   X temp;

// perform some operation on temp, then "move" it over result
// if X is a simple type, use simply "result = temp"
// however, if X is, say, a container, swap(temp, result) could be faster
}
```

and in implementing exception-safe assignment operator in terms of copy constructor:

```
class X
{
public:
   X(X&);
   void swap(X&);
   ~X();

   X& operator=(const X& that)
   {
      X temp(that);          // if an exception occurs here, *this is unchanged
      temp.swap(*this);      // no exception can occur here
      return *this;          // now temp is destroyed and releases resources
   }
};
```

If we perform an unconditional swap, then the most efficient solution is to take the argument by value:

```
   X& operator=(X that)
   {
      that.swap(*this);
      return *this;
   }
```

On the opposite, we may want to perform additional checks before invoking the copy constructor by hand, even if it might be less efficient: [37]

[37] Some objects may want to check in advance if overwrite is feasible: for example, if T is `std::string` whose `size()==that.size()` then it might be able to perform a safe `memcpy`.

```
X& operator=(const X& that)
{
   if (this != &that)
   {
      X temp(that);
      temp.swap(*this);
   }
   return *this;
}
```

The drawback is that at some point, both `that` and `temp` are alive, so we may need more free resources (e.g. more memory).

2.4.3. bool T::empty() const; void T::clear()

The first tests if an object is empty, the second makes it empty. If an objects has a member function `size()`, then a call to `empty()` is expected to be not slower than `size()==0`.

Note that an object may be empty but still control resources: for example an empty `vector` might hold a raw block of memory, where in fact no element has yet been constructed.
In particular, it's unspecified if a `clear` function will or won't release object resources; `clear` is a synonym of `reset`.
To enforce resource cleanup of an auto variable, the usual technique is to swap the instance with a temporary:

```
T x;
// now x holds some resources...
T().swap(x);
```

2.4.4. X T::get() const; X T::base() const

The name `get` is used when type T wraps a simpler type X: a smart pointer's `get` would thus return the internal plain pointer.
`base` instead is used to return a copy of the wrapped object, when the wrapper is just a different interface. Since a smart pointer typically adds some complexity (e.g. a reference count), the name `base` would not be as appropriate as `get`; on the opposite, `std::reverse_iterator` is an interface that swaps ++ and -- of an underlying iterator, so it has a `base()`.

2.4.5. X T::property() const; void T::property(X)

In this paragraph, "property" is a symbolic name.
The first member returns the current value of the property for current instance; the second sets the property to some new value.
The property-set function can also have the form:

```
X T::property(X newval)
{
    const X oldval = property();
    set_new_val(newval);
    return oldval;
}
```

This convention is elegant, but not universally used; it is present in `std::iostream`.

2.4.6. action(value); action(range)

In this paragraph, "action" is a symbolic name.
If an object's own action – for example `container.insert(value)` – is likely to be invoked sequentially, an object may provide one or more range equivalents, in other words, member functions with two or more parameters that identify a series of elements at a time; some familiar examples are:

- an element and a repeat counter
- two iterators pointing to [begin…end)
- an array and two indexes

It's up to the implementation to take advantage of the range being known in advance: as usual, the range-equivalent function should never be worse than the trivial implementation `action(range) := for (x in range) { action(x); }`

2.4.7. Manipulators

Manipulators are one of the least known and more expressive piece of the C++ standard.
They are simply functions that take a stream as argument; since their signature is fixed, streams have a special insertion operator that runs them:

```
class ostream
{
public:

   ostream& operator<<(ostream& (*F)(ostream&))
   {
      return F(*this);
   }

   //...
```

```
inline ostream& endl(ostream& os)
{
   os << '\n';
   return os.flush();
}
```

```
// later...

int main()
{
   cout << "Hello world" << endl;     // executes endl(cout << "Hello world")
}
```

Some manipulators have an argument: the implementation may use a template proxy object to transport this argument to the stream:

```
struct precision_proxy_t
{
   int prec;
};

inline ostream& operator<<(ostream& o, precision_proxy_t p)
{
   o.precision(p.prec);
   return o;
}
```

```
precision_proxy_t setprecision(int p)
{
   precision_proxy_t result = { p };
   return result;
}
```

```
cout << setprecision(12) << 3.14;
```

Note that a more realistic implementation may wish to *embed* a function pointer in the proxy, so to have only one insertion operator:

```
class ostream;

template <typename T, ostream& (*FUNC)(ostream&, T)>
struct proxy
{
   T arg;

   proxy(const T& a)
      : arg(a)
   {
   }
};

class ostream
{
public:

   template <typename T, ostream& (*FUNC)(ostream&, T)>
   ostream& operator<<(proxy<T, FUNC> p)
   {
      return FUNC(*this, p.arg);
   }
```

```
ostream& global_setpr(ostream& o, int prec)
{
   o.precision(prec);
   return o;
}

proxy<int, global_setpr> setprecision(int p)
{
   return p;
}
```

```
cout << setprecision(12) << 3.14;
```

Note that in classic C++ `FUNC` would just be a member:

```
template <typename T>
struct proxy
{
   T arg;
   ostream& (*FUNC)(ostream&, T);
};

class ostream
{
public:

   template <typename T>
   ostream& operator<<(proxy<T> p)
   {
      return p.FUNC(*this, p.arg);
```

In principle, a function template could be used as a manipulator, i.e.

```
stream << manip1;
stream << manip2(argument);
stream << manip3<N>;
stream << manip4<N>(argument);
```

But in practice this is discouraged, as many compilers won't accept `manip3`.

2.4.8. Position of operators

It's important to understand the difference between member and non-member operators.
When member operators are invoked, the left side has already been statically determined, so if any adjustment is necessary, it's performed only on the right side.
Vice versa, non-member operators will only match exactly or give errors.

Suppose we are rewriting `std::pair`...

```
template <typename T2, typename T2>
struct pair
{
   T1 first;
   T2 second;

   template <typename S1, typename S2>
   pair(const pair<S1, S2>& that)
   : first(that.first), second(that.second)
   {
   }
```

Now let's add `operator==`. First as a member:

```
struct pair
{
   // ...

   inline bool operator== (const pair<T1,T2>& that) const
   {
      return (first == that.first) && (second == that.second);
   }
```

Then we compile the following code:

```
   pair<int, std::string> P(1,"abcdefghijklmnop");
   pair<const int, std::string> Q(1,"qrstuvwxyz");
   if (P == Q)
      // ...
```

This will work, and call `pair<int, string>::operator==`; this function requires a constant reference to `pair<int, string>` and instead it was given `pair<const int, string>`, so it will silently invoke the template copy constructor and make a copy of the object on the right, which is undesirable, as it will make a temporary copy of the `string`.

It is slightly better to put the operator outside the class:

```
template <typename T1, typename T2>
bool operator== (const pair<T1,T2>& x, const pair<T1,T2>& y)
{
    return (x.first == y.first) && (x.second == y.second);
}
```

At least, the code above will now fail to compile, since equality now requires identical pairs; explicit failure is always more desirable than a subtle problem.

Analogous to the classic C++ rule "if you write a custom copy constructor, then you'll need a custom assignment operator", we could say that if you write a universal copy constructor, you'll *likely* need universal operators, to avoid the cost of temporary conversions: in this case, either a template member function with two parameters, or a global operator with four; some programmers will prefer global operators when it's possible to implement them using only the public interface of the class (as above).

```
struct pair
{
   // ...

   template <typename S1, typename S2>
   inline bool operator== (const pair<S1, S2>& that) const
   {
      return (first == that.first) && (second == that.second);
   }
```

This will work if `this->first` and `that.first` are comparable (e.g. `int` and `const int`); note that we may still have temporary conversions, because we are delegating to an unspecified `T1::operator==`.[38]

2.4.9. Secret inheritance

Public derivation from a concrete class can be used as a sort of "strong typedef":

```
class A
{
   // concrete class
   // ...
};
```

```
class B : public A
{
};

// now B works "almost" as A, but it's a different type
```

We may need to implement one or more "forwarding constructors" in B.
This is one of the strategies to simulate template typedefs (which do not exist yet in C++):

```
template <typename T1, typename T2>
class A
{
   // ...
```

[38] Note that the best option is to demand that the paired objects provide suitable operators, so we delegate the comparison; for example `pair<const char*, int>` and `pair<std::string, int>` are unlikely to trigger the construction of temporary strings, because we expect the STL to supply a `operator==(const char*, const std::string&)`

```
template <typename T>
class B : public A<T, T>
{
```

However this is acceptable only if A is a private class, whose existence is unknown or undocumented:

```
template <typename T>
class B : public std::map<T, T>    // bad idea
```

```
namespace std
{

template <...
class map : public _Tree<...       // ok: class _Tree is invisible to the user
{
```

A secret base class is often a good container of operators that are independent on some template parameters. For example, it may be reasonable to test equality between two objects, ignoring all the parameters that are purely cosmetic:

```
template <typename T, int INITIAL_CAPACITY = 16>
class C;
```

```
template <typename T>
class H
{
public:
   H& operator==(const H&) const;
};

template <typename T, int INITIAL_CAPACITY>
class C : public H<T>
{
```

So comparisons between two containers C with a different `INITIAL_CAPACITY` will succeed and call their common base `H::operator==`.

2.4.10. Literal zero

Sometimes we need to write a function or an operator that behaves differently when a literal zero is passed. This is often the case of smart pointers:

```
template <typename T>
class shared_ptr
{
   ...
};

shared_ptr<T> P;
T* Q;

P == 7; // should not compile
P == 0; // should compile
P == Q; // should compile
```

We can distinguish 0 from a generic `int` writing an overload that accepts a pointer to member of a class that has... no members:

```
class dummy {};

typedef int dummy::*literal_zero_t;
```

```
template <typename T>
class shared_ptr
{
   // ...

   bool operator==(literal_zero_t) const
   {
```

The user has no way of creating a `literal_zero_t`, because `dummy` has no members of type `int`, so the only valid argument is an implicit cast of a literal zero (unless a more specialized overload exists).

2.4.11. Boolean type

Some types, such as `std::stream`, have a cast-to-boolean operator; if implemented naively, this can lead to inconsistencies:

```
class stream
{
   // ...

   bool operator() const
   {
      // ...
```

```
stream s;

if (s)              // ok, that's what we want
{
   int i = s + 2;   // unfortunately, this compiles
```

A classic workaround was to implement cast to `void*`

```
class stream
{
   // ...

   void* operator() const
   {
      // return 'this' when true or '0' when false
```

```
stream s;

if (s)                     // ok, that's what we want
{
   int i = s + 2;          // good, this does not compile...
   free(s);                // ...but this goes on
```

A better solution is again a pointer to member:

```
struct boolean_type_t
{
   int true_;
};

typedef int boolean_type_t::*boolean_type;

#define mxt_boolean_true    &boolean_type_t::true_
#define mxt_boolean_false   0
```

```
class stream
{
   // ...

   boolean_type operator() const
   {
      // return mxt_boolean_true or mxt_boolean_false
```

2.4.12. Default and Value initialization

If T is a type, then the construction of a default instance does not imply anything about the initialization of the object itself: the exact effect of

```
   T x;
```

depends heavily on T: if T is a fundamental type or a POD, then its initial value is undefined; also, if T is a class, it's possible that some of its members are still undefined:

```
class A
{
   std::string s_;
   int i_;

public:

   A() {}     // this will default-construct s_ but leave i_ uninitialized
};
```

On the opposite, the line

```
T x = T();
```

will initialize T with 0, say for all fundamental types, but it may crash if T is A, because it's illegal to copy the uninitialized member i_ from the temporary on the right into x.
So to sum up:

```
T a();          // error: a is a function taking no argument and returning T
                // equivalent to T (*a)()

T b;            // ok only if T is a class with default constructor
                // otherwise T is uninitialized

T c(T());       // error: c is a function taking a function and returning T
                // equivalent to T (*c)(T (*)())

T d = {};       // ok only if T is a POD

T e = T();      // requires a non-explicit copy constructor
                // and may yield undefined behaviour at runtime
```

Value initialization (cfr. paragraphs 8.5.1-7 of the Standard) is a way to work around this problem: since it works only for class members we have to write

```
template <typename T>
struct initialized_value
{
   T result;

   initialized_value()
      : result()
   {
   }
};
```

If T is a class with a default constructor, that will be used; otherwise, the storage for T will be set to zero. If T is an array, each element will be recursively initialized:

```
initialized_value<double> x;          // x.result is 0.0
initialized_value<double [5]> y;      // y.result is {0.0, 0.0, 0.0, 0.0, 0.0}
initialized_value<std::string> z;     // z.result is std::string()
```

2.5. Code safety

The spirit of TMP is "elegance first". In theory, some techniques can open vulnerabilities in source code, which a malicious programmer could exploit to crash a program.
Consider the following situations:

```
#include <functional>

class unary_F : public std::unary_function<int,float>
{
public:
   // omitted...
};

int main()
{
   unary_F u;

   std::unary_function<int,float>* ptr = &u;      // legal!
   delete u;                                      // undefined behaviour!

   return 0;
}
```

System header <functional> could make the counterexample above fail by defining a protected destructor in `unary_function`:

```
template<class _Arg, class _Result>
struct unary_function
{
   typedef _Arg argument_type;
   typedef _Result result_type;

protected:
   ~unary_function()
   {
   }
};
```

But this in general does not happen.[39]
The following idea is due to Sutter ([4]):

[39] See paragraph 2.6

```
myclass.h
class MyClass
{
   private:
      double x_;
      int z_;

   public:
      template <typename stream_t>
         void write_x_to(const stream_t& y)
      {
         y << x_;
      }
};
```

Is it possible to legally read/modify the private member `MyClass::z_`? Just add a specialization somewhere after including `myclass.h`

```
struct MyClassHACK
{
};

template <>
void MyClass::write_x_to(const MyClassHACK&)
{
   // as a member of MyClass, you can do anything...
   z_ = 3;
}
```

Finally, there are problems when declaring template friendship.
First, there's no standard and portable way to declare friendship with a template parameter (refer to [5] for more details)

```
template <typename T, int N>
class test
{
   friend class T; // uhm...
};
```

Second, there is no way to make `test<T,N>` friend of `test<T,J>` (there is nothing like partial template friendship); a common workaround is to declare `test<T,N>` friend of `test<X,J>` for any other type X.

```
template <typename T, int N>
class test
{
   template <typename X, int J>
      friend class test;        // ok, but every test<X,J> has access
};
```

The same malicious user, who wrote `MyClassHACK`, can add:

```
template <>
class test<MyClassHACK, 0>
{
   public:
      template <typename T, int N>
         void manipulate(test<T,N>& x)
      {
          // a friend can do anything!
      }
};
```

We'll see that TMP sometimes makes use of techniques, which are correctly labeled bad practice in conventional C++, including (but not limiting to):

- Lack of non-virtual protected destructor in (empty) base class
- Implementing cast operators `operator T() const`
- Declaring a non-explicit constructor with a single argument

2.6. Compiler assumptions

Heavy usage of templates implies a massive work for the compiler. Not all standard-conforming techniques behave identically on every ***platform***.[40]

We denote by ***language-neutral idioms*** all the language features that don't have a standard-prescribed behavior but only a reasonable expected behavior: this is what an optimal compiler would usually do on that code.

> For example, the C++ standard prescribes that `sizeof(T)>0` for any type T, but does not require the size of a compound type to be minimal: an empty struct could have size 64, but we expect it to have size 1 (or at worst, size not larger than a pointer).

A standard-conforming compiler can legally violate the optimality condition, but in practice, such a situation is rare; in other words, a language-neutral idiom is a language construction that does not make a program worse, but gives a nice opportunity of optimization to a good compiler.

Several possible problems can arise from a perfect standard-conforming code fragment:

- Unexpected compiler errors
- Failures at runtime (access violations, core dumps, blue screens, panic reactions)
- Huge compilation/link time
- Suboptimal runtime speed

[40] By platform, usually we mean the set { processor, operating system, compiler, linker }

Issues #1 and #2 are due to compiler bugs, and involve finding a language workaround (but #2 is usually met when it's too late).
Problem #3 mostly depends on poorly written template code.
Problem #4 involves finding language-neutral idioms, which are not recognized by the optimizer, and so slow down unnecessarily the program execution.

An example of expected behavior we do care about is the addition of an empty destructor to a base class.

```
class base
{
    public:
        void do_something() {}

    protected:
        ~base() {}
};

class derived : public base
{
};
```

Since the empty destructor adds no code, we expect the executable to be identical both with and without it.[41]
Our optimizing compiler will be assumed able to understand and deal optimally with the situations listed in the next paragraphs.

2.6.1. Inline

The compiler must be able to manage function inlining by itself, ignoring our inline directives and our code positioning (i.e. where the body of member functions is written).
The all-inline style places definitions and declarations inside the body of the class; every member function is implicitly inline:

```
template <typename T>
class vector
{
public:
    bool empty() const
    {
        // definition and declaration
    }
};
```

The merged header style splits definitions and declarations of non-inline member functions, but keeps them in the same file:

[41] From empirical analysis, it looks like sometimes a protected empty destructor inhibits optimizations. Some measurements have been published in [3]

```
template <typename T>
class vector
{
public:
   bool empty() const;    // definition, non inline
};

template <typename T>
bool vector <T>::empty() const
{
   // declaration
}
```

In any case, whether we explicitly write it or not, the inline directive is just more than a hint. Some popular compilers have indeed an option to inline any function at the compiler's discretion.

Specifically, we assume that

- a sequence of inline functions is always "optimal" if the functions are simple enough, no matter how long the sequence is:

```
template <typename T, int N = 0>
class recursive
{
   recursive<T,N-1> r_;

public:
   int size() const
   {
      return 1 + r_.size();
   }
};

template <typename T>
class recursive<T, 0>
{
public:
   int size() const
   {
      return 0;
   }
};
```

In the construction above, `recursive<T,N>::size()` will be inlined and the optimizer will simplify the call down to return `N`.

- the compiler is able to optimize a call to a (const) member function of a stateless object, the typical case being binary relation's `operator()`.

It's a common STL idiom to let a class hold a copy of a functor as a private member:

```
template <typename T>
struct less
{
   bool operator()(const T& x, const T& y) const
   {
      return x<y;
   }
};
```

```
template < typename T, typename less_t = std::less<T> >
class set
{
   less_t less_;                 // the less functor is a member

public:

   set(const less_t& less = less_t())
      : less_(less)
   {
   }

   void insert(const T& x)
   {
      // …
      if (less_(x,y))            // invoking less_t::operator()
      // …
   }

};
```

If the functor is indeed stateless and `operator()` is const, the code above should be equivalent to:

```
template <typename T>
struct less
{
   static bool apply(const T& x, const T& y)
   {
      return x<y;
   }
};
```

```
template < typename T, typename less_t = std::less<T> >
class set
{
public:

   void insert(const T& x)
   {
      // …
      if (less_t::apply(x,y))
```

However, we pay for the greater generality since the `less_` member will consume at least 1 byte of space. We can solve both issues if the compiler implements the EBO (***empty base optimization***)

```
class stateless_base
{
};

class derived : public stateless_base
{
   // ...
```

In other words, any derivation from a stateless base will not make the derived class larger.[42]

If `less` is actually a stateless structure, the EBO will not add extra bytes to the layout of `set`.

```
template <typename T>
struct less
{
   bool operator()(const T& x, const T& y) const
   {
      return x<y;
   }
};
```

```
template < typename T, typename less_t = std::less<T> >
class set : private less_t
{
   inline bool less(const T& x, const T& y) const
   {
      return static_cast<const less_t&>(*this)(x,y);
   }

public:

   set(const less_t& l = less_t())
      : less_t(l)
   {
   }

   void insert(const T& x)
   {
      // ...
      if (less(x,y))          // invoking less_t::operator() through *this
```

Note the auxiliary member function `less`, which is intended to prevent conflicts with any other `set::operator()`.

2.6.2. Error messages

We would like a compiler to give precise and useful error diagnostics, especially when dealing with templates. Unfortunately, the meaning of "precise" and "useful" may not be the same for a human and a compiler.

Sometime TMP techniques specifically induce the compiler to output some hint in the error message; the user, on the other hand, should be ready to figure out the ex-

42 Most compilers implement this optimizazion, at least in the case of single inheritance.

act error from some keywords contained in the compiler log, ignoring all the noise: here's an example of noise

```
\include\algorithm(21) : error 'void DivideBy10<T>::operator ()(T &) const' : cannot convert parameter
1 from 'const int' to 'int &'
        with
        [
            T=int
        ]
        Conversion loses qualifiers
        f:\TEST\iterator.cpp(41) : see reference to function template instantiation '_Fn1
std::for_each<XT::pair_iterator<iterator_t,N>,DivideBy10<T>>(_InIt,_InIt,_Fn1)' being compiled
        with
        [
            _Fn1= DivideBy10<int>,

iterator_t=std::_Tree<std::_Tmap_traits<int,double,std::less<int>,std::allocator<std::pair<const
int,double>>,false>>::iterator,
            N=1,
            T=int,

_InIt=XT::pair_iterator<std::_Tree<std::_Tmap_traits<int,double,std::less<int>,std::allocator<std::pair
<const int,double>>,false>>::iterator,1>
        ]
```

Here's what the user should see:

```
f:\TEST\iterator.cpp(41) : error in 'std::for_each (iterator, iterator, DivideBy10<int>)'
        with
            iterator = XT::pair_iterator<std::map<int, double>::const_iterator, 1>

 'void DivideBy10<T>::operator ()(T &) const' : cannot convert parameter 1 from 'const int' to 'int &'
```

This means that the caller of `for_each` wants to alter (maybe divide by 10?) the (constant) keys of a `std::map`, which is illegal. While the original error points to `<header>`, the true problem is in `"iterator.cpp"`.

Unfriendly entries in error messages happen because the "bare bone error" that the compiler sees may be "distant" from the semantic error.

Long template stack

As above, a function template can report an error, due to a parameter passed from its callers; modern compilers will list the whole chain of template instantiations. Since function templates usually rely on template frameworks, these errors are often several levels deep in the stack of function calls.

Implementation details

In the example above, the compiler shows `std::_Tree` instead of `std::map` because map::iterator happens to be defined in a separate base class (named `_Tree`); `std::map` has a public typedef that borrows iterator from its base class:

```
typedef typename _Tree<...>::iterator iterator;
```

These implementation details, which are usually hidden from the user of `std::map`, may leak in the error log.

Expanded typedefs

An error with `std::string` may show up as `std::basic_string<char, ...>` because some compilers will replace typedefs with their definition. The substitution may introduce a type which is unknown to the user.
However it is truly impossible for the compiler to decide whether it's convenient or not to perform these substitutions.

Suppose there are two metafunctions `F<T1>::type` and `G<T2>::type`,

```
typedef typename G<T>::type GT;
typedef typename F<GT>::type FGT;
```

An error may occur

- when T is not a valid argument for G, and in this case we'd like to read

```
error "F<GT> [where GT=G<int>::type]...".
```

- because `G<T>::type` (which is defined, but unknown to the user) is rejected by F, so it may be more useful

```
error "F<GT> [where GT=double]...".
```

However, if we don't know the result of G, a log entry such as "F<X> [where X=double]..." can be misleading (we may be not even aware that we are invoking F<double>).

Incomplete types

If wisely used, an incomplete type can be used to cause a specific error (cfr. Section 3.2); however, there are situations where a type is *not yet* complete and this may cause bizarre errors: a long, instructive example is in appendix 12.1.2.

As a rule, when a compiler says that "a constant is not a constant" or that "a type is not a type", this usually means that we are either defining a constant recursively, or that we are using a not-yet-complete class template.

2.6.3. Miscellanea Tips

Regardless of assumptions, real compilers can do any sort of things, so here are a few generic tips:

Don't blame the compiler

Bugs can lie:

- In the code, with probability (100-ε)%
- In the optimizer, with probability slightly greater than (ε/2)%
- In the compiler, with probability less than (ε/2)%

Even problems that show up only in release builds are rarely due to optimizer bugs: there are some natural differences between debug and release builds, and this may hide some errors in the program. Common factors are `#ifdef` sections, uninitialized variables, zero-filled heap memory returned by debug allocators, and so on.

Compilers do have bugs, but a common misconception is that they show up only in release builds: the following code, compiled by MSVC7.1 produces the right values in release and not in debug:

```
#include <iostream>

int main()
{
    unsigned __int64 x = 47;
    int y = -1;
    bool test1 = (x+y)<0;
    x += y;
    bool test2 = (x<0);
    bool test3 = (x<0);

    std::cout << test1 << test2 << test3;    // it should print 000

    return 0;
}
```

GCC4 in MacOSX in debug builds does not warn the user that there are multiple "main" functions in a console program and it silently produces a do-nothing executable.[43]

Keep warnings at the default level

A warning is just a guess. All compilers can recognize "idioms" that can be, with some probability, symptom of human errors; the higher the probability is, the lower the warning level. Displaying top-level warnings is very unlikely to reveal an error, but it will flood the compiler log with innocuous messages.[44]

---

[43] Mac OS X 10.4.8, XCode 2.4.1, GCC 4.01

[44] Set warnings at maximum level only once, in the very last development phase or when hunting for mysterious bugs.

Do not silence warnings with "dirty" code modifications.

If some particular warning is annoying, legitimate and provably not an error, don't modify the code; place a compiler-specific `#pragma` disable-warning directive around the line. This will be useful to future code reviewers.
However, this solution should be used with care (a warning in a deeply-nested function template might generate many long spurious entries in the compiler log).

One of the most dangerous warnings that should *not* be fixed is the "signed/unsigned comparison".
Many binary operations between mixed operands involve the promotion of both to unsigned, and negative numbers become positive and very large:[45] compilers will warn in some - not all - situations.

```
bool f(int a)
{
   unsigned int c = 10;
   return ((a+5)<c);
}
```

```
test01.cpp(4) : warning C4018: '<' : signed/unsigned mismatch
```

The function returns `true` for a∈{-5,-4,...,4}; if we change `c` to `int`, the warning disappears, but the function will behave differently.
The same code in a metafunction produces no warning at all:

```
template <int A>
class BizarreMF
{
   static const int B = 5;
   static const unsigned int C = 10;

public:
   static const bool value = ((A+B)<C);
};
```

```
bool t = BizarreMF<-10>::value;          // returns false
```

In real code, two situations are likely vulnerable to "signedness bugs":

- Updating a metafunction return type from enum to static unsigned constant:

```
static const bool value = (A+5) < OtherMF<B>::value; // unpredictable result
```

- Changing a container:

[45] Cfr. [4.7.2] in the standard

The C++ standard does not define univocally an integer type for array indices: if `p` has type `T*`, then `p[i] == *(p+i)`, so `i` should have type `ptrdiff_t`, which is signed; `vector<T>::operator[]` however takes an unsigned index.

To sum up, warnings are:

- compiler specific
- not related to code correctness (there exist both correct code that produces warnings and incorrect code that compiles cleanly)

Write code that produces the least warnings possible, but not less.

Maintain a catalogue of compiler bugs

This will be most useful when upgrading the compiler.

Avoid non-standard behaviour

This advice is in every book about C++, but we repeat it here. Programmers[46] tend to use their favorite compiler as the main tool to decide if a program is correct, instead of the C++ Standard; a reasonable empirical criterion is to use two or more compilers, then if they disagree, check the standard.

Don't be afraid of language features

Whenever there's a native C++ keyword, function or `std::` object assume that it's impossible to do better, unless trading some features.[47]
It's usually true that serious bottlenecks in C++ programs are related to a *misuse* of language features (and some features are more easily misused than other: candidates are virtual functions and dynamic memory allocation), but this does not imply that these features should be avoided.

Any operating system can allocate heap memory fast enough that a reasonable number of calls to `operator new` will get unnoticed.[48]
Some compilers allow to take a little memory from the stack via a function named `alloca`; in principle, `alloca` followed by a placement `new` (and an explicit destructor call) is roughly equivalent to `new`, but it incurs in alignment problems: while the standard grants that heap memory is suitably aligned for any type, this does not hold for stack. Even worse, building objects on unaligned memory, may work by

---

[46] Including the author of this book.

[47] Of course there are known exceptions to this rule: some C runtime functions (`sprintf`, `floor`) and even a few STL functions (`string::operator+`)

[48] Releasing memory may be a totally different matter, anyway.

chance on some platforms and, totally unobserved, may slow down all data operations.[49]

The opposite case is trading features: it is sometimes possible to do better than `new` under strong extra hypotheses, for example in a single threaded program where the allocation/deallocation pattern is known:

```
// assume T1 and T2 are unspecified concrete types, not template parameters

std::multimap<T1, T2> m;

while (m.size()>1)
{
   std::multimap<T1, T2>::iterator first  = ...;     // pick an element
   std::multimap<T1, T2>::iterator second = ...;     // pick another element

   std::pair<T1,T2> new_element = merge_elements(*first, *second);

   m.erase(first);                // line #1
   m.erase(second);               // line #2

   m.insert(new_element);         // line #3
}
```

Here we may hope to outperform the default new-based allocator, since two deletions are always followed by a single allocation; roughly speaking, when this is handled by system new/delete, the operating system has to be notified that more memory is available in line #2, but line #3 immediately reclaims the same amount of memory back.[50]

2.7. Include guards

As we already mentioned, a project is usually spread across many source files. Each file must be organized such that all dependencies and prerequisites are checked by the included file, not by the caller; in particular, header inclusion should never depend on the order of `#include` statements.

---

[49] On AMD processors, `double` should be aligned to 8 byte boundary, otherwise the CPU will perform multiple unnecessary load operations; on different processors, accessing an unaligned double will instantly crash the program

[50] In an empirical test on a similar algorithm, a map with a custom allocator improved the whole program by 25%; a general strategy is to reserve memory in chunks, and free them with some degree of laziness.

```
file "container.hpp"

#include <vector>                   // dependency is resolved here, not outside

#ifdef _WIN32                       // preconditions are checked here
#error This file requires a 128-bit operating system. Please, upgrade ASAP
#endif

template <typename T>
class very_large_container
{
   // internally uses std::vector...
};
```

Most frameworks end-up having a sort of ***root file***, which takes care of preparing the environment:

- Detection of current platform
- Translation of compiler-specific macros to framework macros
- Definition of general macros (such as `MXT_NAMESPACE_BEGIN`)
- Inclusion of STL headers
- Definition of lightweight structures, typedefs and constants

All other headers begin by including the root file, which is rarely modified; this will often decrease compilation time, since compilers can be instructed to distil a pre-compiled header from the root file.
An example follows:

```
////////////////////////////////////////////////////////////////////////
// platform detection

#if defined(_MSC_VER)
#define MXT_INT64     __int64
#elif defined(__GNUC__)
#define MXT_INT64     long long
#else
// ...
#endif

////////////////////////////////////////////////////////////////////////
// macro translation
// the framework will rely on MXT_DEBUG and MXT_RELEASE

#if defined(DEBUG) || defined(_DEBUG) || !defined(NDEBUG)
#define MXT_DEBUG
#else
#define MXT_RELEASE
#endif

////////////////////////////////////////////////////////////////////////
// general framework macros

#define MXT_NAMESPACE_BEGIN(x)      namespace x {
#define MXT_NAMESPACE_END(x)        }

////////////////////////////////////////////////////////////////////////
// STL

#include <complex>
#include <vector>
#include <map>
#include <utility>

////////////////////////////////////////////////////////////////////////

using std::swap;
using std::size_t;

typedef std::complex<double> dcmplx;
typedef unsigned int uint;

////////////////////////////////////////////////////////////////////////

struct empty
{
};
```

The basic ***include guard*** idiom prescribes to enclose each header in preprocessor directives which will prevent multiple inclusions in the same translation unit:

```
#ifndef MXT_filename_
#define MXT_filename_

// put code here

#endif //MXT_filename_
```

As a small variation of this technique, we can store something in `MXT_filename_`: After all, the whole point of this book is storing information in unusual places…

```
#ifndef MXT_filename_
#define MXT_filename_ 0x1020    // version number

// put code here

#endif //MXT_filename_
```

```
#include "filename.hpp"

#if MXT_filename_ < 0x1010
#error You are including an old version!
#endif
```

Anyway such a protection is ineffective against inclusion loops.
Loops happen more frequently in TMP, where there are only headers and no *.cpp file, so declarations and definitions either coincide or lie in the same file.

Suppose A.hpp is self-contained, B.hpp includes A.hpp and C.hpp includes B.hpp

```
file "A.hpp"

#ifndef MXT_A_
#define MXT_A_ 0x1010

template <typename T>    class A {};

#endif
```

```
file "B.hpp"

#ifndef MXT_B_
#define MXT_B_ 0x2020

#include "A.hpp"
template <typename T>    class B {};      // B uses A

#endif
```

Later, a developer modifies A.hpp so it includes C.hpp.

```
file "A.hpp"

#ifndef MXT_A_
#define MXT_A_ 0x1020
#include "C.hpp"
...
```

Now unfortunately, the preprocessor will produce a file that contains a copy of B before A:

```
// MXT_A_ is not defined, enter the #ifdef
#define MXT_A_ 0x1020

// A.hpp requires including "C.hpp"


  // MXT_C_ is not defined, enter the #ifdef
  #define MXT_C_ 0x3030

  // C.hpp requires including "B.hpp"

    // MXT_B_ is not defined, enter the #ifdef

    #define MXT_B _ 0x2020
    // B.hpp requires including A.hpp
    // however MXT_A_ is already defined, so do nothing!

    template <typename T> class B {};

    // end of include "B.hpp"

  template <typename T>   class C {};

  // end of include "C.hpp"

template <typename T> class A {};
```

This usually gives bizarre error messages (see also appendix 12.1.2).
To sum up, we should detect circular inclusion problems where a file includes (indirectly) a copy of itself before it has been fully compiled.
The following skeleton header helps (indentation is for illustration purposes only)

```
#ifndef MXT_filename_
#define MXT_filename_ 0x0000        // first, set version to "null"

   #include "other_header.hpp"

   ///////////////////////////////////////////////////////////////
   MXT_NAMESPACE_BEGIN(framework)
   ///////////////////////////////////////////////////////////////

   // write code here

   ///////////////////////////////////////////////////////////////
   MXT_NAMESPACE_END(framework)
   ///////////////////////////////////////////////////////////////

   #undef MXT_filename_             // finished! remove the null guard
   #define MXT_filename_ 0x1000     // define actual version number and quit

#else                               // if guard is defined...

   #if MXT_filename  == 0x0000      // ...but version is null
   #error Circular Inclusion        // ...then something is wrong!
   #endif

#endif //MXT_filename_
```

Such a header won't *solve* the circular inclusion (which is a design problem), but the compiler will *diagnose* it as soon as possible. Anyway, sometimes it might suffice to replace the `#error` statement with some forward declarations:

```
#ifndef MXT_my_vector_
#define MXT_my_vector_ 0x0000

   template <typename T>
   class my_vector
   {
      public:

         // ...

   };

   #undef MXT_my_vector_
   #define MXT_my_vector_ 0x1000

#else

   #if MXT_my_vector_ == 0x0000

   template <typename T>
   class my_vector;

   #endif

#endif //MXT_my_vector_
```

3. Small Object Toolkit

In previous chapters, we focused on the connection between template programming and style. In short, templates are elegant, as they allow writing efficient code that 'looks' simple and hide the complexity.

Recalling the introductory example of `sq` from section 2, it's clear that the first problem of TMP is the choice of the best C++ entity that models a concept, and that simultaneously makes code look clear at the point of instantiation.

Most classic functions use internally temporary variables and return a result; temporary variables are cheap, so we give a name to intermediate results to increase the readability of the algorithm:

```
int n_dogs = GetNumberOfDogs();
int n_cats = GetNumberOfCats();

int n_food_portions = n_dogs + n_cats;

BuyFood(n_food_portions);
```

In TMP, the moral equivalent of a temporary variable is an auxiliary type.
To model a concept, we will freely use lots of different types; most of them will do nothing, except "carry a meaning in their name", exactly as `n_food_portions` in the sample above.
This will be the main topic of section 3.3.

First, in the following paragraphs, we list some extremely simple objects that naturally come up as building blocks of complex patterns. These are called hollow, because they carry no data (they may have no members at all).

3.1. Hollow Types

3.1.1. instance_of

One of the most versatile tools in metaprogramming is `instance_of`:

```
template <typename T>
struct instance_of
{
   typedef T type;

   instance_of(int = 0)
   {
   }
};
```

The constructor allows us to declare global constants and quickly initialize them.

```
const instance_of<int> I_INT = instance_of<int>();   // fine but cumbersome
const instance_of<double> I_DOUBLE = 0;              // also fine.
```

> Remember that a const object must either be explicitly initialized, or have a user-defined default constructor; however if one simply writes
>
> ```
> struct empty
> {
>    empty() {}
> };
>
> const empty EMPTY;
> ```
>
> the compiler will likely warn that `EMPTY` is unused; a nice workaround to suppress the warning is in fact:
>
> ```
> struct empty
> {
>    empty(int = 0) {}
> };
>
> const empty EMPTY = 0;
> ```

3.1.2. Selector

The moral equivalent of a `bool` in template metaprogramming is a `selector`:

```
template <bool PARAMETER>
struct selector
{
};
```

Since their construction is inexpensive, both `instance_of` and `selector` are useful to replace explicit template parameter invocation:

```
template <bool B, typename T>
void f(const T& x)
{
}

int main()
{
   double d = 3.14;
   f<true>(d);                  // force B=true and deduce T=double
```

Or equivalently:

```
template <typename T, bool B>
void f(const T& x, selector<B>)
{
}

int main()
{
   double d = 3.14;
   f(d, selector<true>());             // deduce B=true and T=double
```

One of the advantages of the latter implementation is that we can give a meaningful name to the second parameter, using a (cheap) constant:

```
   const selector<true> TURN_ON_DEBUG_LOGGING;
   // ...
   f(d, TURN_ON_DEBUG_LOGGING);       // deduce B=true and T=double
```

3.1.3. Static value

The generalization of a selector is a static value:

```
template <typename T, T VALUE>
struct static_parameter
{
};
```

```
template <typename T, T VALUE>
struct static_value : static_parameter<T, VALUE>
{
   static const T value = VALUE;
};
```

Note that we could replace `selector<B>` with `static_value<bool, B>`.
In a `static_value`, T must be an integer type, otherwise the static const initialization becomes illegal; instead, in `static_parameter`, T can be a pointer (and `VALUE` can be a literal zero).

A member cast operator may be added, to allow switching from a static constant to a runtime integer:[51]

```
template <typename T, T VALUE>
struct static_value
{
   static const T value = VALUE;

   operator T () const
   {
      return VALUE;
   }

   static_value(int = 0)
   {
   }
};
```

So we can pass an instance of `static_value<int, 3>` to a function that requires `int`. However it's usually safer to write an external function:

```
template <typename T, T VALUE>
inline T static_value_cast(static_value<T, VALUE>)
{
   return VALUE;
};
```

3.1.4. Sizeof constraints

The C++ standard does not impose strict requirements on the size of elementary types[52] and compound types can have internal padding anywhere between members.

Given a type T, one wants to obtain another type T_2 whose `sizeof` is different. A very simple solution is:

```
template <typename T>
class larger_than
{
   T body_[2];    // private, not meant to be used
};
```

It must hold that `sizeof(T)<2*sizeof(T)≤sizeof(larger_than<T>)`; however the second inequality can be indeed strict, if compiler adds padding (suppose T is `char` and any struct has minimum size 4 bytes).

---

[51] See for example paragraph 5.1.2

[52] Only weak ordering is granted: `1=sizeof(char)≤sizeof(short)≤sizeof(int)≤sizeof(long)`

The most important usage of this class is to define two types (see section 5.2.1):

```
typedef char no_type;
typedef larger_than<no_type> yes_type;
```

Warning: the definitions above are not compatible with C++0x `std::false_type` and `std::true_type`, which instead are equivalent to `static_value<bool, false>` and `static_value<bool, true>`

In practice, we can safely use `char`, whose size is 1 by definition, and `ptrdiff_t` (as in most platforms a pointer is larger than 1 byte).
It is possible to declare a type having exactly size N (with N>0):

```
template <size_t N>
struct fixed_size
{
   typedef char type[N];
};
```

So that `sizeof(fixed_size<N>::type) == N`.
Note that `fixed_size<N>` itself can have any size (at least N, but possibly larger).

Remember that it's illegal to declare a function that returns an array, but a *reference* to array is fine and has the same size:[53]

```
fixed_size<3>::type f();    // error: illegal

int three = sizeof(f());
```

```
fixed_size<3>::type& f();   // ok

int three = sizeof(f());    // ok, three == 3
```

3.2. Static assertions

Static assertions are simple classes whose purpose is to induce a (compiler) error when a template parameter does not meet some specifications.
We illustrate here only the most elementary variations on the theme.
Usually we exploit the fact that an incomplete type cannot be constructed, or that `sizeof(T)` causes a compiler error if `T` is incomplete.

[53] This remark will be clear in view of the material presented in section 5.2.1.

3.2.1. Boolean assertions

The easiest way to verify a statement is to use a selector-like class, whose body is not present if the condition is false:

```
template <bool STATEMENT>
struct static_assert
{
};

template <>
struct static_assert<false>;
```

```
int main()
{
   static_assert<sizeof(int)==314> ASSERT_LARGE_INT;
   return 0;
}
```

```
1> test.cpp(28) : error C2079: 'ASSERT_LARGE_INT' uses undefined struct 'static_assert<false>'
```

All variations of the idiom try to trick the compiler into emitting more user-friendly error messages. Some enhancements have been proposed by Alexandrescu: here's an example.

```
template <bool STATEMENT>
struct static_assert;

template <>
struct static_assert<true>
{
   static_assert()
   {}

   template <typename T>
   static_assert(T)
   {}
};

template <> struct static_assert<false>;
```

```
struct error_CHAR_IS_UNSIGNED {};

int main()
{
   const static_assert<sizeof(double)!=8> ASSERT1("invalid double");
   const static_assert<(char(255)>0)> ASSERT2(error_CHAR_IS_UNSIGNED());
}
```

If condition is false, the compiler will report something like: cannot build `static_assert<false>` from `error_CHAR_IS_UNSIGNED`.

Each assertion wastes some bytes on the stack, but it can be wrapped in a macro-directive using `sizeof`:

```
#define MXT_ASSERT(statement)      sizeof(static_assert<(statement)>)
```

The invocation

```
    MXT_ASSERT(sizeof(double)!=8);
```

will translate to `[[some integer]];` if successful and to an error otherwise. Since `1;` is a no-op, the optimizer will ignore it.

The very problem with macro-assertions is the *comma*:

```
    MXT_ASSERT(is_well_defined< std::map<int, double> >::value);
    //                                      ^
    //                                  comma here
    //
    // warning or error! MXT_ASSERT does not take 2 parameters
```

The argument of the macro in this case is probably the string up to the first comma (i.e. `is_well_defined< std::map<int`) so even if the code compiles, it won't behave as intended.
Two workarounds are possible: either typedef'ing away the comma, or putting extra brackets around the argument:

```
    typedef std::map<int, double> map_type;
    MXT_ASSERT( is_well_defined<map_type>::value );

    MXT_ASSERT(( is_well_defined< std::map<int, double> >::value ));
```

The C++ preprocessor will be confused only by commas which are at the same level[54] as the argument of the macro:

```
    assert( f(x,y)==4 ); // comma at level 2: ok
    assert( f(x),y==4 ); // comma at level 1: error
```

`static_assert` can be used to make assertions in classes using private inheritance:

```
template <typename T>
class small_object_allocator : static_assert<(sizeof(T)<64)>
{
};
```

[54] The level of a character is the number of open brackets minus the number of close brackets in the string from the beginning of the line up to the character itself.

static_assert is a keyword in the next C++ Standard; here we use the same name for a class for illustration purposes, but a C++0x conformant compiler will reject the code.

C++0x static_assert behaves like a function that takes a constant boolean expression and a string literal, that contains an error message that the compiler will print:

```
static_assert(sizeof(T)<64, "T is too large");
```

Similarly to the private inheritance described above, C++0x static_assert can also be a class member.

3.2.2. Assert legal

A different way of making assertions is to require that some C++ expression represents valid code for type T, returning non void (most often, to state that a constructor or an assignment is possible).

```
#define MXT_ASSERT_LEGAL(statement)        sizeof(statement)
```

If instead void is allowed, just put a comma operator inside sizeof:

```
#define MXT_ASSERT_LEGAL(statement)        sizeof((statement), 0)
```

For example:

```
template <typename T>
void do_something(T& x)
{
   MXT_ASSERT_LEGAL(static_cast<bool>(x.empty()));

   If (x.empty())
   {
      // ...
```

The example above will compile, and thus it will not reject T if x.empty(), whatever it means, returns (anything convertible to) bool: T could have a member function named empty returning int, or a member named empty whose operator() takes no argument and returns bool.

Here's another application:

```
#define MXT_CONST_REF_TO(T)          (*static_cast<const T*>(0))
#define MXT_REF_TO(T)                (*static_cast<T*>(0))
```

```
template <typename obj_t, typename iter_t>
class assert_iterator
{
   enum
   {
      verify_construction =
         MXT_ASSERT_LEGAL( obj_t( *MXT_CONST_REF_TO(iter_t) ) ),

      verify_assignment =
         MXT_ASSERT_LEGAL( MXT_REF_TO(obj_t) = *MXT_CONST_REF_TO(iter_t) ),

      verify_preincr =
         MXT_ASSERT_LEGAL( ++MXT_REF_TO(iter_t) ),

      verify_postincr =
         MXT_ASSERT_LEGAL( MXT_REF_TO(iter_t)++ )
   };
};
```

A human programmer should read: "I assert it's legal to construct an instance of `obj_t` from the result of dereferencing a (const) instance of `iter_t`" and similarly for the remaining constants.

> Note that some standard iterators may fail the first test, for example a `back_insert_iterator` may return itself when dereferenced (a special assignment operator will take care of making `*i = x` equivalent to `i = x`)

`assert_iterator<T,I>` will compile only if `I` acts like an iterator having value type (convertible to) `T`; for example, if `I` does not support postincrement, the compiler will stop and report an error in `assert_iterator<T,I>::verify_postincr`. Remember that, with the usual restrictions on comma characters in macros, `MXT_ASSERT_LEGAL` does never instantiate objects, since `sizeof` performs only a dimensional check on its arguments.[55]

Also, note the special use of a macro directive: `MXT_ASSERT_LEGAL` should take the whole line, but since it resolves to a compile-time integer constant, we can use enums to "label" all the different assertions about a class (as we did in `assert_iterator`) and make the code more friendly.

The compiler might also emit useful warnings pointing to our assertions: if `obj_t` is `int` and `iter_t` is `double*`, the compiler will refer to the `verify_assignment` enumerator and emit a message similar to:

---

[55] However a few compilers will anyway generate a warning on `MXT_INSTANCE_OF`, reporting that a null reference is not allowed.

```
iterator.hpp(27) : warning C4244: '=' : conversion from 'double' to 'int', possible loss of data
        : see reference to class template instantiation 'XT::assert_iterator<obj_t,iter_t>' being
compiled
        with
        [
            obj_t=int,
            iter_t=double *
        ]
```

Using the very same technique, we are able to mix static assertions of different kind:

```
#define MXT_ASSERT(statement)        sizeof(static_assert<(statement)>)
```

```
   enum
   {
      construction =
         MXT_ASSERT_LEGAL( obj_t( *MXT_CONST_REF_TO(iter_t) ) ),
      size =
         MXT_ASSERT( sizeof(int)==4 )
   };
```

As an exercise, we list here some more heuristic assertions on iterators.
As is, class `assert_iterator` validates forward `const_iterators`; we may remove const-ness:

```
template <typename obj_t, typename iter_t>
class assert_nonconst_iterator : public assert_iterator<obj_t, iter_t>
{
   enum
   {
      write =
         MXT_ASSERT_LEGAL(*MXT_REF_TO(iter_t) = MXT_CONST_REF_TO(obj_t))
   };
};
```

Sometimes, an algorithm that works on iterators does not need to know the actual type of the underlying objects, and that makes the code even more general. For example, `std::count` could look like this:

```
template <typename iter_t, typename object_t>
int count(iter_t begin, const iter_t end, const object_t& x)
{
   int result = 0;
   while (begin != end)
   {
      if (*begin == x)
         ++result;
   }
   return result;
}
```

We don't need to know if `*begin` has the same type of `x`: regardless of what exactly `*begin` is, we assume that it defines an `operator==` suitable for comparing against an `object_t`.
Suppose instead we have to store the result of `*begin` before comparison.
We may require the iterator type to follow the STL conventions, thus enforcing that `object_t` and `iterator::value_type` are somehow compatible:[56]

```
template <typename obj_t, typename iter_t>
class assert_stl_iterator
{
   typedef typename std::iterator_traits<iter_t>::value_type value_type;

   enum
   {
      assign1 =
        MXT_ASSERT_LEGAL(MXT_REF_TO(obj_t) = MXT_CONST_REF_TO(value_type)),

      assign2 =
        MXT_ASSERT_LEGAL(MXT_REF_TO(value_type) = MXT_CONST_REF_TO(obj_t))

   };
};
```

Finally, we can perform a rough check on the iterator type, either using `indicator_traits` to get its tag, or writing operations with `MXT_ASSERT_LEGAL`:

```
enum
{
   random_access = MXT_ASSERT_LEGAL(
      MXT_CONST_REF_TO(iter_t) + int() == MXT_CONST_REF_TO(iter_t))
```

3.2.3. Assertions with overloaded operators

`sizeof` can evaluate the size of an arbitrary expression.
We can thus create assertions of the form `sizeof(f(x))` where f is an overloaded function, which may return an incomplete type.
Here we just present an example, but the technique will be explained in section 5.2.1.

Suppose we want to check an array length:

```
T arr[] = { ... };

// later, assert that lengthof(arr) is some constant
```

Since static assertions need a compile-time constant, we cannot define 'lengthof' as a function.

---

[56] Actually, dereferencing the iterator returns `std::iterator_traits<iterator_t>::reference`, but `value_type` can be constructed from a reference.

```
template <typename T, size_t N>
size_t lengthof(T (&)[N])
{
   return N;
}
```

```
MXT_ASSERT(lengthof(arr) == 7);     // error: not a compile-time constant
```

A macro would work:

```
#define lengthof(a)     sizeof(a)/sizeof(a[0])
```

But it's risky, because it can be invoked on an unrelated type that supports `operator[]` (e.g. `std::vector`), with nasty implications.

However we can write:

```
class incomplete_type;
class complete_type {};

template <size_t N>
struct compile_time_const
{
   complete_type& operator==(compile_time_const<N>) const;

   template <size_t K>
   incomplete_type& operator==(compile_time_const<K>) const;
};
```

```
template <typename T>
compile_time_const<0> lengthof(T)
{
   return compile_time_const<0>();
}

template <typename T, size_t N>
compile_time_const<N> lengthof(T (&)[N])
{
   return compile_time_const<N>();
}
```

Unfortunately invocation is not trivial:

```
sizeof(lengthof(arr) == compile_time_const<7>());
```

3.2.4. Modeling concepts with function pointers

The following idea has been documented by Bjarne Stroustrup.
A concept is a set of logical requirements on a type that can be translated in syntactic requirements.
For example, a "less-than comparable" type must implement some form of `operator<`: we don't care about the exact meaning of `a<b`, but only that such an expression can be used as a boolean. Complex concepts may require several syntactic constraints at once.

To impose a complex constraint on a tuple of template parameters, we simply write a static member function, where all code lines together model the concept (in other words, if all the lines compile successfully, the constraint is satisfied); then we induce the compiler to emit the corresponding code simply initializing a dummy function pointer in the constructor of a dedicated assertion class (the concept function itself never runs):

```
template <typename T1, typename T2>
struct static_assert_can_copy_T1_to_T2
{
    static void concept_check(T1 x, T2 y)
    {
       T2 z(x);          // T2 must be constructable from T1
       y = x;            // T2 must be assignable from T1
    }

    static_assert_can_copy_T1_to_T2()
    {
       void (*f)(T1, T2) = concept_check;
    }
};
```

The concept check can be triggered when either building an instance on the stack, or deriving:

```
template <typename T>
T sqrt(T x)
{
   static_assert_can_copy_T1_to_T2<T, double> CHECK1;
```

```
template <typename T>
class math_operations : static_assert_can_copy_T1_to_T2<T, double>
{
```

3.3. Tagging techniques

Assume we have a class with a member function `swap` and we need to add an "unsafe swap" (regardless of what it means); this is a variation of an existing function, but it can be modeled as:

- A different function with a similar name (and - hopefully - a similar signature)

```
public:
   void swap(T& that);
   void unsafe_swap(T& that);
```

- An overload of the original function with an extra runtime argument

```
private:
   void unsafe_swap(T& that);

public:
   void swap(T& that);

   enum swap_style { SWAP_SAFE, SWAP_UNSAFE };

   void swap(T& that, swap_style s)
   {
      if (s == SWAP_SAFE)
         this->swap(that);
      else
         this->unsafe_swap(that);
   }
```

- An overload of the original function with an extra static *useless* argument

```
public:
   void swap(T& that);
   void swap(T& that, int);   // unsafe swap: call as x.swap(y, 0)
```

None of these options is completely satisfactory: the first is clear, but it does not scale well, as the interface could grow too much; the second may pay a penalty at runtime; the last is not intuitive and should be documented.

Instead, TMP makes heavy use of ***language-neutral idioms***, i.e. language constructs that have no impact on code generation.
A basic technique for the issue above is overload resolution via ***tag objects***; each member of the overload set has a formal unnamed parameter of different static type.

```
struct unsafe {};

class X
{
public:
   void swap(T& that);
   void swap(T& that, unsafe);
```

Here's a different example:

```
struct naive_algorithm_tag {};
struct precise_algorithm_tag {};

template <typename T>
inline T log1p(T x, naive_algorithm_tag)
{
   return log(x+1);
}

template <typename T>
inline T log1p(T x, precise_algorithm_tag)
{
   const T xp1 = x+1;
   return xp1==1 ? x : x*log(xp1)/(xp1-1);
}
```

```
// later...

double t1 = log1p(3.14, naive_algorithm_tag());
double t2 = log1p(0.00000000314, precise_algorithm_tag());
```

Building a temporary tag is inexpensive (most optimizing compilers will do nothing and behave as if we had two functions named `log1p_naive` and `log1p_precise`, with one parameter each).

We dig a bit further in the mechanisms of overload selection.
Recall that we are facing the problem of picking the right function at compile time, supplying a meaningful (for a human) extra parameter.

The extra parameter is usually an unnamed instance of an empty class:

```
template <typename T>
inline T log1p(T x, selector<true>);

template <typename T>
inline T log1p(T x, selector<false>);
```

```
// code #1
return log1p(x, selector<PRECISE_ALGORITHM>());
```

One could wander why a type is necessary, when the same effect can be achieved with a simpler syntax:

```
// code #2
if (USE_PRECISE_ALGORITHM)
   return log1p_precise(x);
else
   return log1p_standard(x);
```

The key principle in tag dispatching is that the program compiles only the functions that are strictly necessary: in code #1 the compiler sees one function call, but in the

second fragment, there are two; the "if" decision is fixed, but this is irrelevant (as is the fact that the optimizer may simplify the redundant code later).
Tag dispatching allows in fact selecting between a function that works and one that would not even compile (see the paragraph below about iterators).

This does not imply that *every* if with a static decision variable must be turned to a function call: typically, in the middle of a complex algorithm, an explicit statement may be cleaner:

```
do_it();
do_it_again();

if (my_options<T>::need_to_clean_up)
   std::fill(begin, end, T());
```

3.3.1. Type tags

The simplest tags are just empty structures:

```
struct naive_algorithm_tag {};
struct precise_algorithm_tag {};

template <typename T>
inline T log1p(T x, naive_algorithm_tag);

template <typename T>
inline T log1p(T x, precise_algorithm_tag);
```

We can use template tags to transport extra parameters to the function:

```
template <int N>
struct algorithm_precision_level {};

template <typename T, int N>
inline T log1p(T x, algorithm_precision_level<N>);

// ...

double x = log1p(3.14, algorithm_precision_level<4>());
```

We can use derivation to build a tag hierarchy.
This example sketches what actual STL implementations do:

```
struct input_iterator_tag {};
struct output_iterator_tag {};
struct forward_iterator_tag : public input_iterator_tag {};
struct bidirectional_iterator_tag : public forward_iterator_tag {};
struct random_access_iterator_tag : public bidirectional_iterator_tag {};

template <typename iter_t>
void somefunc(iter_t begin, iter_t end)
{
   return somefunc(begin, end,
      typename std::iterator_traits<iter_t>::iterator_category());
}

template <typename iter_t>
void somefunc(iter_t begin, iter_t end, std::bidirectional_iterator_tag)
{
   // do the work here
}
```

bidirectional and random_access iterators will use the last overload of somefunc; vice versa, if somefunc is invoked on any other iterator, the compiler will produce an error.

We can add a generic implementation that processes all tags which do not have an exact match:[57]

```
template <typename iter_t, typename tag_t>
void somefunc(iter_t begin, iter_t end, tag_t)
{
   // generic implementation:
   // any tag for which there's no *exact* match, will fall here
}
```

This generic implementation can be made compatible with the tag hierarchy using pointers:

```
template <typename iter_t>
void somefunc(iter_t begin, iter_t end)
{
   typedef typename std::iterator_traits<iter_t>::iterator_category cat_t;
   return somefunc(begin, end, static_cast<cat_t*>(0));
}

template <typename iter_t>
void somefunc(iter_t begin, iter_t end, std::bidirectional_iterator_tag*)
{
   // do the work here
}

template <typename iter_t>
void somefunc(iter_t begin, iter_t end, void*)
{
   // generic
}
```

[57] In particular, this will process also random_access iterators, i.e. it blindly ignores the base/derived tag hierarchy

The overload resolution rules will try to select the match that loses less information: thus the cast `derived*-to-base*` is a better match than a cast to `void*`. So, whenever possible (i.e. whenever the iterator category is at least bidirectional) the second function will be taken.
Another valuable option would be:

```
template <typename iter_t>
void somefunc(iter_t begin, iter_t end, ...)
{
   // generic
}
```

The ellipsis operator is the worst match at all, but it cannot be used when the tag is a class (and this is exactly the reason why we had to switch to pointers tags).

3.3.2. Tagging with functions

A slightly more sophisticated option is to use function pointers as tags:

```
enum algorithm_tag_t
{
   ALGO_NAIVE,
   ALGO_PRECISE
};

inline static_value<algorithm_tag_t, ALGO_NAIVE> naive_algorithm_tag()
{
   return 0; // dummy function body: calls static_value(int)
}

inline static_value<algorithm_tag_t, ALGO_PRECISE> precise_algorithm_tag()
{
   return 0; // dummy function body: calls static_value(int)
}
```

The tag is not the return type, but the function itself. The idea comes somehow from STL stream manipulators (which however have all a common signature).

```
typedef static_value<algorithm_tag_t, ALGO_NAIVE> (*naive_algorithm_tag_t)();
typedef static_value<algorithm_tag_t, ALGO_PRECISE>
(*precise_algorithm_tag_t)();

template <typename T>
inline T log1p(T x, naive_algorithm_tag_t);
```

```
// later
// line 4: pass a function as a tag

double y = log1p(3.14, naive_algorithm_tag);
```

Since we gave each function a different unique signature, we can use the function name (equivalent to a function pointer) as a global constant. Inline functions are the only "constants" that can be written in a header file, without causing linker errors.

This has the advantage we can omit brackets from tags (compare line 4 above with its equivalent in the previous example). Function tags can be grouped in a namespace, or be static members of a struct:

```
namespace algorithm_tag
{
   inline static_value<algorithm_tag_t, ALGO_NAIVE> naive()
   { return 0; }

   inline static_value<algorithm_tag_t, ALGO_PRECISE> precise()
   { return 0; }
}
```

Or:

```
struct algorithm_tag
{
   static static_value<algorithm_tag_t, ALGO_NAIVE> naive()
   { return 0; }

   static static_value<algorithm_tag_t, ALGO_PRECISE> precise()
   { return 0; }
};
```

```
double y = log1p(3.14, algorithm_tag::naive);
```

Another dramatic advantage of function pointers is that we can adopt a uniform syntax for the same runtime and compile-time algorithm:

```
enum binary_operation
{
   sum,   difference,   product,   division
};
```

```
#define mxt_SUM    x+y
#define mxt_DIFF   x-y
#define mxt_PROD   x*y
#define mxt_DIV    x/y
```

```
// define both the tag and the worker function with a single macro

#define mxt_DEFINE(OPCODE, FORMULA)                                      \
                                                                         \
inline static_value<binary_operation, OPCODE> static_tag_##OPCODE()     \
{                                                                        \
   return 0;                                                             \
}                                                                        \
                                                                         \
template <typename T>                                                    \
T binary(T x, T y, static_value<binary_operation, OPCODE>)              \
{                                                                        \
   return (FORMULA);                                                     \
}
```

```
mxt_DEFINE(sum, mxt_SUM);
mxt_DEFINE(difference, mxt_DIFF);
mxt_DEFINE(product, mxt_PROD);
mxt_DEFINE(division, mxt_DIV);
```

```
template <typename T, binary_operation OP>
inline T binary(T x, T y, static_value<binary_operation, OP> (*)())
{
   return binary(x, y, static_value<binary_operation, OP>());
}
```

This is the usual machinery needed for the static selection of the function: due to the way we defined overloads, the following calls give identical results (otherwise it would be quite surprising for the user), even if they are not identical (the first is preferred):

```
   double a1 = binary(8.0, 9.0, static_tag_product);
   double a2 = binary(8.0, 9.0, static_tag_product());
```

However with the same tools, we can further refine the function and add a similar runtime algorithm:[58]

```
template <typename T>
T binary(T x, T y, const binary_operation op)
{
   switch (op)
   {
   case sum:        return mxt_SUM;
   case difference: return mxt_DIFF;
   case product:    return mxt_PROD;
   case division:   return mxt_DIV;
   default:
      throw std::runtime_error("invalid operation");
   }
}
```

The latter would be invoked as:

[58] This example anticipates ideas from section 8.3.

```
double a3 = binary(8.0, 9.0, product);
```

This may look similar, but it's a completely different function: it shares some implementation (in this case, the four kernel macros), but it selects the right one *at run time*.
However, usage syntax is totally similar.

Manipulators (see 2.4.7) are similar to functions used as compile-time constants, however:

- manipulators are more generic: all operations have a similar signature (which must be supported by the stream object), any user can supply more of them, but they involve some runtime dispatch.
- function constants are a fixed set, but since there's a one-to-one match between signatures and overloaded operators, there is no runtime work

3.3.3. Tag iteration

A useful feature of functions tagged with static values is that, playing with bits and compile-time computations, it's possible to write functions that automatically unroll some "iterative calls".

For example, the following function fills a C-array with zeroes:

```
template <typename T, int N>
void zeroize_helper(T* const data, static_value<int, N>)
{
   zeroize_helper(data, static_value<int, N-1>());
   data[N-1] = T();
}

template <typename T>
void zeroize_helper(T* const data, static_value<int, 1>)
{
   data[0] = T();
}

template <typename T, int N>
void zeroize(T (&data)[N])
{
   zeroize_helper(data, static_value<int, N>());
}
```

We can swap two lines and iterate backwards:

```
{
    data[N-1] = T();
    zeroize_helper(data, static_value<int, N-1>());
}
```

As a more complex case, we can iterate over a set of values, not necessarily 1...N. Assume an enumeration describes some heuristic algorithms in increasing order of complexity:

```
enum
{
    ALGORITHM_1,
    ALGORITHM_2,
    ALGORITHM_3,
    ALGORITHM_4,
    // ...
```

For each value in the enumeration, we are given a function that performs a check and returns true when everything is ok, or false if it detects a problem:

```
bool heuristic([[args]], static_value<size_t, ALGORITHM_1>);
bool heuristic([[args]], static_value<size_t, ALGORITHM_2>);

// ...
```

We would like to run some or all the checks, in increasing order, with a single function call.
First, modify the enumeration using powers of 2:

```
enum
{
    ALGORITHM_1 = 1,
    ALGORITHM_2 = 2,
    ALGORITHM_3 = 4,
    ALGORITHM_4 = 8,
    // ...
};
```

The user will use a static value as a tag, and algorithms will be combined with "bitwise or" (or +)

```
typedef static_value<size_t, ALGORITHM_1 | ALGORITHM_4> mytag_t;
```

```
// this is the public function

template <size_t K>
bool run_heuristics([[args]], static_value<size_t, K>)
{
  return
   heuristic([[args]], static_value<size_t, K>(), static_value<size_t, 0>());
}
```

And here are the "private" implementation details:

```
template <size_t K, size_t J>
bool heuristic([[args]], static_value<size_t, K>, static_value<size_t, J>)
{
   static const size_t JTH_BIT = K & (size_t(1) << J);

   // JTH_BIT is either 0 or a power of 2.
   // try running the corresponding algorithm, first
   // if it succeeds, the && will continue with new tags,
   // with the J-th bit turned off in K and J incremented by 1

   return
    heuristic([[args]], static_value<size_t, JTH_BIT>()) &&
    heuristic([[args]], static_value<size_t, K-JTH_BIT >(),
                                          static_value<size_t, J+1>());
}

template <size_t J>
bool heuristic([[args]], static_value<size_t, 0>, static_value<size_t, J>)
{
   // finished, all bits have been removed from K

   return true;
}

template <size_t K>
bool heuristic([[args]], static_value<size_t, K>)
{
   // this is invoked for all bits in K that do not have a corresponding
   // algorithm, and when K=0 i.e. when a bit in K is off

   return true;
}
```

3.3.4. Tags and inheritance

Some classes inherit additional overloads from their bases. So an object that dispatches a tagged call may not know which of the bases will answer.

Suppose we are given a simple allocator class, which, given a fixed size, will allocate one block of memory of that length.

```
template <size_t SIZE>
struct fixed_size_allocator
{
   void* get_block();
};
```

We now wrap it up in a larger allocator: assuming for simplicity that most memory requests have size equal to a power of 2, we assemble a `compound_pool<N>` that will contain a `fixed_size_allocator<J>` for J=1,2,4,8... And it will resort to `::operator new` when no suitable J exists (all at compile-time).
The syntax for allocation will be:[59]

```
compound_pool<64> A;
double* p = A.allocate<double>();
```

The sketch of the idea is: `compound_pool<N>` contains a `fixed_size_allocator<N>` and derives from `compound_pool<N/2>`; so it can honor directly allocation requests of N bytes and it will dispatch all other tags to base classes; if the last base, `compound_pool<0>`, takes the call, no better match exists, so we will call `operator new`.
More precisely, every class has a pick function that returns either an allocator reference or a pointer.

The call tag is `static_value<size_t, N>` where N is the size of the requested memory block.

```
template <size_t SIZE>
class compound_pool;
```

```
template < >
class compound_pool<0>
{
protected:

   template <size_t N>
   void* pick(static_value<size_t, N>)
   {
      return ::operator new(N);
   }
};
```

[59] Deallocation has been omitted on purpose, but it easily follows.

```
template <size_t SIZE>
class compound_pool : compound_pool<SIZE/2>
{
   fixed_size_allocator<SIZE> p_;

protected:

   using compound_pool<SIZE/2>::pick;

   fixed_size_allocator<SIZE>& pick(static_value<SIZE>)
   {
      return p_;
   }

public:

   template <typename object_t>
   object_t* allocate()
   {
      typedef static_value<size_t, sizeof(object_t)> selector_t;
      return static_cast<object_t*>(get_pointer(this->pick(selector_t())));
   }

private:

   template <size_t N>
   void* get_pointer(fixed_size_allocator<N>& p)
   {
      return p.get_block();
   }

   void* get_pointer(void* p)
   {
      return p;
   }
};
```

Note the using declaration that makes visible all the overloaded `pick` functions in every class.

`compound_pool<0>::pick` has a lower priority because it's a function template, but it always succeeds: furthermore, since it returns a different object, it ends selecting a different `get_pointer`.

#include <prerequisites>

#include <techniques>

#include <applications>

4. Static Programming

Templates are exceptionally good in forcing the compiler and the optimizer to perform some work only once: when the executable program is being generated. By definition, this is called ***static*** work, as opposite to dynamic work, which refers to what is being done when the program runs.
Some activities must be performed entirely before runtime (computing integer constants) and some activities have an impact on runtime (generating machine code for a function template, which is later executed).

TMP can produce two different types of code: metafunctions, entirely static (e.g. a metafunction `unsigned_integer<N>::type` that returns an integer holding at least N bits), and mixed algorithms, part static and part runtime (e.g. STL algorithms relying on `iterator_category` or the `zeroize` function in section 5.1.2 below).

This section deals with techniques for writing efficient metafunctions.

4.1. Static programming with the preprocessor

The classic way to write a program that takes decisions about itself is through preprocessor directives. The C++ preprocessor can perform some integer computations tests and *cut off* portions of code that are not appropriate.

Consider the following example: we want to define fixed-length unsigned integer types, such as `uint32_t` being exactly 32-bit wide, and similarly for any bit length which is a power of 2.
Define

```
template <size_t S>
struct uint_n;

#define mXT_UINT_N(T,N)      template <> struct uint_n<N> { typedef T type; }
```

and specialize `uint_n` for all sizes that are indeed supported on current platform.
If the user tries `uint_n<16>::type` and there's no suitable type, she will get a proper and intelligible compiler error (missing template specialization).
So we ask the preprocessor to work out the sizes by trial and error:[60]

[60] Remember that the preprocessor runs *before* the compiler, and so in particular it cannot rely on `sizeof`.

```
#include <climits>

#define MXT_I32BIT      0xffffffffU
#define MXT_I16BIT      0xffffU
#define MXT_I8BIT       0xffU

#if (UCHAR_MAX == MXT_I8BIT)
mXT_UINT_N(unsigned char,8);
#endif

#if (USHRT_MAX == MXT_I16BIT)
mXT_UINT_N(unsigned short,16);
#elif UINT_MAX == MXT_I16BIT
mXT_UINT_N(unsigned int,16);
#endif

#if (UINT_MAX == MXT_I32BIT)
mXT_UINT_N(unsigned int,32);
#elif (ULONG_MAX == MXT_I32BIT)
mXT_UINT_N(unsigned long,32);
#endif
```

The above code works, but it's rather fragile, because interaction between the preprocessor and the compiler is limited.[61]

Note that this is not merely a generic style debate (macro versus templates), but a matter of correctness: if the preprocessor removes portions of the source file, the compiler does not have a chance to diagnose all errors, until macro definitions change; on the opposite, TMP decisions rely on the fact that the compiler sees a whole set of templates, then it instantiates only some of them.

> The preprocessor is not "evil"; however bugs caused by a misuse of the preprocessor are quite hard to detect.
> We should mention that preprocessor-based "metaprogramming", like the example above, usually compiles much faster and it's more portable: many high-end servers still ship with old or custom compilers that do not truly support language-based (template) metaprogramming.

An implementation of `uint_n` that does not rely on the preprocessor is given in section 4.6.10.

4.2. Compilation complexity

When a class template is instantiated, the compiler generates:

- every member signature at class level
- all static constants and typedefs
- only strictly necessary function bodies

[61] Read the previous note again ☺

If the same instance is needed again in the same compilation unit, then it's found via lookup (which need not be particularly efficient, but it's anyway faster than instantiation).
For example, given the following code:

```
template <size_t N>
struct sum_of_integers_up_to
{
   static const size_t value = N + sum_of_integers_up_to<N-1>::value;
};

template <>
struct sum_of_integers_up_to<0>
{
   static const size_t value = 0;
};
```

```
int n9 = sum_of_integers_up_to<9>::value;
int n8 = sum_of_integers_up_to<8>::value;
```

```
    int n9 = sum_of_integers_up_to<9>::value;
    mov          dword ptr [n9],2Dh

    int n8 = sum_of_integers_up_to<8>::value;
    mov          dword ptr [n8],24h
```

The initialization of `n9` has a cost of 10 template instantiations, but the subsequent initialization of `n8` has a cost of *one* lookup (not 9); both instructions have zero runtime impact, as the assembly code shows.

As a rule, most metafunctions are implemented using recursion. The compilation complexity is the number of template instances recursively required by the metafunction itself.
The example above has linear complexity, because the instantiation of `X<N>` needs `X<N-1>... X<0>`. While we usually look for the implementation with the lowest complexity (to reduce compilation times, not execution times), we may skip this optimization if there's a large code reuse: due to lookups, the first instantiation of `X<N>` will be costly, but it allows instantiation of `X<M>` for free in the same translation unit if `M<N`.
Let's see an example of an optimized low-complexity implementation:

```
template <size_t N, size_t K>
struct static_raise
{
   static const size_t value = /* N raised to K */;
};
```

The trivial implementation has linear complexity:

```
template <size_t N, size_t K>
struct static_raise
{
   static const size_t value = N * static_raise<N, K-1>::value;
};

template <size_t N>
struct static_raise<N, 0>
{
   static const size_t value = 1;
};
```

To obtain `static_raise<N, K>::value`, the compiler needs to produce K instances: `static_raise<N, K-1>`, `static_raise<N, K-2>`, ...
Eventually `static_raise<N, 1>` needs `static_raise<N, 0>` which is already known (because there's an explicit specialization): this stops the recursion. However there's a better formula that needs only about log(K) intermediate types:

> If the exponent is a power of 2, we can save a lot of multiplications via repeated squaring: to compute X^8, only 3 multiplications are needed, if only we can store the intermediate results: since $X^8 = ((X^2)^2)^2$, we need to execute
>
> `t = x*x; t = t*t; t = t*t; return t;`
>
> In general, we use recursively the identity:
> $$X^N = X^{N \bmod 2} \cdot \left(X^{\lfloor N/2 \rfloor} \right)^2$$

```
template <size_t N, size_t K>
struct static_raise;

template <size_t N>
struct static_raise<N, 0>
{
   static const size_t value = 1;
};

template <size_t N, size_t K>
struct static_raise
{
private:
   static const size_t v0 = static_raise<N, K/2>::value;

public:
   static const size_t value = MXT_M_SQ(v0)*(K % 2 ? N : 1);
};
```

Note the use of `MXT_M_SQ` (cfr. paragraph 2.3.1).

4.3. Classic metaprogramming idioms

Metafunctions can be seen as functions that take one or more types and return either types or constants. We'll see in this section how to implement some basic operations.

Binary operators are replaced by metafunctions of two variables: the concept `T1 == T2` becomes `typeequal<T1, T2>::value`

```
template <typename T1, typename T2>
struct typeequal
{
   static const bool value = false;
};


template <typename T>
struct typeequal<T, T>
{
   static const bool value = true;
};
```

Whenever possible, we derive from an elementary class that holds the result, rather than introducing a new type/constant: remember that `public` inheritance is implied by `struct`

```
template <typename T1, typename T2>
struct typeequal : public selector<false>      // redundant
{
};

template <typename T>
struct typeequal<T, T> : selector<true>        // public
{
};
```

The ternary operator `TEST ? T1 : T2` becomes `typeif<TEST, T1, T2>::type`

```
template <bool STATEMENT, typename T1, typename T2>
struct typeif
{
   typedef T1 type;
};

template <typename T1, typename T2>
struct typeif<false, T1, T2>
{
   typedef T2 type;
};
```

Or, according to the guideline above:

```
template <bool STATEMENT, typename T1, typename T2>
struct typeif : instance_of<T1>
{
};

template <typename T1, typename T2>
struct typeif<false, T1, T2> : instance_of<T2>
{
};
```

The strong motivation for derivation is an easier use of tagging techniques: since we will often "embed" the metafunction result in a selector, it will be easier to use the metafunction itself as a selector. Suppose we have two functions that fill a range with random elements:

```
template <typename iterator_t>
void random_fill(iterator_t begin, iterator_t end, selector<false>)
{
    for (; begin != end; ++begin)
        *begin = rand();
}

template <typename iterator_t>
void random_fill(iterator_t begin, iterator_t end, selector<true>)
{
    for (; begin != end; ++begin)
        *begin = 'A' + (rand() % 26);
}
```

Compare the invocation:

```
random_fill(begin, end, selector<typeequal<T, char*>::value>());
```

With the simpler:[62]

```
random_fill(begin, end, typeequal<T, char*>());
```

> Note, as a curiosity, that header files that store a version number in their guard macro can be used in a `typeif`: compare the following snippets

[62] We will not always use the derivation notation in the book, mainly for sake of clarity; however we strongly encourage adopting it in production code, as it truly boosts code reuse.

```
#include "myheader.hpp"

typedef
typename typeif<MXT_MYHEADER_==0x1000, double, float>::type
float_t;

#if MXT_MYHEADER_ == 0x1000
typedef double float_t;
#else
typedef float float_t;
#endif
```

The first will not compile if `MXT_MYHEADER_` is undefined.
The preprocessor instead would behave as if the variable were 0.

4.3.1. Static short circuit

As a case study of template recursion, let's compare a static and a dynamic operator pseudo-code:

```
template <typename T>
struct F : typeif<[[CONDITION]], T, typename G<T>::type>
{
};
```

```
int F(int x)
{
   return [[CONDITION]] ? x : G(x);
}
```

These statements are *not* analogous:

- The run-time statement is short-circuited: it will not *execute* code unless necessary, so `G(x)` might never run.
- The static operator will always *compile* all the mentioned entities, as soon as one of their members is mentioned: so the first `F` will trigger the compilation of `G<T>::type`, regardless of the fact that the result is used (i.e. even when the condition is true).

There is no automatic static short-circuit: if underestimated, this may increase the build times, without extra benefits, and it may not be noticed, because results would be correct anyway.
The expression may be rewritten using an extra "indirection":

```
template <typename T>
struct F
{
   typedef typename typeif<[[CONDITION], instance_of<T>, G<T> >::type aux_t;
   typedef typename aux_t::type type;
};
```

Here only `G<T>` is mentioned, not `G<T>::type`. When the compiler is processing `typeif`, it needs only to know that the 2nd and the 3rd parameters are valid types, i.e. that they have been declared. If the condition is false, `aux_t` is set to `G<T>`, else it is set to `instance_of<T>`; since no member has been requested yet, nothing else has been compiled; finally, the last line triggers compilation of either `instance_of<T>` or `G<T>`.
So, if `CONDITION` is true, `G<T>::type` is never used: `G<T>` may even lack a definition, or it may not contain a member named `type`.

To summarize:
- delay accessing members as long as possible
- wrap items to leverage the interface

An identical optimization applies to constants:

```
static const size_t value = [[CONDITION]] ? 4 : alignment_of<T>::value;
```

```
typedef typename
 typeif<[[CONDITION]], static_value<size_t, 4>, alignment_of<T>>::type aux_t;

static const size_t value = aux_t::value;
```

At first, it may look like there's no need for some special logic operator, since inside templates all default operators on integers are allowed:[63]

```
template <typename T1, typename T2>
struct naive_OR
{
   static const bool value = (T1::value || T2::value);    // ok, valid
};
```

The classic logical operators in C++ are short-circuited, i.e. they don't *evaluate* the second operator if the first alone is enough to return a result; similarly, we can write a static OR which does not *compile* unnecessarily its second argument: if `T1::value` is true, `T2::value` is never accessed, it might even not exist (`AND` is obtained similarly).

```
if (T1::value is true)
   return true;
else
   return T2::value;
```

63 Except casts to non-integer types. For example N*1.2 is illegal, but N+N/5 is fine

```
template <bool B, typename T2>
struct static_OR_helper;

template <typename T2>
struct static_OR_helper<false, T2> : selector<T2::value>
{
};

template <typename T2>
struct static_OR_helper<true, T2> : selector<true>
{
};

template <typename T1, typename T2>
struct static_OR : static_OR_helper<T1::value, T2>
{
};
```

4.4. Hidden template parameters

Some class templates may have undocumented template parameters, generally auto-deduced, that silently select the right specialization; this is the dual technique of tag dispatching:

```
template <typename T, bool IS_SMALL_OBJ = (sizeof(T)<sizeof(void*))>
class A;

template <typename T>
class A<T, true>
{
   // implementation follows
};

template <typename T>
class A<T, false>
{
   // implementation follows
};
```

The user of `A` will accept the default, as a rule:

```
   A<char> c1;
   A<char, true> c2;   // exceptional case. do at own risk
```

The following is a variation of an example that appeared in [3].

```
template <size_t N>
struct fibonacci
{
   static const size_t value = fibonacci<N-1>::value + fibonacci<N-2>::value;
};

template <>
struct fibonacci<0>
{
   static const size_t value = 0;
};

template <>
struct fibonacci<1>
{
   static const size_t value = 1;
};
```

It can be rewritten using a hidden template parameter:

```
template <size_t N, bool TINY_NUMBER = (N<2)>
struct fibonacci
{
   static const size_t value = fibonacci<N-1>::value + fibonacci<N-2>::value;
};

template <size_t N>
struct fibonacci<N, true>
{
   static const size_t value = N;
};
```

To prevent the default from being changed, we can rename the original class, say appending suffix "_helper", and thus introduce a layer in the middle:

```
template <size_t N, bool TINY_NUMBER>
struct fibonacci_helper
{
   // all as above
};
```

```
template <size_t N>
class fibonacci : fibonacci_helper<N, (N<2)>
{
};
```

4.4.1. Static recursion on hidden parameters

Let's compute the highest bit of an unsigned integer x; assume that x has type `size_t` and if x==0 we'll conventionally return -1.
A non-recursive algorithm would be: set N = the number of bits of `size_t`; test bit N-1, then N-2… until a nonzero bit is found.
First, as usual, a naive implementation:

```
template <size_t X, size_t K>
struct highest_bit_helper
{
   static const int value =
      ((X >> K) % 2) ? K : highest_bit_helper<X, K-1>::value;
};

template <size_t X>
struct highest_bit_helper<X, 0>
{
   static const int value = ((X % 2) ? 0 : -1;
};
```

```
template <size_t X>
struct static_highest_bit : highest_bit_helper<X, CHAR_BIT*sizeof(size_t)-1>
{
};
```

As written, it works, but the compiler might need to generate a large number of different classes per static computation (i.e. for any X we pass to `static_highest_bit`).

First, we rework the algorithm using bisection: assume X has N bits, divide it in an upper and a lower half U and L, having respectively (N-N/2) and (N/2) bits; if U is 0, replace X with L, otherwise replace X with U and remember to increment the result by (N/2):[64]
In pseudo-code:

```
size_t hibit(size_t x, size_t N = CHAR_BIT*sizeof(size_t))
{
   size_t u = (x>>(N/2));
   if (u>0)
      return hibit(u, N-N/2) + (N/2);
   else
      return hibit(x, N/2);
}
```

This means:

```
template <size_t X, int N>
struct helper
{
   static const size_t U = (X >> (N/2));

   static const int value =
         U ? (N/2)+helper<U, N-N/2>::value : helper<X, N/2>::value;
};
```

As written, each `helper<X, N>` induces the compiler to instantiate the template again *twice*: `helper<U, N-N/2>` and `helper <X, N/2>`, even if only one will be used.

[64] In practice, N is always even, so N-N/2 == N/2

Compilation time may be reduced either with the static short circuit, or even better: moving all the arithmetic inside the type.[65]

```
template <size_t X, int N>
struct helper
{
   static const size_t U = (X >> (N/2));

   static const int value = (U ? N/2 : 0) +
         helper<(U ? U : X), (U ? N-N/2 : N/2)>::value;
};
```

This is definitely less clear, but more convenient for the compiler.

Since N is the number of bits of X, initially N>0.
We can terminate the static recursion when N==1

```
template <size_t X>
struct helper<X, 1>
{
   static const int value = X ? 0 : -1;
};
```

Finally, we use derivation from `static_value` to store the result:

```
template <size_t X>
struct static_highest_bit
: static_value<int, helper<X, CHAR_BIT*sizeof(size_t)>::value>
{
};
```

The recursion depth is fixed and logarithmic: `static_highest_bit<X>` instantiates at most 5 or 6 classes for every value of X.

4.4.2. Accessing the primary template

A dummy parameter can allow specializations to call back the primary template. Suppose we have two algorithms, one for computing cos(x) and another for sin(x), where x is any floating-point type; initially, the code is organized as follows:

[65] See also the double check stop in section 8.2

```
template <typename float_t>
struct trigonometry
{
   static float_t cos(const float_t x)
   {
      // ...
   }

   static float_t sin(const float_t x)
   {
      // ...
   }
};

template <typename float_t>
inline float_t fast_cos(const float_t x)
{
   return trigonometry<float_t>::cos(x);
}

template <typename float_t>
inline float_t fast_sin(const float_t x)
{
   return trigonometry<float_t>::sin(x);
}
```

Later, someone writes another algorithm for `cos<float>`, but not for `sin<float>`. We can either specialize/overload `fast_cos` for `float`, or use a hidden template parameter, as shown:

```
template <typename float_t, bool = false>
struct trigonometry
{
   static float_t cos(const float_t x)
   {
      // ...
   }

   static float_t sin(const float_t x)
   {
      // ...
   }
};
```

```
template <>
struct trigonometry<float, false>
{
   static float_t cos(const float_t x)
   {
      // specialized algorithm here
   }

   static float_t sin(const float_t x)
   {
      // calls the general template
      return trigonometry<float, true>::sin(x);
   }
};
```

Note that, specializing the class, it's not required to write `<float, false>`, we can simply enter:

```
template <>
struct trigonometry<float>
{
```

because the default value for the second parameter is known from the declaration. Any specialization can access the corresponding general function setting explicitly the boolean to `true`.

This technique will appear again in section 8.1.

A similar trick comes handy to make partial specializations unambiguous.
C++ does not allow specializing a template twice, even if specializations are identical; in particular, if we mix cases for both standard typedefs and integers, the code becomes subtly non-portable:

```
template <typename T>
struct is_integer
{
   static const bool value = false;
};

template < > struct is_integer<short>
{ static const bool value = true; };

template < > struct is_integer<int>
{ static const bool value = true; };

template < > struct is_integer<long>
{ static const bool value = true; };

template < > struct is_integer<ptrdiff_t>          // problem:
{ static const bool value = true; };               // may or may not compile
```

If `ptrdiff_t` is a fourth type, say `long long`, then all the specializations are different; vice versa, if `ptrdiff_t` is simply a typedef for `long`, the code is incorrect. Instead this works:

```
template <typename T, int = 0>
struct is_integer
{
   static const bool value = false;
};

template <int N> struct is_integer<short, N>
{ static const bool value = true; };
template <int N> struct is_integer<int  , N>
{ static const bool value = true; };
template <int N> struct is_integer<long , N>
{ static const bool value = true; };

template <>
struct is_integer<ptrdiff_t>
{
   static const bool value = true;
};
```

Since `is_integer<ptrdiff_t, 0>` is more specialized than `is_integer<long, N>`, it will be used unambiguously.[66]

This technique does not scale well[67], but it might be extended to a small number of typedefs, adding more unnamed parameters; we use `int`, but anything would do: `bool = false` or `typename = void`.

```
template <typename T, int = 0, int = 0>
struct is_integer
{
   static const bool value = false;
};

template <int N1, int N2>
struct is_integer<long, N1, N2>
{ static const bool value = true; };

template <int N1>
struct is_integer<ptrdiff_t, N1>
{ static const bool value = true; };

template < >
struct is_integer<time_t>
{ static const bool value = true; };
```

4.5. Traits

Traits classes (or simply, traits) are a collection of static functions, types and constants that abstract the public interface of a type T. More precisely, for all T repre-

[66] We insist that the problem is solvable because the implementations of `is_integer<long>` and `is_integer<ptrdiff_t>` are identical, otherwise it is ill-formed. For a counterexample, consider the problem of converting a `time_t` and a `long` to string; even if `time_t` *is* `long`, we wish the strings to be different, and thus this issue cannot be solved by TMP techniques.
[67] This is a good thing, because a well-built template class shouldn't need it.

senting the same concept, `traits<T>` is a class template that allows operating on T uniformly: in particular, all `traits<T>` have the same public interface.[68]

Using traits, it's possible to deal with type `T` ignoring partially or completely its public interface; this makes traits an optimal building layer for algorithms.
Why ignore the public interface of `T`? The main reason is: because it could have none, or it could be inappropriate.
Suppose T represents a "string" and we want to get the length of an instance of `T`; `T` may be `const char*` or `std::string`, but we wish the same call to be valid for both, otherwise it will be impossible to write template string functions; furthermore, 0 may have a special meaning as a "character" for some T, but not for all.

The first rigorous definition of traits is an article by Nathan Myers[69], dated 1995. The motivation for the technique is that writing a class template or a function, we realize that some types, constants or atomic actions are a parameter of the "main" template argument.
So we can either put additional template parameters, but this is usually impractical; or we can group these parameters in a traits class. Both the example and the following sentences are quotes from Myers' article[70]:

> Because the user never mentions it, [traits class] name can be long and descriptive.
>
> ```
> template <typename char_t>
> struct ios_char_traits
> {
> };
>
> template <>
> struct ios_char_traits<char>
> {
>     typedef char char_type;
>     typedef int  int_type;
>     static inline int_type eof() { return EOF; }
> };
>
> template <>
> struct ios_char_traits<wchar_t>
> {
>     typedef wchar_t char_type;
>     typedef wint_t  int_type;
>     static inline int_type eof() { return WEOF; }
> };
> ```

---

68 "Same" does not mean "with identical signature", but "independent of T": trivially, functions may take arguments by value or by const reference.
69 Available here: http://www.cantrip.org/traits.html. The article cites as previous bibliography [10], [11] and [12]
70 The sentences have been slightly rearranged.

The default traits class template is empty; what can anyone say about an unknown character type? However, for real character types, we can specialize the template and provide useful semantics.

To put a new character type on a stream, we need only specialize ios_char_traits for the new type.

Notice that ios_char_traits has no data members; it only provides public definitions. Now we can define our streambuf template:

```
template <typename char_t>
class basic_streambuf
```

Notice that it only has one template parameter, the one that interests users.

In fact, Myers concludes his article with a formal definition, and an interesting observation:

Traits class:
A class used in place of template parameters. As a class, it aggregates useful types and constants; as a template, it provides an avenue for that "extra level of indirection" that solves all software problems.

This technique turns out to be useful anywhere that a template must be applied to native types, or to any type for which you cannot add members as required for the template's operations.

Traits classes may be "global" or "local". Global traits are simply available in the system and they can be freely used anywhere; in particular, all specializations of a global traits class have system-scope (i.e. specializations are automatically used everywhere). This approach is in fact preferred when traits express properties of the platform.

```
template <typename char_t>
class basic_streambuf
{
   typedef typename ios_char_traits<char_t>::int_type int_type;
   ...
};
```

For example, one could access the largest unsigned integer, of float, available: consider the following pseudo-code:

```
template <typename T>
struct largest;

template <>
struct largest<int>
{
   typedef long long type;
};

template <>
struct largest<float>
{
   typedef long double type;
};

template <>
struct largest<unsigned>
{
   typedef unsigned long long type;
};
```

Evidently, a call such as `largest<unsigned>::type` is expected to return a result which is constant in the platform, so all customizations - if any - should be global to keep client code coherent.

A more flexible approach is to use local traits, passing the appropriate type to each template instance as an additional parameter (which defaults to the global value).

```
template <typename char_t, typename traits_t = ios_char_traits<char_t> >
class basic_streambuf
{
   typedef typename traits_t::int_type int_type;
   ...
```

In the rest of the section, we focus on a special kind of traits: pure static traits, which do not contain functions, but only types and constants.
The second half of the section is in chapter 5.2

4.5.1. Type traits

Some traits classes provide typedefs only, so they are indeed multi-value metafunctions: as an example, we mention again `std::iterator_traits`.
Type traits[71] are a collection of metafunctions that provide information about qualifiers of a given type and/or alter such qualifiers. Information can be either deduced

[71] The term type traits, introduced by John Maddock and Steve Cleary, is used here as a common name, but it appears it's also a proper name, referring to the boost implementation. See http://www.boost.org/doc/html/boost_typetraits/background.html for a complete review.

by a static mechanism inside traits, or be explicitly supplied with a full/partial specialization of the traits class, or being supplied by the compiler itself.[72]

```
template <typename T>
struct is_const : selector<false>
{
};

template <typename T>
struct is_const<const T> : selector<true>
{
};
```

Today type traits are split to reduce compile times, but historically they were large monolithic classes with many static constants

```
template <typename T>
struct all_info_together
{
   static const bool is_class = true;

   static const bool is_pointer = false;
   static const bool is_integer = false;
   static const bool is_floating = false;
   static const bool is_unsigned = false;

   static const bool is_const = false;
   static const bool is_reference = false;
   static const bool is_volatile = false;
};
```

In general, traits have a general implementation, which gives conservative answers; then partial specializations give answers for classes of types and finally full specializations.

[72] The new C++ standard will include a new `<type_traits>` header; some of the metafunctions that will appear there cannot be replicated in current C++, for example `has_trivial_destructor<T>` is indeducible, and current implementations always return false, except for built-in types.

```
template <typename T>
struct add_reference
{
   typedef T& type;
};

template <typename T>
struct add_reference<T&>
{
   typedef T& type;
};

template < >
struct add_reference<void>
{
   // reference to void is illegal. don't put anything here73
};
```

Often traits are recursive:

```
template <typename T>
struct is_unsigned_integer : selector<false>
{
};

template <typename T>
struct is_unsigned_integer<const T> : is_unsigned_integer<T>
{
};

template <typename T>
struct is_unsigned_integer<volatile T> : is_unsigned_integer<T>
{
};

template < >
struct is_unsigned_integer<unsigned int> : selector<true>
{
};

template < >
struct is_unsigned_integer<unsigned long> : selector<true>
{
};

// add more specializations...
```

Traits may use inheritance, and then selectively hide some members:

[73] It's possible to define `add_reference<void>::type` to be `void`

```
template <typename T>
struct integer_traits;

template <>
struct integer_traits<int>
{
   typedef long long largest_type;
   typedef unsigned int unsigned_type;
};

template <>
struct integer_traits<long> : integer_traits<int>
{
   // keeps integer_traits<int>::largest_type
   typedef unsigned long unsigned_type;
};
```

In C++, a template base class is not in scope of name resolution:

```
template <typename T>
struct BASE
{
   typedef T type;
};

template <typename T>
struct DER : public BASE<T>
{
   type t;  // error: 'type' is not in scope
};
```

However from a static point of view, `DER` *does* contain a `type` member:

```
template <typename T>
struct typeof
{
   typedef typename T::type type;
};

typeof< DER<int> >::type i = 0;      // ok: int i = 0
```

Type traits, if not carefully designed, will be vulnerable to hard conceptual problems, as the C++ type system is a lot more complex than it seems:

```
template <typename T>
struct is_const : selector<false>
{
};

template <typename T>
struct is_const<const T> : selector<true>
{
};
```

```
template <typename T>
struct add_const : instance_of<const T>
{
};

template <typename T>
struct add_const<const T> : instance_of<const T>
{
};
```

Here are some oddities:

- If `N` is a compile-time constant and `T` is a type, then we can form two distinct array types: `T [N]` and `T []`.[74]
- Qualifiers such as `const` applied to array types behave a bit oddly: if `T` is an array, e.g. `double [4]`, `const T` is "array of 4 `const double`", not "`const` array of 4 `double`"; in particular `const T` is *not* `const`:

```
typedef double T1;
typedef add_const<T1>::type T2;
T2 x = 3.14;                        // x has type const double
bool b1 = is_const<T2>::value;      // b1 is true
```

```
typedef double T3[4];
typedef add_const<T3>::type T4;     // T4 is "array of 4 const double"…
T4 a = { 1,2,3,4 };
bool b2 = is_const<T4>::value;      // …which does not match "const T"
                                    // so b2 is false
```

So, we should add more specializations:

```
template <typename T, size_t N>
struct is_const<const T [N]>
{
   static const bool value = true;
};

template <typename T >
struct is_const<const T []>
{
   static const bool value = true;
};
```

There are two possible criteria we can verify on types:

- A match is satisfied, for example `const int` matches `const T` with `T==int`.
- A logical test is satisfied, for example we could say that `T` is `const` if `const T` and `T` are the same type.

---

[74] This is actually used: some smart pointers use `operator delete []` when type matches `T[]` and single deletion in any other case.

For any T, `is_const<T&>::value` is false, because `T&` does not satisfy a match with a `const` type, however `add_const<T&>::type` is again `T&` (qualifiers applied to a reference are ignored): does this mean that references are `const`?
Should we add a specialization of `is_const<T&>` that returns true?
Or what we really wish is `add_const<T&>::type` to be `const T&`?

In C++ objects can have different degrees of const-ness: more specifically, they can be

- assignable
- immutable
- const

Being *assignable* is a syntactic property: an assignable object can live on the left side of `operator=`; a const reference is not assignable: in fact `T&` is assignable whenever `T` is (incidentally, an assignment would change the referenced object, not the reference, but this is irrelevant).
Being *immutable* is a logical property: an immutable object cannot be changed after construction, either because it is not assignable or because assignment does not alter the state of the instance; since we cannot make a reference "point" to another object, a reference is immutable.
Being *const* is a pure language property: an object is const if its type matches `const T` for some `T`; a const object may have a reduced interface and operator= is *likely* one of the restricted member functions.

References are not the only entities both immutable and assignable; this can be reproduced with a custom `operator=`.

```
template <typename T>
class fake_ref
{
   T* const ptr_;

public:

   // ...

   const fake_ref& operator=(const T& x) const
   {
      *ptr_ = x;         // ok, does not alter the state of this instance
      return *this;
   }
};
```

This also shows that const objects may be assignable[75], but it does not imply that references are const: only that they can be simulated with const objects.

---

[75] On the opposite, `std::pair<const int, double>` is neither `const`, nor assignable.

So the standard approach is to provide type traits that operate atomically, with minimal logic, and just a match; and `is_const<T&>::value` should be false.
However type traits are also easy to extend in user code: if an application requires it, we can introduce more concepts, such as "intrusive const-ness"

```
template <typename T>
struct is_const_intrusive : selector<false>
{
};

template <typename T>
struct is_const_intrusive<const T> : selector<true>
{
};

template <typename T>
struct is_const_intrusive<const volatile T> : selector<true>
{
};

template <typename T>
struct is_const_intrusive<T&> : is_const_intrusive<T>
{
};
```

Type traits have infinite applications; we pick the simplest.
Assume that C<T> is a class template that holds a member of type T, initialized by the constructor; however T has no restriction, and in particular it may be a reference.

```
template <typename T>
class C
{
   T member_;

public:

   explicit C(argument_type x)
   : member_(x)
   {
   }
};
```

We still need to define `argument_type`: if `T` is a value type, we would like to pass it by reference-to-const; but if `T` is a reference, writing `const T&` is illegal. So we write:

```
typedef typename add_reference<const T>::type argument_type;
```

`add_reference<T>` returns `const T&`, as desired.
If `T` is reference or reference-to-const, `const T` is `T`, and `add_reference` returns `T`, so argument type is again `T`.

4.5.2. Type dismantling

A type in C++ can generate infinitely many "variations", adding qualifiers, considering references, pointers, arrays... But it can happen that we have to recursively remove all the additional attributes, one at a time, digging in the composite type. This recursive process is usually called ***dismantling***.[76]

We shall write a metafunction, named `copy_q`, that shifts all the "qualifiers" from type `T1` to type `T2`; so `copy_q<const double&, int>::type` shall be `const int&`.

Type deduction is entirely recursive: we dismantle one attribute at a time and we move the same attribute to the result. To continue the example above, `const double&` matches `T&` where `T` is `const double`, so the result is "reference to the result of `copy_q<const double, int>`"; which in turn is "const result of `copy_q<double, int>`"; since this does not match any specialization, it gives `int`.

[76] The expression "type dismantling" has been introduced by Stephen C. Dewhurst

```
template <typename T1, typename T2>
struct copy_q
{
   typedef T2 type;
};

template <typename T1, typename T2>
struct copy_q<T1&, T2>
{
   typedef typename copy_q<T1, T2>::type& type;
};

template <typename T1, typename T2>
struct copy_q<const T1, T2>
{
   typedef const typename copy_q<T1, T2>::type type;
};

template <typename T1, typename T2>
struct copy_q<volatile T1, T2>
{
   typedef volatile typename copy_q<T1, T2>::type type;
};

template <typename T1, typename T2>
struct copy_q<T1*, T2>
{
   typedef typename copy_q<T1, T2>::type* type;
};

template <typename T1, typename T2, int N>
struct copy_q<T1 [N], T2>
{
   typedef typename copy_q<T1, T2>::type type[N];
};
```

A more complete implementation could address the problems caused by T2 being a reference:

```
   copy_q<double&, int&>::type err1;    // error: reference to reference
   copy_q<double [3], int&>::type err2; // error: test is an array of 'int&'
```

However it's questionable if such classes should silently resolve the error or stop compilation.

Let's just note that declaring a `std::vector<int&>` is illegal, but the compiler error is not "trapped":

```
Native Build of Target "StarX" using Build Configuration "Debug"

/usr/include/gcc/darwin/4.0/c++/ext/new_allocator.h: In instantiation of
'__gnu_cxx::new_allocator<int&>':
/usr/include/gcc/darwin/4.0/c++/bits/allocator.h:83:   instantiated from 'std::allocator<int&>'
/usr/include/gcc/darwin/4.0/c++/bits/stl_vector.h:80:   instantiated from 'std::_Vector_base<int&,
std::allocator<int&> >::_Vector_impl'
/usr/include/gcc/darwin/4.0/c++/bits/stl_vector.h:113:   instantiated from 'std::_Vector_base<int&,
std::allocator<int&> >'
/usr/include/gcc/darwin/4.0/c++/bits/stl_vector.h:149:   instantiated from 'std::vector<int&,
std::allocator<int&> >'
//StarX/main.cpp:94:   instantiated from here
/usr/include/gcc/darwin/4.0/c++/ext/new_allocator.h:55: error: forming pointer to reference type 'int&'
```

4.6. Type Containers

So what is a Typelist? It's got to be one of those weird template beasts, right?
Andrei Alexandrescu

The maximum number of template parameters is implementation-defined but it's usually large enough to use a class template as ***a container of types***.[77]
Here we show how some elementary ***static algorithms*** work, because we'll reuse the same techniques many times in the future. Actually, it's possible to implement in TMP most STL concepts: containers, algorithms, iterators and functors, where complexity requirements are translated at compilation time.[78]
In this section, we'll show first the ideas of the elementary techniques, and we'll consider applications later.

The simplest type containers are *pairs*, which are the static equivalent of linked lists, and *arrays*, which resemble C-style arrays of fixed length.

```
template <typename T1, typename T2>
struct typepair
{
   typedef T1 head_t;
   typedef T2 tail_t;
};

struct empty
{
};
```

In fact, we can easily store a list of arbitrary (?) length using pairs of pairs: in principle we could form a binary tree, but for simplicity we represent the list of types `(T1, T2... Tn)` as `typepair<T1, typepair<T2, ...> >`, i.e. we allow the second component to be a pair; actually we force the second component to be either a `typepair` or an `empty`, which is the list terminator. In pseudo-code:

```
P0 = empty
P1 = typepair<T1, empty >
P2 = typepair<T2, typepair<T1, empty> >
// ...
Pn = typepair<Tn, Pn-1>
```

This incidentally shows that the easiest operation with `typepair`-sequences is `push_front`.
Following Alexandrescu notation (see [1]), we will call such an encoding a ***typelist***.
We say that the first accessible type `Tn` is the ***head*** of the list and P_{n-1} is the ***tail***.

---

[77] The C++ Standard contains an informative section, "implementation quantities", where a recommended minimum is suggested for the number of template arguments (1024) and for nested template instantiations (1024), but compilers do not need to respect these numbers.
[78] The reference on the argument is [3]

On the opposite, if we fix the maximum length to a reasonable number, we can store all types in a row; due to the default value (which can be `empty` or `void`), we can declare any number of parameters on the same line:

```
#define MXT_GENERIC_TL_MAX          32

template
<
   typename T1  = empty,
   typename T2  = empty,
   // ...
   typename T32 = empty
>
struct typearray
{
};

typedef typearray<int, double, std::string> array_1;  // 3 items
typedef typearray<int, int, char, array_1> array_2;   // 4 items
```

The properties of these containers are different: a typelist with J elements requires the compiler to produce J different types, while arrays are direct-access: so writing algorithms for type arrays involves writing many (say, 32) specializations, while typelists are shorter and recursive but will take more time to compile.

> Before the theoretical establishment made by Abrahams in [3], there was some naming confusion; the original idea of type pairs was fully developed by Alexandrescu (in [1] and subsequently in CUJ), and he introduced the name typelist.
> Apparently Alexandrescu was also the first to use type arrays as wrappers for declaring long typelists in an easy way:
>
> ```
> template <typename T1, typename T2, ..., typename Tn>
> struct cons
> {
>    typedef typepair<T1, typepair<T2, ...> > type;
> };
> ```
>
> However the name typelist is still widely used as a synonym of a more generic type container.

4.6.1. at

`typeat` is a metafunction that extracts the N-th type from a container.

```
struct Error_UNDEFINED_TYPE;        // no definition!

template <size_t N, typename CONTAINER, typename ERR = Error_UNDEFINED_TYPE>
struct typeat;
```

if the N-th type does not exist, the result is ERR.

The same metafunction can process both type arrays and typelists; as anticipated, arrays require all the possible specializations: the generic template simply returns an error, then the metafunction is specialized first on type arrays, then on type lists.

```
template <size_t N, typename CONTAINER, typename ERR = Error_UNDEFINED_TYPE>
struct typeat
{
   typedef ERR type;
};
```

```
template <typename T1, ... typename T32, typename ERR>
struct typeat<0, typearray<T1, ... T32>, ERR>
{
   typedef T1 type;
};

template <typename T1, ... typename T32, typename ERR>
struct typeat<1, typearray<T1, ... T32>, ERR>
{
   typedef T2 type;
};

// write all 32 specializations
```

The same code for typelists is more concise: the N-th type of the list is declared equal to the (N-1)th type in the tail of the list; if N is 0, the result is the head type, but if we meet an empty list, the result is `ERR`.

```
template <size_t N, typename T1, typename T2, typename ERR>
struct typeat<N, typepair<T1, T2>, ERR>
{
   typedef typename typeat<N-1, T2, ERR>::type type;
};

template <typename T1, typename T2, typename ERR>
struct typeat<0, typepair<T1, T2>, ERR>
{
   typedef T1 type;
};

template <size_t N, typename ERR>
struct typeat<N, empty, ERR>
{
   typedef ERR type;
};
```

Observe however that, whatever index we use, `typeat<N, typearray<...> >` requires just one template instantiation; `typeat<N, typepair<...> >` may require N different instantiations.

Note also the shorter implementation:

```
template <size_t N, typename T1, typename T2, typename ERR>
struct typeat<N, typepair<T1, T2>, ERR> : typeat<N-1, T2, ERR>
{
};
```

4.6.2. Returning an error

In cases when a metafunction `F<T>` is undefined, such as `typeat<N, empty, ERR>`, common options for returning an error are:

- remove entirely the body of `F<T>`
- give `F<T>` an empty body, with no result (type or value)
- define `F<T>::type` such that it will cause compilation errors, if used (void, or a class that has no definition)
- define `F<T>::type` using an user-supplied error type (as above).

Remember that the choice to cause a compiler error is quite drastic: analogous to throwing exceptions, it's hard to ignore; on the opposite, a bogus type is more like a `return false`.
A false can be easily converted to a throw and a bogus type can be converted to a compiler error (a static assertion would suffice).

4.6.3. depth

Dealing with type arrays can be easier with the help of some simple macros:[79]

```
#define MXT_LIST_0(T)
#define MXT_LIST_1(T)    T##1
#define MXT_LIST_2(T)    MXT_LIST_1(T), T##2
#define MXT_LIST_3(T)    MXT_LIST_2(T), T##3
// …
#define MXT_LIST_32(T)    MXT_LIST_31(T), T##32
```

Surprisingly, we can write class declarations that look extremely simple and concise: below an example (before and after preprocessing).

```
template <MXT_LIST_32(typename T)>
struct depth< typelist<MXT_LIST_32(T)> >
```

```
template <typename T1, … , typename T32>
struct depth< typelist<T1, … T32> >
```

`depth` is a metafunction that returns the length of type lists:

[79] The `boost` preprocessor library would be more suitable, anyway, but its description would require another chapter. Here, the focus is on the word *simple*: a strategic hand-written macro can improve noticeably the esthetics of code

```
template <typename CONTAINER>
struct depth;
```

```
template <>
struct depth< empty > : static_value<size_t, 0>
{
};

template <typename T1, typename T2>
struct depth< typepair<T1, T2> > : static_value<size_t, depth<T2>::value+1>
{
};
```

- The primary template is undefined, so `depth<int>` is unusable.
- If the depth of a type list is K, the compiler must generate K different intermediate types (namely `depth<P1>` ... `depth<Pn>` where `Pj` is the j-th tail of the list);

For type arrays, we use macros again: the depth of `typearray<>` is 0; the depth of `typearray<T1>` is 1; and in fact the depth of `typearray<MXT_LIST_N(T)>` is N.

```
template <MXT_LIST_0(typename T)> struct depth< typearray<MXT_LIST_0(T)> >
: static_value<size_t, 0> {};

template <MXT_LIST_1(typename T)> struct depth< typearray<MXT_LIST_1(T)> >
: static_value<size_t, 1> {};

// ...

template <MXT_LIST_32(typename T)> struct depth< typearray<MXT_LIST_32(T)> >
: static_value<size_t, 32> {};
```

Note that even if a malicious user inserts a fake `empty` delimiter in the middle, `depth` returns in any case the position of the last non-`empty` type:

```
typedef typearray<int, double, empty, char> t4;
depth<t4>::value; // returns 4
```

In fact the above call will match `depth<T1, T2, T3, T4>` where it happens that `T3 = empty`.
However, `empty` should anyway be confined in an inaccessible namespace.

4.6.4. front and back

We are going to extract the first and the last type from both structures.

```
template <typename CONTAINER>
struct front;
```

```
template <typename CONTAINER>
struct back;
```

First, when the container is `empty`, we cause an error:

```
template <>
struct back<empty>;
```

```
template <>
struct front<empty>
{
};
```

While `front` is trivial, `back` iterates all over the list:

```
template <typename T1, typename T2>
struct front< typepair<T1, T2> >
{
   typedef T1 type;
};
```

```
template <typename T1>
struct back< typepair<T1, empty> >
{
   typedef T1 type;
};

template <typename T1, typename T2>
struct back< typepair<T1, T2> >
{
   typedef typename back<T2>::type type;
};
```

Or simply:

```
template <typename T1, typename T2>
struct back< typepair<T1, T2> > : back<T2>
{
};
```

For type arrays specialization, we exploit the fact that `depth` and `typeat` are very fast and we simply do what is natural with, say, a vector: the `back` element is the one at `size-1`; in principle this would work for typelists too, but it would "iterate" several times over the whole list (where each "iteration" causes the instantiation of a new type).

```
template <MXT_LIST_32(typename T)>
struct back< typearray<MXT_LIST_32(T)> >
{
   typedef typelist<MXT_LIST_32(T)> aux_t;
   typedef typename typeat<depth<aux_t>::value - 1, aux_t>::type type;
};

template <>
struct back< typearray<> >
{
};
```

```
template <MXT_LIST_32(typename T)>
struct front< typearray<MXT_LIST_32(T)> >
{
   typedef T1 type;
};

template <>
struct front< typearray<> >
{
};
```

4.6.5. find

```
template <typename T, typename CONTAINER>
struct typeindex;
```

We can perform a sequential search and return the index of the (first) type that matches a given type `T`; if `T` does not appear in `CONTAINER`, we return a conventional number (say -1), as opposite to causing a compiler error.

The code for the recursive version basically reads:

- nothing belongs to an empty container
- the first element of a pair has index 0
- the index is one plus the index of T in the tail, unless this latter index is undefined

```
template <typename T>
struct typeindex<T, empty>
{
   static const int value = (-1);
};

template <typename T1, typename T2>
struct typeindex< T1, typepair<T1, T2> >
{
   static const int value = 0;
};

template <typename T, typename T1, typename T2>
struct typeindex< T, typepair<T1, T2> >
{
   static const int aux_v = typeindex<T, T2>::value;
   static const int value = (aux_v==-1 ? -1 : aux_v+1);
};
```

The first implementation for type arrays is:

```
/* tentative version */

template <MXT_LIST_32(typename T)>
struct typeindex< T1, typearray<MXT_LIST_32(T)> >
{
   static const int value = 0;
};

template <MXT_LIST_32(typename T)>
struct typeindex< T2, typearray<MXT_LIST_32(T)> >
{
   static const int value = 1;
};

// ...
```

If the type we are looking for is identical to the first type in the array, then value is 0; if it is the second, value is 1, and so on. Unfortunately this is *incorrect*:

```
typedef typearray<int, int, double> t3;

int i = typeindex<int, t3>::value;
```

There's more than one match (namely, the first two), and this gives a compilation error. We defer the solution of this problem after the next paragraphs.

4.6.6. push and pop

It was already mentioned that the easiest operation with type pairs is `push_front`: it is simply a matter of wrapping the new head type in a pair with the old container:

```
template <typename CONTAINER, typename T>
struct push_front;
```

```
template <typename T>
struct push_front<empty, T>
{
   typedef typepair<T, empty> type;
};

template <typename T1, typename T2, typename T>
struct push_front<typepair<T1, T2>, T>
{
   typedef typepair< T, typepair<T1, T2> > type;
};
```

Quite naturally, also `pop_front` is straightforward:

```
template <typename CONTAINER>
struct pop_front;
```

```
template <>
struct pop_front<empty>;

template <typename T1, typename T2>
struct pop_front< typepair<T1, T2> >
{
   typedef T2 type;
};
```

To implement the same algorithm for type arrays, we adopt a very important technique named ***template rotation:*** the rotation shifts all template parameters by one position to the left (or to the right).

```
template <P1, P2, = some_default, …, PN = some_default>
struct container
{
   typedef container<P2, P3, …, PN, some_default> tail_t;80
};
```

The type resulting from a `pop_front` is exactly what we called the ***tail***. Parameters need not be types: the following class computes the maximum in a list of positive integers.

```
#define MXT_M_MAX(a,b)        ((a)<(b) ? (b) : (a))
```

```
template <size_t S1, size_t S2=0, … , size_t S32=0>
struct typemax : typemax<MXT_M_MAX(S1, S2), S3, …, S32>
{
};

template <size_t S1>
struct typemax<S1,0,0,…,0> : static_value<size_t, S1>
{
};
```

As a side note, whenever it's feasible, it's convenient to *accelerate* the rotation: in the above example, we would write

```
template <size_t S1, size_t S2=0, … , size_t S32=0>
struct typemax
: typemax<MXT_M_MAX(S1, S2), MXT_M_MAX(S3, S4), …, MXT_M_MAX(S31, S32)>
{
};
```

so to compute the maximum of N constants, we need only log2(N) instances of `typemax`, instead of N.

[80] In principle, `some_default` should not be explicitly specified: all forms of code duplication can lead to maintenance errors; here we show it to emphasize the rotation

It's easy to combine rotations and macros with elegance:

```
template <typename T0, MXT_LIST_31(typename T)>
struct pop_front< typearray<T0, MXT_LIST_31(T)> >
{
   typedef typearray<MXT_LIST_31(T)> type;
};
```

```
template <MXT_LIST_32(typename T), typename T>
struct push_front<typearray<MXT_LIST_32(T)>, T>
{
   typedef typearray<T, MXT_LIST_31(T)> type;
};
```

Using `pop_front`, we can implement a generic sequential find: note that for clarity we typedef temporary objects; typedefs in metaprogramming are the equivalent of variables in classic C++; however `private` and `public` sections help separating "temporary" variables from the results:
The procedure we follow is:

- the index of `T` in an empty container is -1
- the index of `T1` in `array<T1, ...>` is 0 (this unambiguously holds, even T1 appears more than once)
- to obtain the index of `T` in `array<T1, T2, T3, ...>`, we compute its index in a rotated array and add 1 to the result

```
template <typename T>
struct typeindex<T, typearray<> >
{
   static const int value = (-1);
};

template <MXT_LIST_32(typename T)>
struct typeindex< T1, typearray<MXT_LIST_32(T)> >
{
   static const int value = 0;
};


template <typename T, MXT_LIST_32(typename T)>
struct typeindex< T, typearray<MXT_LIST_32(T)> >
{
private:
   typedef typearray<MXT_LIST_32(T)> argument_t;
   typedef typename pop_front<argument_t>::type tail_t;

   static const int aux_v = typeindex<T, tail_t>::value;

public:
   static const int value = (aux_v<0) ? aux_v : aux_v+1;
};
```

4.6.7. More on template rotation

Template arguments can be easily rotated, however it's usually simpler to consume them left-to-right: suppose we want to compose an integer entering all its digits in base 10. Here's some pseudo-code.

```
template <int D1, int D2 = 0, ... , int Dn = 0>
struct join_digits
{
   static const int value = join_digits<D2, ..., Dn>::value * 10 + D1;
};

template <int D1>
struct join_digits<D1>
{
   static const int value = D1;
};
```

```
join_digits<3,2,1>::value;       // compiles, but yields 123, not 321
```

Observe instead that it's not so easy to consume `Dn` in the rotation: this will not compile, because whenever D9==0, `value` is defined in terms of itself.

```
template <int D1, int D2 = 0, ..., int D8 = 0, int D9 = 0>
struct join_digits
{
   static const int value = join_digits<D1, D2, ..., D8>::value * 10 + Dn;
```

Rotation to the right won't produce the correct result:

```
template <int D1, int D2 = 0, ..., int D8 = 0, int D9 = 0>
struct join_digits
{
   static const int value = join_digits<0, D1, D2, ..., D8>::value * 10 + Dn;
```

The solution is simply to store some auxiliary constants, and borrow them from the tail:

```
template <int D1 = 0, int D2 = 0, ..., int Dn = 0>
struct join_digits
{
   typedef join_digits<D2, ..., Dn> next_t;
   static const int pow10 = 10 * next_t::pow10;
   static const int value = next_t::value + D1*pow10;
};

template <int D1>
struct join_digits<D1>
{
   static const int value = D1;
   static const int pow10 = 1;
};
```

```
join_digits<3,2,1>::value;        // now really gives 321
```

Template rotation can be used in two different ways:

- direct rotation of the main template (as above)

```
template <int D1 = 0, int D2 = 0, ..., int Dn = 0>
struct join_digits
{ ... };

template <int D1>
struct join_digits<D1>
{ ... };
```

- rotation on a parameter; this adds an extra "indirection"

```
template <int D1 = 0, int D2 = 0, ..., int Dn = 0>
struct digit_group
{
   // empty
};
```

```
template <typename T>
struct join_digits;       // primary template not defined

template <int D1, int D2, ..., int Dn>
struct join_digits< digit_group<D1, ..., Dn> >
{
   // as above
};

template <>
struct join_digits< digit_group<> >
{
   // as above
};
```

The first solution is usually simpler to code; however the second has two serious advantages:

- type T that "carries" the tuple of template parameters can be reused; T will be usually a type container of some kind
- suppose for the moment that `join_digits<...>` is a true class (not a meta-function), and it is actually instantiated; it will be easy to write generic templates accepting any instance of `join_digits`: they just need to take `join_digits<X>`; vice versa, if `join_digits` has a long and unspecified number of parameters, clients will have to manipulate it as `X`.[81]

4.6.8. Agglomerates

The rotation technique encapsulated in `pop_front` can be used to create tuples as ***agglomerate objects***.

In synthesis, an agglomerate A is a class, which has a type container C in its template parameters; the class uses `front<C>` and recursively inherits from `A< pop_front<C> >`; the simplest way to "use" the front type is to declare a member of that type. In pseudo code:

```
template <typename C>
class A : public A<typename pop_front<C>::type>
{
   typename front<C>::type member_;

public:

   // ...
};
```

[81] This need not be a problem: if `join_digits` were a functor, clients would likely take it as X anyway.

```
template < >
class A<empty>
{
};
```

```
template < >
class A< typearray<> >
{
};
```

- Inheritance can be public, private or even protected
- There are two possible recursion stoppers: `A<empty typelist>` and `A<empty typearray>`

So, an agglomerate is a package of objects, whose type is listed in the container; if C is `typearray<int, double, std::string>` the layout of A would be as in picture.

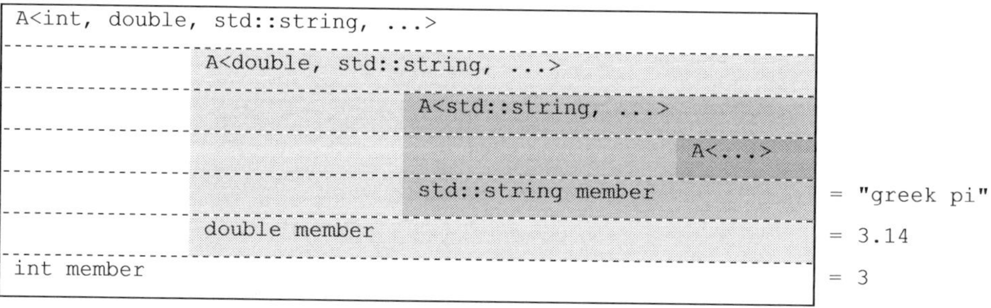

Figure 4-1: layout of the agglomerate A

Note that in the implementation under review, the memory layout of the objects is reversed with respect to the type container.

To access the elements of the package, we use rotation again. Assume for the moment that all members are public. We'll get a reference to the N-th member of the agglomerate via a global function and the collaboration of a suitable traits class. There are two equally good development strategies: ***intrusive traits*** and ***non-intrusive traits***.

Intrusive traits require the agglomerate itself to expose some auxiliary information:

```
template <typename C>
struct A : public A<typename pop_front<C>::type>
{
   typedef typename front<C>::type value_type;
   value_type member;

   typedef typename pop_front<C>::type tail_t;
};
```

```
template <typename agglom_t, size_t N>
struct reference_traits
{
   typedef reference_traits<typename agglom_t::tail_t, N-1> next_t;
   typedef typename next_t::value_type value_type;

   static value_type& ref(agglom_t& a)
   {
      return next_t::ref(a);
   }
};

template <typename agglom_t>
struct reference_traits<agglom_t, 0>
{
   typedef typename agglom_t::value_type value_type;

   static value_type& ref(agglom_t& a)
   {
      return a.member;
   }
};
```

```
template <size_t N, typename agglom_t>
inline typename reference_traits<agglom_t,N>::value_type& ref(agglom_t& a)
{
   return reference_traits<agglom_t, N>::ref(a);
}
```

A quick usage example:

```
typedef typearray<int, double, std::string> C;
A<C> a;

ref<0>(a) = 3;
ref<1>(a) = 3.14;
ref<2>(a) = "3.14";
```

Non-intrusive traits instead would figure out the information with partial specializations:

```
template <typename agglom_t, size_t N>
struct reference_traits;

template <typename C, size_t N>
struct reference_traits< A<C>, N >
{
   typedef reference_traits<typename pop_front<C>::type, N-1> next_t;
   typedef typename front<C>::type value_type;
```

When feasible, non-intrusive traits are preferred: it's not obvious that the author of `reference_traits` can modify the definition of `A`. However it's common for traits to require a reasonable "cooperation" from objects; furthermore, auto-deduction code is a duplication of class A internals and auto-deduced values tend to be "rigid", so intrusiveness is not a clear loser.

A special case is an agglomerate modeled on a typelist *containing no duplicates*; the implementation is much simpler, because instead of rotation, a pseudo-cast suffices:

```
template <typename T, typename tail_t>          // cast-like syntax
T& ref(A< typepair<T, tail_t> >& a)             // T is non-deduced
{
   return a.member;
}
```

```
typedef typepair<int, typepair<double, typepair<std::string, empty> > > C;
A<C> a;

ref<double>(a) = 3.14;
ref<std::string>(a) = "greek pi";
ref<int>(a) = 3;
```

The cast works because the syntax `ref<T>(a)` fixes the first type of the pair and lets the compiler match the tail that follows; this is indeed possible, due to the uniqueness hypothesis.
In fact the C++ standard allows one derived-to-base cast before argument deduction, if it's a necessary and sufficient condition for an exact match.
Here, the only way to bind an argument of type `A<C>` to a reference to `A< typepair<std::string, tail_t> >` is to cast it to `typepair<std::string, empty>` then deduce `tail_t = empty`.

To store a value extracted from an agglomerate, declare an object of type `reference_traits<agglom_t,N>::value_type`.

Finally, with a little more intrusiveness, we just add a member function to A

```
template <typename C>
struct A : public A< typename pop_front<C>::type >
{
   typedef typename front<C>::type value_type;
   value_type member;

   typedef typename pop_front<C>::type tail_t;

   tail_t& tail() { return *this; }
};
```

```
template <typename agglom_t, size_t N>
struct reference_traits
{
   // ...

   static value_type& get_ref(agglom_t& a)
   {
      return next_t::get_ref(a.tail());
   }
};
```

Invoking a member function, instead of an implicit cast allows us to switch to private inheritance or even to a has-relationship:

```
template <typename C>
class A
{
public:
   typedef typename pop_front<C>::type tail_t;
   typedef typename front<C>::type value_type;

private:
   A<tail_t> tail_;
   value_type member;

public:
   tail_t& tail() { return tail_; }

   // ...
};
```

Now the memory layout of the object is exactly in the same order as the type container.

4.6.9. Conversions

Many algorithms in fact require a linear number of recursion steps, both for typelists and for type arrays; in practice, the `typepair` representation suffices for most practical purposes, except one: the declaration of a typelist is indeed unfeasible. Anyway, as anticipated, it's very easy to convert from type array to typelist, and vice versa
It is an interesting exercise to provide a unified implementation:[82]

[82] It's another exercise of type dismantling; note also that using `push_back` instead of `push_front` would reverse the container

```
template <typename T>
struct convert
{
   typedef typename pop_front<T>::type tail_t;
   typedef typename front<T>::type head_t;

   typedef
     typename push_front<typename convert<tail_t>::type, head_t>::type type;
};

template <>
struct convert< typearray<> >
{
   typedef empty type;
};

template <>
struct convert< empty >
{
   typedef typearray<> type;
};
```

Note that T in the code above is a generic type container, not a generic type. Before, we used partial template specialization as a protection against ***bad static argument types***: for example, if one tries `front<int>::type`, the compiler will output that `front` cannot be instantiated on `int` (if we did not define the main template) or that it does not contain a member `type` (if it's empty).
However, such a protection is not necessary here: `convert` is built atop of `front` and `pop_front`, and they will perform the required argument validation; in case, the compiler will diagnose that `front<int>`, instantiated inside `convert<int>`, is illegal.

The problem is just a less clear debug message; among the options we have, we can write type traits to identify type containers, and then place assertions:

```
template <typename T>
struct type_container
{
   static const bool value = false;
};

template <typename T1, typename T2>
struct type_container< typepair<T1, T2> >
{
   static const bool value = true;
};

template <>
struct type_container<empty>
{
   static const bool value = true;
};

template <MXT_LIST_32(typename T)>
struct type_container< typearray<MXT_LIST_32(T)> >
{
   static const bool value = true;
};
```

```
template <typename T>
struct convert
   : static_assert< type_container<T>::value >
{
   …
```

Very likely, the compiler will emit the first error pointing to the assertion line.

> Section 6.2 is fully devoted to bad static argument types and we will meet function templates which restrict statically their template parameters to those having a particular interface.

It can be useful to extend type container traits inserting a type representing the empty container of that kind (the primary template is unchanged).

```
template <typename T1, typename T2>
struct type_container< typepair<T1, T2> >
{
   static const bool value = true;
   typedef empty type;
};

template <>
struct type_container<empty>
{
   static const bool value = true;
   typedef empty type;
};

template <MXT_LIST_32(typename T)>
struct type_container< typearray<MXT_LIST_32(T)> >
{
   static const bool value = true;
   typedef typearray<> type;
};
```

When enough "low-level" metafunctions, such as `front`, `back`, `push_front`, etc. are available, most meta-algorithms will just work both on arrays and on lists; we just need two different recursion terminations, a specialization for `typearray<>` and one for `empty`.

Another option is ***the empty-empty idiom***: let a helper class take the original type container as T and a second type, which is the empty container of the same kind (obtained from traits); when these are equal, we stop.

```
template <typename T>
struct some_metafunction
: static_assert<type_container<T>::value>
, helper<T, typename type_container<T>::type>
{
};

template <typename T, typename E>
struct helper
{
   // general case:
   // T is a non-empty type container of any kind
   // E is the empty container of the same kind
};

template <typename E>
struct helper<E, E>
{
   // recursion terminator
};
```

4.6.10. Meta-functors

User functors, predicates and binary operations can be replaced by template-template parameters. Here is a simple meta-functor:

```
template <typename T>
struct size_of
{
   static const size_t value = CHAR_BIT*sizeof(T);
};

template <>
struct size_of<void>
{
   static const size_t value = 0;
};
```

Here is a simple binary meta-relation:

```
template <typename X1, typename X2>
struct less_by_size : selector<(sizeof(X1) < sizeof(X2))>
{
};

template <typename X>
struct less_by_size<void, X> : selector<true>
{
};

template <typename X>
struct less_by_size<X, void> : selector<false>
{
};

template <>
struct less_by_size<void, void> : selector<false>
{
};
```

And here's the skeleton of a metafunction that might use it:

```
template <typename T, template <typename X1, typename X2> class LESS>
struct static_stable_sort
: static_assert< type_container<T>::value >
{
   // write LESS<T1, T2>::value instead of "T1<T2"

   typedef [[RESULT]] type;
};
```

Instead of describing an implementation, we sketch a possible application of `static_stable_sort`: out source code includes a collection of random generators, returning unsigned integers:

```
class linear_generator
{
   typedef unsigned short random_type;
   ...
};

class mersenne_twister
{
   typedef unsigned int random_type;
   ...
};

class mersenne_twister_64bit
{
   typedef /* ... */ random_type;
   ...
};
```

The user will list all the generators in a type container, in order from the best (i.e. the preferred algorithm) to the worst; this container can be sorted by `sizeof(typename T::random_type)`; finally when the user asks for a random number of type X, we scan the sorted container and stop on the first element whose `random_type` has at least the same size as X and we use that generator to return a value; since sorting is stable, the first suitable type is also the best in the user preferences.

As promised earlier, we turn now to the problem of selecting unsigned integers by size (in bit).
First we put all candidates in a type container:

```
typedef typearray<unsigned char, unsigned short, unsigned int,
                  unsigned long, unsigned long long> all_unsigned;
```

We are going to scan the list from left to right and use the first type which has a specified size (it's also possible to append to the list whatever compiler-specific type).

A little algebra is necessary: by definition of the sign function, for any integer we have the identity $\delta \cdot \mathrm{sign}(\delta)=|\delta|$; vice versa, if S is a prescribed constant in {-1, 0, 1}, the equality $\delta \cdot S=|\delta|$ implies respectively $\delta \leq 0$, $\delta=0$, $\delta \geq 0$; this elementary relation allows to represent three predicates (less-or-equal-to-zero, equal-to-zero and greater-or-equal-to-zero), with an integer parameter.

In the code below, T is any type container:

```
#define MXT_M_ABS(a)        ((a)<0 ? -(a) : (a))
```

```
enum
{
   LESS_OR_EQUAL = -1,
   EQUAL = 0,
   GREATER_OR_EQUAL = +1
};

template
<
   typename T,
   template <typename X> class SIZE_OF,
   int SIGN,
   size_t SIZE_BIT_N
>
struct static_find_if
   : static_assert< type_container<T>::value >
{
   typedef typename front<T>::type head_t;

   static const int delta = (int)SIZE_OF<head_t>::value - (int)SIZE_BIT_N;

   typedef typename typeif
   <
      SIGN*delta == MXT_M_ABS(delta),
      front<T>,
      static_find_if<typename pop_front<T>::type, SIZE_OF, SIGN, SIZE_BIT_N>
   >::type aux_t;

   typedef typename aux_t::type type;
};
```

```
// define an unsigned integer type which has exactly 'size' bits

template <size_t N>
struct uint_n
: static_find_if<all_unsigned, size_of, EQUAL, N>
{
};
```

```
// defines an unsigned integer type which has at least 'size' bits

template <size_t N>
struct uint_nx
: static_find_if<all_unsigned, size_of, GREATER_OR_EQUAL, N>
{
};
```

```
typedef uint_n<8>::type uint8;
typedef uint_n<16>::type uint16;
typedef uint_n<32>::type uint32;
typedef uint_n<64>::type uint64;

typedef uint_nx<32>::type uint32x;
```

Note that the order of template parameters was chosen so to make clear the line that *uses* `static_find_if`, not `static_find_if` itself.[83]

What does it happen if a suitable type is not found? Any invalid use will unwind a long error cascade (it has been edited to suppress most of the noise):

```
uint_n<25>::type i0 = 8;
uint_nx<128>::type i1 = 8;
```

```
typelist.hpp(109) : error C2039: 'type' : is not a member of 'front<typearray<>>'
                    : see declaration of 'front<typearray<>>'

typelist.hpp(120) : see reference to class template instantiation
'static_find_if<T,SIZE_OF,SIZE_BIT_N,SIGN>' being compiled
        with
        [

T=pop_front<pop_front<pop_front<pop_front<pop_front<all_unsigned>::type>::type>::type>::type>::type,
        ]
typelist.hpp(120) : see reference to class template instantiation
'static_find_if<T,SIZE_OF,SIZE_BIT_N,SIGN>' being compiled
        with
        [
            T=pop_front<pop_front<pop_front<pop_front<all_unsigned>::type>::type>::type>::type,
        ]
typelist.hpp(120) : see reference to class template instantiation
'static_find_if<T,SIZE_OF,SIZE_BIT_N,SIGN>' being compiled
        with
        [
            T=pop_front<pop_front<pop_front<all_unsigned>::type>::type>::type,
        ]
[…]
typelist.hpp(85) : see reference to class template instantiation
'static_find_if<T,SIZE_OF,SIZE_BIT_N,SIGN>' being compiled
        with
        [
            T=all_unsigned,
        ]
Main.cpp(48) : see reference to class template instantiation 'uint_n<SIZE_BIT_N>' being compiled
        with
        [
            SIZE_BIT_N=25
        ]
```

Basically, the compiler is saying that, during deduction of `uint_n<25>::type`, after applying 5 times `pop_front` to the type array, it ended up with an empty container, which has no `front` type.
However it's easy to get a more manageable report, just adding an undefined type as a result of the recursion terminator:

[83] We adopted the name `find_if` with some abuse of notation; a genuine `static_find_if` would be `static_find_if<typename T, template <typename X> class F>`, which returns the first type in `T` where `F<X>::value` is true.

```
template
<
   template <typename X> class SIZE_OF,
   int SIGN,
   size_t SIZE_BIT_N
>
struct static_find_if<typearray<>, SIZE_OF, SIGN, SIZE_BIT_N>
{
   typedef error_UNDEFINED_TYPE type;
};
```

Now the error message is very likely more concise:

```
Main.cpp(48) : error C2079: 'i0' uses undefined class 'error_UNDEFINED_TYPE'
Main.cpp(49) : error C2079: 'i1' uses undefined class 'error_UNDEFINED_TYPE'
```

4.7. A summary of styles

When programming metafunctions, identify:

- a suggestive name and syntax
- which template parameters are needed to express the concept
- which atomic actions the algorithm depend on
- a recursive efficient implementation
- special cases that must be isolated

About the metafunction name, if it's similar to a classic algorithm (say, `find_if`), then we can adopt a similar name (`static_find_if`), or even identical if it resides in a specific namespace (say, `typelist::find_if`).
Some authors append an underscore to pure static algorithms, because this allows to mimic existing keywords (`typeif` would be called `if_`).

If several template parameters are necessary, write code such that the user will be able to remember their meaning and their order. An idea is to give a syntax hint through the name:

```
: static_find_if<all_unsigned, size_of, GREATER_OR_EQUAL, N>
```

Many unrelated parameters should be grouped in a traits class, which however should have a default implementation that is easy to copy.

Finally, the following table may help in translating a classic algorithm in a static one.

	Classic C++ Function	Static Metaprogramming
What they manipulate	Instances of objects	Types
Argument handling	Via argument public interface	Via metafunctions
Deal with different arguments	Function overload	Partial template specializations
Return result	Zero or one return statement	Zero or more static data (type or constant), usually inherited
Error trapping	`try...catch` block	extra template parameter with `ERR` type
User-supplied callbacks	Functors	Template-template parameters
Temporary objects	Local variables	Private typedef / static const
Function calls	Yes, as subroutines	Yes, also via derivation
Algorithm structure	Iteration or recursion	Static recursion, stopped with suitable full/partial template specializations
Conditional decisions	Language constructs (if, switch)	Partial specializations
Error handling	o Throw an exception o Return false	o Abort compilation o Return no result o Set result to an incomplete type

5. Overload Resolution

In this chapter, we present some TMP techniques based on overload resolution. The common underlying schema is as follows:

- we want to test if type T satisfies a condition;
- we write several static functions with the same name, say `test`, and we feed them with T;
- the compiler selects the best candidate, according to C++ language rules
- we deduce which function was used, either using the return type or indirectly, from a property of this type, and eventually we make a decision.

First, we introduce some definitions.

5.1. Groups

A group is a class that provides optimized variants of a single routine; from the outside, a group acts as a monolithic function that automatically picks the best implementation for every call.
A group is composed by two entities:

- a template struct, containing variants of a (single) static member function
- a companion global function template that just forwards the execution to the right member of the group, performing a static decision based on the auto-deduced template parameter and on some framework-supplied information.

The group itself is usually a template, even if formally unnecessary (it may be possible to write the group as a normal class with template member functions).

Finally, observe that groups and traits are somehow orthogonal:

Traits<T1>	Traits<T2>		Group_F1	Group_F2
{ F1(); F2(); }	{ F1(); F2(); }	←→	{ F1(T1); F1(T2); }	{ F2(T1); F2(T2); }

5.1.1. From overload to groups

A group is the evolution of a set of overloaded functions.
Step 1: we realize that a default template implementation can handle most cases, so we just add overloaded variants:

```
template <typename T>
bool is_product_negative(T x, T y)
{
   return x<0 ^ y<0;
}

bool is_product_negative(short x, short y)
{
   return int(x)*int(y) < 0;
}

bool is_product_negative(unsigned int x, unsigned int y)
{
   return false;
}

bool is_product_negative(unsigned long x, unsigned long y)
{
   return false;
}
```

Step 2: implementation is clustered in several templates, which are picked using tags.

```
template <typename T>
bool is_product_negative(T x, T y, selector<false>)
{
   return x<0 ^ y<0;
}

template <typename T>
bool is_product_negative(T x, T y, selector<true>)
{
   return int(x)*int(y) < 0;
}

template <typename T>
bool is_product_negative(T x, T y)
{
   typedef selector<(sizeof(T)<sizeof(int))> small_int_t;
   return is_product_negative(x, y, small_int_t());
}
```

Step 3: group all the auxiliary functions in a class.

```
// companion function

template <typename T>
bool is_product_negative(T x, T y)
{
   return is_product_negative_t<T>::doIt(x, y);
}

template <typename T>
struct is_product_negative_t
{
   static bool doIt(T x, T y)
   {
      ...
   }
};
```

Here is another very simple group:

```
struct maths
{
   template <typename T>
   inline static T abs(const T x)
   {
      return x<0 ? -x : x;
   }

   inline static unsigned int abs(unsigned int x)
   {
      return x;
   }
};
```

```
template <typename T>
inline T absolute_value(const T x)
{
   return maths::abs(x);
}
```

> Remember that the group class, being a non-template, is always fully instantiated.
> Furthermore, a non-template function in a header file must be declared inline.

Suppose further we have a metafunction named `has_abs_method`, such that `has_abs_method<T>::value` is true if the absolute value of an object `x` of type `T` is given by `x.abs()`.[84]
This allows our group to grow a bit more complex: in the next example, we specialize the whole group for `double`, and the specialization ignores the actual result of `has_abs_method<double>`.[85]

---

[84] Paragraph 5.2.1 will show how to detect if T has a member function `T T::abs() const`.
[85] Of course, we could have written a method taking `selector<false>`, but using a template as a replacement for C ellipsis can be of some interest.

```
template <typename scalar_t>
struct maths
{
   static scalar_t abs(const scalar_t& x, selector<false>)
   {
      return x<0 ? -x : x;
   }

   static scalar_t abs(const scalar_t& x, selector<true>)
   {
      return x.abs();
   }
};

template <>
struct maths<double>
{
   template <bool DON_T_CARE>
   static double abs(const double x, selector<DON_T_CARE>)
   {
      return std::fabs(x);
   }
};
```

```
template <typename scalar_t>
inline scalar_t absolute_value(const scalar_t& x)
{
   typedef selector< has_abs_method<scalar_t>::value > select_t;
   return maths<scalar_t>::abs(x, select_t());
}
```

Too many overloads will likely conflict: remember that a non-template function is preferred to a matching template, but this does not hold for a member function that uses the template parameter of the class:

```
template <typename scalar_t>
struct maths
{
   static scalar_t abs(const scalar_t& x, selector<false>)
   {
      return x<0 ? -x : x;
   }

   static int abs(const int x, selector<false>)
   {
      return std::abs(x);
   }
```

```
error: ambiguous call to overloaded function, during instantiation of absolute_value<int>
```

This is precisely the advantage of a "double-layer" template selection: "layer one" is the automatic deduction of `scalar_t` in the companion function; "layer two" is the overload selection, performed inside a class template (the group), whose parameter has already been fixed:

```
template <typename scalar_t>
inline scalar_t absolute_value(const scalar_t& x)
{
   // collect auxiliary information, if needed
   return math<scalar_t>::abs(x, ...);
}
```

Combining both, we have fewer global function templates (too many overloads are likely to cause "ambiguous calls") and in addition, the group may have subroutines (private static member functions).

The user has several expansion choices:

- specialize the whole group (if it's a template)
- specialize the global companion function
- model types to take advantage of the existing framework (e.g. specialize `has_abs_method`)

The selection part can be even more subtle, with additional layers in the middle. As the following example shows, the right member of the group is chosen via an implicit argument promotion:

```
struct tag_floating
{
   tag_floating() {}
   tag_floating(instance_of<float>) {}
   tag_floating(instance_of<double>) {}
   tag_floating(instance_of<long double>) {}
};

struct tag_signed_int
{
   tag_signed_int() {}
   tag_signed_int(instance_of<short>) {}
   tag_signed_int(instance_of<int>) {}
   tag_signed_int(instance_of<long>) {}
};

struct tag_unsigned_int
{
   tag_unsigned_int() {}
   tag_unsigned_int(instance_of<unsigned short>) {}
   tag_unsigned_int(instance_of<unsigned int>) {}
   tag_unsigned_int(instance_of<unsigned long>) {}
};
```

```
template <typename scalar_t>
struct maths
{
   inline static scalar_t abs(const scalar_t x, tag_signed_int)
   {
      return x<0 ? -x : x;
   }

   inline static scalar_t abs(const scalar_t x, tag_unsigned_int)
   {
      return x;
   }

   inline static scalar_t abs(const scalar_t x, tag_floating)
   {
      return fabs(x);
   }
};

template <typename scalar_t>
inline scalar_t absv(const scalar_t& x)
{
   return maths<scalar_t>::abs(x, instance_of<scalar_t>());
}
```

The same effect could be obtained with a reversed selector hierarchy (e.g. letting `instance_of<double>` derive from `scalar_floating`), but `instance_of` is a general-purpose template, and we treat it as non modifiable.

We can also introduce intermediate selectors (unfortunately, we have to write the constructors by hand):

```
struct tag_int
{
   tag_int() {}
   tag_int(instance_of<short>) {}
   tag_int(instance_of<int>) {}
   tag_int(instance_of<long>) {}
   tag_int(instance_of<unsigned short>) {}
   tag_int(instance_of<unsigned int>) {}
   tag_int(instance_of<unsigned long>) {}
};
```

```
template <typename scalar_t>
struct maths
{
   static scalar_t mod(const scalar_t x, const scalar_t y, tag_int)
   {
      return x % y;
   }

   static scalar_t mod(const scalar_t& x, const scalar_t& y, tag_floating)
   {
      return fmod(x, y);
   }
};

template <typename scalar_t>
inline scalar_t mod(const scalar_t& x, const scalar_t& y)
{
   return maths<scalar_t>::mod(x, y, instance_of<scalar_t>());
}
```

Note that, in the above code, `maths<double>` contains a method that must not be called (there's no `operator%` for double): had `operation` been a non-template class, it would have been instantiated anyway, thus yielding a compiler error. However, when parsing an expression depending on a template parameter, the compiler, not knowing the actual type involved, will accept any formally legal C++ statement[86]; so if at least one between `x` and `y` has generic type `T`, then `x % y` is to be considered valid, until instantiation time.
Also the former example works unambiguously because the companion function restricts the call to members of `maths<double>` named `mod`, and for any type T, `instance_of<T>` can be promoted to at most one of `tag_int` or `tag_floating`.

Sometimes groups are associated with a special header file that detects platform information using macro blocks and translates it in C++ using typedefs:

```
// file "root.hpp"

struct msvc {};
struct gcc {};

#if defined(__MSVC)              // preprocessor compiler detection...
typedef msvc compiler_type;      // ...translated in c++
#elif defined(__GCC__)
typedef gcc compiler_type;
#endif

// from here on, there's a global type tag named "compiler_type"
```

[86] An illegal statement would be for example a call to an undeclared function. We remark once again that compilers are not required to diagnose errors in templates that are not instantiated; MSVC skips even the basic syntax checks, while GCC does forbid usage of undeclared functions and types. See also 5.2.3 about “Platform-specific traits”

In different platforms, the same function could have a different "best" implementation, so we can select the most suitable using `compiler_type` as a tag (but *all* functions must be legal C++ code):

```
template <typename scalar_t, typename compiler_t>
struct maths
{
    static scalar_t multiply_by_two(const scalar_t x)
    {
        return 2*x;
    }
}

template < >
struct maths<unsigned int, msvc>
{
    static unsigned int multiply_by_two(const unsigned int x)
    {
        return x << 1;
    }
}
```

```
template <typename scalar_t>
inline scalar_t multiply_by_two(const scalar_t& x)
{
    return maths<scalar_t, compiler_type>::multiply_by_two(x);
}
```

Note that we can branch the selection of member functions as we wish: either simultaneously on multiple tags, or hierarchically.

As a rule, we may want to use the "compiler tag" whenever we need to manipulate the result of a standard function that is defined as compiler-specific to some extent. For example, pretty-print a string given by `typeid(...).name()`.

5.1.2. Runtime decay

A type tag may implement a special cast operator so that if no overload in the group matches the tag exactly, the execution continues in a default function, which usually performs some work at runtime.
The prototype is a static integer, which, if there's no better match, decays into a normal integer.

Suppose we want to fill a C-array with zeroes:

```
template <typename T, T VALUE>
struct static_value
{
   operator T() const
   {
      return VALUE;
   }
};
```

```
template <typename T>
struct zeroize_helper
{
   static void apply(T* const data, static_value<int, 1>)
   {
      *data = T();
   }

   static void apply(T (data&)[2], static_value<int, 2>)
   {
      data[0] = data[1] = T();
   }

   static void apply(T* const data, const int N)
   {
      std::fill_n(data, N, T());
   }
};

template <typename T, int N>
void zeroize(T (&data)[N])
{
   zeroize_helper<T>::apply(data, static_value<int, N>());
}
```

- Instead of 0, we write T(), which works for a broader range of types
- If N is larger than 2, the best match is the third member.
- each function in the group can decide freely to cast, or even to ignore, the `static_value`.
- The default case may accept every `static_value` not necessarily performing all the work at runtime, but with another template function:

```
template <>
struct zeroize_helper<char>
{
   template <int N>
   struct chunk
   {
      char data[N];
   };

   template <int N>
   static void apply(char* const data, static_value<int, N>, selector<true>)
   {
      *reinterpret_cast<chunk<N>*>(data) = chunk<N>();
   }

   template <int N>
   static void apply(char* const data, static_value<int, N>, selector<false>)
   {
      memset(data, N, 0);
   }

   template <int N>
   static void apply(char* const data, static_value<int, N> S)
   {
      apply(data, S, selector<sizeof(chunk<N>) == N>());
   }
};
```

5.2. More traits

In this section we complete the review of traits.
This time we are going to use traits restricted for static programming, but also as function groups; at first, we present a

5.2.1. A function set for strings

Suppose we are going to write some generic algorithms for strings. Surely we can use iterators, in particular random-access iterators; most STL implementations have char-optimized algorithms, such as `std::find`, `std::copy`, etc.
The only burden on the user is a large number of calls to `strlen` to find the end of range: `strlen` is a *very* fast function, but this is a violation of STL assumptions, as "end" is assumed to be obtained in constant time, not linear time.

```
const char* c_string = "this is an example";

// can we avoid this?
std::copy(c_string, c_string+strlen(c_string), destination);
```

We can squeeze even more optimization using traits:

```
template <typename string_t>
struct string_traits
{
   typedef /* dependent on string_t */ const_iterator;
   typedef const string_t& argument_type;

   const_iterator begin(argument_type s);
   const_iterator end  (argument_type s);

   static bool is_end_of_string(const_iterator i, argument_type s);
};
```

Assuming that for every meaningful string, `string_traits` has the same interface, we can write an algorithm as follows:

```
template <typename string_t>
void loop_on_all_chars(const string_t& s)
{
   typedef string_traits<string_t> traits_t;

   typename traits_t::const_iterator i = traits_t::begin(s);
   while (!traits_t::is_end_of_string(i, s))
   {
      std::cout << *(i++);
   }
}
```

The code above is verbose, but clear; yet at this point it may not be evident what we accomplished: the semi-opaque interface of `string_traits` gives more freedom in doing comparisons:

```
template <typename char_t>
struct string_traits< std::basic_string<char_t> >
{
   typedef char_t char_type;
   typedef
      typename std::basic_string<char_type>::const_iterator const_iterator;

   typedef const std::basic_string<char_type>& argument_type;

   static const_iterator begin(argument_type text)
   {
      return text.begin();
   }

   static const_iterator end(argument_type text)
   {
      return text.end();
   }

   static bool is_end_of_string(const_iterator i, argument_type s);
   {
      return i == s.end();
   }
```

```
template <>
struct string_traits<const char*>
{
   typedef char char_type;

   typedef const char* const_iterator;
   typedef const char* argument_type;

   static const_iterator begin(argument_type text)
   {
      return text;
   }

   static const_iterator end(argument_type text)
   {
      return 0;    // constant-time
   }

   static bool is_end_of_string(const_iterator i, argument_type s);
   {
      // a constant-time "C" test for end of string
      return (i==0) || (*i==0);
   }
```

Since end is now constant-time, we save a linear-time pass (we'll meet again the very same problem and solve it with a different technique in section 7.2.2).

`string_traits` can be easily extended to a full interface (some words have been renamed for ease of reading)

```
template <typename string_t>
struct string_traits
{

typedef /* ... */ char_type;

typedef /* ... */ const_iterator;
typedef /* ... */ argument_type;      // either string_t or const string_t&

static size_t npos();

static size_t find1st(arg_t txt, const char_t c, size_t offset=0);
static size_t find1st(arg_t txt, const arg_t s, size_t offset=0);

static size_t findlast(arg_t txt, const char_t s, size_t offset);
static size_t findlast(arg_t txt, const arg_t s, size_t offset);

static size_t find1st_in(arg_t txt, const char_t* charset, size_t offs=0);
static size_t find1st_out(arg_t txt, const char_t* charset, size_t offs=0);

static size_t size(arg_t txt);

static const_iterator begin(arg_t txt);
static const_iterator end(arg_t txt);

static const char_t* c_str(arg_t txt);

static bool empty(const_iterator begin, const_iterator end);
static bool less(const_iterator begin, const_iterator end);
static size_t distance(const_iterator begin, const_iterator end);
};
```

To leverage the interface and take advantage of `std::string` member functions, we introduce the following convention:

- all iterators are random-access
- find functions return either the index of the character (which is portable in all kind of strings), or `npos()`, which means "not found"

```
static size_t find1st(arg_t text, const char_type c, size_t offset=0)
{
   const char_t* pos = strchr(text+offset, c);
   return pos ? (pos-text) : npos();
}
```

In the specialization for `const char*`, we carry on the ambiguity on the end iterator, which can be a null pointer to mean "until `char 0` is found"; thus, we could implement distance like:

```
static size_t distance(const_iterator begin, const_iterator end)
{
   return end ? end-begin : (begin ? strlen(begin) : 0);
}
```

Finally, we can inherit function sets via public derivation, as usual with traits, because they are stateless (so the protected empty destructor can be omitted):

```
template <>
struct string_traits<char*> : string_traits<const char*>
{
};
```

5.2.2. Concept traits

As we repeatedly noticed in the first chapters, traits classes prescribe syntax, not precise entities: code may borrow from traits in such a way that several different implementations may be possible.

Suppose we have some kind of smart pointer class, which is given an extra parameter

```
template <typename T, typename traits_t = smart_ptr_traits<T> >
class smart_ptr
{
   typedef typename traits_t::pointer pointer;
    pointer p_;

   // ...

   traits_t::release(p_);
```

`traits::release` can be:

- a public static function:

```
template <typename T>
struct smart_ptr_traits
{
   typedef T* pointer;

   static void release(pointer p)
   {
      delete p;
   }
};
```

- a type, whose constructor executes some code:

```
template <typename T>
struct smart_ptr_traits
{
   typedef T* pointer;

   struct release
   {
      explicit release(pointer p)
      {
         delete p;
      }
   };
};
```

- something that triggers a conversion operator:

```
template <typename T>
struct smart_ptr_traits
{
   struct release
   {
   };

   class pointer
   {
      // ...
      public:

         operator release()
         {
            delete p_;
            return release();
         }
   };
};
```

```
template <typename T>
struct smart_ptr_traits
{
   static void release(bool)
   {
   };

   class pointer
   {
      // ...
      public:

         operator bool()
         {
            // ...
         }
   };
};
```

All the implementations above are valid.
If `traits::release` is provided as a type, it may have static data that is easily shared with the rest of the program (we could, for example, log all the released pointers).

5.2.3. Platform-specific traits

Recall that traits classes may be "global" or "local": global traits classes are visible everywhere and local traits should be passed as parameters.
Global traits are preferred to make some platform properties easily accessible to clients:

```
template <typename char_t>
struct textfile_traits
{
   static char_t get_eol() { return '\n'; }
```

We now provide a full example, representing a timer object with a class template, borrowing additional information from a "timer traits" class:

- how to get current time
- how to convert a time into seconds (i.e. a frequency)

```
template <typename traits_t>
class basic_timer
{
   typedef typename traits_t::time_type tm_t;
   typedef typename traits_t::difference_type diff_t;

   tm_t start_;
   tm_t stop_;

   inline static tm_t now()
   {
      return traits_t::get_time();
   }

   double elapsed(const tm_t end) const
   {
      static const tm_t frequency = traits_t::get_freq();
      return double(diff_t(end-start_))/frequency;
   }

public:

   typedef tm_t time_type;
   typedef diff_t difference_type;

   basic_timer()
      : start_()
   {
   }

   difference_type lap() const
   {
      return now()-start_;
   }

   time_type start()
   {
      return start_ = now();
   }

   difference_type stop()
   {
      return (stop_ = now())-start_;
   }

   difference_type interval() const
   {
      return stop_-start_;
   }

   double as_seconds() const
   {
      return elapsed(stop_);
   }

   double elapsed() const
   {
      return elapsed(now());
   }
};
```

Here is a sample traits class that measures clock time (in seconds)

```
struct clock_time_traits
{
   typedef size_t time_type;
   typedef ptrdiff_t difference_type;

   static time_type get_time()
   {
      time_t t;
      return std::time(&t);
   }

   static time_type get_freq()
   {
      return 1;
   }
};
```

Here's a different traits class that accounts CPU time:

```
struct cpu_time_traits
{
   typedef size_t time_type;
   typedef ptrdiff_t difference_type;

   static time_type get_time()
   {
      return std::clock();
   }

   static time_type get_freq()
   {
      return CLOCKS_PER_SEC;
   }
};
```

And a short use case:

```
   basic_timer<clock_time_traits> t;
   t.start();
   // ...
   t.stop();
   std::cout << "I run for " << t.as_seconds() << " seconds.";
```

The fundamental restriction to traits is that all member functions must contain valid C++ code, even if unused: we cannot use compiler-specific code in one of the functions.
Since different operating systems can expose more precise API for time measurement, we are tempted to write specialized traits:

```
#include <windows.h>

struct windows_clock_time_traits
{
   typedef ULONGLONG time_type;
   typedef LONGLONG difference_type;

   static time_type get_time()
   {
      LARGE_INTEGER i;
      QueryPerformanceCounter(&i);
      return i.QuadPart;
   }

   static time_type get_freq()
   {
      LARGE_INTEGER value;
      QueryPerformanceFrequency(&value);
      return value.QuadPart;
   }
};
```

```
#include <sys/time.h>

struct macosx_clock_time_traits
{
   typedef uint64_t time_type;
   typedef int64_t difference_type;

   static time_type get_time()
   {
      timeval now;
      gettimeofday(&now, 0);
      return static_cast<time_type>(now.tv_sec) * get_freq() + now.tv_usec;
   }

   static time_type get_freq()
   {
      return 1000000;
   }
};
```

Apart from the typedefs for large integers, the traits interface above is purely standard C++, so we are tempted to isolate the preprocessor in a "factory header" and rely entirely on template properties later:

```
platform_detect.hpp

struct windows {};
struct macosx {};
struct other_os {};

#if defined(WIN32)
typedef windows platform_type;
#elif defined(__APPLE__)
typedef macosx platform_type;
#else
typedef other_os platform_type;
#endif
```

```
timer_traits.hpp

template <typename platform_t>
struct clock_time_traits;

template < >
struct clock_time_traits<windows>
{
   // implementation with QPC/QPF
};

template < >
struct clock_time_traits<macosx>
{
   // implementation with gettimeofday
};

template < >
struct clock_time_traits<other_os>
{
   // implementation with std::time
};
```

```
typedef basic_timer< clock_time_traits<platform_type> > native_timer_type;
```

Unfortunately, the code above is *non-portable* (if it compiles, however, it runs correctly).
According to the standard, a compiler is not required to diagnose errors in unused template member functions, but if it does, it will require that all mentioned entities are well-defined.
In particular, GCC may (likely, it will) report an error in `clock_time_traits<windows>::get_time`, because no function named `QueryPerformanceCounter` has been declared.

As the approach is attractive, some workarounds are possible:

- define a macro with the same name and as many arguments as the function

```
// define as nothing because the return type is void
// otherwise define as an appropriate constant, e.g. 0

#define QueryPerformanceCounter(X)

#if defined(WIN32)
#undef QueryPerformanceCounter      // remove the fake…
#include <windows.h>                // …and include the true function
#endif
```

- declare - but do not define - the function

```
#if !defined(WIN32)
   void QueryPerformanceCounter(void*);
#endif
```

This is the preferred solution, because windows traits should not link in other operating systems.

A common trick, if the function returns void, is to define the name of the function itself to <nothing>: the comma-separated argument list will be parsed as comma operator.
This allows also ellipsis functions to be used:

```
#define printf

printf("Hello world, %f", cos(3.14));
```

The macro changes the return type of the expression to double (the last argument); furthermore, the program is still evaluating `cos(3.14)`; an alternative that also cares for runtime - but not totally bulletproof - would be:

```
inline bool ellipsis_replacement(...) { return false };

#define printf    false && ellipsis_replacement
```

5.2.4. Merging traits

Especially when dealing with large traits, we would like the user to be able to customize only a smaller part.
Typically the problem is solved splitting the traits class in sub-parts and recombining them by public inheritance to form a traits default value.

Suppose we are grouping some comparison operators in traits:

```
template <typename T>
struct binary_relation_traits
{
   static bool gt(const T& x, const T& y)    { return x>y; }
   static bool lt(const T& x, const T& y)    { return x<y; }

   static bool gteq(const T& x, const T& y)    { return x>=y; }
   static bool lteq(const T& x, const T& y)    { return x<=y; }

   static bool eq(const T& x, const T& y)      { return x==y; }
   static bool ineq(const T& x, const T& y)    { return x!=y; }
};
```

The general implementation of `binary_relation_traits` assumes that `T` defines all six comparison operators; but we'd like to support two important special cases, namely:

- `T` defines only `operator<`
- `T` defines only `operator<` and `operator==`

Without our support, in both cases, the user will have to implement all traits structure from scratch. So we rearrange the code as follows:

```
template <typename T>
struct b_r_ordering_traits
{
   static bool gt(const T& x, const T& y)    { return x>y; }
   static bool lt(const T& x, const T& y)    { return x<y; }

   static bool gteq(const T& x, const T& y)    { return x>=y; }
   static bool lteq(const T& x, const T& y)    { return x<=y; }
};

template <typename T>
struct b_r_equivalence_traits
{
   static bool eq(const T& x, const T& y)       { return x==y; }
   static bool ineq(const T& x, const T& y)     { return x!=y; }
};

template <typename T>
struct binary_relation_traits
   :
      public b_r_ordering_traits<T>,
      public b_r_equivalence_traits<T>
{
};
```

Then we write the alternative blocks, which can be combined:

```
template <typename T>
struct b_r_ordering_less_traits
{
   static bool gt(const T& x, const T& y)    { return y<x; }
   static bool lt(const T& x, const T& y)    { return x<y; }

   static bool gteq(const T& x, const T& y)    { return !(x<y); }
   static bool lteq(const T& x, const T& y)    { return !(y<x); }
};

template <typename T>
struct b_r_equivalence_equal_traits
{
   static bool eq(const T& x, const T& y)       { return x==y; }
   static bool ineq(const T& x, const T& y)     { return !(x==y); }
};

template <typename T>
struct b_r_equivalence_less_traits
{
   static bool eq(const T& x, const T& y)       { return !(x<y) && !(y<x); }
   static bool ineq(const T& x, const T& y)     { return x<y || y<x; }
};
```

Finally we combine the pieces via derivation and a hidden template parameter.

```
enum
{
   HAS_JUST_OPERATOR_LESS,
   HAS_OPERATOR_LESS_AND_EQ,
   HAS_ALL_6_OPERATORS
};

template <typename T, int = HAS_ALL_6_OPERATORS>
struct binary_relation_traits
: b_r_ordering_traits<T>
, b_r_equivalence_traits<T>
{
};

template <typename T>
struct binary_relation_traits<T, HAS_JUST_OPERATOR_LESS>
: b_r_ordering_less_traits<T>
, b_r_equivalence_less_traits<T>
{
};

template <typename T>
struct binary_relation_traits<T, OPERATOR_LESS_AND_EQ>
: b_r_ordering_less_traits<T>
, b_r_equivalence_equal_traits<T>
{
};
```

Further, traits can be chained using appropriate enumerations and "bitwise-or" syntax.[87]

We would like to provide an enumeration set, containing powers of 2 which will be combined using the standard ***flags idiom*** but at compile time:

```
   fstream fs("main.txt", ios::in | ios:out);
```

```
   typedef binary_relation<MyType, native::less | native::eq> MyTraits;
```

First we let the flags start from 1, since we need powers of 2.

```
namespace native
{
   enum
   {
      lt       = 1,
      lt_eq    = 2,
      gt       = 4,
      gt_eq    = 8,
      eq       = 16,
      ineq     = 32
   };
}
```

Second, we split our traits class in atoms, using partial specialization:

[87] Cfr. section 3.3.3

```
template <typename T, int FLAG>
struct binary_relation;                    // no body!

template <typename T>
struct binary_relation<T, native::lt>
{
   static bool lt(const T& x, const T& y)    { return x<y; }
};

template <typename T>
struct binary_relation<T, native::lt_eq>
{
   static bool lteq(const T& x, const T& y)    { return x<=y; }
};

// and so on...
```

If the user sets `FLAG` to (`native::ineq | ...`) then `binary_relation<T,FLAGS>` should derive from `binary_relation<T, native::ineq>` and `binary_relation<T, FLAGS - native::ineq>`.

We need an auxiliary metafunction, `static_highest_bit<N>::value` that returns the index of the highest bit set in a (positive) integer N, i.e. the exponent of the largest power of 2 less or equal to N.[88]
Having this tool at our disposal, we come up with an implementation:

```
template <typename T, unsigned FLAG>
struct binary_relation;

template <typename T>
struct binary_relation<T, 0>
{
   // empty!
};

template <typename T>
struct binary_relation<T, native::lt>
{
   static T lt(const T& x, const T& y)    { return x<y; }
};

template <typename T>
struct binary_relation<T, native::gt>
{
   static T gt(const T& x, const T& y)    { return x>y; }
};
```

```
// write all remaining specializations
// then finally...
```

[88] The details of `static_highest_bit` are in chapter 4.4.1

```
template <typename T, unsigned FLAG>
struct binary_relation
:
  binary_relation_traits<T, FLAG & (1 << static_highest_bit<FLAG>::value)>,
  binary_relation_traits<T, FLAG - (1 << static_highest_bit<FLAG>::value)>
{
   // empty!
};
```

Now the user can select `binary_relation_traits` members at compile time:

```
   typedef binary_relation<MyType, native::less | native::eq> MyTraits;

   MyType a, b;
   MyTraits::lt(a,b);      // ok.
   MyTraits::lteq(a,b);    // error: undefined
```

This technique is interesting in itself, but it does not yet solve our original requirements, since we can only pick "native" operators. But we can add more flags:

```
namespace native
{
   enum
   {
      lt       = 1,
      lt_eq    = 2,
      gt       = 4,
      gt_eq    = 8,
      eq       = 16,
      ineq     = 32
   };
}

namespace deduce
{
   enum
   {
      ordering    = 64,
      equivalence = 128,
      ineq        = 256
   };
}
```

```
template <typename T>
struct binary_relation_traits<T, deduce::ordering>
{
   static bool gt(const T& x, const T& y)      { return y<x; }

   static bool gteq(const T& x, const T& y)    { return !(x<y); }
   static bool lteq(const T& x, const T& y)    { return !(y<x); }
};

template <typename T>
struct binary_relation_traits<T, deduce ::ineq>
{
   static bool ineq(const T& x, const T& y)    { return !(x==y); }
};

template <typename T>
struct binary_relation_traits<T, deduce::equivalence>
{
   static bool eq(const T& x, const T& y)      { return !(x<y) && !(y<x); }
   static bool ineq(const T& x, const T& y)    { return x<y || y<x; }
};
```

```
typedef
binary_relation_traits
<
   MyType,
   native::less | deduce::ordering | deduce::equivalence
>
MyTraits;
```

Note that any unnecessary duplication (such that `native::ineq | deduce::ineq`) will trigger a compiler error *at the first use*: if `traits<T,N>` and `traits<T,M>` both have a member `x`, then `traits<T,N+M>::x` is an ambiguous call.

5.3. SFINAE

The "Substitution failure is not an error" principle is a guarantee that the C++ standard offers; we will see precisely what it means and how to remove conditionally function templates from an overload set.

Remember that when a class template is instantiated, the compiler generates:

- every member signature at class level
- only strictly necessary function bodies

As a consequence, this does not compile:

```
template <typename T>
struct A
{
   typename T::pointer f() const
   {
      return 0;
   }
};
```

```
A<int> x;
```

As soon as `A<int>` is met, the compiler will try to generate a signature for *every* member function, and it will give an error because `int::pointer` is not a valid type.
Instead, this would work:

```
template <typename T>
struct A
{
   int f() const
   {
      typename T::type a = 0;
      return a;
   }
```

```
A<int> x;
```

As long as `A<int>::f()` is unused, the compiler will ignore its body (and it is good news, because it contains an error).

Furthermore, when the compiler meets `f(x)` and `x` has type `X`, it should decide which particular `f` is being invoked, so it sorts all possible candidates from the best to the worst and it tries to substitute `X` in any template parameter; if this replacement produces a function with an invalid signature (signature, not body!), then the candidate is silently discarded: this is the SFINAE principle.

```
template <typename T>
typename T::pointer f(T*);

int f(void*);
```

```
int* x = 0;
f(x);
```

The first f would be preferred because `T*` is a better match than `void*`; however `int` has no member type called `pointer`, so the second f is used. SFINAE applies only when the substitution produces an expression that is formally invalid (like `int::pointer`); instead, it does not apply when the result is a type that does not compile:

```
template <typename T, int N>
struct B
{
   static const int value = 100/N;
};
```

```
template <typename T>
B<T, 0> f(T*);

int f(void*);
```

`B<T, 0>` is a valid type, but its compilation gives an error: the first f will be picked anyway, and the compiler will stop.

To take advantage of SFINAE, when we want to "enable" or "disable" a particular overload of a function template, we artificially insert in its signature a dependent name that may resolve to an invalid expression (i.e. a non-existent type, like `int::pointer`).
If all candidates have been discarded, we get a compiler error (trivial uses of SFINAE look in fact like static assertions).

There are two big different applications of SFINAE: when f runs after being selected and when f is not executed at all.

5.3.1. SFINAE metafunctions

With SFINAE and `sizeof` we can write metafunctions that take a decision based on the interface of a type T, very close to what is called *reflection* in different programming languages.
The basic ingredients are:

- two (or more) types with different size; we'll call them `YES` and `NO`
- a set of overloaded functions `f`, where at least one must be a template, returning either `YES` or `NO`
- a static constant defined in terms of `sizeof(f(something))`

The following paradigm helps clarifying:

```
template <typename T>
class YES { char dummy[2]; };          // has size > 1

typedef char NO;                       // has size == 1
```

```
template <typename T>
class MF
{
   template <typename X>
   static YES<[[condition on X]]> test(X);

   static NO test(...);


   static T this_type();

public:

   static const bool value = sizeof(test(this_type())) != sizeof(NO);
};
```

The compiler has to decide which test is being called when the argument has type T; it will try to evaluate `YES<[[condition on T]]>` first (because `void*` and the ellipsis "..." have very low priority): if this generates an invalid type, the first overload of `test` is discarded and it will select the other.

We list some important facts:

- the static functions *need not have a body*; only their signature is used in `sizeof`
- `YES<T>` need not have size 2, so it would be an error to write `sizeof(test(this_type())) == 2`; however `char` *must* have size 1, so we could verify if `sizeof(test(this_type()))>1`
- at least one of the test functions should be a template depending on a *new* parameter X; it would be wrong to define `test` in terms of `T` (the parameter of `MF`) since SFINAE would not apply
- we use a dummy function that returns T instead of, say invoking `test(T())` because T may not have a default constructor

Some compilers will emit a warning, because it's illegal to pass an object to an ellipsis function; actually the code does not run, since `sizeof` wraps the whole expression, but warnings may be long and annoying; a good workaround is to pass pointers to functions:

```
   template <typename X>
   static YES<[[condition on X]]> test(X*);

   static NO test(...);

   static T* this_type();
```

If we switch to pointers:

- `void` becomes an admissible type (since `T*` exists)
- references become illegal (a pointer to a reference is an error).

So either way, we'll always have to write some explicit specialization of MF to deal with corner cases.

SFINAE applies if *any* substitution of the template parameter produces an invalid type, not necessarily in the return type; sometimes in fact it's more convenient to use arguments:

```
template <typename T>
class MF
{
   template <typename X>
   static YES<void> test([[type that depends on X]]*);

   template <typename X>
   static NO test(...);

public:
   static const bool value = sizeof(test<T>(0)) != sizeof(NO);
};
```

If the substitution of X in the first expression produces a valid type, thus a valid pointer, then `test<T>(0)` takes it as the preferred call (casts 0 to a typed pointer and returns `YES<void>`, or whatever yes-type), otherwise 0 is passed without any cast (as integer) to `test(...)`, which returns `NO`.
The explicit call `test<T>` works because the ellipsis test function has a dummy template parameter, otherwise it would never match.[89]

As a simple example, we can test if type T has a member type named `pointer`:

```
template <typename T>
class has_pointer_type
{
   template <typename X>
   static YES<typename X::pointer> test(X*);

   static NO test(...);

   static T* this_type();

public:
   static const bool value = sizeof(test(this_type())) != sizeof(NO);
};
```

Or (almost) equivalently:[90]

[89] Cfr. section 2.2.1

[90] This would fail if `X::pointer` were a reference; at the moment, we do not care

```
template <typename T>
class has_pointer_type
{
   template <typename X>
   static YES<void> test(typename X::pointer*);

   template <typename X>
   static NO test(...);

public:
   static const bool value = sizeof(test<T>(0)) == sizeof(YES);
};
```

By modifying the template parameter of YES, we can check if T has a static constant named `value`: once again, it's convenient to derive from a common yes-type:

```
template <int VALUE>
struct YES2 : yes_type
{
};
```

```
template <typename T>
class has_value
{
   template <typename X>
   static YES2<X::value> test(X*);
```

Or we can check the presence of a member function with a fixed name and signature:[91]

```
template <typename T, void (T::*F)(T&)>
struct YES3 : yes_type
{
};
```

```
template <typename T>
class has_swap_member
{
   template <typename X>
   static YES3<X, &X::swap> test(X*);
```

Finally, a popular idiom checks if T is a class or a fundamental type using a fake pointer-to-member (literal zero can be cast to `int T::*` if T is a class, even if it has no member of type `int`).

[91] The swap-detection problem is actually much more difficult; it's discussed later in this section

```
template <typename T>
class is_class
{
   template <typename X>
   static yes_type test(int X::*);

   template <typename X>
   static no_type test(...);

public:

   static const bool value = (sizeof(test<T>(0))!=sizeof(no_type));
};
```

5.3.2. Multiple decisions

The examples shown insofar take a single decision path yes/no, but some criteria can be more complex. Let's write a metafunction that identifies all signed integers:[92]

```
if (T is a class)
    return false

if (T is a pointer)
    return false

if (T is a reference)
    return false

if (we can have a non-type template parameter of type T)
{
    if (the expression "T(0) > T(-1)" is well-formed and true)
        return true
    else
        return false
}
else
{
    return false
}
```

```
template <typename X, bool IS_CLASS = is_class<X>::value>
class is_signed_integer;
```

[92] The "main algorithm" alone would not suffice: it will work when T is a fundamental type; some compilers however evaluate the expression T(0) < T(-1) as true when T is a pointer; other compilers will give errors if T is a type with no constructor, that's why we add explicit specializations for pointers, references and class types. Note however that this approach is superior to an explicit list of specializations, because it's completely compiler/preprocessor independent.

```
template <typename X>
class is_signed_integer<X*, false> : public selector<false>
{
};

template <typename X>
class is_signed_integer<X&, false> : public selector<false>
{
};

template <typename X>
class is_signed_integer<X, true> : public selector<false>
{
};
```

```
template <typename X>
class is_signed_integer<X, false>
{
   template <typename T>
   static static_parameter<T, 0>* decide_int(T*);

   static void* decide_int(...);


   template <typename T>
   static selector<(T(0) > T(-1))> decide_signed(static_parameter<T, 0>*);

   static selector<false> decide_signed(...);

   static yes_type cast(selector<true>);
   static no_type cast(selector<false>);

   static X* getX();

public:

   static const bool value =
         sizeof(cast(decide_signed(decide_int(getX()))))==sizeof(yes_type);
};
```

`cast` maps all possible intermediate return types to either `yes_type` or `no_type`, for the final `sizeof` test.

In general, it's possible to stretch this idea and return an enumeration (more precisely, a `size_t`), instead of `bool`: suppose we had more intermediate decision cases

```
static T1 decide(int*);
static T2 decide(double*);
...
static Tn decide(void*);
```

Then we can map `T1, T2,... Tn` to an enumeration using `fixed_size`

```
    static fixed_size<1>::type& cast(T1);
    static fixed_size<2>::type& cast(T2);
    // ...
public:

    static const size_t value = sizeof(cast(decide(...)));
};
```

5.3.3. only_if

Another interesting usage of SFINAE is in excluding elements from a set of overloaded (member) functions which are not compliant to some condition:

```
template <bool CONDITION>
struct static_assert_SFINAE
{
   typedef void type;
};

template <>
struct static_assert_SFINAE<false>
{
};
```

If a function has an argument of type pointer-to-`static_assert_SFINAE<…>::type`, then clearly substitution of any `T` which makes the condition false, generates an invalid expression; so that particular function is removed from the set of overloads.
The fake pointer argument has a default value of 0, so the user can safely ignore its existence.[93]

```
#define ONLY_IF(COND)    typename static_assert_SFINAE<COND>::type* = 0

template <typename T>
void f(T x, ONLY_IF(is_integer<T>::value))
{
}

void f(float x)
{
}
```

```
// later…

double x = 3.14;
f(x); // calls f(float)
```

[93] Sometimes it's desirable to document C++ code, not literally, but just as the user is supposed to use it. This kind of functional documentation is also a part of C++ style: in the example illustrated here, we will document that f(T) is a single argument function, even if it's not; all the implementation details should be hidden.

This technique is often useful in universal-copy constructors of class templates:

```
template <typename T1>
class MyVector
{
public:
   // not used if T2 is T1

   template <typename T2>
   MyVector(const MyVector<T2>& that)
   {
   }
};
```

Restrictions on `T2` may be easily introduced using `ONLY_IF` (`has_conversion` is fully documented in paragraph 5.4)

```
   template <typename T2>
   MyVector(const MyVector<T2>& that, ONLY_IF((has_conversion<T2,T1>::L2R)))
   {
   }
```

Another application is the "static cast" of `static_value`: we may wish to convert, say, `static_value<int, 3>` to `static_value<long, 3>`:

```
template <typename T, T VALUE>
struct static_value
{
   static const T value = VALUE;

   static_value(const int = 0)
   {
   }

   template <typename S, S OTHER>
      static_value(const static_value<S, OTHER>,
                   typename only_if<VALUE==OTHER, int>::type = 0)
   {
   }
};
```

Sometimes it can be useful to apply the idiom not to arguments, but to the return value:

```
template <bool CONDITION, typename T = void>
struct only_if
{
   typedef T type;
};

template <typename T>
struct only_if<false, T>
{
};
```

```
template <typename T>
typename only_if<is_integer<T>::value, T>::type multiply_by_2(const T x)
{
   return x << 1;
}
```

The function above is either ill-formed, or takes a `const T` and returns `T`.

5.3.4. SFINAE and returned functors

The various `test` functions met so far have no use for their return type, whose size is all that matters. Sometimes instead, they will return a functor that is immediately invoked: consider a simple example, where the function `number_of_elem` returns `x.size()` if x has a type member called `size_type`, otherwise 1.

```
template <typename T, typename S>
struct get_size
{
   S operator()(const T& x) const { return x.size(); }

   get_size(int) {}
};
```

```
struct get_one
{
   template <typename T>
   size_t operator()(const T&) const { return 1; }

   get_one(int) {}
};
```

```
template <typename T>
get_size<T, typename T::size_type> test(const T* x)    // SFINAE
{
   return 0;
}

get_one test(const void*)
{
   return 0;
}
```

```
template <typename T>
size_t number_of_elem(const T& x)
{
   return test(&x)(x);
}
```

```
std::vector<int> v;
std::map<int, double> m;
double x;

number_of_elem(v);      // returns v.size()
number_of_elem(m);      // returns m.size()
number_of_elem(x);      // returns 1
```

We will use some techniques from the previous paragraph to describe a metaprogramming implementation of a logging callback, with a variable log level.
In scientific computing, we can meet functions that may run for a long time: so it's necessary to maintain some interaction with the function even while it's running, for example to get feedback on the progress, or to send an abort signal. Since there is no hypothesis on the environment (computational routines are usually portable), we cannot pass, say, a pointer to a progress bar, and we have to design an equally portable interface.

A possible solution follows: the function internally updates a structure (whose type is known to its caller) with all the meaningful information about the state of the program, and regularly it invokes a user functor on the structure:

```
struct algorithm_info
{
   int iteration_current;
   int iteration_max;

   double best_tentative_solution;

   size_t time_elapsed;
   size_t memory_used;
};
```

```
template <..., typename logger_t>
void algorithm(..., logger_t LOG)
{
   algorithm_info I;
   for (...)
   {
      // do the work...

      I.iteration_current = ...;
      I.best_tentative_solution = ...;

      LOG(I);
   }
}
```

We'll try to design some static interaction between the logger and the algorithm so that only some relevant portion of the information is updated: if LOG does nothing, no time is wasted updating I.

First, all recordable information is partitioned in levels. `logger_t` will declare a static constant named `log_level` and the algorithm loop will not update the objects corresponding to information in ignored levels.
By convention, having no member `log_level` or having `log_level=0` corresponds to skipping the log.

```
template <int LEVEL = 3>
struct algorithm_info;

template <>
struct algorithm_info<0>
{
};

template <>
struct algorithm_info<1> : algorithm_info<0>
{
   int iteration_current;
   int iteration_max;
};

template <>
struct algorithm_info<2> : algorithm_info<1>
{
   double best_value;
};

template <>
struct algorithm_info<3> : algorithm_info<2>
{
   size_t time_elapsed;
   size_t memory_used;
};
```

Second, we use SFINAE to query `logger_t` for a constant named `log_level`

```
template <int N>
struct log_level_t
{
   operator int () const
   {
      return N;
   }
};

template <typename T>
log_level_t<T::log_level> log_level(const T*)
{
   return log_level_t<T::log_level>();
}

inline int log_level(...)
{
   return 0;
}
```

Finally, a simple `switch` will do the work: if `logger_t` does contain `log_level`, SFINAE will pick the first overload of `log_level`, returning an object which is immediately cast to integer; otherwise, the weaker overload will immediately return 0.

```
   switch (log_level(&LOG))
   {
      case 3:
         I.time_elapsed = ...;
         I.memory_used = ...;

      case 2: // fall through
         I.best_value = ...;

      case 1: // fall through
         I.iteration_current = ...;
         I.iteration_max = ...;

      case 0: // fall through
      default:
         break;
   }

   LOG(I);
```

The above implementation is the simplest to code, but `LOG` has still access to the whole object I, even to the part which is not initialized.
The static information about the level is already contained in `log_level_t`, so it's appropriate to transform this object into a functor that performs a cast.

```
template <int N>
struct log_level_t
{
   operator int () const
   {
      return N;
   }

   typedef const algorithm_info<N>& ref_n;
   typedef const algorithm_info< >& ref;

   ref_n operator()(ref i) const
   {
      return i;
   }
};
```

```
template <typename T>
log_level_t<T::log_level> log_level(const T*)
{
   return log_level_t<T::log_level>();
}

inline log_level_t<0> log_level(...)
{
   return log_level_t<0>();
}
```

```
   switch (log_level(&LOG))
   {
      // as above...
   }

   LOG(log_level(&LOG)(I));
```

This enforces `LOG` to implement an `operator()` that accepts exactly the right "slice" of information.

5.3.5. SFINAE and software updates

One of the many uses of SFINAE-based metafunctions is conditional requirement detection.

TMP libraries often interact with user types and user functors, which must usually satisfy some (minimal) interface constraint. New releases of these libraries could in principle impose additional requirements for extra optimizations, but this often conflicts with backward compatibility.

Suppose we sort a range passing a custom binary relation to an external library function, called `nonstd::sort`

```
template <typename T>
struct has_any_NUMBER_OF_THREADS
{
   template <typename X>
   static static_value<size_t, X::NUMBER_OF_THREADS> test(X*);

   static no_type test(void*);

   template <size_t N>
   static yes_type cast(static_value<size_t, N>);

   static no_type cast(no_type);

   static T* getT();

   static const bool value = (sizeof(cast(test(getT()))) > 1);
};
```

```
template <typename REQUIRED_T, typename T, bool>
struct check_NUMBER_OF_THREADS_type;

template <typename REQUIRED_T, typename T>
struct check_NUMBER_OF_THREADS_type<REQUIRED_T, T, true>
{
   static yes_type test(REQUIRED_T);

   template <typename X>
   static no_type test(X);

   static const bool value = sizeof(test(T::NUMBER_OF_THREADS))>1;// line #1
};

template <typename REQUIRED_T, typename T>
struct check_NUMBER_OF_THREADS_type<REQUIRED_T, T, false>
{
   static const bool value = false;                          // line #2
};
```

```
template <typename T>
struct has_valid_NUMBER_OF_THREADS :
check_NUMBER_OF_THREADS_type<size_t, T, has_any_NUMBER_OF_THREADS<T>::value>
{
};
```

5.3.6. Limitations and workarounds

SFINAE techniques ultimately rely on the compiler handling gracefully an error, so they are especially vulnerable to compiler bugs.

If correct code does not compile, here's a checklist of workarounds:

- o give all functions a body
- o move static functions outside of the class, in a private namespace
- o think of a simpler algorithm
- o remove "private" and use "struct"

```
template <typename X>
class is_signed_integer
{
   template <typename T>
   static static_value<T, 0>* decide_int(T*);

   static void* decide_int(...);


   template <typename T>
   static selector<(T(0) > T(-1))>
                              decide_signed(static_value<T, 0>*);

   static selector<false> decide_signed(...);

   static yes_type cast(selector<true>);
   static no_type cast(selector<false>);

   static X* getX();

public:

   static const bool value =
         sizeof(cast(decide_signed(decide_int(getX()))))
         ==sizeof(yes_type);
};
```

```
namespace priv {

template <typename T>
static_value<T, 0>* decide_int(T*);

void* decide_int(...);

template <typename T>
selector<(T(0) > T(-1))> decide_signed(static_value<T, 0>*);

selector<false> decide_signed(...);

yes_type cast(selector<true>);
no_type cast(selector<false>);

template <typename X>
struct is_signed_integer_helper
{
   X* getX();

   static const bool value =
      sizeof(cast(decide_signed(decide_int(getX()))))
      ==sizeof(yes_type);
};

} // end of namespace

template <typename T>
struct is_signed_integer
: public selector<priv::is_signed_integer_helper<T>::value>
{
};
```

A corner case in the standard is a substitution failure inside a `sizeof` that should bind to a template parameter: the following example usually does not compile:

```
template <typename T>
class is_dereferenceable
{
   template <size_t N>
   class YES { char dummy[2]; };

   template <typename X>
      static YES<sizeof(*X())> test(X*);

   static NO test(...);

   static T* this_type();

public:

   static const bool value = sizeof(test(this_type()))>1;
};
```

Detection of member functions is extremely problematic: let's rewrite the meta-function here.

```
template <typename S>
class has_swap_member
{
   template <typename T, void (T::*)(T&) >
   class YES { char dummy[2]; };

   typedef char NO;

   template <typename T>
   static YES<T, &T::swap> test( T* );

   static NO test(...);

   static S* ptr();

public:

   static const bool value = sizeof(test(ptr()))>1;
};
```

Suppose that classes `D1` and `D2` have a public template base `B<T1>` and `B<T2>`, adding no data member; `swap` will likely be implemented only once in B, with signature `void B<T>::swap(B<T>&)`, but the users will see it as `D1::swap` and `D2::swap` (an argument of type `D1` will be cast to `B<T1>&`).[94]
However `has_swap_member<D1>::value` is false, because `YES<D1, &D1::swap>` does not match `YES<T, void (T::*F)(T&)>`: it would match `YES<T1, void (T2::*F)(T2&)>` or even `YES<T1, void (T1::*F)(T2&)>` but this pointer cast is out of scope, because `T2` is unknown.

So the fact that `has_swap_member<T>::value` is false does not imply that the syntax `a.swap(b)` is illegal.

The best we can do is integrate the detection phase with the swap itself, and create a function that swaps two references with the best known method: when swap detection fails, Koenig lookup will usually find an equivalent routine in the right namespace (at least for all STL containers; cfr. paragraph 2.4.2).

[94] This may look like a corner case, but it's quite common: in popular STL implementation let D1=`std::map`, D2=`std::set` and B<T> be an undocumented class that represents a balanced tree.

```
using std::swap;

struct swap_traits
{
   template <typename T>
   inline static void apply(T& a, T& b)
   {
      apply1(a, b, test(&a));
   }

private:

   template <typename T, void (T::*F)(T&)>
   struct yes : public yes_type
   {
      yes(int = 0) {}
   };

   template <typename T>
   static yes<T, &T::swap> test(T*)
   {
      return 0;
   }

   static no_type test(void*)
   {
      return 0;
   }


   template <typename T>
   inline static void apply1(T& a, T& b, no_type)
   {
      swap(a, b);
   }

   template <typename T>
   inline static void apply1(T& a, T& b, yes_type)
   {
      a.swap(b);
   }
};

template <typename T>
inline void smart_swap(T& x, T& y)
{
   swap_traits::apply(x, y);
}
```

Note that all functions have a body, as they are truly invoked.
The workflow is: `smart_swap(x, y)` invokes `apply`, which in turn is `apply1(x, y, [[condition on T]])`; `apply1` is ADL swap when condition is "no", and member swap invocation otherwise.

```
#include <map>

struct swappable
{
   void swap(swappable&)
   {
   }
};

int main()
{
   std::map<int, int> a, b;
   smart_swap(a, b);            // if it fails detection of map::swap
                                // then it uses ADL swap, which is the same

   swappable c, d;
   smart_swap(c, d);            // correctly detects and uses swappable::swap

   int i = 3, j = 4;
   smart_swap(i, j);            // correctly uses std::swap
}
```

The true solution requires the C++0x keyword `decltype`.
See section 13.2

5.4. Other classic metafunctions with sizeof

An overload may be selected because the argument can be cast successfully. We will write a metafunction that returns three boolean constants:
`has_conversion<L,R>::L2R` is true when L is convertible to R;
`has_conversion<L,R>::identity` is true when L and R are the same type.[95]

[95] The left-right notation may not be the most elegant, but it's indeed excellent for remembering how the class works.

```
template <typename L, typename R>
class has_conversion
{
   static yes_type test(R);
   static no_type test(...);
   static L left();

public:

   static const bool L2R = (sizeof(test(left())) == sizeof(yes_type));
   static const bool identity = false;
};


template <typename T>
class has_conversion<T, T>
{
public:

   static const bool L2R = true;
   static const bool identity = true;
};
```

Here we pass a fake instance of L to `test`; if L is convertible to R, the first overload is preferred, and the result is `yes_type`.
Following Alexandrescu, we can deduce if a type publicly derives from another:

```
template <typename B, typename D>
struct is_base_of
{
   static const bool value =
   (
      has_conversion<const D*, const B*>::L2R &&
      !has_conversion<const B*, const void*>::identity
   );
};
```

Implicit promotion techniques have been extensively used by Abrahams[96]: the key point is to overload an operator at namespace level, not at a member.

```
struct fake_incrementable
{
   template <typename T>
   fake_incrementable(T);    // non-explicit constructor takes anything
};

fake_incrementable operator++(fake_incrementable);       // line #1
```

96 `boost::is_incrementable` correctly strips qualifiers from `T`, but it allows `operator++` to return `void`, which in general is not desirable: in this case, the simpler version presented here gives a compile-time error.

```
yes_type test(fake_incrementable);

template <typename T>
no_type test(T);
```

```
template <class T>
struct has_preincrement
{
   static T& getT();

   static const bool value = sizeof(test(++getT())) == sizeof(no_type);
};
```

The statement `++getT()` can either resolve to `x`'s own `operator++` or (with lower priority) to a conversion to `fake_incrementable`, followed by `fake_incrementable` increment; this latter function is visible, because, as anticipated, it is declared as a global entity in the namespace, not as a member function.

To test preincrement, replace line #1 with:

```
fake_incrementable operator++(fake_incrementable, int);
```

Note that the computation of `sizeof(test(++x))` must be done in the namespace where `fake_incrementable` lives, otherwise it will fail:

```
namespace aux {

struct fake_incrementable
{
   template <typename T>
   fake_incrementable(T);
};

fake_incrementable operator++(fake_incrementable);

yes_type test(fake_incrementable);

template <typename T>
no_type test(T);

}
```

```
template <typename T>
struct has_preincrement
{
   static T& getT();
   static const bool value = sizeof(aux::test(++getT())) == sizeof(no_type);
};
```

We can also move the computation inside the namespace, and recall the result outside:

```
namespace aux {

// ... (all as above)

template <typename T>
struct has_preincrement_helper
{
   static T& getT();
   static const bool value = sizeof(test(++getT())) == sizeof(no_type);
};

}
```

```
template <typename T>
struct has_preincrement : selector<aux::has_preincrement_helper<T>::value>
{
};
```

5.5. Overload on function pointers

One of the most convenient tag objects to select an overloaded function is a function pointer, which is then discarded.
A pointer is cheap to build and at the same time it may convey a lot of static information, suitable for template argument deduction.

5.5.1. erase

The following will be our primary example: iterating over an STL container, we need to erase the element pointed by iterator i; erasure should advance (not invalidate) the iterator itself; unfortunately for some containers the right syntax is `i = c.erase(i)`, but for associative containers is `c.erase(i++)`.
Taking advantage of the fact that `C::erase` must exist (otherwise we wouldn't know what to do - and the call to `erase_gap` is ill formed), we just pick the right one with a dummy pointer:

```
template <typename C, typename iterator_t, typename base_t>
void erase_gap2(C& c, iterator_t& i, iterator_t (base_t::*)(iterator_t))
{
   i = c.erase(i);
}

template <typename C, typename iterator_t, typename base_t>
void erase_gap2(C& c, iterator_t& i, void (base_t::*)(iterator_t))
{
   c.erase(i++);
}
```

```
template <typename C>
void erase gap(C& c, typename C::iterator& i)
{
   erase_gap2(c, i, &C::erase);
}
```

```
for (i = c.begin(); i != c.end(); )
{
   if (need_to_erase(i))
      erase_gap(c, i);
   else
      ++i;
}
```

Observe that erasure is *not* invoked via the pointer: it's just the type of the pointer that matters.
Also, the type of erase may not be `... (C::*)(...)`, because a container could have a "hidden base", so the exact type is left open to compiler deduction.

5.5.2. swap

The technique above can be extended via SFINAE to cases where it's unknown if the member function exists or not. To demonstrate, we'll extend `swap_traits` (introduced in section 5.3.6) to perform the following:[97]

- o if T has `void T::swap(T&)`, use `a.swap(b)`
- o if T has `static void swap(T&,T&)`, use `T::swap(a,b)`
- o if T has both swaps, then the call is ambiguous
- o in any other case, use ADL swap

The first part does not contain anything new; all "yes" types derive from a common "yes-base", because the first test is meant only to ensure that any of the possible swap member functions exists.

[97] This extension is to be considered an exercise, not necessarily a good idea.

```
struct swap_traits
{
   template <typename T, void (T::*F)(T&)>
   class yes1 : public yes_type {};

   template <typename T, void (*F)(T&, T&)>
   class yes2 : public yes_type {};


   template <typename T>
   inline static void apply(T& a, T& b)
   {
      apply1(a, b, test(&a));
   }

private:

   // first test: return a yes_type* if any allowed T::swap exists

   template <typename T>
   static yes1<T, &T::swap>* test(T*)
   {
      return 0;
   }

   template <typename T>
   static yes2<T, &T::swap>* test(T*)
   {
      return 0;
   }

   static no_type* test(void*)
   {
      return 0;
   }
```

When the test is false, call ADL swap, otherwise perform a *function-pointer based* test: call `apply2` taking the address of `swap` which is known to be possible, because at least one `swap` exists.

```
private:

   template <typename T>
   inline static void apply1(T& a, T& b, no_type*)
   {
      swap(a, b);
   }

   template <typename T>
   inline static void apply1(T& a, T& b, yes_type*)
   {
      apply2(a, b, &T::swap);
   }
```

```
   template <typename T>
   inline static void apply2(T& a, T& b, void (*)(T&, T&))
   {
      T::swap(a, b);
   }

   template <typename T, typename BASE>
   inline static void apply2(T& a, T& b, void (BASE::*)(BASE&))
   {
      a.swap(b);
   }

   template <typename T>
   inline static void apply2(T& a, T& b, ...)
   {
      swap(a, b);
   }
};
```

6. Interfaces

Templates are used as interfaces in two different ways: to provide sets of atomic functions and to obtain ***compile-time polymorphism***.

If several functions use the same portion of the interface of an object, then we can factor them out in a single template:

```
void do_something(std::vector<double>& v)
{
   if (v.empty())
      // ...

   ... v.size();

   for_each(v.begin), v.end(), my_functor());

   ...
}
```

```
void do_something(std::list<double>& L)
{
   if (L.empty())
      // ...

   ... L.size();

   for_each(L.begin(), L.end(), my_functor());

   ...
}
```

Becomes:

```
template <typename T>
void do_something(T& L)
{
   if (L.empty())
      // ...

   ... L.size();

   for_each(L.begin(), L.end(), my_functor());

   ...
}
```

This is also why it's important to follow common guidelines for containers (as listed in section 2.4)

If necessary, as described in chapter 4.5, we can replace calls to *member* functions with calls to small *global* functions: assume we have a third `do_something` that executes a slightly different test:

```
void do_something(MyContainer<double>& M)
{
   if (M.size() == 0)
```

We'd better extract the notion of emptiness in a function:

```
template <typename T>
bool is_empty(const T& c)
{
   return c.empty();
}

template <typename T>
bool is_empty(const MyContainer<T>& c)
{
   return c.size() == 0;
}
```

```
template <typename T>
void do_something(T& L)
{
   if (is_empty(L))
```

6.1. Wrapping references

A class template and its specialization can be used to make interfaces uniform:

```
class Dog
{
   public:
      void bark();
      void go_to_sleep();
};
```

```
class Professor
{
   public:
      void begin_lesson();
      void end_lesson();
};
```

```
template <typename T>
class Reference
{
   T& obj_;

public:
   Reference(T& obj) : obj_(obj) {}
   void start_talking() { obj_.talk(); }
   void end_talking() { obj_.shut(); }
};

template <typename T>
Reference<T> make_reference(T& obj)
{
   return obj;
}
```

```
template <>
class Reference<Dog>
{
   Dog& obj_;

public:
   Reference(Dog& obj) : obj_(obj) {}

   void start_talking() { for (int i=0; i<3; ++i) obj_.bark(); }
   void end_talking() { obj_.go_to_sleep(); }
};
```

```
template <>
class Reference<Professor>
{
   Professor& obj_;

public:

   Reference(Professor& obj) : obj_(obj) {}

   void start_talking() { obj_.begin_lesson(); }
   void end_talking() { obj_.end_lesson(); }
};
```

Finally:

```
template <typename T>
void DoIt(Reference<T> r)
{
   r.start_talking();
   // ...
   r.end_talking();
}
```

6.2. Static Interfaces

When a function template manipulates an object of unspecified type `T`, it actually forces the object to implement some interface: for example this very simple function contains indeed a lot of hidden assumptions about the (unknown) types involved.

```
template <typename iter1_t, typename iter2_t>
iter2_t copy(iter1_t begin, const iter1_t end, iter2_t output)
{
   while (begin != end)
      *(output++) = *(begin++),

   return output;
}
```

`iter1_t` and `iter2_t` must have a copy constructor, `operator++(int)` and `iter1_t` also needs `operator!=`; furthermore, every `operator++` returns a dereferenceable entity, and in case of `iter2_t`, the final result is an l-value, whose assignment blindly accepts whatever `*(begin++)` returns.
In short, template code pretends that all instructions compile, until the compiler can prove they don't.
In general, it's too verbose or not useful to list the assumptions on a type interface: in the example above, very likely `iter1_t::operator++` will return `iter1_t`, which also implements `operator*`, but it need not be *exactly* the case (copy would work if, say, `iter1_t::operator++` returned `int*`).
So we take a minimal set of ***concepts***, which the template parameter must satisfy; informally, a concept is a requirement on the type, which implies that a C++ statement is legal, whatever its implementation.[98]

For example, this object will happily play the role of `iter2_t`:

[98] The notion of concept was met for the first time in 3.2.4

```
struct black_hole_iterator
{
   const black_hole_iterator& operator++ () const
   {
      return *this;
   }

   const black_hole_iterator& operator++ (int) const
   {
      return *this;
   }

   const black_hole_iterator& operator* () const
   {
      return *this;
   }

   template <typename T>
   const black_hole_iterator& operator= (const T&) const
   {
      return *this;
   }
};
```

Here the concept "the object returned by `operator*` must be an l-value" is satisfied, even if in an unusual way (the assignment does not modify the black hole).

Generally, we don't list the exact concepts for any generic function; however, some sets of concepts have a standard name, so whenever possible, we adopt it, even if it's a superset of what is actually needed.
In the `copy` template above, we would prescribe to use an *input iterator* and an *output iterator*, because these are the smallest universally known labels which identify a (super-)set of the concepts; as we read in chapter 7, a true output iterator satisfies a few more properties (for example, it must provide some typedefs, which are irrelevant here), however this is a fair price for reusability.[99]

Authors of template code often need to make concepts explicit: if they have a simple name, they can be used as template parameters:

```
template <typename FwdIter, typename RandIter>
FwdIter special_copy(RandIter beg, RandIter end, FwdIter output);
```

Note that in the above function, nothing constrains `beg` to be an iterator, except names (which are hints for humans, not for the compiler): the template argument `FwdIter` will match *anything*, say `double` or `void*`, and if we are lucky, the body of the function will report errors; it may happen however that we pass a type that works, but does not behave as expected.[100]

[99] The black hole iterator is a hack, not a perfect output iterator.
[100] This is why, for example, the standard describes carefully what happens to functors passed to STL algorithms, how many times they are copied, etc.

Vice versa, classic C++ does offer a tool to constrain types: inheritance and virtual functions: we write functions that accept a BASE* and at runtime they invoke the right functions.
Static interfaces are the moral equivalent in TMP. They offer less generality than a "flat" type T, but the same level of static optimizations.
A ***static interface*** is a skeleton class that limits the scope of validity of a template to types derived from interface, and at the same time it provides a default (static) implementation of the "virtual" callback mechanism.
The details follow.

6.2.1. Static interfaces

The original language idiom was called the "curiously recurring template" pattern (***CRTP***) and it's based on the following observation: a `static_cast` can traverse a class hierarchy using only compile-time information, as the user - not the compiler - guarantees that the cast is indeed possible.
In other words, `static_cast` will converts `BASE*` to `DERIVED*` and the result will be valid only if the original `BASE*` was pointing to a true `DERIVED` object.
As a special case, there's an easy way to be sure that the cast will succeed: when each derived class inherits from a "personal base":

```
template <typename DERIVED_T>
class BASE
{
   protected:
      ~BASE() {}
};

class DERIVED1 : public BASE<DERIVED1>
{
};

class DERIVED2 : public BASE<DERIVED2>
{
};
```

An object of type `BASE<T>` is guaranteed to be the base of a `T`, because thanks to the protected destructor, nobody except a derived class can build a `BASE<T>`, and only T itself derives from `BASE<T>`.
So `BASE<T>` can cast itself to T and invoke functions:

```
template <typename DERIVED_T>
struct BASE
{
   DERIVED_T& true_this()
   {
      return static_cast<DERIVED_T&>(*this);
   }

   const DERIVED_T& true_this () const
   {
      return static_cast<const DERIVED_T&>(*this);
   }

   double getSomeNumber() const
   {
      return true_this().getSomeNumber();
   }
};
```

```
struct DERIVED_rand : public BASE<DERIVED_rand>
{
   double getSomeNumber() const
   {
      return std::rand();
   }
};

struct DERIVED_circle : public BASE<DERIVED_circle>
{
   double radius_;

   double getSomeNumber() const
   {
      return (constant::Pi)*sq(radius_);
   }
};
```

Exactly as for virtual functions, normal calls via derived class interface are inexpensive:

```
DERIVED_rand d;
d.getSomeNumber();          // normal call; BASE is completely ignored
```

However we can write a function template that takes reference-to-base and makes an inexpensive call to the derived member function: `true_this` will produce no overhead.

```
template <typename T>
void PrintSomeNumber(BASE<T>& b)        // note: argument by referencc
{
   // here BASE methods will dispatch to the correct T equivalent
   std::cout << b.getSomeNumber();
}

DERIVED_circle C = { 2.0 };
DERIVED_rand R;

PrintSomeNumber(C); // prints the area of the circle
PrintSomeNumber(R); // prints a random number
```

Conceptually the function above is identical to the simpler (but more vague):

```
template <typename T>
void PrintSomeNumber(T& b)
{
   std::cout << b.getSomeNumber();
}
```

However the replacement looks acceptable because `PrintSomeNumber` is a named function, not an operator (think about writing a global `operator+` with two arguments of type T); in the following example, we will demonstrate the use of static interfaces with operators.[101]
We will implement only `operator+=` and have `operator+` for free, simply deriving from the `summable<...>` interface.

```
template <typename T>
struct summable
{
   T& true_this()
   {
      return static_cast<T&>(*this);
   }

   const T& true_this () const
   {
      return static_cast<const T&>(*this);
   }

   T operator+ (const T& other) const
   {
      T result(true_this());
      result += other;        // call dispatch to native T::operator+=
      return result;
   }
};
```

[101] The `boost` collection contains a library that generalizes this situation

```
struct complex_number : public summable<complex_number>
{
   complex_number& operator+= (const complex_number& that)
   {
      ...
   }
};
```

```
complex_number a;
complex_number b;
...
complex_number s = a+b;
```

The (apparently simple) last line above performs the following compile-time steps:

- `a` does not have an own `operator+` so cast `a` to its base that has, namely `const summable<complex_number>&`
- `const summable<complex_number>&` can be summed to a `complex_number`, so `b` is fine as is
- `summable<complex_number>::operator+` builds a `complex_number` named `result`, which is a copy of `true_this`, because `true_this` is a `complex_number`
- dispatching execution to `complex_number::operator+=`, the result is computed and returned

Note that we could rewrite the base class as:

```
template <typename T>
struct summable
{
   // ...

   T operator+ (const summable<T>& other) const
   {
      T result(true_this());
      result += other.true_this();
      return result;
   }
};
```

We will call ***interface*** the base class, and ***specializations*** the derived classes.

6.2.2. Common Errors

We just met a situation where the interface class makes a specialized copy of itself:

```
      T result(true_this());
```

This is not a problem, since the interface, being static, by definition knows its "true type".

However the correct behavior of `true_this` can be destroyed by ***slicing***:

```
template <typename DERIVED_T>
void PrintSomeNumber(BASE<DERIVED_T> b)// argument by value
{
   std::cout << b.getSomeNumber();      // error: slicing
                                        // b is not a DERIVED_T any more
}
```

Usually it's necessary to declare BASE destructor non virtual and protected, and sometimes it's a good idea to extend protection to the copy constructor; algorithms should not need to make a copy of the static interface: if they need to clone the object, the correct idiom is to call DERIVED_T constructor on true_this(), as above.

```
template <typename DERIVED_T>
struct BASE
{
   DERIVED_T& true_this()
   {
      return static_cast<DERIVED_T&>(*this);
   }

   const DERIVED_T& true_this() const
   {
      return static_cast<const DERIVED_T&>(*this);
   }

protected:
   ~BASE()
   {
   }

   BASE(const BASE&)
   {
   }
};
```

The interface of DERIVED is visible only inside the body of BASE member functions:

```
template <typename DERIVED_T>
struct BASE
{
   // ...

   typedef DERIVED_T::someType someType;        // compiler error

   void f()
   {
      typedef DERIVED_T::someType someType;     // ok here
   }

};
```

```
class DERIVED : public BASE<DERIVED>
{
```

Typedefs and enums from `DERIVED` are not available at class level in `BASE`; this is obvious, because `DERIVED` is compiled after its base, which is `BASE<DERIVED>`, thus when the latter is processed, `DERIVED` is known, but still incomplete.

It's a good idea (not an error) to make `BASE` expose a `typedef` for `DERIVED_T`. This allows external functions to make a specialized copy of `BASE`.

```
template <typename DERIVED_T>
struct BASE
{
   typedef DERIVED_T static_type;
```

However `DERIVED` cannot access `BASE` members without full qualification, because a template base class is out of scope for the derived objects.[102]

```
template <typename DERIVED_T>
struct BASE
{
   typedef double value_type;

   value_type f() const
   {
      return true_this().f();
   }

   // …
};
```

```
struct DERIVED1 : public BASE<DERIVED1>
{
   value_type f() const       // error: value_type is undefined
   {
      true_this();            // error: true_this is undefined
      return 0;
   }
};
```

```
struct DERIVED2 : public BASE<DERIVED2>
{
   BASE<DERIVED2>::value_type f() const     // ok
   {
      this->true_this();                    // ok
      return 0;
   }
};
```

Note once again that scope restriction holds only "inside" the class: external users will correctly see `DERIVED1::value_type`:

[102] See [2] page. 135

```
template <typename T>
struct value_type_of
{
   typedef typename T::value_type type;
};

value_type_of<DERIVED1>::type Pi = 3.14;        // ok, Pi has type double
```

Finally, the developer must ensure that all derived classes announce correctly their names to the base, i.e. avoid a classic copy & paste error:

```
class DERIVED1 : public BASE<DERIVED1>
{
};

class DERIVED2 : public BASE<DERIVED1>
{
};
```

Benefits	Problems
Write algorithms that take "not too generic objects" and use them with a statically-known interface	The developer must ensure that all algorithms take arguments by reference, and avoid other common errors
Implement only some part of the code in the derived (i.e. specialized) class and move all common code in the base	Experimental measurements suggest that the presence of a non-virtual protected destructors and multiple inheritance may inhibit or degrade code optimizations.

6.2.3. A static_interface implementation

Many of the above ideas can be grouped in a class:

```
template <typename T>
struct clone_of
{
   typedef const T& type;
};
```

```
template <typename static_type, typename aux_t = void>
class static_interface
{
public:
   typedef static_type type;

   typename clone_of<static_type>::type clone() const
   {
      return true_this();
   }

protected:
   static_interface() {}
   ~static_interface() {}

   static_type& true_this()
   {
      return static_cast<static_type&>(*this);
   }

   const static_type& true_this() const
   {
      return static_cast<const static_type&>(*this);
   }
};
```

We'll come back on the extra template parameter later.
The helper metafunction `clone_of` can be customized: returning const reference is a reasonable default choice; for small objects, it may be faster to return a copy:

```
template <typename T, bool SMALL_OBJECT = (sizeof(T)<sizeof(void*))>
struct clone_of;

template <typename T>
struct clone_of<T, true>
{
   typedef T type;
};

template <typename T>
struct clone_of<T, false>
{
   typedef const T& type;
};
```

First we make some macros available to ease interface declaration:
An interface is defined by

```
#define MXT_INTERFACE(NAME)                                    \
                                                               \
template <typename static_type>                                \
class NAME : public static_interface<static_type>
```

```
#define MXT_SPECIALIZED        this->true_this()
```

Here's a practical example: the interface macro is similar to a normal class declaration.[103]

```
MXT_INTERFACE(random)
{
protected:

   ~random()
   {
   }

public:

   typedef double random_type;

   random_type max() const
   {
      return MXT_SPECIALIZED.max();
   }

   random_type operator()() const
   {
      return MXT_SPECIALIZED();    // note operator call
   }
};
```

- random can access true_this() only with explicit qualification (as MXT_SPECIALIZED does).
- random needs to declare a protected destructor
- static_type is a valid type name inside random, even if static_interface is out of scope, because it's the template parameter name.

Now let's implement some random algorithms:

```
#define MXT_SPECIALIZATION(S, I)                class S : public I< S >
```

```
MXT_SPECIALIZATION(gaussian, random)
{
   public:

      double max() const
      {
         return std::numeric_limits<double>::max();
      }

      double operator()() const
      {
         // ...
      }
};
```

[103] The downside of this technique is the macro may confuse some IDEs that parse headers to build a graphical representation of the project

```
MXT_SPECIALIZATION(uniform, random)
{
   public:

      double max() const
      {
         return 1.0;
      }

      // ...
};
```

What if we need a template static interface? Such as:

```
template <typename RANDOM_T, typename SCALAR_T>
class random
{
   public:

      typedef SCALAR_T random_type;

      // ...
};
```

```
template <typename T>
class gaussian : public random<gaussian<T>, T>
{
   // ...
```

It's easy to provide more macros for template static interfaces (with a small number of parameters): the naïve idea is:

```
#define MXT_TEMPLATE_INTERFACE(NAME,T)                          \
                                                                \
template <typename static_type, typename T>                     \
class NAME : public static_interface<static_type>
```

```
#define MXT_TEMPLATE_SPECIALIZATION(S,I,T)                      \
                                                                \
template <typename T>                                           \
class S : public I< S<T> >
```

Which is used like:

```
MXT_TEMPLATE_INTERFACE(pseudo_array, value_t)
{
protected:

   ~array_like()
   {
   }

public:

   typedef value_t value_type;

   value_type operator[](const size_t i) const
   {
      return MXT_SPECIALIZED.read(i, instance_of<value_type>());
   }

   size_t size() const
   {
      return MXT_SPECIALIZED.size(instance_of<value_type>());
   }
};
```

A template static interface can be used by a non-template class: for example we could have a class `bitstring` that behaves like an array of bits, or like an array of nibbles, or like an array of bytes:

```
class bitstring
: public pseudo_array<bitstring, bit_tag>
, public pseudo_array<bitstring, nibble_tag>
, public pseudo_array<bitstring, byte_tag>
{
```

An interface need not respect the same member names as the true specialization: in this case, `operator[]` above dispatches execution to a function template `read`. This makes sense, because the underlying `bitstring` is able to `read` the element at position `i` in many ways, because there are 3 distinct i-th elements; but inside `pseudo_array` the type to retrieve is statically known, so we will see that the `bitstring` interface is simpler.

But when the macro expands, the compiler reads:

```
template <typename static_type, typename value_t>
class pseudo_array : public static_interface<static_type>
```

Thus `bitstring` inherits multiple times from `static_interface<bistring>`, and this will make the `static_cast` in `true_this` ambiguous.

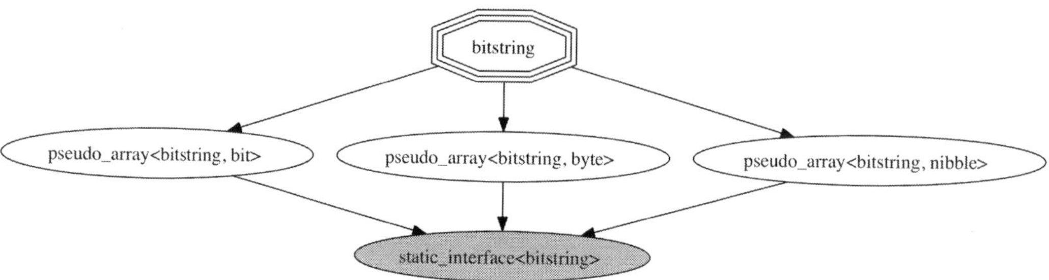

To avoid this issue, use an extra parameter in static interface for disambiguation, and the most unambiguous type names are either `T` or the whole interface (i.e. `pseudo_array<bitstring, T>`). The macro becomes:

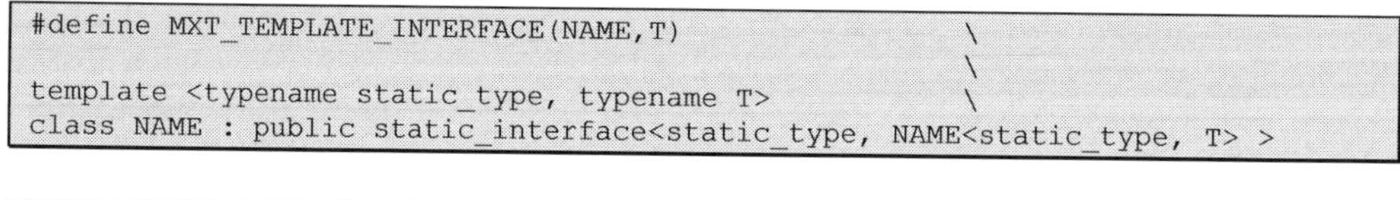

```
#define MXT_TEMPLATE_INTERFACE(NAME,T)                    \
                                                          \
template <typename static_type, typename T>               \
class NAME : public static_interface<static_type, NAME<static_type, T> >
```

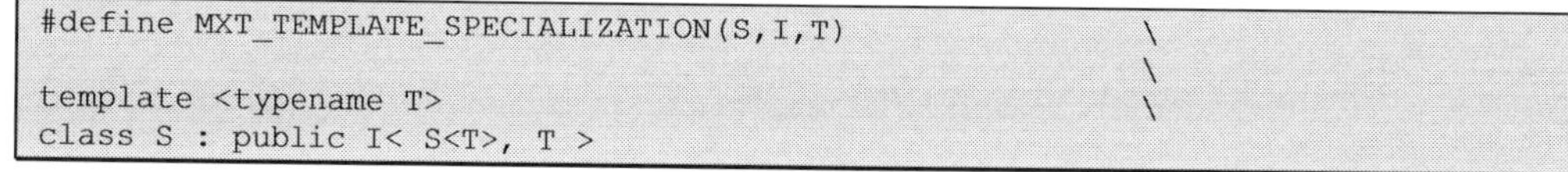

```
#define MXT_TEMPLATE_SPECIALIZATION(S,I,T)                \
                                                          \
template <typename T>                                     \
class S : public I< S<T>, T >
```

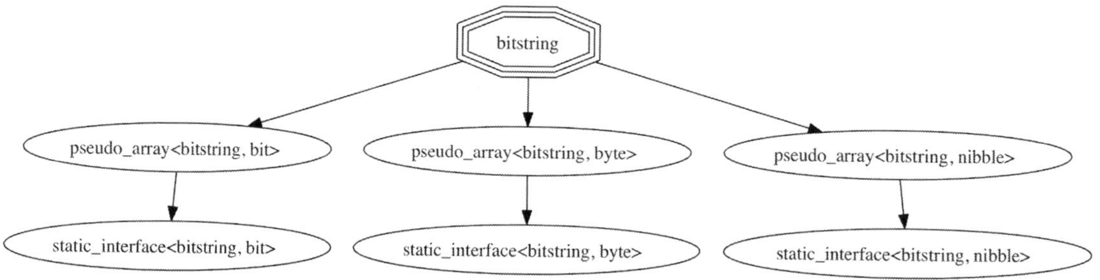

6.2.4. The memberspace problem

Up to now we described static interfaces as a technique to limit the scope of some template parameters: so instead of `F(T)`, we write `F(random<T>)` where `T` will be a special implementation of a random generator; this is especially useful if `F` is indeed a (global) operator.

A second application of static interfaces is the *memberspace* problem.[104]
The name memberspace is the equivalent of a namespace, relative to the member functions of a class; in other words, it's a sort of subspace where a class can put member functions with duplicate names.

---

[104] Apparently the term memberspace was introduced by Joaquín M López Muñoz in "An STL-like bidirectional map" (see http://www.codeproject.com/vcpp/stl/bimap.asp). Also the double-end queue example is due to the same author.

Assume that `C` is a container that follows the STL conventions, so the first element of `C` is `*begin()` and the last is `*rbegin()`.
This is the classic solution to partition an interface: function names have a unique prefix/suffix, such as `push+front`, `push+back`, `r+begin`...
We would prefer instead a real partition, code where both `front` and `back` are containers with their own interface:[105]

```
C MyList;
// ...

first = MyList.front.begin();
last  = MyList.back.begin();

MyList.front.push(3.14);
MyList.back.push(6.28);
MyList.back.pop();
```

Indeed, we can use static interfaces to write code such as:[106]

```
class bitstring
: public pseudo_array<bitstring, bit_tag>
, public pseudo_array<bitstring, nibble_tag>
, public pseudo_array<bitstring, byte_tag>
{
   char* data_;
   size_t nbits_;

public:

   pseudo_array<bitstring, bit_tag>& bit() { return *this; }
   pseudo_array<bitstring, nibble_tag>& nibble() { return *this; }
   pseudo_array<bitstring, byte_tag>& byte() { return *this; }

   size_t size(instance_of<byte_tag>) const
   {
      return nbits_ / CHAR_BITS;
   }

   size_t size(instance_of<bit_tag>) const
   {
      return nbits_;
   }

   size_t size(instance_of<nibble_tag>) const
   {
      return nbits_ / (CHAR_BITS/2);
   }
```

105 In the pseudo-code that follows, we pretend that C is a class; of course a non-template container would be an unusual beast.
106 This code does not compile, because for conciseness, we removed all const versions of the member functions; however the fix should be obvious

```
bitstring b;

int n1 = b.bit().size();
int n2 = b.byte().size();
```

Compare with:

```
bitstring b;

int n1 = b.size(instance_of<bit_tag>());
```

Also `b.bit()` is a sort of container of its own, which can be passed - by reference - to algorithms:

```
template <typename T>
size_t parity(pseudo_array<T>& data)
{
   size_t result = 0;
   for (size_t i=0; i<data.size(); ++i)
      result ^= data[i];

   return result;
}
```

This technique is excellent, but it suffers from a limitation.
As mentioned, *typedefs provided in the specialization are not available in the static interface*, thus we have no way of declaring a member function returning an `iterator`, because the static interface has to borrow the iterator type from the specialization.

```
MXT_INTERFACE(front)
{
   typename static_type::iterator begin()          // <-- error here
   {
      return MXT_SPECIALIZED.begin();
   }

   typename static_type::iterator end()            // <-- error again
   {
      return MXT_SPECIALIZED.end();
   }
};
```

```
MXT_INTERFACE(back)
{
   typename static_type::reverse_iterator begin()    // <-- another error
   {
      return MXT_SPECIALIZED.rbegin();
   }

   typename static_type::reverse_iterator end()      // <-- lots of errors
   {
      return MXT_SPECIALIZED.rend();
   }
};
```

```
class C : public front<C>, public back<C>
{
   // ...

public:

   front<C>& front()
   { return *this; }

   back<C>& back()
   { return *this; }
};
```

```
C MyList;
MyList.front().begin();       // error
MyList.back().begin();        // error
// ...
```

We remark that it's not a matter of syntax: since `C` is still incomplete, `C::iterator` does not exist yet. However there are some *design* fixes:

- define `iterator` before C

```
class C_iterator
{
   // ...
};

class C
{
   // container implementation

   typedef C_iterator iterator;
};
```

- insert an additional layer between `C` and the interfaces, so that the static interface compiles after C (and before the wrapper class)

```
class C
{
   // container implementation

   class iterator { … };
};


MXT_TEMPLATE_INTERFACE(front, impl_t)
{
   typename impl_t::iterator begin()
   {
      return MXT_SPECIALIZED.begin();
   }

   typename impl_t::iterator end()
   {
      return MXT_SPECIALIZED.end();
   }
};
```

```
// …
```

```
class C_WRAPPER : public front<C_WRAPPER, C>, public back<C_WRAPPER, C>
{
      C c_;

   public:

      // reproduce C's interface
      // dispatch all execution to c_

      typename C::iterator begin()
      {
         return c_.begin();
      }
```

6.2.5. Member selection

The same technique used in merging traits (cfr. 5.2.4) can be successfully applied to value objects: the next listing - intentionally incomplete - suggests a possible motivation:

```
enum
{
   empty    = 0,
   year     = 1,
   month    = 2,
   day      = 4,
   // ...
};

template <unsigned CODE> struct time_val;

template <> struct time_val<empty> { }; // empty, I really mean it ☺
template <> struct time_val<year>  { int year; };
template <> struct time_val<month> { short month; };
// ...

template <unsigned CODE>
struct time_val
:
   public time_val<CODE & static_highest_bit<CODE>::value>,
   public time_val<CODE - static_highest_bit<CODE>::value>
{
};
```

```
// an algorithm

template <unsigned CODE>
time_val<(year | month | day)> easter(const time_val<CODE>& t)
{
   time_val<(year | month | day)> result;

   result.year = t.year;
   result.month = compute_easter_month(t.year);
   result.day = compute_easter_day(t.year);

   return result;
}
```

```
   time_val<year | month> tv1;
   time_val<month | day> tv2;

   easter(tv1);   // ok.
   easter(tv2);   // error: tv2.year is undefined.
```

Note that the algorithm acts unconditionally as if any `time_val<CODE>` had a member `year`; where necessary, we can isolate this assumption using a wrapper:

```
template <unsigned CODE>
time_val<year | month | day> easter(const time_val<CODE>& t, selector<true>)
{
   // implementation
}

template <int CODE>
time_val<year | month | day> easter(const time_val<CODE>& t, selector<false>)
{
   // put whatever here: throw exception, static assert...
}

template <int CODE>
time_val<year | month | day> easter(const time_val<CODE>& t)
{
   return easter(t, selector<CODE & year>());
}
```

6.3. Type hiding

Classic C++ programs transform instances of objects into other instances, having possibly different types (via function calls).

```
int i = 314;
double x = f(i);   // transform an instance of int into an instance of double
```

Using templates, C++ can manipulate instances, compile-time constants and types (constants are in the middle because they share some properties with both); we can transform types and constants into instances (trivially), types into types (via traits and metafunctions), types into constants (via metafunctions and other operators, such as `sizeof`), instances into constants (via `sizeof`), but current C++ does not allow to transform an instance into a type, until a new operator is added to the language.[107]

The most common example comes from iterator handling:

```
   T t = *begin;      // store a copy of the first element
                      // who is T?
```

At the moment, a suitable type is provided by metafunctions:

```
     typename std::iterator_traits<iterator_t>::value_type t = *begin;
```

[107] The next revision of the Standard includes `decltype` and `auto`; the former returns the exact type of any expression, similarly to `sizeof`; the latter allows an instance to "copy" the type of its initializer, so `auto i = f()` would declare a variable `i` having the best possible type to store the result of `f()`. See appendix 13 for more details.

There are tricks, which essentially avoid direct knowledge of `T`: the simplest option is to pass `*begin` as a dummy unused parameter, to ensure template type deduction.

```
template <typename iterator_t>
void f(iterator_t beg, iterator_t end)
{
   if (beg == end)
      return;

   f_helper(beg, end, *beg);
}

template <typename iterator_t, typename value_t>
void f_helper(iterator_t beg, iterator_t end, const value_t& )
{
   // for most iterators, value_t ~ iterator_traits<iterator_t>::value_type

   // however if *beg returns a proxy, value_t is the type of the proxy
   // so this may not work with std::vector<bool>
   // because value_t does not store a copy of the value, but a reference
```

In current C++ there are two ways to store an object without knowing its type.

- pass it to a template function, as above; however the lifetime of the object is limited
- cancel its interface, possibly via a combination of templates and virtual functions; in the simples case, the object can be *merely stored* and nothing else:[108]

```
class wrapper_base
{
   public:
      virtual ~wrapper_base() {}

      virtual wrapper_base* clone() const = 0;
};
```

```
template <typename T>
class wrapper : public wrapper_base
{
      T obj_;

   public:

      wrapper(const T& x)
      : obj_(x) {}

      wrapper<T>* clone() const
      {
         return new wrapper<T>(obj_);
      }
};
```

[108] This example is actually important and it will be analyzed again in paragraph 6.4.1

```
template <typename T>
wrapper_base* make_clone(const T& x)
{
   return new wrapper<T>(x);
}
```

Sometimes it's desirable to provide a common interface for several types; the most famous example is given by *variant objects/discriminated unions*: a class, whose static type is fixed, but whose internal storage can transport different types.
In the rest of this section, we'll discuss in details the problem of command-line parsing. Assume we are coding a UNIX utility that gets options from the command line; each option has a name and an associated value of some fixed type.
Options come first, and everything else is an argument:

```
parser.exe -i=7 -f=3.14 -d=6.28 -b=true ARGUMENT1 ARGUMENT2 … ARGUMENTn
```

`i` is an `int`, `f` is a `float`, and so on.
Ideally, we need a sort of `map<string, T>`, where T may possibly vary for each pair; also, we should be able to query such map for values having the right type, so that we will accept `-f=3.14` but reject `-f="hello world"`.

Assume, for extra simplicity, that we start with an array of strings, where each string is either `[prefix][name]` or `[prefix][name]=[value]`[109] and that each parameter value will be obtained via stream extraction (i.e. `operator>>`).

We will produce two containers: the first, named `option_map`, stores pairs name-value, like `std::map`, but where each value has arbitrary type; the second, named `option_parser`, is another map which knows the desired pairing name-type (e.g. "f" is a float) before parsing the command line. Our target is writing code like:

[109] The prefix is a fixed character sequence, usually "-", "--" or "/"

```
int main(int argc, char* argv[])
{
   option_parser PARSER;

   PARSER.declare_as<float>("f");    // we tell the parser what it should
   PARSER.declare_as<int>("i");      // expect, i.e. that "d" is a double,
   PARSER.declare_as<double>("d");   // etc. etc.

   option_map<std::string> CL;       // only key_type is a template parameter

   try
   {
      const char* prefix = "-";

      char** opt_begin = argv+1;
      char** opt_end   = argv+argc;

      // finally we ask the parser to fill a map with the actual values
      // this may throw an exception...

      char** arg_begin = PARSER.parse(CL, opt_begin, opt_end, prefix);

      double d;
      if (!CL.get(d, "d"))
      {
         // the user did not specify a value for "d"
         d = SOME_DEFAULT_VALUE;
      }

   }
   catch (std::invalid_argument& ex)
   {
      // ...
   }
```

6.3.1. Trampolines

The core technique for this kind of "polymorphism" is the use of ***trampolines***. Formally, a trampoline is a local class inside a function template, but the meaning of "local" should not be taken literally.
The class has only static member functions; its public interface accepts parameters of a fixed type (say, `void*`), but being nested in a template, the body of the trampoline is aware of the "outer" template parameter and uses it to perform safe static casts.

Here is a bare bone example: a naked struct that holds untyped pointers and a function template that knows the static type of the object and apparently looses information

```
struct generic_t
{
   void* obj;
   void (*del)(void*);
};
```

```
template <typename T>                       // outer template parameter
generic_t copy_to_generic(const T& value)
{
   struct local_cast                        // local class
   {
      static void destroy(void* p)          // void*-based interface
      {
         delete static_cast<T*>(p);         // static type knowledge
      }
   };

   generic_t p;
   p.obj = new T(value);                    // information loss: copy T* to void*
   p.del = &local_cast::destroy;

   return p;
}
```

Actually, `p.obj` alone does not know how to destroy its attached object, but `p.del` points to (pseudo-code) `copy_to_generic<T>::local_cast::destroy` and this function will do the right thing, namely casting the `void*` back to `T*` just before deleting it.

```
p.del(p.obj);                               // it works!
```

`del` is the moral equivalent of a virtual destructor; the analogy between trampolines and virtual function tables is correct, but:

- trampoline techniques allow to work with *objects*, not with *pointers* (a classic factory would have returned pointer-to-base, while `copy_to_generic` produces an object)
- trampoline pointers can be modified at runtime: for example, `del` can be replaced anytime with a do-nothing function if ownership of the pointer is transferred.
- trampolines are much less clear (i.e. more difficult to maintain) than abstract class hierarchies

The advantage of structures like `generic_t` is that their type is statically known, so they can be used in standard containers, and it's a class, so it can manage its own resources and invariants.
Unfortunately, while type T is known *internally*, it cannot be exposed: function pointers like `del` cannot have T anywhere in their signature. The interface of the trampoline class must be independent of T and it cannot have template member functions (thus, for example, we cannot have a trampoline member that takes a functor and applies it to the pointee).

We'll need another tool: a wrapper for `std::type_info`.

6.3.2. typeinfo wrapper

The `typeid` operator is a less-known C++ operator that determines the type of an expression at run time and returns a constant reference to a system object of type `std::type_info`.

`type_info::before` is a member function that can be used to simulate a total (but unspecified) ordering on types.

Several wrappers have been proposed to give `std::type_info` value semantics; this code is similar to the elegant implementation found in [1], but the comparison operator ensures that a default-constructed (null) `typeinfo` is less than any other instance.[110]

```
class typeinfo
{
   const std::type_info* p_;

public :

   typeinfo()
      : p_(0)
   {}

   typeinfo(const std::type_info& t)
      : p_(&t)
   {}

   inline const char* name() const
   {
      return p_ ? p_->name() : "";
   }

   inline bool operator<(const typeinfo& that) const
   {
      return (p_ != that.p_) &&
         (!p_ || (that.p_ && static_cast<bool>(p_->before(*that.p_))));
   }

   inline bool operator==(const typeinfo& that) const
   {
      return (p_ == that.p_) ||
         (p_ && that.p_ && static_cast<bool>(*p_ == *that.p_));
   }
};
```

6.3.3. option_map

The interface for `option_map` is indeed very simple.

[110] The implementation uses short-circuit to prevent null pointer dereferencing, and it's extremely concise.

```
template <typename userkey_t>
class option_map
{
public:
// typed find:
// MAP.find<T>("name") returns true
// if "name" corresponds to an object of type T

   template <typename T>
      bool find(const userkey_t& name) const;


// typeless find:
// MAP.scan("name") returns true if "name" corresponds to any object

   bool scan(const userkey_t& name) const;


// checked extraction:
// MAP.get(x, "name") returns true
// if "name" corresponds to an object of type T;
// in this case, x is assigned a copy of such object;
// otherwise, x is not changed

   template <typename T>
      bool get(T& dest, const userkey_t& name) const;


// unchecked extraction:
// MAP.get<T>("name") returns either the object of type T
// corresponding to "name", or T().

   template <typename T>
      T get(const userkey_t& name) const;


// insertion
// MAP.put("name", x) inserts a copy of x into the map

   template <typename T>
      bool put(const userkey_t& name, const T& value);

   size_t size() const;

   ~option_map();
};
```

Now the implementation details: we develop the idea of `generic_t` a bit further, giving it the ability to copy and destroy:

```
template <typename userkey_t>
class option_map
{
   struct generic_t
   {
      void* obj;
      void (*copy)(void* , const void*);
      void (*del)(void*);
   };
```

Since we want to search our container both by name and by pair (name, type), we pick the latter structure as key, using our `typeinfo` wrapper class.

```
typedef std::pair<userkey_t, typeinfo> key_t;
typedef std::map<key_t, generic_t> map_t;
typedef typename map_t::iterator iterator_t;

map_t map_;
```

The insertion routine is almost identical to our prototype example:

```
template <typename T>
   bool put(const userkey_t& name, const T& value)
{
   struct local_cast
   {
      static void copy(void* dest, const void* src)
      {
         *static_cast<T*>(dest) = *static_cast<const T*>(src);
      }

      static void destroy(void* p)
      {
         delete static_cast<T*>(p);
      }
   };

   generic_t& p = map_[key_t(name, typeid(T))];

   p.obj = new T(value);
   p.copy = &local_cast::copy;
   p.del = &local_cast::destroy;

   return true;
}
```

Some functions come for free on the top of `std::map`.

```
size_t size() const
{
   return map_.size();
}
```

Here is the typed find:

```
template <typename T>
   bool find(const userkey_t& name) const
{
   return map_.find(key_t(name, typeid(T))) != map_.end();
}
```

Data retrieval uses the `copy` function; first we do a typed find: if it succeeds and the object is non-null, we perform the copy over the user-supplied reference

```
template <typename T>
   bool get(T& dest, const userkey_t& name) const
{
   const typename map_t::const_iterator i
      = map_.find(key_t(name, typeid(T)));

   const bool test = (i != map_.end());
   if (test && i->second.obj)
      i->second.copy(&dest, i->second.obj);

   return test;
}
```

The unchecked retrieval is a shortcut implemented for convenience:

```
template <typename T>
   T get(const userkey_t& name) const
{
   initialized_value<T> v;
   get(v.result, name);
   return v.result;
}
```

At this moment, we simply let the destructor wipe all the objects.[111]

```
~option_map()
{
   iterator_t i = map_.begin();
   while (i != map_.end())
   {
      generic_t& p = (i++)->second;
      if (p.del)
         p.del(p.obj);
   }
}
```

Finally, we take advantage of the ordering properties of `typeinfo` for the typeless find: due to the way pairs are ordered, the map is sorted by name and entries with the same name are sorted by `typeinfo`. First, we search for the upper bound of `(name, typeinfo())`: any other pair with the same name will be larger, because `typeinfo()` is the least possible value; so, if the upper bound exists and has the same name we are looking for, we return true.

```
bool scan(const userkey_t& name) const
{
   const typename map_t::const_iterator i
      = map_.upper_bound(key_t(name, typeinfo()));

   return i != map_.end() && i->first.first == name;
}
```

[111] The implementation here is obviously faulty: `option_map` cannot be safely copied/assigned; to keep the code as simple as possible, and even simpler, the discussion of this topic is deferred to paragraph 6.3.5

Note that our container may hold more objects of different types with the same name.

6.3.4. option_parser

We will not describe `option_parser` in full details, since it does not add anything to the concepts used in building `option_map`. However we point out that a trampoline may have parameters whose type is not `void*`; we leave some details for exercise.

```
class option_parser
{
  typedef option_map<std::string> option_map_t;
  typedef bool (*store_t)(option_map_t&, const char*, const char*);

  typedef std::map<std::string, store_t> map_t;
  map_t map_;

public:

  template <typename T>
     void declare_as(const char* const name)
  {
    struct local_store
    {
      static bool store(option_map_t& m, const char* name, const char* value)
      {
        std::istringstream is(value);
        T temp;
        return (is >> temp) && m.put(name, temp);
      }
    };

    map_[name] = &local_store::store;
  }
```

Note that `local_store::store` does not take `void*` arguments: the only requirement is to publish an interface independent of `T`.

```
template <typename iterator_t>
   iterator_t parse(option_map_t& m, iterator_t begin, iterator_t end)
{
      for every iterator i=begin...end
      {
       get the string S = *i;
       if S has no prefix
             stop and return i;
       else
         remove the prefix

       if S has the form "N=V"
             split S in N and V
       else
             set N = S
             set V = <empty string>

       if N is not contained in map_
             throw exception "unknown option"
       else
             set F := local_store::store
             execute F(m, N, V)
             if it fails, throw exception "illegal value"
      }
}
```

6.3.5. Final additions

Due to the way `declare_as` works, every type which can be extracted from a string stream is acceptable in this command line parser.
To include parameter-less options, simply add an empty class:

```
struct option
{
};

inline std::istream& operator>>(std::istream& is, option&)
{
   return is;
}
```

This will enable a command line switch, such as:

```
parser.exe -verbose
```

If the name is unique, the simplest way to retrieve the value of the switch is a type-less find: this will yield false if the switch was omitted.

```
PARSER.declare_as<option>("verbose");

char** arg_begin = PARSER.parse(CL, opt_begin, opt_end, prefix);
if (CL.scan("verbose"))
{
   // ...
```

Trampoline techniques can be easily optimized for space: instead of one pointer for each "virtual function", we can group functions for type T in a static instance of a structure and so have a single pointer, exactly as in the traditional implementation of virtual function tables.

This approach is also scalable: should we need to add an extra "ability" to the interface, it requires less modifications and almost no extra memory (since we have a single pointer table, as opposed to many pointers per instance).

```
struct virtual_function_table
{
    void (*copy)(void* , void*);
    void (*del)(void*);
    void* (*clone)(const void*);
};
```

```
   struct generic_t
   {
      void* obj;
      const virtual_function_table* table;      // single pointer-to-const
   };
```

```
// identical implementation, but not a local class any more...

   template <typename T>
   struct local_cast
   {
      static void copy(void* dest, void* src)
      {
         *static_cast<T*>(dest) = *static_cast<T*>(src);
      }

      static void destroy(void* p)
      {
         delete static_cast<T*>(p);
      }

      static void* clone(const void* p)
      {
         return new T(*static_cast<const T*>(p));
      }
   };
```

```
   template <typename T>
      bool put(const userkey_t& name, const T& value)
   {
      static const virtual_function_table pt =
      {
         &local_cast<T>::copy,
         &local_cast<T>::destroy,
         &local_cast<T>::clone
      };

      generic_t& p = map_[key_t(name, typeid(T))];

      p.obj = new T(value);
      p.table = &pt;

      return true;
   }
```

Of course, instead of `p.del` we shall write `p.table->del` and pay an extra indirection.

Finally, we make `generic_t` a true value by the rule of three: implementing copy constructor, assignment and destructor.

```
struct generic_t
{
   void* obj;
   const fptbl_t* table;

   generic_t()
      : obj(0), table(0)
   {
   }

   generic_t(const generic_t& that)
      : table(that.table)
   {
      if (table)
         obj = table.clone(that.obj);
   }

   generic_t& operator=(const generic_t& that)
   {
      generic_t temp(that);
      swap(obj, temp.obj);
      swap(table, temp.table);
      return *this;
   }

   ~generic_t()
   {
      if (table && obj)
         table.del(obj);
   }
};
```

6.3.6. Boundary crossing with trampolines

Let's summarize briefly the last paragraphs. A trampoline function is used as a companion to a void pointer, when it contains enough information to recover the original type:

```
void* myptr_;
void (*del_)(void*);
```

```
template <typename T>
struct secret_class
{
   static void destroy(void* p)
   {
      delete static_cast<T*>(p);
   }
};
```

```
   myptr_ = [[a pointer to T]];
   del_ = &secret_class<T>::destroy;
```

The information about T cannot be returned to the caller, because T cannot be present in the trampoline interface.
So we generally tackle the issue requiring the caller to specify a type T, and the trampoline just ensures it's the same as the original type (calling `typeid`, for example: see the "typed find"). This is informally called an ***exact cast***.
A second possibility is to throw an exception:

```
   template <typename T>
   struct secret_class
   {
      static void throw_T_star(void* p)
      {
         throw static_cast<T*>(p);
      }
   };
```

```
struct myobj
{
   void* myptr_;
   void (*throw_)(void*);

   template <typename T>
   myoby(T* p)
   {
      myptr_ = p;
      throw_ = &secret_class<T>::throw_T_star;
   }

   template <typename T>
   T* cast_via_exception() const
   {
      try
      {
         (*throw_)(myptr_);
      }
      catch (T* p)    // yes, it was indeed a T*
      {
         return p;
      }
      catch (...)     // no, it was something else
      {
         return 0;
      }
   }
```

This approach is several orders of magnitude slower (a `try...catch` block may not be cheap), but it adds an interesting new feature: we can cast not only to the original type T, but also to any *base class* of T. When the trampoline function throws `DERIVED*`, the exception handler will succeed catching `BASE*`.

Remember that it's not possible to `dynamic_cast` a `void*` directly, so this is actually the best we can do; if efficiency is an issue, in practice we might want to adopt a scheme where we perform an exact cast to `BASE*` using trampolines, and leave outside a dynamic cast on the result.

Observe also that, depending on the precise application semantics, sometimes we can limit the number of "destination" types to a small set, and hardcode them in the trampoline:

```
struct virtual_function_table
{
   bool (*safe_to_double)(void*, double&);
   std::string (*to_string)(void*);
};
```

```
template <typename T1, typename T2>
struct multi_cast
{
   static T2 cast(void* src)
   {
      return has_conversion<T1,T2>::L2R ? T2(*static_cast<T1*>(src)) : T2();
   }

   static bool safe_cast(void* p, T2& dest)
   {
      if (has_conversion<T1,T2>::L2R)
         dest = *static_cast<T1*>(src);

      return has_conversion<T1,T2>::L2R;
   }
};
```

```
   to_double = &multi_cast<T, double>::safe_cast;
   to_string = &multi_cast<T, std::string>::cast;
```

6.4. Variant

The key point in type-hiding techniques is deciding who remembers the correct type of the objects. In our example, the client of `option_map` is responsible for declaring and querying the right types, calling `option_map::get<T>("name")`.
But in some cases the client needs or prefers to ignore the type and blindly delegate the "opaque" object, so that it performs the right action, whatever the stored object is.

6.4.1. Parameter deletion with virtual calls

If we just need to transport a copy of an object of arbitrary type, then we can wrap it in a custom class template, "hiding" the template parameter behind a non-template abstract base class.
The following rough sketch will help clarifying:

```
struct wrapper_base
{
   virtual ~wrapper_base()
   {
   }

   virtual wrapper_base* clone() const = 0;

   // add more virtual functions if needed

   virtual size_t size() const = 0;
};
```

```
template <typename T>
struct wrapper : wrapper_base
{
   T obj_;

   wrapper(const T& that)
      : obj_(that)
   {
   }

   virtual wrapper_base* clone() const
   {
      return new wrapper<T>(obj_);
   }

   // implement virtual functions delegating to obj_

   virtual size_t size() const
   {
      return obj_.size();
```

```
class transporter
{
   wrapper_base* myptr_;

public:

   ~transporter()
   {
      delete myptr_;
   }

   transporter(const transporter& that)
   : myptr_(that.myptr_ ? that.myptr_->clone() : 0)
   {
   }

   transporter()
   : myptr_(0)
   {
   }

   template <typename T>
   transporter(const T& that)
      : myptr_(new wrapper<T>(that))
   {
   }

   // implement member functions delegating to wrapper_base

   size_t size() const
   {
      return myptr_ ? myptr_->size() : 0;
   }
```

We can also add a custom (friend) dynamic cast:

```
   template <typename T>
   static T* transporter_cast(transporter& t)
   {
      if (wrapper<T>* p = dynamic_cast<wrapper<T>*>(t.myptr_))
         return &(p->obj_);
      else
         return 0;
   }
```

6.4.2. Variant with visitors

Opaque interfaces make often use of the visitor pattern; the visitor is a functor of unspecified type that is accepted by the interface and it is allowed to communicate with the real objects, whose type is otherwise hidden.
In other words we need a way to pass a generic functor through the non-template trampoline interface.

As a prototype problem, we will code a concept class that can store any object of size not greater than a fixed limit.[112]

```
template <size_t N>
class variant
```

First we define the required trampolines: `variant` will have some fixed-size storage, where we place objects:

```
template <size_t N>
class variant
{
   char storage_[N];
   const vtable* vt;
```

Again from the rule of three, the tentative interface has three functions:

```
struct vtable
{
   void (*construct)(void*, const void*);
   void (*destroy)(void*);
   void (*assign)(void*, const void*);
};
```

[112] This is also known as an *unbounded discriminated union*. The code should be taken as a proof-of-concept, not as production ready. Two big issues are not considered: const-ness and aligned storage; we simply suggest as a quick and dirty fix to put `variant::storage_` in a union with a dummy structure having a single member `double`. Cfr. A. Alexandrescu, "An Implementation of Discriminated Unions in C++"

```
template <typename T>
struct vtable_impl
{
   static void construct(void* dest, const void* src)
   {
      new(dest) T(*static_cast<const T*>(src));
   }

   static void destroy(void* dest)
   {
      static_cast<T*>(dest)->~T();
   }

   static void assign(void* dest, const void* src)
   {
      *static_cast<T*>(dest) = *static_cast<const T*>(src);
   }
};

template <>
struct vtable_impl<void>
{
   static void construct(void* dest, const void* src)
   {
   }

   static void destroy(void* dest)
   {
   }

   static void assign(void* dest, const void* src)
   {
   }
};
```

```
template <typename T>
struct vtable_singleton
{
   static const vtable* get()
   {
      static const vtable v =
      {
         &vtable_impl<T>::construct,
         vtable_impl<T>::destroy,
         &vtable_impl<T>::assign
      };

      return &v;
   }
};
```

```
template <size_t N>
class variant
{
   char storage_[N];
   const vtable* vt;

public:

   ~variant()
   {
      (vt->destroy)(storage_);
   }
```

```
   variant()
      : vt(vtable_singleton<void>::get())
   {
   }

   variant(const variant& that)
      : vt(that.vt)
   {
      (vt->construct)(storage_, that.storage_);
   }

   template <typename T>
   variant(const T& that)
      : vt(vtable_singleton<T>::get())
   {
      MXT_STATIC_ASSERT(sizeof(T)<=N);
      (vt->construct)(storage_, &that);
   }
```

The constructors initialize the "virtual function table pointer" and invoke the construction over raw memory.[113]

The assignment operator depends on a subtle issue: exceptions. If a constructor throws an exception, since the object was never fully constructed it won't be destroyed either, and that's exactly what we need; however if we need to overwrite an instance of T1 with an instance of T2, we destroy T1 first, but construction of T2 may fail.

Thus we need to reset the virtual table pointer first to a no-op version, destroy T1, construct T2 then eventually store the right pointer.

```
   void rebuild(const void* src, const vtable* newvt)
   {
      const vtable* oldvt = vt;
      vt = vtable_singleton<void>::get();
      (oldvt->destroy)(storage_);

// if construct throws, then variant will be in a consistent (null) state

      (vt->construct)(storage_, src);
      vt = newvt;
   }
```

[113] We got rid of the « if pointer is null » tests initializing members with a dummy trampoline

Thanks to `rebuild` we can both copy another `variant` and any other object of type T:

```
    variant& operator=(const variant& that)
    {
        if (vt == that.vt)
            (vt->assign)(storage_, that.storage_);
        else
            rebuild(that.storage_, that.vt);

        return *this;
    }

    template <typename T>
    variant& operator=(const T& that)
    {
        MXT_STATIC_ASSERT(sizeof(T)<=N);

        if (vt == vtable_singleton<T>::get())
            (vt->assign)(storage_, &that);
        else
            rebuild(&that, vtable_singleton<T>::get());

        return *this;
    }
};
```

This variant is only pure storage, but we would like to add:

```
class variant
{
    // ...

    template <typename visitor_t>
    void accept_visitor(visitor_t& v)
    {
        // ???
```

Since trampolines need to have a fixed non-template signature, here the solution is *virtual inheritance*: we define an interface for any unspecified visitor and another interface for a visitor that visits type T; since the trampoline knows T, it will try one dynamic cast.
Virtual inheritance is necessary because visitors may want to visit more than one type (see below).

```
class variant_visitor_base
{
public:

    virtual ~variant_visitor_base()
    {
    }
};
```

```
template <typename T>
class variant_visitor : public virtual variant_visitor_base
{
public:

   virtual void visit(T&) = 0;

   virtual ~variant_visitor()
   {
   }
};

struct bad_visitor
{
};
```

```
struct vtable
{
   // ...

   void (*visit)(void*, variant_visitor_base*);
};
```

```
template <typename T>
struct vtable_impl
{
   // ...

   static void visit(void* dest, variant_visitor_base* vb)
   {
      if (variant_visitor<T>* v = dynamic_cast<variant_visitor<T>*>(vb))
         v->visit(*static_cast<T*>(dest));
      else
         throw bad_visitor();
   }
};
```

```
template <>
struct vtable_impl<void>
{
   // ...

   static void visit(void* dest, variant_visitor_base* vb)
   {
   }
};
```

```
template <size_t N>
class variant
{
public:

   variant& accept_visitor(variant_visitor_base& v)
   {
      (vt->visit)(storage_, &v);
      return *this;
   }
```

Finally, here's a concrete visitor (which in fact will visit three types, hence the importance of the virtual base class):

```
struct MyVisitor
: public variant_visitor<int>
, public variant_visitor<double>
, public variant_visitor<std::string>
{
   virtual void visit(std::string& s)
   {
      std::cout << "visit: {s}" << s << std::endl;
   }

   virtual void visit(int& i)
   {
      std::cout << "visit: {i}" << i << std::endl;
   }

   virtual void visit(double& x)
   {
      std::cout << "visit: {d}" << x << std::endl;
   }
};
```

```
      variant<64> v1, v2, v3;
      std::string s = "hello world!";
      double x = 3.14;
      int j = 628;

      v1 = s;
      v2 = x;
      v3 = j;

      MyVisitor mv;

      v1.accept_visitor(mv);
      v2.accept_visitor(mv);
      v3.accept_visitor(mv);
```

```
visit: {s}hello world!
visit: {d}3.14
visit: {i}628
```

We just mention for the sake of completeness that *bounded* discriminated unions, such as `boost::variant`, adopt a different approach: `variant` is a class template with N type parameters `T1...Tn` and at any time it holds exactly an instance of one of the `Tj`. The constructor can take any object of type T having unambiguous conversion to exactly one of the Tj, or it fails.

6.5. Wrapping Containers

New containers are often built atop of classical STL objects:

```
template <typename T, typename less_t = std::less<T> >
class sorted_vector
{
   typedef std::vector<T> vector_t;
   vector_t data_;
```

The sorted vector basically is equivalent to a set of functions that manipulate a vector, enforcing some invariant (namely, preserving the ordering): so, we will call `sorted_vector` a ***container adapter***, because it delegates the actual storage, and it only alters the way data are stored.

Suppose we already have a vector and we want to treat it as a sorted vector for some time. Remember that it's a bad idea to expose the internals of the class (recall paragraph 2.4.4):

```
template <typename T, typename less_t = std::less<T> >
class sorted_vector
{
public:

   vector_t& base()                    // very bad
   { return data_; }

   const vector_t& base() const        // moderately bad
   { return data_; }
};
```

```
void causeDamage(sorted_vector<double>& s)
{
   std:random_shuffle(s.base().begin(), s.base().end());
   laugh();    // Ah! Ah! Ah!
}
```

We can instead have an additional parameter that defines the storage, analogous to the container type of `std::stack` and similar to the allocator parameter for `std::vector`.

```
template <typename T, typename less_t = …, typename vector_t = std::vector<T>
>
class sorted_vector
{
   vector_t data_;

public:

   sorted_vector(vector_t data)
      : data_(data)
   {
   }
};
```

```
void treatVectorAsSorted(vector<double>& v)
{
   sorted_vector<double, less<double>, vector<double>&> sorted_v(v);
   // …
}
```

The author of `sorted_vector` should behave as if `vector_t` were `std::vector`, whose interface is defined unambiguously.
Anyway this solution is the most complex to code, since we need reference-aware functions; we should explicitly support the case of `vector_t` being a reference to some vector, and this is likely to cause problems when deciding to take arguments by value/by reference: this is a call for traits.

```
template <typename T>
struct s_v_storage_traits
{
   typedef const T& argument_type;
   typedef T value_type;
};

template <typename T>
struct s_v_storage_traits<T&>
{
   typedef T& argument_type;
   typedef T& value_type;
};
```

```
template <typename T, typename less_t = …, typename vector_t = vector<T> >
class sorted_vector
{
   typename s_v_storage_traits<vector_t>::value_type data_;

public:

   sorted_vector(typename s_v_storage_traits<vector_t>::argument_type data)
      : data_(data)
   {
   }
};
```

A strong need to isolate the storage parameter comes from serialization: modern operating systems can easily map memory from arbitrary storage devices into the program address space at no cost.
In other words, we can get a pointer (or a pointer-to-const) from the OS, which *looks* like ordinary memory, but it's actually pointing somewhere else, for example, to the hard drive.
But now we can create a `sorted_vector` that points directly to the mapped memory, plugging a suitable class as `vector_t`:[114]

```
template <typename T>
class read_only_memory_block
{
   const T* data_;
   size_t size_;

public:

   // constructor, etc....

   // now implement the same interface as a const vector

   typedef const T* const_iterator;

   const_iterator begin() const { return data_; }
   const_iterator end() const { return data_ + size_; }

   const T& operator[](size_t i) const { return data_[i]; }

   // ...
```

Observe that we don't need a true drop-in replacement for vector: if we limit to calling const member functions, a subset of the interface will suffice.

[114] The mapped memory area is usually not resizable; merely for simplicity, here we assume it's `const`, but it need not be the case. A vector needs to store three independent data and all the rest is deduced: "begin", "size" and "capacity"; a `read_write_memory_block` also would need these members, but the capacity would be a constant and equal to "max size" from the beginning.

7. Algorithms

The implementation of an algorithm needs a generic I/O interface: we have to decide how and where functions get data and write results, how and what intermediate results they keep. Iterators are an existing abstraction that help solving this problem.
An iterator is a small data type that offers a sequential view over a dataset; putting it simply, it's a class that implements a subset of the operations that pointers can perform.
The importance of iterators is that they decouple functions from the actual data storage: an algorithm sees its input via a couple of iterators `[begin...end)` of unspecified type, and often it writes its output to another range:

```
template <typename iterator_t>
... sort(iterator_t begin, iterator_t end);
```

```
template <typename iter1_t, typename iter2_t >
... copy(iter1_t input_begin, iter1_t input_end, iter2_t output_begin);
```

It's possible to sketch a rough classification of algorithms by I/O interface.

- ***non-mutating algorithms*** iterate on one or more read-only ranges; there are two sub-families:
  - "find" algorithms return an iterator that points to the result (e.g. `std::min_element`), or `end` if no result exist
  - "accumulate" algorithms return an arbitrary value, which need not correspond to any element in the range
- ***selective copying algorithms*** take an input read-only range and an output range, where the results are written. The output range is assumed to be writable; if the output range can store an arbitrary number of elements or simply as many elements as the input range, only the leftmost position is given (e.g. `std::copy`).
  - Usually each algorithm describes what happens if input and output ranges overlap; "transform" algorithms accept an output range which is either disjoint or entirely coincident with `begin...end`
- ***reordering algorithms*** shuffle the elements of the input range and ensure that the result will be in some special position, or equivalently, that the result will be a particular sub range (e.g. `std::nth_element`, `std::partition`).
  - "shrinking" algorithms (e.g. `std::remove_if`) rearrange the data in `begin...end`, and if the result is shorter than the input sequence, they return a new `end'`, leaving unspecified elements in range `end'...end`

Writing algorithms in terms of iterators can offer significant advantages:

- all containers, standard or nonstandard, can easily provide iterators, so it's a way to decouple algorithm and data storage
- iterators have a default and convenient way to signal "failure", namely returning `end`
- it may be feasible, depending on the algorithm details, to ignore the actual "pointed type" under the iterators

On the opposite, there are two difficulties:

- The exact type of the iterator should be avoided whenever possible; the code becomes less generic and obscure:

```
for (vector<string>::const_iterator i = v.begin(); i != v.end(); ++i)
```

To accomplish this, we will often move pieces of code into subroutines:[115]

```
std::for_each(v.begin(), v.end(), ...);
```

> The lines above are not identical, since the latter runs on a couple of non-const iterators.
> In classic C++ we should cast v to const reference, which obviously defeats the benefit of ignoring the iterator type.
>
> ```
> std::for_each(
>  static_cast<const std::vector<std::string>&>(v).begin(),..)
> ```
>
> In C++0x instead we may just use the const-iterator versions of `begin` and `end`:
>
> ```
> for (auto i = v.cbegin(); i != v.cend(); ++i)
> ```

- We will need often to adapt a given view to a pre-existing algorithm: we may need a sequence of X and a sequence of Y, but get a sequence of `pair<X, Y>`. In some cases, changing the view consistently requires a lot of effort.

7.1. Algorithm I/O

Usually algorithms are functions that perform their input/output operations via generic ranges; a range is represented by a pair of iterators of generic type `iterator_t`, and the function assumes that `iterator_t` supports all the required operations; we'll see however that this assumption is not only a convenient simpli-

[115] Apart from visual clarity, the importance of standard algorithms is that they offer subtle optimizations: an explicit for-loop may recompute `v.end()` at every iteration, while `for_each` will store the result.

fication, but it's often the best we have, as it's extremely hard to *detect* if a generic type `T` is an iterator.
The hypotheses are:

- `*i` returns `std::iterator_traits<T>::reference` which behaves like a reference to the underlying object[116].
- whatever `*i` returns, a copy of the pointed value can be stored as a `std::iterator_traits<T>::value_type`; often, we'll impose further that this type is assignable or swappable[117]
- any elementary manipulation of `i` (copy, dereference, increment...) is inexpensive
- we can dispatch specialized algorithms for iterators of different type using `std::iterator_traits<T>::iterator_category` as a type tag
- all increment/decrement operators which are valid on `i` return a dereferenceable object (usually, another instance of `T`); this allows us to write safely `*(i++)`

Sometimes we implicitly assume that two copies of the same iterator are independent: this is usually violated by I/O-related iterators, e.g. objects that read/write files or memory, such as `std::back_insert_iterator`, because `*i` conceptually allocates space for a new object, it does not retrieve an existing element of the range.

7.1.1. swap-based or copy-based

As a consequence of the basic assumptions, most (if not all) I/O within the algorithm should be written without explicitly declaring types: the usage of `reference` and `value_type` should be minimized, if possible, usually via swaps and direct dereference-and-assign.
For example, `copy` tackles the problem of output: it simply asks a valid iterator where the result is written:

```
template <typename iter1_t, typename iter2_t>
iter2_t copy(iter1_t begin, iter1_t end, iter2_t output)
{
   while (begin != end)
      *(output++) = *(begin++);       // dereference-and-assign

   return output;
}
```

---

116 The C++ Standard guarantees that `*i` is a real reference, but it may be useful not to assume this unless necessary; not all containers are standard-compliant, and in fact not even `std::vector<bool>` is.

117 `value_type` is granted by the standard to be non-const qualified, but this is not enough: for example, `std::map`'s `value_type` is `pair<const key_type, mapped_type>` which is not assignable; more about this problem is in paragraph 7.3

Not knowing what the range elements are, we can assume that a swap operation is less heavy than ordinary assignment: a POD swap performs 3 assignments, so it is slightly worse, but if objects contain resource handles (e.g. pointers to heap allocated memory), swap is usually optimized to avoid construction of a temporary object (which may fail or throw); if `s1` is a short string and `s2` is a very long string, the assignment `s1 = s2` will require a large amount of memory, while `swap(s1, s2)` will cost nothing.

For example, an implementation of `std::remove_if` could overwrite out-of-place elements with a `smart_swap`.
`move` is a destructive copy process, where the original value is left in a state which is consistent, but unknown to the caller.

```
template <typename iterator_t>
void move_iter(iterator_t dest, iterator_t source)
{
   if (dest == source)
      return;

   if (is_class<std::iterator_traits<iterator_t>::value_type>::value)
      smart_swap(*dest, *source);
   else
      *dest = *source;
}

template <typename iterator_t, typename func_t>
iterator_t remove_if(iterator_t begin, iterator_t end, func_t F)
{
   iterator_t i = begin;

   while (true)
   {
      while (i != end && F(*i))
         ++i;

      if (i == end)
         break;

      move_iter(begin++, i++);
   }

   return begin;
}
```

The algorithm above returns the new end of range; it will use an assignment to "move" a primitive type, and a swap to "move" a class; since the decision rule is hidden[118], it follows that the algorithm will leave unpredictable objects between the new and the old end of range:

[118] And possibly suboptimal, but this is not really relevant here.

```
struct less_than_3_digits
{
   bool operator()(const std::string& x) const
   {
      return x.size()<3;
   }

   bool operator()(const int x) const
   {
      return x <= 99;
   }
};
```

```
std::string A1[] = { "111", "2", "3", "4444", "555555", "66" };
int          A2[] = {  111 ,  2 ,  3 ,  4444 ,  555555 ,  66  };

remove_if(A1, A1+6, less_than_3_digits());
remove_if(A2, A2+6, less_than_3_digits());
```

After executing the code above, the arrays A1 and A2 will be different: the trailing range is filled with unspecified objects, and they do vary.

[0]	111	"111"
[1]	4444	"4444"
[2]	555555	"555555"
[3]	4444	"2"
[4]	555555	"3"
[5]	66	"66"

C++0x has a language construct for move semantics: R-value references.
A function argument declared as R-value reference-to-T (written `T&&`) will bind to a non-constant temporary object; being temporary, the function can freely steal resources from it. In particular, we can write a special "move constructor" that initializes an object from a temporary.
Furthermore, casting a reference to R-value reference has the effect of marking an existing object as "moveable" (this cast is encapsulated in the STL function `std::move`).
Combining these features, the three-copy swap will be rewritten as:

```
void swap(T& a, T& b)
{
   T x(std::move(a));
   a = std::move(b);
   b = std::move(x);
}
```

So if T implements a move constructor, the function above has the same complexity as a native swap.

Other implementations of `move_iter` could:

- *o* test `if (!has_trivial_destructor<...>::value)`: it's worth swapping a class that owns resources, and such a class should have a non-trivial destructor;

observe however that if the type is not swappable, this approach may be slower, because it will end calling the three-copy swap, instead of one assignment

o test the presence of a swap member function and use assignment in any other case.

```
template <typename iterator_t>
void move_iter(iterator_t dest, iterator_t source, selector<true>)
{
   dest->swap(*source);
}

template <typename iterator_t>
void move_iter(iterator_t dest, iterator_t source, selector<false>)
{
   *dest = *source;
}
```

```
template <typename iterator_t>
void move_iter(iterator_t dest, iterator_t source)
{
   if (dest != source)
      move_iter(dest, source,
                 has_swap<std::iterator_traits<iterator_t>::value_type>());
}
```

7.1.2. Classification of algorithms

Recall the distinction between non-mutating, selective copy and reordering algorithms. In this section, we show how sometimes, even when the mathematical details of the algorithm are clear, several implementations are possible, and we will discuss the side effects of each.

We want to find simultaneously the minimum and the maximum over a range: if the range has N elements, a naïve algorithm uses ~2N comparisons, but it's possible to do better. While iterating, we examine two consecutive elements at a time, then compare the larger with the max and the smaller with the min, thus using 3 comparisons per 2 elements, or about 1.5*N comparisons in total.

First, we consider a non-mutating function (the macro is only for conciseness)

```
#define VALUE_T        typename std::iterator_traits<iterator_t>::value_type

template <typename iterator_t, typename less_t>
std::pair<VALUE_T, VALUE_T> minmax(iterator_t b, iterator_t e, less_t less)
```

`minmax(begin, end)` scans the range once from `begin` to `end`, without changing any element and it returns a `pair` (min, max); if the range is empty, we can either return a default-constructed pair, or break the assumption that `result.first < result.second`, using `std::numeric_limits`.

Here's a reasonable implementation, which needs only forward iterators:

```
template <typename scalar_t, typename less_t>
inline scalar_t& mmax(scalar_t& a, const scalar_t& b, less_t less)
{
   return (less(a, b) ? a=b : a);
}

template <typename scalar_t, typename less_t>
inline scalar_t& mmin(scalar_t& a, const scalar_t& b, less_t less)
{
   return (less(b, a) ? a=b : a);
}
```

```
template <typename iterator_t, typename less_t>
   std::pair<…> minmax(iterator_t begin, const iterator_t end, less_t less)
{
     typedef
       typename std::iterator_traits<iterator_t>::value_type value_type;

     std::pair<value_type, value_type> p;

     if (begin != end)
     {
        p.first = p.second = *(begin++);
     }

     while (begin != end)
     {
        const value_type& x0 = *(begin++);
        const value_type& x1 = (begin != end) ? *(begin++) : x0;

        if (less(x0, x1))
        {
           mmax(p.second, x1, less);
           mmin(p.first , x0, less);
        }
        else
        {
           mmax(p.second, x0, less);
           mmin(p.first , x1, less);
        }
     }

     return p;
}
```

As a rule, it's more valuable to return iterators, for two reasons: first, the objects may be expensive to copy, second because if no answer exists, we return `end`. So, given that dereferencing an iterator is inexpensive, a possible refinement can be:

```
template <typename iterator_t, typename less_t>
   std::pair<iterator_t, iterator_t> minmax(...)
{
      std::pair<iterator_t, iterator_t> p(end, end);

      if (begin != end)
      {
         p.first = p.second = begin++;
      }

      while (begin != end)
      {
         iterator_t i0 = (begin++);
         iterator_t i1 = (begin != end) ? (begin++) : i0;

         if (less(*i1, *i0))
            swap(i0, i1);

         // here *i0 is less than *i1

         if (less(*i0, *p.first))
            p.first = i0;

         if (less(*p.second, *i1))
            p.second = i1;

      }
      return p;
}
```

Note that we never mention `value_type` any more.
Finally, we can sketch the reordering variant:

```
template <typename iterator_t>
void minmax(iterator_t begin, iterator_t end);
```

The function reorders the range so that, after execution, `*begin` is the minimum and `*(end-1)` is the maximum; all the other elements will be moved to an unspecified position; iterators are bidirectional, so `end-1` is just a formal notation.

Suppose `F` takes a range `[begin...end)`, it compares the first and the last element, it swaps them if they are not in order, then it moves to the second and the second last; when the iterators cross, it stops and it returns an iterator `H` which points to the half of the range. `F` does about N/2 "compare and swap" operations, where N is the length of the range.
Obviously the maximum cannot belong to the left half and the minimum cannot belong to the right half; we invoke again `F` on the both half-intervals, and let `HL=F(begin, HL)` and `HR=F(HR, end)`.
When there's a single element in one of the intervals, it has to be the extreme.
If a unit of complexity is a single "compare and swap", the algorithm performs: N/2 at iteration 0 to find H, 2*(N/4) for the second partition, 2*(N/8) for the third... so the total number of operations is again about 3/2*N.

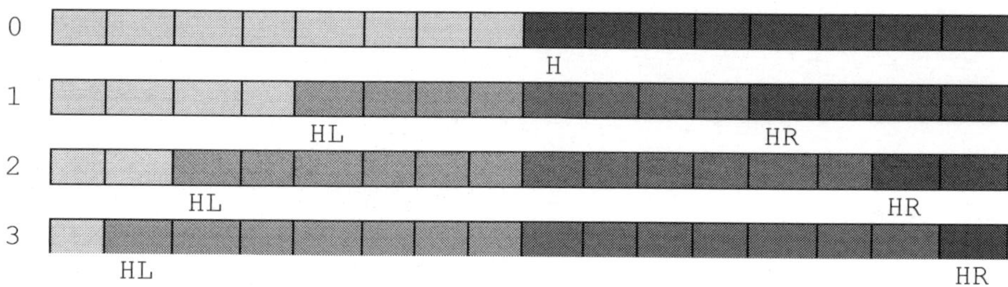

7.1.3. Iterator requirements

Algorithms have requirements about the kind of operation the iterator must provide. As a rule of thumb, the "average" iterator is bidirectional[119]: it supports single increment and decrement (`++` and `--`), equality/inequality (`==` and `!=`); however it does not offer additions of arbitrary integers, difference and `operator<`; random-access iterators are used wherever maximum speed is needed, and for sorting, so they usually deserve a special treatment with specialized algorithms.

As previously mentioned, we can ensure that a requirement on the iterator is met, by dispatching to another function that accepts an additional formal argument of type "iterator category":

```
template <typename iter_t>
void do_something(iter_t begin, iter_t end)
{
   return do_something(begin, end,
      typename std::iterator_traits<iter_t>::iterator_category());
}

template <typename iter_t>
void do_something(iter_t begin, iter_t end, std::bidirectional_iterator_tag)
{
   // do the work here
}
```

This technique was born for invoking optimized versions of the algorithm for any iterator type, but it can be used to restrict the invocation as well; standard iterator tags form a class hierarchy, so a "strong" tag can be cast nicely to a "weaker" requirement.

Here are some guidelines:

- Sometimes we write an algorithm first, and *then* we deduce which iterator is required for the algorithm to work; while deduction a posteriori is perfectly acceptable, it is easy to underestimate the requirements imposed by subroutines.

[119] This is of course fair, but arbitrary. About half STL containers have bidirectional iterators and half random-access; however if we weight them by usage, and include plain pointers, the average iterator would be more random-access.

- It's usually good design to separate algorithms that have different requirements. For example, instead of sorting *and then* iterating, just prescribe that the range should be already sorted; this may bring down the requirements to bidirectional iterators.

```
template <typename iterator_t>
void do_something(iterator_t begin, iterator_t end)
{
   // the following line has stronger requirements than all the rest

   std::sort(begin, end, std::greater<...>());
   std::for_each(begin, end, ...);
```

```
template <typename iterator_t>
void do_something_on_sorted_range(iterator_t begin, iterator_t end)
{
   // much better: all lines has the same complexity

   std::reverse(begin, end);
   std::for_each(begin, end, ...);
```

7.1.4. An example: set partitioning

Suppose we are given a set of integers X, and we need to partition it in two subsets so that the sum in each has roughly the same value.[120]
For this problem, heuristic algorithms are known, which quickly find an acceptable partition (possibly suboptimal); the simplest is the greedy algorithm, which states that:

```
Let P1={} and P2={} be empty sets;
While X is not empty, repeat:
{
   Assign the largest remaining integer in X to the set Pi which currently has the lower sum
   (break ties arbitrarily);
}
```

This description sounds like reordering, so we consider a mutating algorithm: reorder the input range and return an iterator `h`, so that `[begin, h)` and `[h, end)` are the required partitions. Also, as an additional bonus we compute the difference of the sums of both partitions $\left|\sum_{i\in[begin,h)} *i - \sum_{i\in[h,end)} *i\right|$, which is the objective to be minimized; thus the result will be `std::pair<iterator, value_type>`.

The implementation behaves like this:

- the range is divided in three logical blocks: partition A `[begin, end_of_A)` on the left; partition B on the right `[begin_of_B, end)` and a residual middle block M

[120] Ideally, we would like these sums to differ by 0 or 1. This is an NP-Hard problem, anyway.

- initially A and B are empty and M = `[begin, end)`
- while M is non-empty, repeat:
    - elements of M are sorted in decreasing order
    - iterate over the elements of M: objects assigned to A are swapped to the right of A (in position "end of A"); objects assigned to B are swapped to the left of B (in position "begin of B minus 1")[121]

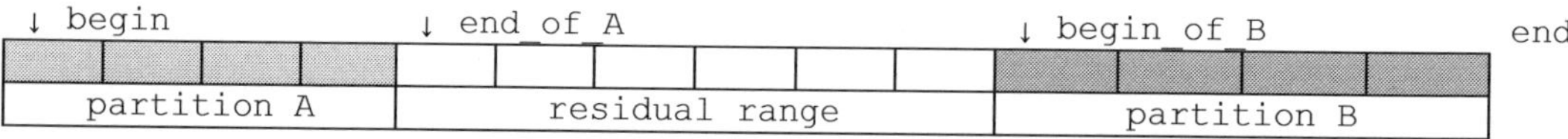

This code is a concise example of a mutating algorithm:

- it does not allocate temporary memory
- it's runtime complexity is documented

[121] The swapping process will leave some elements behind, that's the reason for the loop on the size of M; in the worst case, about one half of the members of M will be skipped, so the algorithm complexity is still superlinear, i.e. it takes time proportional to ~ n·log(n) when processing n elements.

```
#define mxt_value_type(T)      typename std::iterator_traits<T>::value_type

template <typename iterator_t>
std::pair<iterator_t, mxt_value_type(iterator_t)>
            equal_partition (iterator_t begin, iterator_t end)
{
   typedef mxt_value_type(iterator_t)> scalar_t;

   scalar_t sum_a = 0;
   scalar_t sum_b = 0;

   iterator_t end_of_A = begin;
   iterator_t beg_of_B = end;

   while (end_of_A != beg_of_B)
   {
      std::sort(end_of_A, beg_of_B, std::greater<scalar_t>());

      iterator_t i = end_of_A;
      do
      {
         if (sum_b < sum_a)
         {
            sum_a = sum_a - sum_b;
            sum_b = *i;
            smart_swap(*i, *(--beg_of_B));
         }
         else
         {
            sum_b = sum_b - sum_a;
            sum_a = *i;
            smart_swap(*i, *(end_of_A++));
         }
      }
      while ((i != beg_of_B) && (++i != beg_of_B));
   }

   return std::make_pair(end_of_A, sum_a<sum_b ? sum_b-sum_a : sum_a-sum_b);
}
```

Let's examine the implementation to determine the requirements on iterators and types.

- At a first glance, it may look like a bidirectional `iterator_t` suffices, because the code only uses copy construction, inequality, `++` and `--`; however `std::sort` requires random access iterators[122]
- The underlying `scalar_t` needs to implement `operator<` and binary `operator-`; note that there's a small difference between these lines:

```
sum_b = sum_b - sum_a;
sum_b -= sum_a;
```

[122] The fastest classical algorithms, quicksort and heapsort, can sort a random-access container in place in superlinear time (usually `std::sort` is a combination of both); mergesort is a third superlinear method that works with forward iterators, but it requires extra memory to hold a copy of the whole input: in practice however, if such extra memory is available, it may be convenient to copy/swap the input in a vector, sort the vector and put the result back.

The second option would introduce a new requirement (namely `operator-=`).

7.1.5. Identifying iterators

`std::iterator_traits<T>` is a metafunction that returns several types if `T` is an iterator or a pointer (in this case, types are trivially deduced);
`std::iterator_traits` is also the most reliable way to ensure that `T` is an iterator, because for most other types it will not compile:

```
template
<
   typename T,
   typename IS_ITERATOR = std::iterator_traits<T>::value_type
>
class require_iterator
{
   // similar to a static assertion,
   // this will compile only if T is a compliant iterator
};
```

We can take an educated guess if a type is a conforming iterator, using the ***5 basic typedefs*** which iterators are required to supply.[123]
Using again SFINAE techniques, we would write:

```
template <typename T>
struct is_iterator
{
   static const bool value =
      static_AND
      <
         has_type_value_type<T>,
         static_AND
         <
            has_type_reference<T>,
            static_AND
            <
               has_type_pointer<T>,
               static_AND
               <
                  has_type_iterator_category<T>,
                  has_type_difference_type<T>
               >
            >
         >
      >::value;
};

template <typename T>
struct is_iterator<T*>
{
   static const bool value = true;
};
```

The rational for the heuristic is as follows:

[123] Refer to the excellent description in the 3rd chapter of [6].

- `std::map` is not an iterator, but defines all types except `iterator_category`; so we really need to test that all 5 types are present
- we cannot test if `std::iterator_traits` is well defined, because it will not even compile if T is invalid
- there exist types where `is_iterator` is true but they are not even dereference-able (trivially, let `T` be `std::iterator_traits<int*>`).

Here's a test that, with a good precision, will identify non const-iterators.[124]
The key motivation is the following:

- an iterator will define a value type `T` and a reference type, usually `T&` or `const T&`
- `T&` is convertible to `T` but not vice versa
- `const T&` and `T` are mutually convertible.[125]

There are several possible cases:

- If `T` is not an iterator, it's not even a mutable iterator (that's handled by the last partial specialization)
- If `reference` is `value_type&` then the answer is true (this case is handled by the helper class)
- If `reference` is convertible to `value_type`, but not vice-versa, the answer is again true

```
template <typename T1, typename T2>
struct is_mutable_iterator_helper
{
   static const bool value = false;
};

template <typename T>
struct is_mutable_iterator_helper<T&, T>
{
   static const bool value = true;
};
```

[124] Of course, if a metafunction is known to fail for some specific type, it's always possible for the user to specialize it explicitly. Note also that the boost library takes another approach: if x is an instance of T, it checks if `*x` can be converted to T's `value_type`. See `boost::is_readable_iterator`.

[125] Remember that `X` is convertible to `Y` if given two functions `void F(X)` and `Y G()`, the call `F(G())` is legal; if `X=T` and `Y=T&` or `Y=const T&`, the call is fine; viceversa, if `X=T&` and `Y=T` the call is invalid; that's precisely the way `has_conversion` works.

```
template <typename T, bool IS_ITERATOR = is_iterator<T>::value>
class is_mutable_iterator
{
   typedef typename std::iterator_traits<T>::value_type val_t;
   typedef typename std::iterator_traits<T>::reference ref_t;

public:

   static const bool value =
      static_OR
      <
         is_mutable_iterator_helper<ref_t, val_t>,
         selector
         <
            has_conversion<ref_t, val_t>::L2R &&
            !has_conversion<val_t, ref_t>::L2R
         >
      >::value;

};

template <typename T>
class is_mutable_iterator<T, false>
{
public:
   static const bool value = false;
};
```

- `has_conversion<ref_t, val_t>::L2R` should be true by definition of `value_type`.
- we wrapped a static bool in a `selector`, since `static_OR` needs two types, not constants.

Some iterators are known to be views on sorted sets, for example `set<T>::iterator`. Can we detect them?
As is, the question is ill-formed: `set<T>::iterator` is a dependent type, and in C++ there's no "reverse matching" to deduce `T`, given `iterator`[126]

```
template <typename T>
void wrong(std::set<T>::iterator i)       // error: T is non-deducible
{
}
```

However we can make the problem less hard, if we just limit to some special candidates; in fact a set is declared as `set<T, L, A>` but in some contexts we may take a guess on L and A.

A practical example is given in the following code:

---

[126] As remarked in chapter 2. There is actually a way to do this, but it does not scale well and it's intrusive, i.e. it requires cooperation from the author of `std::set`; such a technique is the topic of section 7.6

```
template <typename T, typename less_t, typename alloc_t = std::allocator<T> >
class sorted_vector
{
   std::vector<T, alloc_t> data_;
   less_t less_;

public:

   template <typename iterator_t>
   sorted_vector(iterator_t begin, iterator_t end, less_t less = less_t())
      : data_(begin, end), less_(less)
   {
      // this is unnecessary if begin...end is already sorted

      std::sort(data_.begin(), data_.end(), less_);
```

Since the underlying `sort` algorithm will consume CPU time even when the range is already sorted, we shall try to guess if this step can be avoided.[127]

> Testing if a range is already sorted takes linear time.
> In C++0x, there's a dedicated algorithm:
>
> ```
> template <typename FwdIter>
> bool is_sorted(FwdIter begin, FwdIter end);
>
> template <typename FwdIter, typename less_t>
> bool is_sorted(FwdIter begin, FwdIter end, less_t LESS);
> ```
>
> In classic C++, this function can be implemented in a single line:
>
> ```
> return
>    std::adjacent_find
>    (
>       std::reverse_iterator<FwdIter>(end),
>       std::reverse_iterator<FwdIter>(begin),
>       LESS
>    ) == std::reverse_iterator<FwdIter>(begin);
> ```

We can combine both the static and the runtime test in this order:

```
if (!is_sorted_iterator<iterator_t, less_t>::value)
{
   if (!is_sorted(begin, end, less_)
      std::sort(begin, end, less_);
}
```

`is_sorted_iterator<iterator_t, less_t>` is allowed to return false negatives but not false positives: we tolerate to sort unnecessarily, but we must not let an unsorted range pass.

---

[127] Among all superlinear algorithms, only some mergesort variant may take advantage of a sorted input; quicksort and heapsort, on the opposite, do not depend significantly on the “entropy” of the initial data.

`is_sorted_iterator<iterator_t, less_t>` simply tries to match `iterator_t` against some special standard iterators:

```
#define ITER(C,T1)          typename std::C<T1,less_t>::iterator
#define CONST_ITER(C,T1)    typename std::C<T1,less_t>::const_iterator

template
<
   typename iter_t,
   typename less_t,
   typename value_t = typename std::iterator_traits<iter_t>::value_type
>
struct is_sorted_iterator
{
static const bool value =
   static_OR
   <
      static_OR
      <
       typeequal<iter_t, ITER(set, value_t)>,
       typeequal<iter_t, CONST_ITER(set, value_t)>
      >,
      static_OR
      <
       typeequal<iter_t, ITER(multiset, value_t)>,
       typeequal<iter_t, CONST_ITER(multiset, value_t)>
      >
   >::value;
};
```

There's a partial specialization for maps:

```
#define ITER(C,T1,T2)         typename std::C<T1,T2,less_t>::iterator
#define CONST_ITER(C,T1,T2)   typename std::C<T1,T2,less_t>::const_iterator


template
<
   typename iter_t,
   typename less_t,
   typename T1,
   typename T2
>
struct is_sorted_iterator< iter_t, less_t, std::pair<const T1, T2> >
{
   static const bool value =
   static_OR
   <
      static_OR
      <
         static_OR
         <
          typeequal<iter_t, ITER(map,T1,T2)>,
          typeequal<iter_t, CONST_ITER(map,T1,T2)>
         >,
         static_OR
         <
          typeequal<iter_t, ITER(multimap,T1,T2)>,
          typeequal<iter_t, CONST_ITER(multimap,T1,T2)>
         >
      >,
      static_OR
      <
         static_OR
         <
          typeequal<iter_t, ITER(map,const T1,T2)>,
          typeequal<iter_t, CONST_ITER(map,const T1,T2)>
         >,
         static_OR
         <
          typeequal<iter_t, ITER(multimap,const T1,T2)>,
          typeequal<iter_t, CONST_ITER(multimap,const T1,T2)>
         >
      >
   >::value;

};
```

7.1.6. Selection by iterator value type

A function that takes iterators may want to dispatch to another template, tagging the call with the iterator value type; in particular, this allows some mutating algorithms to deal with anomalies, such as mutable iterators that have constant references (e.g. `std::map`).

```
template <typename iterator_t>
iterator_t F(iterator_t b, iterator_t e)
{
   typedef typename std::iterator_traits<iterator_t>::value_type value_type;
   return F(b, e, instance_of<value_type>());
}

template <typename iterator_t, typename T1, typename T2>
iterator_t F(iterator_t b, iterator_t e, instance_of< std::pair<const T1, T2>
>)
{
   // modify only i->second
}

template <typename iterator_t, typename T>
iterator_t F(iterator_t b, iterator_t e, instance_of<T>)
{
   // modify *i
}
```

Selective-copy algorithms may use the *output* iterator value type to decide what to return. Suppose a computation produces a series of values and the corresponding weights; if the output type is a pair, the dump writes both, otherwise only the value:

```
template <..., typename iterator_t>
void do_it([[...]], iterator_t out_begin, iterator_t out_end)
{
   typedef typename std::iterator_traits<iterator_t>::value_type value_type;

   // ...

   dump([[...]], out_begin, out_end, instance_of<value_type>());
}

private:

template <..., typename iterator_t, typename T1, typename T2>
void dump([[...]], iterator_t b, iterator_t e, instance_of< std::pair<T1, T2>
>)
{
   for (i=b; i!=e; ++i)
      // write value in b->first and weight in b->second
}

template <typename iterator_t, typename T>
void dump([[...]], iterator_t b, iterator_t e, instance_of<T>)
{
   for (i=b; i!=e; ++i)
      // write value in *b
}
```

Note that the implementations may be unified using accessors. See the next section for details.

7.2. Generalizations

In this section we discuss alternative ways of coding functions, with different I/O interfaces; since iterators offer a view over data, they may not be flexible enough, especially for algorithms that have special semantics.
Some computation may be described in terms of properties, such as "find the object whose *price* is minimum"; surely we will need iterators to scan the objects, but how does a price is read?

7.2.1. Properties and Accessors

An algorithm that accepts iterators may not use the actual interface of the pointed type: usually they have two versions, one where the required operations are handled directly by the pointed type, and one that takes an extra functor that completely supersedes the object interface.
For example, `std::sort(b, e)` assumes that the pointed type is less-than comparable and it uses the pointee's `operator<` while `std::sort(b, e, LESS)` uses an external binary predicate for all the comparisons, and `operator<` may not exist at all.

As a generalization of this concept, algorithms may be defined in terms of *properties*.
Properties generalize data members: a (read only) ***property*** is simply a non-void function of a single (const) argument, which by default invokes a const member function of the argument or returns a copy of a data member of the argument: here's a trivial example.

```
template <typename T>
struct property_size
{
   typedef size_t value_type;

   value_type operator()(const T& x) const
   {
      return x.size();
   }
};
```

An instance of `property_size` passed to an algorithm is called the ***accessor*** of the property.
Many computational algorithms can be defined in terms of properties: they ignore the pointed type, but they need to read "its size", thus they require a suitable accessor.
By hypothesis, applying an accessor is inexpensive.

A property is a functor, thus the right typedef should be `result_type`, but the user needs to store a copy of the property value, which conceptually lies in the object and is only "accessed" by the functor, hence `value_type` is preferred.

A ***read-write property*** has an additional member that writes back a value:

```
template <typename T>
struct property_size
{
   typedef size_t value_type;

   value_type operator()(const T& x) const
   {
      return x.size();
   }

   value_type operator()(T& x, const value_type v) const
   {
      x.resize(v);
      return x.size();
   }
};
```

Accessors are useful in different contexts: in the simplest case, they avoid a call to `std::transform` or to write custom binary operators.
Suppose we have a range of `std::string`, and we need to find the total size and the maximum size.
Using the classical STL, we will write a custom "sum" and a custom "less": the transformation from string to integer (the size) is performed inside these functors.

```
struct sum_size
{
   size_t operator()(size_t n, const std::string& s) const
   {
      return n + s.size();
   }
};

struct less_by_size
{
   bool operator()(const std::string& s1, const std::string& s2) const
   {
      return s1.size() < s2.size();
   }
};
```

```
// assume beg!=end

size_t tot = std::accumulate(beg, end, 0U, sum_size());
size_t max = std::max_element(beg, end, less_by_size())->size();
```

Using accessors, we would have more code reuse:

```
#define VALUE   typename accessor_t::value_type

template <typename iterator_t, typename accessor_t>
VALUE accumulate(iterator_t b, iterator_t e, accessor_t A, VALUE init = 0)
{
   while (b != e)
      init = init + A(*b++);

   return init;
}
```

```
template <typename iterator_t, typename accessor_t>
iterator_t max_element(iterator_t b, iterator_t e, accessor_t A)
{
   if (b == e)
      return e;

   iterator_t result = b;
   while ((++b) != e)
   {
      if (A(*result) < A(*b))
         result = b;
   }

   return result;
}
```

```
size_t tot = accumulate(beg, end, property_size<std::string>());
size_t max = max_element(beg, end, property_size<std::string>());
```

The default accessor returns the object itself:

```
template <typename T>
struct default_accessor
{
   typedef T value_type;

   T& operator()(T& x) const
   {
      return x;
   }
};
```

Accessors offer a good degree of abstraction in complex computational algorithms that need several "named properties" at a time. We cite the knapsack problem as an example.
Each object has a (nonnegative) price and a (nonnegative) quality, we are given an amount of money and our objective is to buy the subset of objects having maximal total quality.

At the end of the computation, (part of) the result is a subset of the original range, so we choose a reordering algorithm: we return an iterator that partitions the range, paired with an additional by-product of the algorithm, in this case, the total quality. The function prototype in terms of accessors is long, but extremely clear:

```
#define QUALITY    typename quality_t::value_type
#define PRICE      typename price_t::value_type

template <typename price_t, typename quality_t, typename iterator_t>
std::pair<iterator_t, QUALITY> knapsack(iterator_t begin, iterator_t end,
                                         PRICE budget, price_t price,
                                           quality_t quality)
```

`price_t` and `quality_t` are accessors for the required properties.
So the price of the element `*i` is simply `price(*i)`, and it can be stored as a `typename price_t::value_type`.

To illustrate the usage, here's a non-mutating function which simply evaluates the total quality of the solution, assuming that we buy all elements possible starting from `begin`

```
template <typename price_t, typename quality_t, typename iterator_t>
QUALITY knapeval(iterator_t begin, iterator_t end, PRICE money,
                 price_t price, quality_t quality)
{
   typename quality_t::value_type total_q = 0;
   while (begin != end)
   {
      const typename price_t::value_type p = price(*begin);
      if (p > money)
         break;

      money -= p;
      total_q += quality(*begin++);
   }
   return total_q;
}
```

For algorithm testing, we will usually have the accessors fixed; then, it can be convenient to generate a placeholder structure that fits:

```
struct property_price
{
   typedef unsigned value_type;

   template <typename T>
   value_type operator()(const T& x) const
   {
      return x.price();
   }
};
```

```
struct price_tag_t {};
struct quality_tag_t {};

struct knapsack_object
{
   property<unsigned, price_tag_t> price;
   property<unsigned, quality_tag_t> quality;
};
```

Class `property` is described below.
The extra tag forbids assignment between different properties having the same underlying type (e.g. `unsigned int`).

```
template <typename object_t, typename tag_t = void>
class property
{
   object_t data_;

public:
   property()
      : data_()    // default-constructs fundamental types to zero
   {}

   property(const object_t& x)
      : data_(x)
   {}

   const object_t& operator()() const
   {
      return data_;
   }

   const object_t& operator()(const object_t& x)
   {
      return data_ = x;
   }

   const char* name() const
   {
      return typeid(tag_t).name();
   }
};
```

7.2.2. Mimesis

Some general-purpose algorithms accept a range, that is two iterators `[begin, end)` and an additional value OR a unary predicate. These algorithms are implemented twice: the latter version uses the predicate to test the elements, the former tests for "equality with the given value".
A classical example is `std::find` versus `std::find_if`.

```
template
<typename iter_t, typename object_t>
iter_t find(
iter_t begin, iter_t end,
object_t x)
{
        for (; begin != end; ++begin)
        {
                if (*begin == x)
                        break;
        }
        return begin;
}
```

```
template
<typename iter_t, typename functor_t>
iter_t find_if(
iter_t begin, iter_t end,
functor_t f)
{
        for (; begin != end; ++begin)
        {
                if (f(*begin))
                        break;
        }
        return begin;
}
```

In principle, `find` could be rewritten in terms of `find_if`

```
template <typename iter_t, typename object_t>
iter_t find(iter_t begin, const iter_t end, object_t x)
{
   return std::find_if(begin, end, std::bind2nd(std::equal_to<object_t>(),
x));
}
```

But also the converse is possible:

```
template <typename functor_t>
class wrapper
{
   functor_t f_;

public:

   wrapper(functor_t f = functor_t())
      : f_(f)
   {
      // verify with a static assertion that functor_t::result_type is bool
   }

   bool operator==(const typename functor_t::argument_type& that) const
   {
      return f_(that);
   }
};
```

```
template <typename iter_t, typename functor_t>
iter_t find_if(iter_t begin, const iter_t end, functor_t F)
{
   return std::find(begin, end, wrapper<functor_t>(F));
}
```

A ***mimesis object*** for type T, informally, behaves like an instance of T, but internally it's a unary predicate. A mimesis implements `operator==(const T&)`, `operator!=(const T&)` and operator "cast to T" (all operators being `const`).
To invoke a predicate, one writes:

```
if (f(x))
```

To invoke a mimesis, the equivalent syntax would be:

```
if (f == x)
```

The requirements above are slightly incomplete:

- o equality and inequality should take the mimesis itself and a T in any order, to prevent the undesired usage of "cast to T" for comparisons (we'll come on this later).
- o the cast operator should return a prototype value which satisfies the same criteria.

In other words if M is a mimesis for type T, then the fundamental property for M is:

```
   M<T> m;
   assert(m == static_cast<T>(m));
```

The simplest mimesis for type T is T itself.

As a very simple case, let's implement a mimesis that identifies positive numbers:

```
template <typename scalar_t >
struct positive
{
   bool operator==(const scalar_t& x) const
   {
      return 0<x;
   }

   bool operator!=(const scalar_t& x) const
   {
      return !(*this == x);
   }

   operator scalar_t() const
   {
      return 1; // an arbitrary positive number
   }
};
```

Here's the first application: we don't need `find_if` any more.

```
double a[] = { -3.1, 2.5, -1.0 };
std::find(a, a+3, positive<double>());        // fine, returns pointer to 2.5
```

The key is that the value parameter in find has independent template type, so `positive<double>` is passed over as is, without casting.
A deduced template type, such as:

```
template <typename I>
iter_t find(I, I, typename std::iterator_traits<I>::value_type x)
```

would have caused the mimesis to decay into its default value (and consequently, a wrong find result).

The mimesis interface can in fact be richer:

```
template <typename scalar_t, bool SIGN = true>
struct positive
{
   bool operator==(const scalar_t& x) const
   {
      return (0<x) ^ (!SIGN);
   }

   bool operator!=(const scalar_t& x) const
   {
      return !(*this == x);
   }

   operator scalar_t() const
   {
      return SIGN ? 1 : -1; // arbitrary positive and non-positive numbers
   }

   positive<scalar_t, !SIGN> operator!() const
   {
      return positive<scalar_t, !SIGN>();
   }
};
```

```
template <typename scalar_t, bool SIGN>
inline bool operator==(const scalar_t& x, const positive<scalar_t, SIGN> p)
{
   return p == x;
}

template <typename scalar_t, bool SIGN>
inline bool operator!=(const scalar_t& x, const positive<scalar_t, SIGN> p)
{
   return p != x;
}
```

Thus `positive<double, true>` will compare equal to any strictly positive double and it will convert to 1.0 when needed; on the opposite, `positive<double, false>` will compare equal to non-positive numbers, and it will return -1.0. Note that the user will simply write `positive<T>()` or `!positive<T>()`.

```
std::find(a, a+3, !positive<double>());
```

We have seen that writing a mimesis takes more effort than a functor, but it's worth especially for generalizing functions that take a special value as an argument. The next section offers another application.

7.2.3. End of range

Iterator-based algorithms cannot compute dynamically the end of range; for example, we cannot express the concept "find 5.0 but stop on the first negative number", as the range is pre-computed: we need two function calls.

```
using namespace std;
find(begin, find_if(begin, end, bind2nd(less<double>(), 0.0)), 5.0)
```

The canonical example of range inefficiency is given by C-strings: suppose we are copying a C-string, and we get an output iterator to the destination:

```
const char* c_string = "this is an example";

// can we avoid strlen?
std::copy(c_string, c_string+strlen(c_string), destination);
```

`strlen` has to traverse the string looking for the terminator, then `copy` traverses it again. The process in practice is extremely fast, but it does an unnecessary pass.

Suppose for a moment we rewrite `copy`: we don't change the function body, but just allow the endpoints of the range to have different types.

```
template <typename iter1_t, typename iter2_t, typename end_t>
iter2_t copy_2(iter1_t begin, end_t end, iter2_t output)
{
   while (begin != end)
      *(output++) = *(begin++),

   return output;
}
```

This is equivalent to asking that `end` is a mimesis for type `iter1_t`. Compare with the following code:

```
template <typename char_t, char_t STOP = 0>
struct c_string_end
{
   typedef char_t* iterator_t;

   operator iterator_t() const { return 0; }

   bool operator!=(const iterator_t i) const
   {
      return !(*this == i);
   }

   bool operator==(const iterator_t i) const
   {
      return i==0 || *i==STOP;
   }
};

// implement operator== and != with arguments in different order
// ...
```

```
const char* begin = "hello world!";
copy_2(begin, c_string_end<const char>(), output);     // ok and efficient!
copy_2(begin, begin+5, output);                         // also ok!
```

The latter invocation of `copy_2` is totally equivalent to `std::copy`.

To sum up, a mimesis has two usages:

- algorithms that accept a "test", which can be either a value or a predicate
- algorithms that process a range `begin...end`, where `end` is just a termination criteria (i.e. it's not decremented)

We stress the difference: the "test" mentioned in the first point is a skip-and-continue condition *on elements*; `end` is a terminate-and-exit criterion *on iterators*.

The cast operator in the interface of a mimesis turns out to be useful when the object acts as a skip-and-continue filter: assume we are computing the average of all the elements that satisfy some criteria; first, we write a tentative "classical" version.

```
template <class iter_t, class predicate_t>
typename std::iterator_traits<iter_t>::value_type average_if(iter_t begin,
iter_t end, predicate_t f)
{
   size_t count = 0;
   typename std::iterator_traits<iter_t>::value_type result = 0;

   for (; begin != end; ++begin)
   {
      if (f(*begin))
      {
         result += *begin;
         ++count;
      }
   }
   return count>0 ? result/count : [[???]];
}
```

If the predicate rejects all elements, we don't know what to return, except possibly `std::numeric_limits<...>::quiet_NaN()` (hoping that `has_quiet_NaN` is true).

However the best choice is to ask the functional what to return: if F is seen as the rejection logic (not the acceptance), it should be also responsible for providing a prototype of the rejected element, and that's exactly the fundamental property for a mimesis.
That's why we rewrite the algorithm using a mimesis standing for a `quiet_NaN`:[128]

```
template <typename iter_t, typename end_t, typename nan_t>
typename std::iterator_traits<iter_t>::value_type
   average(iter_t begin, const end_t end, nan_t NaN)
{
   size_t count = 0;
   typename std::iterator_traits<iter_t>::value_type result = 0;

   for (; begin != end; ++begin)
   {
      if (NaN != *begin)
      {
         result += *begin;
         ++count;
      }
   }
   return count>0 ? result/count : NaN;
}
```

To represent an "exclusion filter" is a typical role of a mimesis:

[128] the algorithm should now be named `average_if_not`

```
template <typename scalar_t>
struct ieee_nan
{
   operator scalar_t() const
   {
      return std::numeric_limits<scalar_t>::quiet_NaN();
   }

   bool operator!=(const scalar_t& x) const
   {
      return x == x;
   }

   bool operator==(const scalar_t& x) const
   {
      return x != x;
   }
};
```

The dangerous downside of a cast operator is that it can be called unexpectedly. Consider again the example on page 302:

```
template <typename iterator_t, char STOP = 0>
struct c_string_end
{
   // ...
};

// ooops...
// forgot to implement operator== and != with arguments in different order
```

```
// later...
while (begin != end)
{
```

`begin!=end` will actually call `bool operator!=(const char*, const char*)` with arguments `begin`, which is already a pointer, and `end` cast to (null) pointer. Thus the loop will never exit.

We finally remark that it's possible to wrap a mimesis and turn it to a predicate, and vice versa.

7.3. Iterator wrapping

Writing STL-compliant iterators is a complex activity and it involves a lot of code duplication. Luckily, writing `const_iterators` is far easier.

A wrapped iterator, const or non-const, is a class which contains another iterator as a member: the wrapper forwards every "positioning operation" (e.g. increments and decrements) to the member, but it intercepts dereferencing, changing the result so to express a logical view on the underlying data set.

Since the end user may not see actual data, but a custom-forged value, it's often impossible to modify the original objects through the view, so wrapped iterators are mostly const_iterators.

Suppose we have a vector of integers, and an iterator wrapper that returns the actual value multiplied by 5.

```
template <typename iterator_t>
class multiplier_iterator
{
   // ...
```

```
// Later...

   std::vector<int> data;
   data.push_back(8);

   multiplier_iterator<std::vector<int>::iterator> i(data.begin(), 5);

   int a = *i;            // now a = 5*8
   *i = 25;               // what about data[0] now???
   assert(*i == 25);

   *i = 24;               // what about data[0] now???
   assert(*i == 25);      // are you serious?
```

Even if `multiplier_iterator` could physically write an integer at position `data[0]`, what should it do? Were it smart enough, it would write 25/5=5, so that `*i` returns again 25 from that point on.
However the instruction `*i = 24` is even more problematic: should it throw an exception? Or do nothing? Or set `data[0]=(24+(5-1))/5` anyway?

A correct implementation of `operator->` is indeed the hardest issue: a lucky wrapper will simply dispatch recursively the execution to the wrapped iterator, but since this usually reveals the "real" data underneath, it may not be compatible with the wrapping logic.
Consider instead *omitting* operators that are less likely to be used, `operator->` being the first candidate, unless their implementation is both trivial and correct[129]

The arrow operator is used to access members of the pointed type, but in portions of code where this type is generic (e.g. a template parameter, maybe deduced), these members are usually *not known*, so the arrow should not be used.[130]

---

[129] As a rule, iterator wrappers need not be 100% standard-conforming, as there are some common issues that won't compromise their functionality: the most common are lack of `operator->` and `operator*` returning a value and not a reference (in other words: `iterator::reference` and `iterator::value_type` are the same). On the opposite, the implementation with these simplified features may be much easier: see the `random_iterator` example later in the chapter.
[130] An exception is `std::map`, which could legitimately call i->first and i->second.

For example, std::vector::assign will generally work even on iterators having no operator->.

7.3.1. Iterator expander

Iterator wrappers will delegate most operations to the wrapped object, such as operator++.
The dispatching part is extremely easy to automate using a static interface[131], which we name iterator_expander:

```
class wrapper :
      public iterator_expander<wrapper>,
      public std::iterator_traits<wrapped>
{
   wrapped w_;

public:

   wrapped& base()
   {
      return w_;
   }

   const wrapped& base() const
   {
      return w_;
   }

   wrapper(wrapped w)
      : w_(w)
   {
   }

   [[...]] operator* () const
   {
      // write code here
   }

   [[...]] operator-> () const
   {
      // write code here
   }
};
```

The iterator_expander interface (listed below) is responsible for all possible positioning (++, ++, +=, -=, +, -) and comparison operators; they are all implemented, and as usual, they will be compiled only if used and if wrapped does not support any of them, an error will be emitted (no static assertion is necessary, as the cause of the error will be evident).

[131] As usual, the Boost library actually offers a more complete solution, but this is simpler and fully functional

Note also that every operator in the interface return `true_this()`, not `*this`, because otherwise a combined expression such as `*(i++)` would not work: `iterator_expander` does not implement `operator*`, but `true_this()` returns the actual wrapper.

```
template <typename iterator_t, typename diff_t = ptrdiff_t>
class iterator_expander
{
protected:

// the static interface part, cfr. chapter 6.2

~iterator_expander() {}
 iterator_expander() {}

iterator_t& true_this()
{
   return static_cast<iterator_t&>(*this);
}

const iterator_t& true_this() const
{
   return static_cast<const iterator_t&>(*this);
}

public:

iterator_t& operator++() { ++true_this().base(); return true_this(); }
iterator_t& operator--() { --true_this().base(); return true_this(); }

iterator_t& operator+=(diff_t i)
{ true_this().base() += i; return true_this(); }
iterator_t& operator-=(diff_t i)
{ true_this().base() -= i; return true_this(); }

iterator_t operator++(int)
{ iterator_t t(true_this()); ++(*this); return t; }
iterator_t operator--(int)
{ iterator_t t(true_this()); --(*this); return t; }

iterator_t operator+(diff_t i) const
{ iterator_t t(true_this()); t+=i; return t; }
iterator_t operator-(diff_t i) const
{ iterator_t t(true_this()); t-=i; return t; }

diff_t operator-(const iterator_expander& x) const
{ return true_this().base() - x.true_this().base(); }

bool operator<(const iterator_expander& x) const
{ return true_this().base() < x.true_this().base(); }

bool operator==(const iterator_expander& x) const
{ return true_this().base() == x.true_this().base(); }

bool operator!=(const iterator_expander& x) const { return !(*this == x); }
bool operator> (const iterator_expander& x) const { return x < *this; }
bool operator<=(const iterator_expander& x) const { return !(x < *this); }
bool operator>=(const iterator_expander& x) const { return !(*this < x); }
};


template <typename iterator_t, typename diff_t>
iterator_t operator+(diff_t n, iterator_expander<iterator_t, diff_t> i)
{
   return i+n;
}
```

Note that `difference_type` is taken, not deduced: `iterator_expander<T>` cannot read types defined in T, because, being a base of T, it is compiled before T.

So the wrapper will be declared as:

```
template <typename iterator_t>
class wrapper
: public iterator_expander
        <
           wrapper<iterator_t>,
           typename std::iterator_traits<iterator_t>::difference_type
        >
{
   // ...
```

Here's a trivial practical example, which also shows that the iterator base can be a simple integer.

```
class random_iterator
: public iterator_expander<random_iterator>
, public std::iterator_traits<const int*>
{
   int i_;

public:

   int& base() { return i_; }
   const int& base() const { return i_; }

   explicit random_iterator(const int i=0)
      : i_(i)
   {
   }

   int operator*() const
   {
      return std::rand();
   }
};
```

```
std::vector<int> v;
v.assign(random_iterator(0), random_iterator(25));

// now v contains 25 random numbers
```

Note that we skipped the arrow operator and dereferencing returns a value, not a reference (but since the class inherits `const int*` traits, it's still possible to bind a `reference` to `*iterator`, as `reference` is `const int&`)

> Don't store copies of values in iterators; while this actually allows returning genuine references and pointers, the referenced entity has a lifetime that is bound to the iterator, not to the "container" (in other words, destroying the iterator, the reference becomes invalid), and this will lead to subtle bugs. Here's some *bad* code:

```
class random_iterator
: public iterator_expander<random_iterator>
, public std::iterator_traits<const int*>
{
   int i_;
   int val_;                              // bad

public:

   const int& operator*() const
   {
      return val_ = std::rand();          // bad
   }

   const int* operator->() const
   {
      return &*(*this);                   // even worse
   }
};
```

Iterator wrappers solve the problem of iterating over values in a map (or equivalently, the problem of const-iterating over keys); this time it's going to be a true non-const iterator implementation, because we iterate over existing elements, so we can return pointers and references.

```
template <typename T, int N>
struct component;

template <typename T1, typename T2>
struct component<std::pair<T1, T2>, 1>
{
   typedef T1 value_type;
   typedef T1& reference;
   typedef const T1& const_reference;
   typedef T1* pointer;
   typedef const T1* const_pointer;
};

template <typename T1, typename T2>
struct component<std::pair<const T1, T2>, 1>
{
   typedef T1 value_type;
   typedef const T1& reference;
   typedef const T1& const_reference;
   typedef const T1* pointer;
   typedef const T1* const_pointer;
};

template <typename T1, typename T2>
struct component<std::pair<T1, T2>, 2> : component<std::pair<T2, T1>, 1>
{
};
```

We will assume that `iterator_t` (the wrapped type) points to a `std::pair`-like class; if that's not the case, the compiler will give an error compiling one of the `ref` overloads.

```
template <typename iterator_t, int N>
class pair_iterator
: public iterator_expander< pair_iterator<iterator_t, N> >
{
   static const bool    IS_MUTABLE = is_mutable_iterator<iterator_t>::value;

   iterator_t i_;

   typedef std::iterator_traits<iterator_t> traits_t;
   typedef component<typename traits_t::value_type, N> component_t;

   typedef typename component_t::reference ref_t;
   typedef typename component_t::const_reference cref_t;

   typedef typename component_t::pointer ptr_t;
   typedef typename component_t::const_pointer cptr_t;

   template <typename pair_t>
   static ref_t ref(pair_t& p, static_value<int, 1>)
   { return p.first;   }

   template <typename pair_t>
   static ref_t ref(pair_t& p, static_value<int, 2>)
   { return p.second; }

   template <typename pair_t>
   static cref_t ref(const pair_t& p, static_value<int, 1>)
   { return p.first; }

   template <typename pair_t>
   static cref_t ref(const pair_t& p, static_value<int, 2>)
   { return p.second; }

public:

   explicit pair_iterator(iterator_t i)
      : i_(i)
   {}

   iterator_t& base() { return i_; }
   const iterator_t& base() const { return i_; }

   typedef typename typeif<IS_MUTABLE, ref_t, cref_t>::type reference;
   typedef typename typeif<IS_MUTABLE, ptr_t, cptr_t>::type pointer;
   typedef typename component_t::value_type value_type;
   typedef typename traits_t::iterator_category iterator_category;
   typedef typename traits_t::difference_type difference_type;

   reference operator* () const
   {
      return ref(*i_, static_value<int, N>());
   }

   pointer operator->() const
   {
      return &*(*this);
   }
};
```

Here's a driver function:

```
template <int N, typename iterator_t>
inline pair_iterator<iterator_t, N> select(iterator_t i)
{
   return pair_iterator<iterator_t, N>(i);
}
```

And finally some example code: the syntax for the driver is `select<N>(i)` where `N` is 1 or 2 and `i` is an iterator, whose `value_type` is a pair:

```
template <typename T>
struct Doubler
{
   void operator()(T& x) const
   {
      x *= 2;
   }
};

template <typename T>
struct User
{
   void operator()(const T& x) const
   {
      std::cout << x << ';';
   }
};
```

```
   typedef std::map<int, double> map_t;

   MXT_ASSERT(!is_mutable_iterator<map_t::const_iterator>::value);
   MXT_ASSERT(is_mutable_iterator<map_t::iterator>::value);

   map_t m;
   const map_t& c = m;

   m[3] = 1.4;
   m[6] = 2.8;
   m[9] = 0.1;

// print 3;6;9; via iterator
   std::for_each(select<1>(m.begin()), select<1>(m.end()), User<int>());

// print 3;6;9; via const_iterator
   std::for_each(select<1>(c.begin()), select<1>(c.end()), User<int>());

// multiplies by 2 each value in the map
   std::for_each(select<2>(m.begin()), select<2>(m.end()),
Doubler<double>());

   std::vector<double> v1;
   v1.assign(select<1>(c.begin()), select<1>(c.end()));

   std::vector< std::pair<int, double> > v2(m.begin(), m.end());

// multiplies by 2 each key in the vector (the key is not constant)
   std::for_each(select<1>(v2.begin()), select<1>(v2.end()), Doubler<int>());
```

```
//   these two lines should give an error:
//   std::for_each(select<1>(m.begin()), select<1>(m.end()), Doubler<int>());
//   std::for_each(select<1>(c.begin()), select<1>(c.end()), Doubler<int>());
```

7.3.2. Fake pairs

The inverse problem is "merging" two logical views and obtaining a single iterator that makes them look like pairs: with `pair_iterator`, we can build a vector of keys and a vector of values reading a map, but not the other way.

```
std::vector<int> key;
std::vector<double> value;

std::map<int, double> m = /* ??? */;
```

Actually, we can extend the interface of iterator expander, to allow the possibility that the derived class has more than one `base`. Simply let `base` have N overloads, taking a `static_value<size_t, N>`, and each can possibly return a (reference to an) iterator of different kind.
We isolate the elementary modifiers to be applied to the `base`s and code a very simple statically-recursive method.[132]
Note the template member function, since we do not know in advance what `base(static_value<size_t, K>)` returns:

```
struct plusplus
{
   template <typename any_t>
      void operator()(any_t& x) const { ++x; }
};
```

```
class pluseq
{
   const diff_t i_;

public:
   pluseq(const diff_t i) : i_(i) {}

   template <typename any_t>
      void operator()(any_t& x) const { x += i_; }
};
```

[132] For brevity, we omit all "subtractive" functions

```
template <typename iterator_t, size_t N, typename diff_t>
class iterator_pack
{
protected:

   typedef static_value<size_t, N> n_times;

   ~iterator_pack() {}
   iterator_pack() {}

   iterator_t& true_this()
   {
      return static_cast<iterator_t&>(*this);
   }

   const iterator_t& true_this() const
   {
      return static_cast<const iterator_t&>(*this);
   }
```

```
   /* static recursion */

   template <typename modifier_t, size_t K>
      void apply(const modifier_t modifier, const static_value<size_t, K>)
   {
      modifier(true_this().base(static_value<size_t, K-1>()));
      apply(modifier, static_value<size_t, K-1>());
   }

   template <typename modifier_t>
      void apply(const modifier_t modifier, const static_value<size_t, 0>)
   {
   }

public:

   typedef diff_t difference_type;

   iterator_t& operator++()
   {
      apply(plusplus(), n_times());
      return true_this();
   }

   iterator_t& operator+=(const diff_t i)
   {
      apply(pluseq(i), n_times());
      return true_this();
   }
```

Difference and comparison are based (arbitrarily) on the first base: [133]

[133] In synthesis, an iterator pack is an iterator-like class that maintains synchronization between N different iterators; if `P` is such a pack, you can call `P += 2` only if all iterators are random-access, however if only the first is random-access, then the pack will have a constant-time difference.

```
typedef static_value<size_t, 0> default_t;

diff_t operator-(const iterator_pack& x) const
{
  return true_this().base(default_t()) - x.true_this().base(default_t());
}

bool operator<(const iterator_pack& x) const
{
  return true_this().base(default_t()) < x.true_this().base(default_t());
}

bool operator==(const iterator_pack& x) const
{
  return true_this().base(default_t()) == x.true_this().base(default_t());
}
```

All other operators derive from the basic ones in the usual way: postfix `++` and `operator+` from prefix `++` and `+=`, comparison from `<` and `==`.

With the new tool at our disposal, here's a not-fully-standard iterator that pretends to move over `std::pair`

First, some highlights:

- `pointer` is `void`, because we don't want to support `operator->`, but to compile `std::iterator_traits< iterator_couple<...> >pointer` needs to be defined; however this definition will prevent any use.
- `iterator_category` is the weakest of the two categories, however we statically-assert that both categories should be comparable so to avoid unusual pairs (such as input/output iterators); of course, the restriction could be removed.
- the main problem is how to define `reference`; obviously we have to rely on `r1_t` and `r2_t` but we cannot use `std::pair<r1_t, r2_t>` mainly because, in current C++ standard, `std::pair` does not support it and it will not compile.[134]

[134] `std::pair` takes arguments in the constructor by const reference, but if either type is a reference, this makes a reference to a reference, and that's forbidden

```
#define TRAITS(N)   std::iterator_traits<iterator##N##_t>

template <typename iterator1_t, typename iterator2_t>
class iterator_couple
: public iterator_pack
        <
            iterator_couple<iterator1_t, iterator2_t>,
            2,
            typename TRAITS(1)::difference_type
        >
{
   typedef typename TRAITS(1)::value_type v1_t;
   typedef typename TRAITS(2)::value_type v2_t;

   typedef typename TRAITS(1)::reference r1_t;
   typedef typename TRAITS(2)::reference r2_t;

   typedef typename TRAITS(1)::iterator_category cat1_t;
   typedef typename TRAITS(2)::iterator_category cat2_t;

public:

   iterator_couple(iterator1_t i1, iterator2_t i2)
      : i1_(i1), i2_(i2)
   {
   }

   typedef typename
      typeif
      <
         is_base_of<cat1_t, cat2_t>::value,
         cat1_t,
         cat2_t
      >::type iterator_category;


   typedef std::pair<v1_t, v2_t> value_type;

   typedef void pointer;

   struct reference
   {
      /* see below... */
   };

   iterator1_t& base(static_value<size_t, 0>) { return i1_; }
   iterator2_t& base(static_value<size_t, 1>) { return i2_; }

   const iterator1_t& base(static_value<size_t, 0>) const { return i1_; }
   const iterator2_t& base(static_value<size_t, 1>) const { return i2_; }

   reference operator* () const
   {
      MXT_ASSERT
      (
         (is_base_of<cat1_t, cat2_t>::value
             || is_base_of<cat2_t, cat1_t>::value)
      );
      return reference(*i1_, *i2_);
   }

private:
   iterator1_t i1_;
   iterator2_t i2_;
};
```

We have to emulate a pair of references, which `std::pair` does not allow:

```
struct reference
{
   r1_t first;
   r2_t second;

   reference(r1_t r1, r2_t r2)
      : first(r1), second(r2)
   {
   }

   operator std::pair<v1_t, v2_t>() const
   {
      return std::pair<v1_t, v2_t>(first, second);
   }

   template <typename any1_t, typename any2_t>
      operator std::pair<any1_t, any2_t>() const
   {
      return std::pair<any1_t, any2_t>(first, second);
   }

   reference& operator= (const std::pair<v1_t, v2_t>& p)
   {
      first = p.first;
      second = p.second;
      return *this;
   }

   void swap(reference& r)
   {
      swap(first, r.first);
      swap(second, r.second);
   }

   void swap(std::pair<v1_t, v2_t>& p)
   {
      swap(first, p.first);
      swap(second, p.second);
   }
};
```

The template cast-to-pair operator is needed since `std::map` will likely cast our reference not to `pair<V1, V2>` but to `pair<const V1, V2>`.
This implementation may suffice to write code like this:

```
template <typename iterator1_t, typename iterator2_t>
iterator_couple<iterator1_t, iterator2_t> make_couple(iterator1_t i1,
iterator2_t i2)
{
   return iterator_couple<iterator1_t, iterator2_t>(i1, i2);
}
```

```
std::vector<int> k;
std::list<double> v1;
std::vector<double> v2;

std::map<int, double> m;

std::pair<int, double> p = *make_couple(k.begin(), v1.begin());

m.insert(make_couple(k.begin(),v1.begin()),make_couple(k.end(),v1.end()));

std::vector< std::pair<int, double> > v;
v.assign(make_couple(k.begin(), v2.begin()),make_couple(k.end(), v2.end()));
```

Note that the first `insert` gets a bidirectional iterator, while the last `assign` gets a random-access iterator.[135]

7.4. Receipts

Receipts are empty classes that can be created only by "legally authorized entities" and unlock the execution of functions, as required parameters. Some receipts can be stored for later usage, some instead must be passed on immediately.
In a very simple case, when we need to enforce that function F is called before G, we modify F and let it return a receipt R, which cannot be constructed otherwise; finally, G takes R as an additional – formal – parameter.

Receipts are mostly useful in connection to hierarchy of classes, when a virtual member function `foo` in every `DERIVED` should invoke `BASE::foo` at some point. Assume for the moment that `foo` returns `void`.

There are two similar solutions:

- the public non-virtual/protected virtual technique: the base class implements a public nonvirtual `foo`, which calls a protected virtual function when appropriate

```
class BASE
{
protected:
   virtual void custom_foo()
   {
   }

public:
   void foo()
   {
      /* whatever */
      custom_foo();
   }
};
```

- receipts: `BASE::foo` returns a secret receipt, private to `BASE`

[135] Interestingly, the use of a global helper function avoids all the nasty ambiguities between a constructor and a function declaration: the problem is described and solved in “Item 6” of [7].

```
class BASE
{
protected:
   class RECEIPT_TYPE
   {
      friend class BASE;

      RECEIPT_TYPE() {}        // constructor is private
   };

public:
   virtual RECEIPT_TYPE foo()
   {
      /* whatever */
      return RECEIPT_TYPE();
   }
};
```

```
class DERIVED : public BASE
{
public:
   virtual RECEIPT_TYPE foo()
   {
      /* whatever */

      // the only way to return is...
      return BASE::foo();
   }
};
```

If `RECEIPT_TYPE` has a public copy constructor, `DERIVED` can store the result of `BASE::foo` at any time; otherwise, it's forced to invoke it on the return line.

Note that a non-void return type `T` can be changed into `std::pair<T,RECEIPT_TYPE>`, or a custom class, which needs a receipt, but ignores it.

Receipts are particularly useful in objects, where we want to control the execution order of member functions (*algors* will be described in section 9.6):

```
class an_algor
{
   public:
      bool initialize();

      void iterate();

      bool stop() const;

      double get_result() const;
};
```

```
double execute_correctly_algor(an_algor& a)
{
   if (!a.initialize())
      throw std::logic_error("something bad happened");

   do
   {
      a.iterate();
   } while (!a.stop());

   return a.get_result();
}
```

```
double totally_crazy_execution(an_algor& a)
{
   if (a.stop())
      a.iterate();

   if (a.initialize())
      return a.get_result();
   else
      return 0;
}
```

In general we want `initialize` to be called before `iterate`, and `get_result` after at least one iteration. So we modify the interface as follows:

```
template <int STEP, typename T>
class receipt_t : receipt_t<STEP-1>
{
   friend class T;

private:
   receipt_t()
   {
   }
};

template < typename T>
class receipt_t<0, T>
{
   friend class T;

private:
   receipt_t()
   {
   }
};
```

```
class a_better_algor
{
public:

   typedef receipt_t<0, a_better_algor> init_ok_t;
   typedef receipt_t<1, a_better_algor> iterate_ok_t;

   init_ok_t initialize();

   iterate_ok_t iterate(init_ok_t);

   bool stop(iterate_ok_t) const;

   double get_result(iterate_ok_t) const;
};
```

With the necessary evil of a template friendship declaration (which is non-standard yet), the idea should be clear: since the user cannot forge receipts, she must store the return value of `initialize` and pass it to `iterate`; finally, to get the result, it's necessary to prove that at least one iteration was performed:

```
   a_better_algor A;
   a_better_algor::init_ok_t RECEIPT1 = A.initialize();

   while (true)
   {
      a_better_algor::iterate_ok_t RECEIPT2 = a.iterate(RECEIPT1);
      if (a.stop(RECEIPT2))
         return a.get_result(RECEIPT2);
   }
```

7.5. Algebraic requirements

7.5.1. Less and NaN

Objects of generic type T are often assumed *LessThanComparable*.
This means that either `T::operator<` is defined, or an instance of a binary predicate "less" is given as an extra argument.[136]

An algorithm should avoid mixing different comparison operators, such as `operator<=` and `operator>`, because they could be inconsistent; the best solution is to replace them with `operator<` (or with the binary predicate "less")

[136] As a rule of thumb: if T is such that there's a single way to decide if A<B, because the comparison is trivial or fixed, then we should supply `T::operator<` (e.g. T = `RomanNumber`); conversely, if there's more than one feasible comparison, we should not implement `operator<` and pass the right functional every time, to make our intentions explicit (e.g. T = `Employee`). These functionals however may be defined inside T

X<Y	(assumed valid)
X>Y	Y<X
X≤Y	!(Y<X)
X≥Y	!(X<Y)
X==Y	!(X<Y) && !(Y<X)
X!=Y	(X<Y) || (Y<X)

It's questionable if `operator==` should be assumed valid or replaced with the *equivalence test*: in fact two calls to `operator<` may be significantly slower (as in `std::string`).
Under additional hypothesis, one of the tests may be elided.
For example, if a range is sorted, a test with iterators `*i == *(i+k)` can be replaced by `!less(*i, *(i+k))`.

A NaN (Not-a-Number) is an instance of T that causes any comparison operator to "fail": in other words if at least one of x and y is NaN, then `x OP y` returns false if OP is <,>,<=,>=,== and returns true if OP is !=.
In fact a NaN can be detected by this simple test:

```
template <typename T>
bool is_nan(const T& x)
{
    return x != x;
}
```

Types `double` and `float` have a native NaN.
If T has a NaN, then it can create problems to sorting algorithms: two elements are equivalent if neither is less than the other[137]; so a NaN is equivalent to any other element. If we write, for example:

```
std::map<double, int> m;
// insert elements...
m[std::numeric_limits<double>::quiet_NaN()] = 7;
```

Then we are effectively overwriting a random (i.e. implementation dependent) value with 7.
The right way to deal with a range than may contain NaN is to `partition` them out before sorting, or modify the comparison operator, so for example they fall at the beginning of range:

[137] Vice versa, if both x<y and y<x are true, then it's an error in the comparison operator.

```
template <typename T>
struct LessWithNAN
{
   bool operator()(const T& x, const T& y) const
   {
      if (is_nan(x))
         return !is_nan(y);
      else
         return x<y;
   }
};
```

7.6. The Barton-Nackman trick

Knuth wrote that a *trick* is a clever idea that is used once and a *technique* is a trick that is used at least twice. The Barton-Nackman *technique*, also known as ***restricted template expansion***, is a way to declare global functions and operators inside a class, marking them as friends:

```
template <typename T>
class X
{
public:

   friend int f(X<T> b)                          // global function #1
   {
      return 0;
   }

   friend bool operator==(X<T> a, X<T> b)        // global operator #2
   {
      return ...;
   }
};
```

```
X<double> x;
f(x);          // calls #1
x == x;        // calls #2
```

The *global* function and operator above are *non-template* functions that are injected in the scope of X<T>, when the class is instantiated. In other words, they are found with Koenig lookup, so at least one of the arguments must have type X<T>.

The main use of this technique is to declare global functions that take an inner class of a template class.

```
template <typename T>
struct outer
{
   template <int N>
   struct inner {};
};
```

We cannot write a template that takes `outer<T>::inner<N>` for arbitrary T, because T is non-deducible. However the Barton-Nackman trick will do:

```
template <typename T>
struct outer
{
   template <int N>
   struct inner
   {
      friend int f(inner<N>)
      { return N; }
   };
};
```

Regardless of the fact that `f` is not a template, we can manipulate the template parameters at will:

```
template <typename T>
struct outer
{
   template <int N>
   struct inner
   {
      friend inner<N+1> operator++(inner<N>)
      { return inner<N+1>(); }
   };
};
```

```
outer<double>::inner<0> I1;
++I1; // returns outer<double>::inner<1>
```

We can also write template functions in the same way, but *all parameters should be deducible* because Koenig lookup does not find functions with explicit template parameters; the following code is correct:

```
template <typename T>
struct outer
{
   template <int N>
   struct inner
   {
      inner(void*) {}

      template <typename X>
      friend inner<N+1> combine(inner<N>, X x)
      { return inner<N+1>(&x); }
   };
};
```

```
outer<double>::inner<0> I;
combine(I, 0);
```

Instead, this example works only when `outer` is in the global scope, but not if it's enclosed in a namespace:

```
template <typename T>
struct outer
{
   template <typename S>
   struct inner
   {
      template <typename X>
      friend inner<X> my_cast(inner<S>)
      { return inner<X>(); }
   };
};
```

```
outer<double>::inner<int> I;
outer<double>::inner<float> F = my_cast<float>(I);
```

The only workaround for having a functional `my_cast` as above would be a static interface, with the base class at namespace level, but the required machinery is non-negligible:

```
// note: global scope

template <typename T, typename S>
struct inner_interface
{
};
```

```
namespace XYZ
{
   template <typename T>
   struct outer
   {
      template <typename S>
      struct inner : inner_interface<T, S>
      {
         inner(int = 0) {}
      };
   };
}
```

```
// note: global scope

template <typename X, typename T, typename S>
typename XYZ::outer<T>::template inner<X>
                                          my_cast(const inner_interface<T,S>& x)
{
   // cast x to outer<T>::inner<S> if necessary
   return 0;
}
```

Finally:

```
XYZ::outer<double>::inner<int> I;
my_cast<float>(I);
```

Obviously, `my_cast` could be simply a template member function of `inner`, but this may force clients to introduce a `template` keyword between the dot and the function name:

```
template <typename S>
struct inner
{
    template <typename X>
    inner<X> my_cast() const
    { return inner<X>(); }
};
```

```
outer<double>::inner<int> I;
outer<double>::inner<float> F = I.my_cast<float>();    // Ok.
```

```
template <typename T>
void f(outer<T>& o)
{
   o.get_inner().my_cast<float>(); // error: should be
                                   // o.get_inner().template my_cast<float>()
```

8. Code Generators

In this chapter we'll deal with templates that generate code that is partly static, partly executed at runtime.
Suppose we have to perform a simple comparison of powers

```
int x = ...;
if (3^4 < x^5 < 4^7)
```

Clearly, we would like to have static constants for 3^4 and 4^7, and a corresponding runtime powering algorithm to obtain x^5; however a call to `std::pow(x, 5)` may be suboptimal, since 5 is a compile time constant that might possibly be "embedded" in the call.
One of the goals of TMP is in fact to make the maximum information available to the compiler, so that it can take advantage of it.

8.1. Static code generators

Iteration can be used in a purely static context; recall here the repeated squaring algorithm from page 123:

```
template <size_t X, size_t Y>
struct static_raise;

template <size_t X> struct static_raise<X,2>
{ static const size_t value = X*X; };

template <size_t X> struct static_raise<X,1>
{ static const size_t value = X; };

template <size_t X> struct static_raise<X,0>
{ static const size_t value = 1; };

template <size_t X, size_t Y>
struct static_raise
{
   static const size_t v0 = static_raise<X, Y/2>::value;
   static const size_t value = ((Y % 2) ? X : 1U) * MXT_M_SQ(v0);
};
```

```
double data[static_raise<3, 4>::value];       // an array with 81 numbers
```

`static_raise` does not generate any code, only a compile-time result (namely, a numeric constant).

The same algorithm is now used to implement ***static code generation***: the static recursion generates a *function* for any specified value of the exponent.
We just have to assume that 1 is a valid scalar.

```
template <typename scalar_t, size_t N>
struct static_pow
{
   static inline scalar_t apply(const scalar_t& x)
   {
      return ((N % 2) ? x : 1) *
         static_pow<scalar_t, 2>::apply(static_pow<scalar_t, N/2>::apply(x));
   }
};

template <typename scalar_t>
struct static_pow<scalar_t, 2>
{
   static inline scalar_t apply(const scalar_t& x)
   { return x*x; }
};


template <typename scalar_t>
struct static_pow<scalar_t, 1>
{
   static inline scalar_t apply(const scalar_t& x)
   { return x; }
};


template <typename scalar_t>
struct static_pow<scalar_t, 0>
{
   static inline scalar_t apply(const scalar_t& x)
   { return 1; }
};
```

```
size_t x = 3;
size_t n = static_pow<size_t, 4>::apply(x);    // yields 81
```

Here template recursion does not produce a compile-time result, but a compile-time algorithm; in fact `static_pow` is a ***code generator template***.
Note also that we can avoid multiplication by 1, which is implied by the ternary operator:

```
template <typename scalar_t, size_t N>
struct static_pow
{
   static inline scalar_t apply(const scalar_t& x, selector<false>)
   {
      return static_pow<2>::apply(static_pow<N/2>::apply(x));
   }

   static inline scalar_t apply(const scalar_t& x, selector<true>)
   {
      return x*apply(x, selector<false>());
   }

   static inline scalar_t apply(const scalar_t& x)
   {
      return apply(x, selector<(N % 2)>());
   }
```

In particular, this code generator is ***strongly typed***: the user must specify in advance the argument type; this is not necessary for the algorithm to work properly, in fact a weaker version which deduces its arguments is fine too:

```
template <size_t N>
struct static_pow
{
   template <typename scalar_t>
      static inline scalar_t apply(const scalar_t& x)
   { … }
};

template <>
struct static_pow<2>
{
   template <typename scalar_t>
      static inline scalar_t apply(const scalar_t& x) { return x*x; }
};

// ...
```

The invocation of strongly typed templates is more verbose, since the user explicitly writes a type that could be deduced:

```
size_t x = 3;
size_t n1 = static_pow<size_t, 4>::apply(x);      // boring
size_t n2 = static_pow<4>::apply(x);              // nicer
```

However it sometimes pays to be explicit, as a cast on the argument is quite different from a cast of the result, because the code generator will produce an entirely new function:

```
double x1 = static_pow<double, 4>::apply(10000000);   // correct
double x2 = static_pow<4>::apply(10000000);           // wrong (it overflows)

double x3 = static_pow<4>::apply(10000000.0);         // correct again
```

Usually it's possible to code both a strong and a weak code generator at the same time, borrowing a trick from groups: move the weak generator in a partial specialization, which is recalled by the general template.

```
struct deduce
{
};

template <size_t N, typename scalar_t = deduce>
struct static_pow;
```

```
template <>
struct static_pow<2, deduce>
{
   template <typename scalar_t>
   static inline scalar_t apply(const scalar_t& x)
   { … }
};

template <size_t N>
struct static_pow<N, deduce>
{
   template <typename scalar_t>
   static inline scalar_t apply(const scalar_t& x)
   { … }
};
```

```
// primary template comes last

template <size_t N, typename scalar_t>
struct static_pow
{
   static inline scalar_t apply(const scalar_t& x)
   {
      return static_pow<N>::apply(x);
   }
};
```

Strict argument check is actually performed only by the primary template, which immediately calls the `deduce` specialization. The order of declarations matters: `static_pow<N, deduce>` will likely use `static_pow<2, deduce>`, so the latter must precede the former in source file.

8.2. Double-checked stop

Usually compile-time recursion is obtained having a template call 'itself' with a different set of template parameters. Actually there's no recursion at all, since a change in template parameters generates a different entity: what we get is static "loop unrolling".
The advantage of the static recursion is that explicitly unrolled code is easier to optimize.

The snippets below perform a vector-sum of two arrays of known length;

```
template <size_t N, typename T>
void vector_sum_LOOP(T* a, const T* b, const T* c)
{
   for (int i=0; i<N; ++i)
      a[i] = b[i] + c[i];
}
```

```
template <size_t N, typename T>
void vector_sum_EXPLICIT(T* a, const T* b, const T* c)
{
   a[0] = b[0] + c[0];
   a[1] = b[1] + c[1];
   // ...
   // assume that it's possible to generate exactly N of these lines
   // ...
   a[N-1] = b[N-1] + c[N-1];
}
```

The explicitly unrolled version will be faster for small N, because modern processors can execute some arithmetic/floating point operations in parallel, so even without specific optimizations from the compiler, the processor will perform the sums, say, four at a time.[138]
However for large N, the code would exceed the size of the processor cache, so the first version will be faster from some point on.
The ideal solution in fact would be a mixture of both:

[138] Usually this requires the additional assumption that a, b and c point to unrelated areas of memory. Modern optimizers however are more powerful than we even suspect.

```
static const int THRESHOLD = /* platform-dependent */;

template <size_t N, typename T>
void vector_sum(T* a, const T* b, const T* c)
{
    if (N>THRESHOLD)
    {
        int i=0;
        for (; (i+4)<N; i+=4)
        {
            a[i+0] = b[i+0] + c[i+0];       // --+
            a[i+1] = b[i+1] + c[i+1];       //   | the number of lines here
            a[i+2] = b[i+2] + c[i+2];       //   | is platform-dependent
            a[i+3] = b[i+3] + c[i+3];       // --+
        }
        for (; i<N; ++i)                    // residual loop
            a[i] = b[i] + c[i];
    }
    else
    {
        vector_sum_EXPLICIT<N>(a, b, c);
    }
}
```

The implementation above has a problem anyway: suppose `THRESHOLD` is 1000; when the compiler instantiates, say, `vector_sum<1000, double>` it wastes time generating 1000 lines which will never be called:

```
    if (true)
    {
        // ...
    }
    else
    {
        a[0] = b[0] + c[0];
        a[1] = b[1] + c[1];
        // ...
        a[999] = b[999] + c[999];
    }
```

To fix this issue, we add a *double check*:

```
    else
    {
        vector_sum_EXPLICIT<(N>THRESHOLD ? 1 : N)>(a, b, c);
    }
```

The double check is not simply an optimization: static recursion can yield an *unlimited* number of lines: assume again we have an array of length N and we need to fill it with consecutive integers.

We hope to be able to write a function template `integrize` whose call produces native machine code which is logically equivalent to:

```
    {
        data[0] = 0;
        data[1] = 1;
        // ...
        data[N-1] = N-1;
    }
```

But we guess that when N is very large, due to the effect of processor caches, the unrolled loop will generate a huge amount of bytes, whose mass will eventually slow down the execution.[139]

So we would like `integrize` to select a compile-time strategy or a run-time strategy:

```
template<typename T, int N>
void integrize(T (&data)[N])
{
    if (N<STATIC_LOWER_BOUND)
        integrize_helper<N>(data);
    else
        for (size_t i=0; i<N; ++i)
            data[i] = i;
}
```

First, we start with an incorrect function:

```
template <int N, typename T>
    void integrize(T* const data)
{
    data[N-1] = N-1;
    integrize<N-1>(data);
}
```

The recursion has no limit, so it will never compile successfully.

So we are tempted to make the following improvement:

```
template <int N, typename T>
    void integrize(T* const data)
{
    data[N-1] = N-1;
    if (N>1)
        zeroize<N-1>(data);
}
```

This version still doesn't work, since the compiler will produce a sequence of calls with unlimited depth. From some point on, the `if (N>1)` condition is always false, but it doesn't matter: such code would be pruned by the optimizer, but the compiler will complain and stop much earlier!

[139] This is commonly called code bloat.

```
    data[2-1] = 2-1;              // here N=2
    if (true)                     // 2>1?
    {                             // integrize<2-1>
        data[1-1] = 1-1;          // here N=1
        if (false)                // 1>1?
        {                         // integrize<1-1>
            data[0-1] = 0-1;      // here N=0
            if (false)            // 0>1?
            {
                ...
```

In other words, the compiler sees that `integrize<1>` depends on `integrize<0>`, hence the unlimited recursion (at compile time).
The ***double checked stop*** idiom is again the solution:

```
template <int N, typename T>
    void integrize(T* const data)
{
    data[N-1] = N-1;
    if (N>1)
        integrize<(N>1) ? N-1 : 1>(data);
}
```

Note the extra parentheses around N>1 (otherwise the ">" between N and 1 will be parsed as the angle bracket that closes the template).
Thanks to the double check, the compiler will expand code like this:

```
    data[2-1] = 2-1;              // here N=2
    if (true)                     // 2>0?
    {                             // integrize<2-1>
        data[1-1] = 1-1;          // here N=1
        if (1>1)
            call again integrize<1>
```

The expansion is finite, since `integrize<1>` mentions only itself (which is a well defined entity, not a new one) and the recursion stops. Of course `integrize<1>` will never call itself at runtime: the optimizer will streamline the `if (true)` branches and remove the last `if (false)`.

In general the double checked stop idiom prescribes to stop a recursion, mentioning a template that has been already instantiated (instead of a new one), but at the same time preventing its execution.

Finally, we apply again the idiom as an optimization against code bloat:

```
template<typename T, int N>
void integrize(T (&data)[N])
{
   if (N<STATIC_LOWER_BOUND)
      integrize_helper<(N<STATIC_LOWER_BOUND) ? N : 1>(data);
   else
      ...
}
```

8.3. Static and Dynamic hashing

Sometimes it's possible to share an algorithm between a static and a runtime implementation via kernel macros: the following example shows how to statically hash a string.

Assume as usual that a hash is an integer stored in a `size_t` and that we have a macro, taking "x", the old hash and a new character "c"; we list some possibilities:

```
#define MXT_HASH(x, c)        ((x) << 1) ^ (c)
#define MXT_HASH(x, c)        (x) + ((x) << 5) + (c)
#define MXT_HASH(x, c)        ((x) << 6) ^ ((x) & ((~size_t(0)) << 26)) ^ (c)
```

The hashing macros require that `c` is a positive number. We could replace `c` with `(c-CHAR_MIN)`, but this would make the hash platform-dependent: where `char` is signed, `'a'-CHAR_MIN` equals 97-(-128) = 225 and where `char` is unsigned, the same expression yields 97-0 = 97. Furthermore, the same text in a `std::string` and in a `std::wstring` should not return two different hash codes.

Given that we disregard what happens for non-ASCII characters, an elegant workaround is: cast `char` c to `unsigned char`.

Constants should not be hard-coded, but rather generated at compile-time.

We would like to replace classic code

```
const char* text = ...;
if (strcmp(text, "FIRST")==0)
{
   //...
}
else if (strcmp(text, "SECOND")==0)
{
   //...
}
else if (strcmp(text, "THIRD")==0)
{
   // ...
```

With something like:

```
const char* text = …;
switch (dynamic_hash(text))
{
   case static_hash<'F','I','R','S','T'>::value:
      // ...
      break;

   case static_hash<'S','E','C','O','N','D'>::value:
      // ...
      break;
```

- Hashing will save a lot of string comparisons, even if it could produce false positives[140]
- if `static_hash` produces duplicate values, the switch won't compile, so it will never produce false negatives (i.e. the words "FIRST", "SECOND"... will always be matched without ambiguities)

The static algorithm uses template rotation and a very neat implementation:

```
template
<
   char C0=0, char C1=0, char C2=0, char C3=0, char C4=0, …, char C23=0,
   size_t HASH = 0
>
struct static_hash
: static_hash<C1,C2…,C23,0, MXT_HASH(HASH, static_cast<unsigned char>(C0))>
{
};

template <size_t HASH>
struct static_hash<0,0,0,0,…,0, HASH> : static_value<size_t, HASH>
{
};
```

The only degree of freedom in `dynamic_hash` is the function signature.
Here's a fairly general one, with some plain old vanilla C tricks:

140 There are 26^N sequences of N letters, and "only" say 2^{64} different hash values, so for N>14 no hash can be injective; however if the algorithm is fair, conflicts are "scattered", so strings having the same hash are *really* different.

```
std::pair<size_t, const char*>
   dynamic_hash(const char* text, const char* separ = 0, const char* end = 0)
{
   size_t h = 0

   const char* const end1 = (separ ? text+strcspn(text, separ) : end);
   const char* const end2 = (end && end<end1) ? end : end1;

   while (end2 ? text<end2 : (*text != 0))
   {
      const size_t c = static_cast<unsigned char>(*(text++));
      h = MXT_HASH(crc, c);
   }
   return std::make_pair(h, text);
}
```

```
dynamic_hash(text);                    // hash all string, up to char(0)
dynamic_hash(text, ";,");              // hash up to any of the separators
dynamic_hash(text, ";,", text+10);     // hash up to separator, at most 10 chars
```

We chose to return a composite result, the hash value and the updated "iterator".

8.3.1. A function set for characters

The selection of the correct function set can be done either by a deduced template parameter (as seen in `string_traits`: paragraph 5.2.1), or by an environment template parameter.
A natural example is the problem of character set: some string-conversion functions can be accelerated, given that some set of characters, say `{'0', '1'...'9'}`, is contiguous: if `c` belongs to the set, we can convert `c` to integer via a simple `c - '0'`, but if the digit character set is arbitrarily scattered, a more complex implementation is needed.

We scan sets of characters with template rotation:

```
template
<
   typename char_t,
   char_t C0,
   char_t C1 = 0,
   char_t C2 = 0,
   // …
   char_t C9 = 0
>
struct is_contiguous
{
   static const bool value = (C0+1==C1) &&
                   is_contiguous<char_t,C1,C2,C3,C4,C5,C6,C7,C8,C9>::value;
};

template <char C0>
struct is_contiguous<char,C0>
{
   static const bool value = true;
};

template <wchar_t C0>
struct is_contiguous<wchar_t,C0>
{
   static const bool value = true;
};
```

Next, the result of a static test can be saved in a global traits structure:

```
struct ascii
{
static const bool value_lowerc =
 charset::is_contiguous<char, 'a','b','c','d','e','f','g','h','i','j'>::value
 &&
 charset::is_contiguous<char, 'j','k','l','m','n','o','p','q','r','s'>::value
 &&
 charset::is_contiguous<char, 's','t','u','v','w','x','y','z'>::value;

static const bool value_upperc =
 charset::is_contiguous<char, 'A','B','C','D','E','F','G','H','I','J'>::value
 &&
 charset::is_contiguous<char, 'J','K','L','M','N','O','P','Q','R','S'>::value
 &&
 charset::is_contiguous<char, 'S','T','U','V','W','X','Y','Z'>::value;

static const bool value_09 =
 charset::is_contiguous<char,'0','1','2','3','4','5','6','7','8','9'>::value;

static const bool value =
 value_09 && value_lowerc && value_upperc;
};
```

Suppose for the moment `ascii::value` is true; let's write a function set to deal with the special case:

```
template <typename T, T lower, T upper>
inline bool is_between(const T c)
{
   return !(c<lower) && !(upper<c);
}
```

```
struct ascii_traits
{
   typedef char char_type;

   static inline bool isupper(const char_type c)
   {
      return is_between<char,'A','Z'>(C);
   }

   static inline bool islower(const char_type c)
   {
      return is_between<char,'a','z'>(c);
   }

   static inline bool isalpha(const char_type c)
   {
      return islower(c) || isupper(c);
   }

   static inline bool isdigit(const char_type c)
   {
      return is_between<char,'0','9'>(c);
   }

   ...

   static inline char tolower(const char c)
   {
      return isupper(c) ? c-'A'+'a' : c;
   }

   static inline char toupper(const char c)
   {
      return islower(c) ? c-'a'+'A' : c;
   }
```

In a different implementation, we use `std::locale`

```
template <typename char_t>
struct stdchar_traits
{
   typedef char_t char_type;

   static inline bool isupper(const char_t c)
   {
      return std::isupper(c, locale());
   }

   static inline bool islower(const char_t c)
   {
      return std::islower(c, locale());
   }

   static inline bool isalpha(const char_t c)
   {
      return std::isalpha(c, locale());
   }

   static inline bool isdigit(const char_t c)
   {
      return std::isdigit(c, locale());
   }

   …

   static inline char_t tolower(const char_t c)
   {
      return std::tolower(c, std::locale());
   }

   static inline char_t toupper(const char_t c)
   {
      return std::toupper(c, std::locale());
   }
```

And eventually we combine these types:

```
struct standard {};
struct fast {};
```

```
template <typename char_t, typename charset_t = fast>
struct char_traits : stdchar_traits<char_t>
{};

template <>
struct char_traits<char, fast>
: typeif<ascii::value, ascii_traits, stdchar_traits<char> >::type
{};
```

The environment parameter `charset_t` is by default set to `fast`: if it's possible in current platform, the fast set is preferred; otherwise the standard set is used.[141]

[141] As an exercise, the reader might generalize the idea to `wchar_t`, which in the above implementation always picks the locale-based function set.

8.3.2. Changing case

We list some utilities to change the case of characters; first, let's introduce some tags: we'll consider "case sensitive" as a "no conversion" label.[142]

```
struct case_sensitive {};
struct upper_case {};
struct lower_case {};
```

We exploit the fact that `char_traits` offer a leveraged interface to mutate characters at runtime (the example is limited to `char`): the classic part of the work is a collection of functors.

```
template <typename mutation_t, typename traits_t = char_traits<char> >
struct change_case;

template <typename traits_t>
struct change_case<case_sensitive, traits_t>
{
   typedef typename traits_t::char_type char_type;

   char_type operator()(const char_type c) const
   {
      return c;
   }
};

template <typename traits_t>
struct change_case<lower_case, traits_t>
{
   typedef typename traits_t::char_type char_type;

   char_type operator()(const char_type c) const
   {
      return traits_t::tolower(c);
   }
};

template <typename traits_t>
struct change_case<upper_case, traits_t>
{
   typedef typename traits_t::char_type char_type;

   char_type operator()(const char_type c) const
   {
      return traits_t::toupper(c);
   }
};
```

```
std::string s = "this is a lower case string";
std::transform(s.begin(), s.end(), s.begin(), change_case<upper_case>());
```

Now we move to the analogous conversion at compile time.

[142] The motivation will be evident when we'll show an application to string hashing, later in the paragraph.

```
template <typename case_t, char C, bool FAST = ascii::value>
struct static_change_case;
```

`FAST` is a hidden parameter; regardless of its value, a case-sensitive conversion should do nothing:

```
template <char C, bool FAST>
struct static_change_case<case_sensitive, C, FAST>
{
   static const char value = C;
};
```

If `FAST` is true, the transformation is trivial. If `FAST` is false, unfortunately, every character that can change case needs its own specialization: macros will save a lot of typing here.

```
template <char C>
struct static_change_case<lower_case, C, true>
{
   static const char value = ((C>='A' && C<='Z') ? C-'A'+'a' : C);
};

template <char C>
struct static_change_case<upper_case, C, true>
{
   static const char value = ((C>='a' && C<='z') ? C-'a'+'A' : C);
};
```

```
template <char C>
struct static_change_case<lower_case, C, false>
{
   static const char value = C;        // a generic char has no case
};

template <char C>
struct static_change_case<upper_case, C, false>
{
   static const char value = C;        // a generic char has no case
};
```

```
#define mxt_STATIC_CASE_GENERIC(C_LO, C_UP)                              \
                                                                         \
template <> struct static_change_case<lower_case, C_UP, false>           \
{ static const char value = C_LO; };                                     \
                                                                         \
template <> struct static_change_case<upper_case, C_LO, false>           \
{ static const char value = C_UP; }
```

```
mxt_STATIC_CASE_GENERIC('a', 'A');
mxt_STATIC_CASE_GENERIC('b', 'B');
...
mxt_STATIC_CASE_GENERIC('z', 'Z');
```

```
#undef mxt_STATIC_CASE_GENERIC
```

This has an immediate application to both `static_hash` and `dynamic_hash` As usual, the macro is merely for convenience: note that we introduce a non-deduced template parameter in

```
#define mxt_FIRST_CHAR(c)           \
      static_cast<unsigned char>(static_change_case<case_t, C>::value)

template
<
   typename case_t,
   char C0=0, char C1=0, char C2=0, char C3=0, char C4=0, …, char C23=0,
   size_t HASH = 0
>
struct static_hash
: static_hash<case_t,C1,C2,…,C23,0, MXT_HASH(HASH, mxt_FIRST_CHAR(C0))>
{
};

template <typename case_t, size_t HASH>
struct static_hash<case_t,0,0,0,0,…,0, HASH> : static_value<size_t, HASH>
{
};
```

```
template <typename case_t>
inline … dynamic_hash(const char* text, …)
{
   const change_case<case_t> CHANGE;
   size_t h = 0;
   const char* const end1 = (separ ? text+strcspn(text, separ) : end);
   const char* const end2 = (end && end<end1) ? end : end1;

   while (end2 ? text<end2 : (*text != 0))
   {
      const size_t c = static_cast<unsigned char>(CHANGE(*(text++)));
      h = MXT_HASH(crc, c);
   }
   return std::make_pair(h, text);
}
```

Such a modified algorithm will alter the case of a string *inside the computation* of the hash value, so an "upper case hash" is effectively a case-insensitive value:

```
switch (dynamic_hash<upper_case>(text).first)
{
   case static_hash<'F','I','R','S','T'>::value:
      // will match "First", "FIRST", "first", "fiRST"…
      break;
```

8.3.3. Mimesis techniques

We rewrite the `dynamic_hash` using mimesis techniques: in the new prototype `end` is not optional, so we shall provide more overloads to get a flexible syntax, as for the original C version:

```
template <typename case_t, typename iterator_t, typename end_t>
std::pair<size_t, iterator_t>
                dynamic_hash(iterator_t begin, const end_t end, size_t h = 0)
{
   typedef typename std::iterator_traits<iterator_t>::value_type char_t;
   const change_case< case_t, char_traits<char_t> > CHANGE;

   while (end != begin)
   {
      const size_t c = static_cast<unsigned char>(CHANGE(*(begin++)));
      h = MXT_HASH(crc, c);
   }
   return std::make_pair(h, begin);
}
```

```
template <typename case_t, typename iterator_t>
inline std::pair<size_t, iterator_t>
                       dynamic_hash(iterator_t begin, size_t h = 0)
{
   return dynamic_hash(begin, c_string_end<iterator_t>(), h);
}
```

We can plug-in some useful mimesis-like objects:[143]

```
template <typename char_t, char_t CLOSE_TAG>
struct stop_at
{
   template <typename iterator_t>
      inline bool operator!=(const iterator_t i) const
   {
      return (*i != 0) && (*i != CLOSE_TAG);
   }
};
```

```
size_t h = dynamic_hash<case_insensitive>(text, stop_at<char, ';'>()).first;
```

```
template <bool (*funct)(const char), bool NEGATE>
struct apply_f
{
   template <typename iterator_t>
      inline bool operator!=(const iterator_t i) const
   {
      return funct(*i) ^ NEGATE;
   }
};

typedef apply_f<char_traits<char>::isspace, true> end_of_word;
typedef apply_f<char_traits<char>::isalpha, false> all_alpha;
```

[143] There's no need for a complete mimesis implementation: cast is not needed.

`end_of_word` stops at the first space, and `all_alpha` stops at the first non-alphabetical character.

8.3.4. Ambiguous overloads

The evolution of the `dynamic_hash` led us to add more template parameters and more overloads. We need to be careful not to cause compilation problems because of ***ambiguous overload*** resolution.

The exact overload resolution rules are described in appendix B of [2], but we sketch here a roughly summary.
When the compiler meets a function call, it must pick, from the set of all functions with the same name, the most specialized that suits, if any; if we have several function templates named F, we'll denote them as F[1], F[2]... F[1] is considered more specialized than F[2] if F[2] could be used wherever F[1] is used, with an exact argument match, but not vice versa.
For example:

```
template <typename T1, typename T2>
void F(T1 a, T2 b);

template <typename T>
void F(T a, T b);

template <typename T>
void F(T a, int b);
```

The second template F[2] is more specialized than F[1], because the call `F(X, X)` can refer to either, but only the first matches exactly `F(X, Y)`. Similarly F[3] is more specialized than F[1].
However this is a partial ordering criterion: if no function is more specialized than the other(s), the compiler will abort, reporting an ambiguous overload. In fact F[2] and F[3] are not comparable: F[3] will not match exactly `F(X, X)` and F[2] will not match exactly `F(X, int)`.[144]

```
    int z = 2;
    F(z, z);        // error
```

Informally, an easy unambiguous special case is total replacement: if a template parameter is completely replaced by fixed types or previous template parameters, then the resulting function is more specialized than the original; take F[1], replace

[144] Another common error is the argument crossover: suppose a class C has two template parameters T1 and T2; if we partially specialize `C<T1, Y>` and `C<X, T2>` for some fixed X and Y, then `C<X,Y>` is ambiguous, so it must be explicitly specialized too.

every occurrence of `T2` with `T1`, and obtain F[2]; replace `T2` with `int`, and obtain F[3].

A library writer usually provides a set of overloads, where one or more elements are function templates; one of the problems, often underestimated or ignored, is to decide in advance if the set is *well-ordered*. A well-ordered set will never generate ambiguity errors.
The combination of default arguments and templates often makes deduction very hard.

```
template <typename case_t, typename iterator_t, typename end_t>
… dynamic_hash(iterator_t begin, const end_t end, size_t crc = 0);

template <typename case_t, typename iterator_t>
… dynamic_hash(iterator_t begin, size_t crc = 0);
```

To determine if this set is well-ordered, we need only to consider the case of a call with 2 arguments, and it's evident that the total replacement condition holds (replace `end_t` with `size_t`).
However, note that `dynamic_hash(T, int)` will invoke `dynamic_hash[1]`

```
dynamic_hash(text, 123);    // invokes (1) [with end_t = int]
```

Obviously, a user-friendly library will try to avoid these ambiguities, first using additional types:

```
struct hash_type
{
   size_t value;

   hash_type() : value(0) {}
   explicit hash_type(const size_t c) : value(c) {}
};

template <typename case_t, typename iterator_t, typename end_t>
[[…]] dynamic_hash(iterator_t begin, end_t end, hash_type h = hash_type());

template <typename case_t, typename iterator_t>
[[…]] dynamic_hash(iterator_t begin, hash_type h = hash_type());
```

While this does not change the way the compiler picks functions, it will make the error more evident to the user, because now `dynamic_hash(text, 123)` is a documented invalid call.

```
dynamic_hash(text, hash_type(123));       // this instead is correct
```

A radical change instead is obtained wrapping the original return type in a `typename only_if<[[condition]], ...>::type` clause (cfr. page 207).

```
template <typename T1, typename T2>
struct different : selector<true>
{};

template <typename T>
struct different<T, T> : selector<false>
{};

template <typename case_t, typename iterator_t, typename end_t>
typename only_if<different<end_t, hash_type>::value, [[...]]>::type
  dynamic_hash(iterator_t begin, const end_t end, hash_type h = hash_type());
```

Suppose finally we add back the C version:

```
template <typename case_t>
… dynamic_hash(const char* text, const char* const separator = 0,
                    const char* const end = 0, size_t h = 0)
```

This function, as is, can generate an ambiguous call: `dynamic_hash(const char*)` matches either `dynamic_hash[2]` (with `iterator_t = const char*`) or `dynamic_hash[3]`; the error depends on both functions being templates, because of `case_t`: had `dynamic_hash[3]` been a classic function, it would have been picked with higher priority.
To avoid the problem, remove default arguments to `separator` and `end`.

8.3.5. Algorithm I/O

We let `dynamic_hash` return a pair, containing the updated iterator position and the hash value.
Often the user will need to store the result, just to split it:

```
std:pair<size_t, const char*> p = dynamic_hash(text);
text = p.second;
switch (p.first)
{
   ...
}
```

This can be boring, especially if the iterator has a long type.[145]

The new keyword `auto` in C++0x would help:

[145] The problem actually falls under the opaque type principle: if the return type of a function is "complex", we should either publish a convenient typedef to the user, or allow to use the object ignoring its type at all (refer to chapter 10 for more details)

```
auto p = dynamic_hash(text);
```

Note that `auto` cannot refer to a part of an object:

```
std::pair<auto, const char*> p = dynamic_hash(text);
```

We could take an iterator by reference and update it, but this is not a fair solution, as it forces the caller to duplicate the iterator, if he wants to save the original value. Instead we modify the return type: it will be an object conceptually similar to a pair, with the option to overwrite a reference with the result:

```
template <typename iterator_t>
struct dynamic_hash_result
{
   size_t value;
   iterator_t end;

   dynamic_hash_result(const size_t v, const iterator_t i)
      : value(v), end(i)
   {
   }

   dynamic_hash_result& operator>>(iterator_t& i)
   {
      i = end;
      return *this;
   }
};
```

Then we replace `std::make_pair(...)` with `dynamic_hash_result(...)`.

The final function call is indeed compact: it updates `text` and returns the hash at the same time; additionally, the `.value` suffix reminds of `static_hash<>::value`. Of course, more variations are possible.[146]

```
switch ((dynamic_hash(text) >> text).value)
{
   case static_hash<'a','b','c'>::value:
   …
}
```

8.3.6. Mimesis interface

Mimesis objects are lightweight objects, conceptually similar to functors, but whose expressivity is close to a scalar. Since they are indeed instantiated, we shall investigate the possibility of combining them with operators:

[146] As follows from the opaque type principle, it's not necessary to document what the exact return type is: just state that it works like a `std::pair`, with an extra `operator>>`. In principle, it would be reasonable to add a conversion operator from `dynamic_hash_result` to `std::pair<size_t, iterator_t>`.

```
size_t h = dynamic_hash<case_insensitive>(text,
                        stop_at<char, ';'>() || stop_at<char, ','>());
```

This is exactly work for a static interface:[147]

```
template <typename static_type>
class hash_end_type
{
public:

   const static_type& true_this() const
   {
      return static_cast<const static_type&>(*this);
   }

   template <typename iterator_t>
      inline bool operator!=(const iterator_t i) const
   {
      return true_this() != i;
   }
};
```

```
template <bool (*funct)(const char), bool NEGATE>
struct apply_f : public hash_end_type< apply_f<funct, NEGATE> >
{
   template <typename iterator_t>
      inline bool operator!=(const iterator_t i) const
   {
      return funct(*i) ^ NEGATE;
   }
};


template <typename char_t, char_t CLOSE_TAG>
struct stop_at : public hash_end_type< stop_at<char_t, CLOSE_TAG> >
{
   template <typename iterator_t>
      inline bool operator!=(const iterator_t i) const
   {
      return (*i != CLOSE_TAG);
   }
};

...
```

Having all objects inherit the same interface, we can define a "combo type" and logic operators:

[147] Since there's a single function in the class, we do not derive from `static_interface`, but we replicate the code.

```
struct logic_AND {};
struct logic_OR {};

template <typename T1, typename T2, typename LOGICAL_OP>
class hash_end_type_combo
: public hash_end_type< hash_end_type_combo<T1, T2, LOGICAL_OP> >
{
   T1 t1_;
   T2 t2_;

public:

   hash_end_type_combo(const T1& t1, const T2& t2)
      : t1_(t1), t2_(t2)
   {
   }

   template <typename iterator_t>
      inline bool operator!=(const iterator_t i) const
   {
      return combine(i, LOGICAL_OP());
   }

private:

   template <typename iterator_t>
      bool combine(const iterator_t i, logic_AND) const
   {
      return (t1_ != i) && (t2_ != i);
   }

   template <typename iterator_t>
      bool combine(const iterator_t i, logic_OR) const
   {
      return (t1_ != i) || (t2_ != i);
   }
};
```

```
template <typename K1, typename K2>
inline hash_end_type_combo<K1, K2, logic_AND>
   operator&& (const hash_end_type<K1>& k1, const hash_end_type<K2>& k2)
{
   return
     hash_end_type_combo<K1, K2, logic_AND>(k1.true_this(), k2.true_this());
}

template <typename K1, typename K2>
inline hash_end_type_combo<K1, K2, logic_OR>
   operator|| (const hash_end_type<K1>& k1, const hash_end_type<K2>& k2)
{
   return
     hash_end_type_combo<K1, K2, logic_OR>(k1.true_this(), k2.true_this());
}
```

Note the counter-intuitive use of the operation tag: we may be tempted to replace `logic_AND` with an "active tag", such as `std::logical_and<bool>`, drop entirely `combine` and just use the tag as a function call to produce the result:

```
template <typename iterator_t>
   inline bool operator!=(const iterator_t i) const
{
   return LOGICAL_OP()(t1_ != i, t2_ != i);
}
```

This is *incorrect*, as it would blow short-circuit.

```
size_t h = dynamic_hash<case_insensitive>(text,
         stop_at<char, ';'>() || stop_at<char, ','>() || stop_at<char, 0>());
```

Note also that, for maniac-level efficiency, we removed the check for null char in `stop_at`: now it has to be added explicitly, but it's performed only once.
The syntax above is an example of *lambda expression*, which is the main topic of section 10.2.

8.4. N-th minimum

We give a step-by-step example of implementation of a simple recursive compile-time function that involves a data structure.
We write a container `nth_min<T, N>`; an instance of this container receives values of type `T`, one at a time[148], via an `insert` member function, and it can be asked for the smallest N elements met so far.
For a reason to be discussed later, we'll impose the extra requirement that the container should not allocate its workspace from dynamic memory.

```
template <typename scalar_t, size_t N>
class nth_min
{
   scalar_t data_[N];

public:

   void insert(const scalar_t& x)
   {
      update(data_, x);
   }

   const scalar_t& operator[](const size_t i) const
   {
      return data_[i];
   }
};
```

[148] This is an *online* problem; in *offline* problems, all the input values are given at the same time. There's a data structure by David Eppstein (see: http://www.ics.uci.edu/~eppstein/pubs/kbest.html) that solves the online problem using memory proportional to N and exhibits amortized constant time operations, but here we focus on how to improve a naive implementation, not on an efficient algorithm.

In the following paragraphs we'll produce a suitable `update` function.[149]

```
template <typename scalar_t, int N>
inline void update(scalar_t (&data)[N], const scalar_t& x)
{
   // now N is known, start iterations here
}
```

First, we need to visualize the algorithm in recursive form. Assume as induction hypothesis that `data_` contains the `N` smallest values met so far, in ascending order.

```
if (x ≥ data_[N-1])
     // x is not in the N minima
     discard x and return;
else
     // here x < data_[N-1], so
     // data_[N-1] will be replaced either by x or by data_[N-2]
     if (x ≥ data_[N-2])
          data_[N-1] = x and return;
     else
          data_[N-1] = data_[N-2];
          if (x ≥ data_[N-3])
               data_[N-2] = x and return;
          else
               data_[N-2] = data_[N-3];
               ...
```

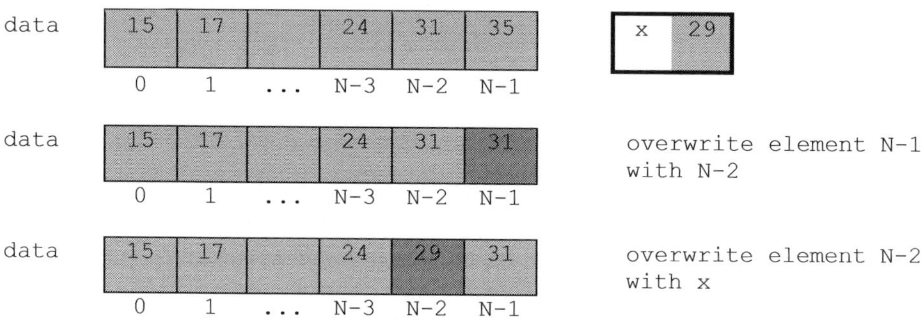

Now observe that "discard x" is equivalent to "write x in the non-existent position N". We factor out the write operation using a custom selector:

[149] Here `update` and its auxiliary subroutines are global functions; this just makes illustration easier, because it allows to focus on one feature at a time. The reader may safely declare all these functions as private static members of the container.

```
template <int N>
struct nth
{
};
```

```
template <typename scalar_t, int N, int SIZE>
void write(scalar_t (&data)[SIZE], const scalar_t& x, nth<N>)
{
   data[N] = x;
}

template <typename scalar_t, int SIZE>
void write(scalar_t (&data)[SIZE], const scalar_t& x, nth<SIZE>)
{
}
```

The second overload uses the dimension of the array; so `write(data, x, nth<I>())` actually means "write x in the I-th position of array data, if possible, otherwise do nothing".
This small abstraction permits to extend the same recursive pattern to the whole algorithm:

```
if (x ≥ data_[N-1])
    // x is not in the N minima
    data_[N] = x and return;
else
    if (x ≥ data_[N-2])
        data_[N-1] = x and return;
    else
        ...
```

```
template <typename scalar_t, int N, int SIZE>
void iterate(scalar_t (&data)[SIZE], const scalar_t& x, nth<N>)
{
   if (x < data[N])
   {
      data[N] = data[N-1];
      iterate(data, x, nth<N-1>());
   }
   else
   {
      write(data, x, nth<N+1>());        // write x at position N+1
   }
}
```

Next, we have to write an iteration terminator. The easiest option, to begin with, is to identify which template parameters become meaningless: when `N==0`, `data[N-1]` is for sure not well-formed, so we specialize/overload the case where `N` is zero: in fact, if we have to track down only the smallest element of the sequence, there's no shift involved:

```
template <typename scalar_t, int SIZE>
void iterate(scalar_t (&data)[SIZE], const scalar_t& x, nth<0>)
{
   // here N=0, after this point, stop iterations
   // if x is less than minimum, keep x, else discard it

   if (x < data[0])
      data[0] = x;
   else
      write(data, x, nth<1>());
}
```

The else branch cannot be omitted, but if `SIZE` is 1, the optimizing compiler will wipe it out.
Finally, the recursion starts backwards, on the last element of the array, so we pass `N-1`:

```
template <typename scalar_t, int N>
void update(scalar_t (&data)[N], const scalar_t& x)
{
   iterate(data, x, nth<N-1>());
}
```

What's not elegant in the implementation above is that `iterate<0>` contains duplicated code from `iterate<N>`; the most elegant solution would end with an empty function.
Another generalization is needed: all write operations involve either a shift `data[K] = data[K-1]` or the insertion `data[K] = x`, respecting array bounds.
Can a single function template represent both?
Yes, if we are able to identify x with an element of data and specify only the index of the element to pick:

```
template <typename scalar_t, int N, int SIZE, int J>
void write(scalar_t (&data)[SIZE], const scalar_t& x, nth<N>, nth<J>)
{
   data[N] = data[J];
}

template <typename scalar_t, int SIZE, int J>
void write(scalar_t (&data)[SIZE], const scalar_t& x, nth<SIZE>, nth<J>)
{
}
```

If we compare the instructions `data[K] = data[K-1]` and `data[0] = x` from the implementation above, we see that x is naturally identified with `data[-1]`.
So we add two more specializations:

```
template <typename scalar_t, int N, int SIZE>
void write(scalar_t (data&)[SIZE], const scalar_t& x, nth<N>, nth<-1>)
{
   data[N] = x;
}

template <typename scalar_t, int SIZE>
void write(scalar_t (data&)[SIZE], const scalar_t& x, nth<SIZE>, nth<-1>)
{
}
```

To sum up, `write(data, x, N, J)` is a complicated way to say `data[N] = data[J]`; `N` and `J` are selectors, not integers; as usual, the function deduces the length of the array, so out-of-bounds accesses become no-ops.

```
template <typename scalar_t, int N, int SIZE>
void iterate(scalar_t (data&)[SIZE], const scalar_t& x, nth<N>)
{
   if (x < data[N])
   {
      write(data, x, nth<N>(), nth<N-1>());
      iterate(data, x, nth<N-1>());
   }
   else
   {
      write(data, x, nth<N+1>(), nth<-1>());    // line #1
   }
}

template <typename scalar_t, int SIZE>
void iterate(scalar_t (data&)[SIZE], const scalar_t& x, nth<-1>)
{
}
```

When `N=0` in the code above, `write` translates to `data[0] = x`, as required and iteration -1 is empty.
Note that we pay the price of generality in line 1, which is rather unclear at first sight, since we have to explicitly use `nth<-1>` to access x.

If N is large, the fastest algorithm would possibly store objects in a large chunk of memory, and sort them when necessary, with a pure-runtime strategy:
In the worst case, if K is the number of items inserted, execution time is proportional to K·N for the static version, but for small values of N and simple POD types (i.e. when `operator<` and assignment do not have significant overhead), the static version will usually perform faster, due to its compactness and absence of hidden constants.[150]

---

[150] It seems that this kind of "greedy compact style" for small values of N gets most benefit from an aggressive optimizing compiler; a primitive stress test with 10.000.000 insertions and N<32 showed a very large runtime difference (30-40%) between a "normal" and an "extreme" release build. Greedy algorithms and compact code take advantage of technological factors, such as processor caches.

Finally, we can replace the `write` function call, whose hidden meaning is an assignment, with a real assignment: just use a proxy

```
struct null_reference
{
   template <typename scalar_t>
   null_reference& operator= (const scalar_t&)
   {
      return *this;
   }
};
```

```
template <int K>
struct nth
{
   template <typename scalar_t, int SIZE>
   static scalar_t& element(scalar_t (&data)[SIZE], const scalar_t& x)
   {
      return data[K];
   }

   template <typename scalar_t>
   static null_reference element(scalar_t (&data)[K], const scalar_t& x)
   {
      return null_reference();
   }
};

template <>
struct nth<0>
{
   template <typename scalar_t, int SIZE>
   static scalar_t& element(scalar_t (&data)[SIZE], const scalar_t& x)
   {
      return data[0];
   }
};

template <>
struct nth<-1>
{
   template <typename scalar_t, int SIZE>
   static const scalar_t& element(scalar_t (&data)[SIZE], const scalar_t& x)
   {
      return x;
   }
};
```

```
struct nth_min
{
   template <typename scalar_t, int SIZE>
      static void update(scalar_t (&data)[SIZE], const scalar_t& x)
   {
      iterate(data, x, nth<SIZE-1>());
   }

private:

   template <typename scalar_t, int N, int SIZE>
      static void iterate(scalar_t (&data)[SIZE], const scalar_t& x, nth<N>)
   {
      if (x < data[N])
      {
         nth<N>::element(data, x) = nth<N-1>::element(data, x);
         iterate(data, x, nth<N-1>());
      }
      else
      {
         nth<N+1>::element(data, x) = nth<-1>::element(data, x);
      }
   }

   template <typename scalar_t, int SIZE>
      static void iterate(scalar_t (&data)[SIZE], const scalar_t& x, nth<-1>)
   {
   }
};
```

8.5. The template factory pattern

Templates are good at taking compile-time decisions, but all programs need to take run-time decisions.

The ***factory pattern*** solves the run-time decision problem via polymorphism: an isolated function, called the *factory*, embeds all the logic and returns a pointer to a dynamically-created object, which drives the program flow with its virtual member function calls:

```
class abstract_task
{
   public:
      virtual void do_it() = 0;

      virtual ~abstract_task()
      {
      }
};

class first_task : public abstract_task
{
   public:
      first_task(/* parameters */)
      {
         // …
      }

      virtual void do_it()
      {
         // …
      }
};
```

```
enum task_type
{
   FIRST_TASK, SECOND_TASK, THIRD_TASK
};

abstract_task* factory(task_type t)
{
   switch (t)
   {
      case FIRST_TASK:   return new first_task(…);
      case SECOND_TASK:  return new second_task(…);
      case THIRD_TASK:   return new third_task(…);
      default:           return 0;
   }
}
```

```
int main()
{
   task_type t = ask_user();
   abstract_task* a = factory(t);
   a->do_it();

   delete a;
   return 0;
}
```

Note that the only `switch…case` construct, i.e. the link between the user choice and the program flow, is hidden inside the factory.

As expected, templates have no exact equivalent, but the following pattern is definitely similar:

```
template <typename TASK_T>
void do_the_work(TASK_T task)
{
   task.loadParameters(...);
   task.run();
   task.writeResult(...);
}

enum task_type
{
   FIRST_TASK, SECOND_TASK, THIRD_TASK
};

void factory(task_type t)
{
   first_task t1;
   second_task t2;
   third_task t3;

   switch (t)
   {
      case FIRST_TASK:   do_the_work(t1); break;
      case SECOND_TASK:   do_the_work(t2); break;
      case THIRD_TASK:   do_the_work(t3); break;
      default:            throw some_exception();
   }
}
```

The function `do_the_work` is an example of ***static polymorphism***: the usage of an object determines its interface, and vice versa, every static type for which the syntax is valid, is automatically usable.

This approach offers the advantage of a unified workflow: there's a single function to debug and maintain; obviously, having three overloads of `do_the_work`, would minimize this benefit.

Here's another example: a function that takes an array and computes either the sum or the product of all elements.

```
enum compute_type { SUM, MULTIPLY };

double do_the_work(compute_type t, const double* data, size_t length)
{
   switch (t)
   {
      case SUM:
      return std::accumulate(data,data+length,0.0);

      case MULTIPLY:
      return std::accumulate(data,data+length,1.0,std::multiplies<double>());

      default:
      throw some_exception();
   }
}
```

We want to rework the code so that it takes numbers from a given text file and performs the requested operation on all elements, and all computations should be performed with a user-supplied precision.
This requires a *multi-layer template factory*: roughly speaking, we have N function templates; the K-th function has N-K arguments and K template parameters, and it uses a switch block to branch execution to one of the possible (K+1)th functions.

```
enum result_type { SUM, MULTIPLY };
enum data_type { FLOAT, DOUBLE };
```

```
template <typename T>
T factory_LAYER3(result_type t, const std::vector<T>& data)
{
   switch (t)
   {
   case SUM:
   return std::accumulate(data.begin(),data.end(),T(0));

   case MULTIPLY:
   return std::accumulate(data.begin(),data.end(),T(1),std::multiplies<T>());

   default:
   throw some_exception();
   }
}
```

```
template <typename T>
T factory_LAYER2(result_type t, std::istream& i)
{
   std::vector<T> data;

   std::copy(std::istream_iterator<T>(i), std::istream_iterator<T>(),
      std::back_inserter(data));

   return factory_LAYER3(t, data);
}
```

```
double ML_factory(result_type t, data_type d, const char* filename)
{
   std::ifstream i(filename);

   switch (d)
   {
      case FLOAT:
         return factory_LAYER2<float>(t, i);
      case DOUBLE:
         return factory_LAYER2<double>(t, i);
      default:
         throw some_exception();
   }
}
```

The hardest design problem in template factories is usually *the type of the result*. Here the code silently exploits the fact that all functions return a result convertible to double.

8.6. Automatic enumeration of types

It's possible to exploit the `__LINE__` macro to create some easily extensible collections of types, which can be accessed as some sort of enumerations.

Consider the following prototype:

```
template <int N>
struct single_value : selector<false>
{
};

template <>
struct single_value<128>          // terminator, equivalent to max size
{
};

//////////////////////////////////////////////////////////////////////////////

template <>
struct single_value<7> : selector<true>        // user supplied case #1
{
};

template <>
struct single_value<13> : selector<true>       // user supplied case #2
{
};

// ...
```

We will write a template class `enum_hunter` that maps indices to user-supplied cases, so that `enum_hunter<1>` derives from `single_value<7>`, `enum_hunter<2>` from `single_value<13>`, and new cases can be easily added to the list.
The key concept in the code is as follows:

- Since a default implementation is given, any `single_value<N>` exists; user-supplied specialization have their `::value == true`
- `enum_hunter<N>` must inspect all `single_value<J>`, starting at J==0, until it finds the N-th user-supplied value
- `enum_hunter<N>` is actually `enum_hunter<N, 0>`
- `enum_hunter<N, J>` inspects `single_value<J>::value`; if it's false, it inherits from `enum_hunter<N, J+1>`, otherwise from `enum_hunter<N-1, J+1>` (except when N-1 would be zero, where we pick `<0, J>`)
- if N is too large, then eventually J will reach the terminator (say, 128), and since the corresponding class is empty, the compiler will complain.

All of this yields to a very short implementation (at the moment we ignore the fact that everything is hardcoded):

```
template <int N, int J=0>
struct enum_hunter
: enum_hunter<N-single_value<J>::value, J+1-(N == single_value<J>::value)>
{
};

template <int N>
struct enum_hunter<0, N> : single_value<N>
{
};

template <>
struct enum_hunter<0, 0> : single_value<0>
{
};
```

This skeleton technique can lead to a couple of different applications: the simplest is to build a sparse compile-time array between arbitrary (but small) integers and types:

```
#define MXT_ADD_ENUMERATION(N, TYPE)   \
template <> struct single_value<N> : public TYPE, selector<true> {}
```

```
struct Mapped1
{
  static double do_it() { return 3.14; }
};

struct Mapped2
{
  static double do_it() { return 6.28; }
};
```

```
MXT_ADD_ENUMERATION(7, Mapped1);
MXT_ADD_ENUMERATION(13, Mapped2);
```

```
double xx1 = enum_hunter<1>::do_it();   // == 3.14
double xx2 = enum_hunter<2>::do_it();   // == 6.28
```

Observe that 7 and 13 in the example above are not needed, except for their ordering. So we can just replace them with `__LINE__`.
Polishing up the macros, we parameterize the name of `enum_hunter` as ENUM and rename `single_value` as ENUM##2.

```
#define MXT_BEGIN_ENUMERATION(ENUM)                                          \
                                                                             \
template <int N> struct ENUM##2 : selector<false> {};                        \
                                                                             \
template <int N, int J=0> struct ENUM                                        \
: ENUM<N - ENUM##2<J>::value, J + 1 - (N == ENUM##2<J>::value)> {};         \
                                                                             \
template <int N> struct ENUM<0, N> : ENUM##2<N> {};                         \
                                                                             \
template <> struct ENUM<0, 0> : ENUM##2<0> {}
```

```
#define MXT_END_ENUMERATION(ENUM)     template <> struct ENUM##2 <__LINE__> {}
```

```
#define MXT_ADD_ENUMERATION(ENUM, TYPE)  \
template <> struct ENUM##2<__LINE__> : TYPE, selector<true> { }
```

When using the macros, every directive in the sequence between begin/end will be added automatically using line numbers as a progressive index; two directives on the same line won't compile, since you cannot specialize a class template twice.

```
MXT_BEGIN_ENUMERATION(enum_hunter);

MXT_ADD_ENUMERATION(enum_hunter, Mapped1);  // this gets index 1
MXT_ADD_ENUMERATION(enum_hunter, Mapped2);  // this gets index 2

MXT_END_ENUMERATION(enum_hunter);
```

8.7. If-less code

Sometimes program logic can be embedded in "smart objects" that just know what to do, thus eliminating the need for if/switch blocks.

8.7.1. Smart constants

Consider the following example: we need to code a suitable print function for a date class:

```
class date
{
   public:
      int day() const;
      int month() const;
      int year() const;
};

enum dateformat_t
{
   YYYYMMDD,
   YYMMDD,
   DDMMYYYY,
   // many more...
};

void print(date d, dateformat_t f)
{
   switch (f)
   {
      case YYYYMMDD:
         // boring...
```

Instead we can write branch-free code: as usual, TMP techniques take advantage from storing information in places where it's not even evident that meaningful data may be stored!

Suppose the format constants like YYYYMMDD are actually numbers with 6 decimal digits of the form `[f1 e1 f2 e2 f3 e3]`, where `fi` is the index of the "date field to print" (say, 0=year, 1=month and 2=day) and `ei` is the width as a number of digits.
For example 041222 would be "year with 4 digits, month with 2 digits, day with 2 digits", or simply `YYYY-MM-DD`; this would enable us to write:

```
const int pow10[] = { 1, 10, 100, 1000, 10000, ... };
const int data[3] = { d.year(), d.month(), d.day() };
const char* sep[] = { "-", "-", "" );

for (int i=0; i<3; ++i)
   std::cout << std::setw(e[i]) << (data[f[i]] % pow10[e[i]]) << sep[i];
```

Generating such constants is easy:

```
enum { Y, M, D };
```

```
template <unsigned F, unsigned W = 2>
struct datefield : static_value<unsigned, F*10 + (W % 10)>
{
};
```

```
template <typename T1, typename T2 = void, typename T3 = void>
struct dateformat
{
   static const unsigned pow10
                        = 100 * dateformat<T2,T3>::pow10;
   static const unsigned value
                        = pow10 * T1::value + dateformat<T2,T3>::value;
};

template < >
struct dateformat<void, void, void>
{
   static const unsigned value = 0;
   static const unsigned pow10 = 1;
};
```

```
enum
{
   YYYYMMDD = dateformat<datefield<Y,4>, datefield<M>, datefield<D> >::value,
   DDMMYY   = dateformat<datefield<D>, datefield<M>, datefield<Y> >::value,
   YYYYMM   = dateformat<datefield<Y,4>, datefield<M> >::value,
   // ...
```

For simplicity the implementation above uses rotation on 3 parameters only.[151] The print function follows:

```
void print(date d, dateformat_t f)
{
   const unsigned pow10[] = { 1, 10, 100, 1000, 10000, ... };
   const int data[3] = { d.year(), d.month(), d.day() };

   for (unsigned int fc = f; fc != 0; fc /= 100)
   {
      unsigned w = fc % 10;
      unsigned j = (fc % 100) / 10;

      std::cout << std::setw(w) << (data[j] % pow10[w]);
```

8.7.2. Self-modifying function tables

Consider a trivial example of a circular container, where elements are "pushed back": (at the moment, pretend anything is public)

[151] So you cannot generate stuff like YYYYMMDDYY.

```
template <typename T, size_t N>
struct circular_array
{
   T data_[N];
   size_t pos_;

   circular_array()
      : data_(), pos_(0)
   {
   }

   void push_back(const T& x)
   {
      data_[pos_] = x;
      if (++pos_ == N)
         pos_ = 0;
   }
```

We can convert `push_back` into a sort of self-modifying function: similar to trampolines (see 6.3.1), we will use a function pointer initialized with a suitable function template.

```
template <typename T, size_t N>
struct circular_array
{
   T data_[N];

   typedef void (*push_back_t) (circular_array<T, N>& a, const T& x);

   push_back_t pb_;


   template <size_t K>
   struct update_element_at
   {
      static void apply(circular_array<T, N>& a, const T& x)
      {
         a.data_[K] = x;
         a.pb_ = &update_element_at<(K+1) % N>::apply;
      }
   };


   circular_array()
      : data_(), pb_(&update_element_at<0>::apply)
   {
   }

   void push_back(const T& x)
   {
      pb_(*this, x);
   }
```

The key point of this pattern is that we have a collection of functions where all elements know which is the action that follows, and so they may update a pointer with this information.

Updating the function pointer is not mandatory: a function may select itself as the next candidate. Suppose we change the container policy so to keep the first N-1 elements and then constantly overwrite the last:

```
if ((K+1)<N)
   a.pb_ = &update_element_at<K+1>::apply;
```

Self-modifying functions are usually elegant, but slightly less efficient than a classic switch, mostly because of technology factors, such as caches or program flow predictors.
Applications include data structures whose behavior during initialization is different (a "warm-up" phase), until a minimum number of elements has been inserted.

9. Functors

In this chapter we focus on several techniques that help in writing (or not writing) functors.
Most STL algorithms require compile-time function objects and this usually requires some manual coding:

```
struct Person
{
   unsigned int age;
   std::string home_address;

   double salary() const;
};
```

```
std::vector<Person> data;
std::sort(data.begin(), data.end(), /* by age */ );
std::partition(data.begin(), data.end(), /* by salary */ );
```

If we can modify `Person`, sometimes an elegant and quick solution is to write both a public static member function and a member functor: this simultaneously attains the maximum efficiency and gives access to private members:

```
struct Person
{
private:
   unsigned int age;

public:
   static bool less_by_age(const Person& a, const Person& b)
   {
      return a.age < b.age;
   }

   struct BY_AGE
   {
      bool operator()(const Person& a, const Person& b) const
      {
         return Person::less_by_age(a, b);
      }
   };
};
```

```
std::sort(data.begin(), data.end(), Person::less_by_age);    // suboptimal
std::sort(data.begin(), data.end(), Person::BY_AGE());       // good
```

A static member function has access to private data; however it will be much harder for the compiler to inline the comparison, so a functor is usually better.
We can even factor out some code that converts the former to the latter:

```
template <typename T, bool (*LESS)(const T&, const T&)>
struct less_compare_t
{
   typedef T first_argument_type;
   typedef T second_argument_type;
   typedef bool result_type;

   bool operator()(const T& x, const T& y) const
   {
      return LESS(x, y);
   }
};
```

```
struct Person
{
private:
   unsigned int age;

public:
   static bool less_by_age(const Person& a, const Person& b)
   {
      return a.age < b.age;
   }

   typedef less_compare_t<Person, Person::less_by_age> BY_AGE;
```

The name of the function/functor is chosen so to make the expression *clear at the point of instantiation*, not at the point of definition.
Note that non-generic functors (whose arguments have a fixed type) are usually members of the class.

It's generally fair to assume that a functor can be freely copied, and pass it by value; if a functor needs many data members, we'd better collect them in a separate structure and store only a reference; the caller of the functor will be responsible for keeping the extra information alive:

```
struct information_needed_to_sort_elements
{
   // ...
};

class my_less
{
   const information_needed_to_sort_elements& ref_;

public:

   explicit functor(const information_needed_to_sort_elements& ref)
      : ref_(ref)
   {
   }

   // ...
```

```
information_needed_to_sort_elements i;
// build a suitable object...

std::sort(v.begin(), v.end(), my_less(i));
```

STL algorithms do not provide any guarantee about the number of copies of function objects.

Another interesting feature is that a functor static type is irrelevant, because it's always deduced: if the functor is returned from a function, it will be used immediately (see section 5.3.4); if it's passed to a function template, it will bind to an argument that accepts anything.
This allows clients to generate anonymous instances of complex function objects at the call site:

```
i = std::find_if(begin, end, std::bind2nd(std::less<double>(), 3.14));

      // the exact type of the functor is irrelevant
      // since find_if has an argument that binds to anything:

      // template <typename I, typename F>
      // I find_if(I begin, I end, F func)
```

> C++0x includes support for creation of lambda objects.
>
> It is a new syntax that can pass anonymous "pieces of code" in curly brackets as if they were functors; this mitigates the problem of name pollution, in other words: it's not necessary to give a name to an entity that is not reused.
> See section 13.4 for more details.

9.1.1. Strong and weak functors

Some functors are strongly typed: this means that the user fixes the argument of the function call when deciding the template arguments. All standard functionals are strongly typed.

```
template <typename T>
struct less
{
   bool operator()(const T& lhs, const T& rhs) const
   {
      return lhs < rhs;
   }
};
```

```
std::sort(begin, end, less<double>());
```

Vice versa, we can have a weak functor that accepts arguments with more freedom:

```
struct weak_less
{
   template <typename T>
   bool operator()(const T& lhs, const T& rhs) const
   {
      return lhs < rhs;
   }
};
```

```
std::sort(begin, end, weak_less());
```

A strongly typed functor blocks statically all types that are incompatible with T, but since this is limited to the interface, it can actually share the implementation with a weak functor:

```
template <typename T>
struct less : private weak_less
{
   bool operator()(const T& lhs, const T& rhs) const
   {
      return static_cast<const weak_less&>(*this)(lhs, rhs);
   }
};
```

9.2. Functor composition tools

The STL offers facilities to compose functors and values, for example `std::bind2nd` turns a binary operation into a unary function. Often, we need tools that perform the reverse.

The prefix "by" in "by age" is actually the composition of a binary relation with an accessor: "age" extracts the age from a person and "by" compares two ages: here's a minimal implementation that abstracts this composition concept.

```
template <typename functor_t>
class by_t
{
   functor_t f_;

public:

   by_t(functor_t f)
      : f_(f)
   {}

   template <typename argument_t>
   bool operator()(const argument_t& a, const argument_t& b) const
   {
      return f_(a) < f_(b);
   }
};
```

```
template <typename functor_t>
inline by_t<functor_t> by(const functor_t& f)
{
   return f;
}

// cfr. section 2.1.4

template <typename R, typename A>
inline by_t<R (*)(A)> by(R (*f)(A))
{
   return f;
}
```

```
struct age_t
{
   unsigned int operator()(const Person& p) const
   {
      return p.age;
   }

   age_t(int = 0)
   {
   }
};
```

```
static const age_t AGE = 0;
```
[152]

```
std::sort(data.begin(), data.end(), by(AGE));
```

`by` is a functor composition tool. It does not impose any requirement on `functor_t`, in particular it will accept suitable static member functions:

[152] Since most functors are stateless, so not affected by initialization problems, global constants can be created in header files

```
struct Person
{
private:
   unsigned int age;

public:
   static int AGE(const Person& a)
   {
      return a.age;
   }
};
```

```
std::sort(data.begin(), data.end(), by(Person::AGE));     // ok!
```

A functor/accessor may be given powerful ***lambda*** semantics.
Here we show just another preview of chapter 10.2: in pseudo-intuitive notation `comparator(A, S)` is a predicate that returns true on object `O` if `A(O)` is "less" than `S`; "less" is a generic binary predicate.

```
template
<
   typename scalar_t,
   typename accessor_t,
   template <typename T> class less_t
>
class comparator
{
   scalar_t x_;
   accessor_t a_;

public:

   comparator(scalar_t x, accessor_t a = accessor_t())
      : x_(x), a_(a)
   {
   }

   template <typename argument_t>
   bool operator()(const argument_t& obj) const
   {
      const less_t<scalar_t> less_;
      return less_(a_(obj), x_);
   }
};
```

Using a template-template parameter instead of a normal binary predicate here saves us from typing twice `scalar_t` and makes an anonymous instance quite clear to read:

```
comparator<double, SALARY, std::greater>(3.0)
```

Another minor point is the class layout: `x_` is declared before `a_`, because `a_` will often be stateless, so a small object, and `x_` might have stronger alignment constraints.

Now we can add operators to the functor and promote it to a lambda predicate:

```
struct age_t
{
 int operator()(const Person& a) const
 {
    return a.age;
 }

 template <typename scalar_t>
 comparator<scalar_t,age_t,std::less> operator<(const scalar_t& x) const
 {
    return comparator<scalar_t,age_t,std::less>(x, *this);
 }

 template <typename scalar_t>
 comparator<scalar_t,age_t,std::equal_to> operator==(const scalar_t& x) const
 {
    return comparator<scalar_t,age_t,std::equal_to>(x, *this);
 }
};
```

```
std::partition(data.begin(), data.end(), Person::AGE < 35);
std::partition(data.begin(), data.end(), Person::AGE == 18);
```

With a little effort, we can add more syntactic tricks to the chaining operator:

```
const selector<true> INCREASING;
const selector<false> DECREASING;

template <typename object_t>
bool oriented_less(const object_t& x, const object_t& y, selector<true>)
{
   return x<y;
}

template <typename object_t>
bool oriented_less(const object_t& x, const object_t& y, selector<false>)
{
   return y<x;
}
```

`oriented_less` can flip `operator<` and simulate `operator>`.

```
template <typename functor_t, bool ASCENDING = true>
class by_t
{
   // ...

   template <typename argument_t>
   bool operator()(const argument_t& a, const argument_t& b) const
   {
      return oriented_less(f_(a), f_(b), selector<ASCENDING>());
   }


   // inversion operators:

   by_t<accessor_t, true> operator+() const
   {
      return f_;
   }

   by_t<accessor_t, false> operator-() const
   {
      return f_;
   }
};
```

And finally, we add another "by" helper function:

```
template <bool DIRECTION, typename functor_t>
by_t< functor_t, DIRECTION> by(selector<DIRECTION>, const functor_t& v)
{
   return by_t<functor_t, DIRECTION>(v);
}
```

All this allows to write:

```
std::sort(data.begin(), data.end(), +by(Person::AGE));
std::sort(data.begin(), data.end(), -by(Person::AGE));
std::sort(data.begin(), data.end(), by(DECREASING, Person::AGE));
```

> We chose operator+ and operator- because `by` deals with numeric properties; the logical inversion of a unary predicate is better expressed with `operator!`
>
> Also, Lines #2 and #3 are identical: it's only a matter of style to pick the clearest.

The last improvement to `by_t` is to perform strict type checking in `operator()`. The function call operator accepts almost anything, so more type checking will trap errors arising from code that compiles merely by chance:

```
std::vector<Animal> data;
std::sort(data.begin(), data.end(), by(Person::AGE));
```

A convenient approach is to exploit cooperation from the functor: if `functor_t` has a member `argument_type`, that will be also the argument of a strong `operator()`; otherwise, we'll use the weak function call operator.
As usual, we hide the decision in a template parameter, and we provide two partial specializations; first, some traits:

```
template <typename T>
struct argument_type_of
{
   typedef typename T::argument_type argument_type;
};

template <typename A, typename R>
struct argument_type_of<R (*)(A)>
{
   typedef A argument_type;
};

template <typename A, typename R>
struct argument_type_of<R (*)(const A&)>
{
   typedef A argument_type;
};
```

```
template <typename T>
struct has_argument_type : selector<[[ true if T::argument_type exists153 ]]>
{
};

template <typename A, typename R>
struct has_argument_type<R (*)(A) > : selector<true>
{
};

//...
```

The first specialization performs strict type checking.

```
template
<
   typename functor_t,
   bool ASCENDING = true,
   bool STRICT_CHECK = has_argument_type<functor_t>::value
>
struct by_t;
```

[153] Details have been described in section 5.2.1

```
template <typename functor_t, bool ASCENDING>
struct by_t<functor_t, ASCENDING, true>
{
   // ...

   typedef typename argument_type_of<functor_t>::argument_type argument_type;

   bool operator()(const argument_type& a, const argument_type& b) const
   {
      return oriented_less(f_(a), f_(b), selector<ASCENDING>());
   }
};
```

```
template <typename functor_t, bool ASCENDING>
struct by_t<functor_t, ASCENDING, false>
{
   //...

   template <typename argument_t>
   bool operator()(const argument_t& a, const argument_t& b) const
   {
      return oriented_less(f_(a), f_(b), selector<ASCENDING>());
   }
};
```

To minimize code duplication, we factor out the function call operator in a template base and use a `static_cast`, as in CRTP:

```
template <typename functor_t, bool ASCENDING = true>
struct by_t;
```

```
template <typename functor_t, bool ASCENDING, bool STRICT_CHECK>
struct by_base_t;
```

```
template <typename functor_t, bool ASCENDING>
struct by_base_t<functor_t, ASCENDING, true>
{
   const functor_t& f() const
   {
      typedef by_t<functor_t, ASCENDING> real_type;
      return static_cast<const real_type&>(*this).f_;
   }

   typedef typename argument_type_of<functor_t>::argument_type argument_type;

   bool operator()(const argument_type& a, const argument_type& b) const
   {
      return oriented_less(f()(a), f()(b), selector<ASCENDING>());
   }
};
```

```
template <typename functor_t, bool ASCENDING>
struct by_base_t<functor_t, ASCENDING, false>
{
   const functor_t& f() const
   {
      typedef by_t<functor_t, ASCENDING> real_type;
      return static_cast<const real_type&>(*this).f_;
   }

   template <typename argument_t>
   bool operator()(const argument_t& a, const argument_t& b) const
   {
      return oriented_less(f()(a), f()(b), selector<ASCENDING>());
   }
};
```

```
template <typename functor_t, bool ASCENDING = true>
struct by_t
: by_base_t< functor_t, ASCENDING, has_argument_type<functor_t>::value> >
{
```

9.3. Inner template functors

Functor wrappers may be used as an interface leveraging tool.
Syntactically, we take advantage of the fact that inner class templates know template parameters of the outer class.

9.3.1. Conversion of functions to functors

Assume for simplicity we have a collection of functions with similar signature `T f(T, T, ..., T)` where the number of argument varies; suppose further that the list of functions to be executed will be known at runtime, so we need a base class with a virtual call, whose unique signature could be `(const T*, size_t)`.[154]
Let's look for an automatic way of performing the conversion:

```
template <typename T>
struct base
{
   virtual T eval(const T*, size_t) const = 0;

   virtual ~base() {}
};
```

Given a function, say `double F(double,double)`, we could embed it in a functor, but we would have to deduce T and F simultaneously:

[154] A careful reader will notice that in the example that follows, we do pass the length of the array, even if it is always ignored

```
template <typename T, T (*F)(T,T)>
struct functor : public base<T>
{
```

Actually, we need T before F, so we can build a class template on T only, and after that an inner template class:

```
template <typename T>
struct outer
{
   template <T (*F)(T,T)>
   struct inner : public base<T>
   {
```

So, first we identify `outer<T>`, then we build `inner`

```
template <typename T>
struct function_call_traits
{
   template <T (*F)()>
   struct eval_0 : public base<T>
   {
      virtual T eval(const T*  , size_t) const { return F(); }
   };

   template <T (*F)(T)>
   struct eval_1 : public base<T>
   {
      virtual T eval(const T* x, size_t) const { return F(x[0]);   }
   };

   template <T (*F)(T, T)>
   struct eval_2 : public base<T>
   {
      virtual T eval(const T* x, size_t) const { return F(x[0], x[1]); }
   };

   // ...
```

```
    template <T (*F)()>
    eval_0<F>* get_ptr() const
    {
       return new eval_0<F>;
    }

    template <T (*F)(T)>
    eval_1<F>* get_ptr() const
    {
       return new eval_1<F>;
    }

    template <T (*F)(T, T)>
    eval_2<F>* get_ptr() const
    {
       return new eval_2<F>;
    }

    // ...
};
```

```
template <typename T>
inline function_call_traits<T> get_function_call(T (*F)())
{
   return function_call_traits<T>();
}

template <typename T>
inline function_call_traits<T> get_function_call(T (*F)(T))
{
   return function_call_traits<T>();
}

template <typename T>
inline function_call_traits<T> get_function_call(T (*F)(T, T))
{
   return function_call_traits<T>();
}

// ...
```

```
#define MXT_FUNCTION_CALL_PTR(F)        get_function_call(F).get_ptr<F>()
```

Note that:

- F is used twice: first as a pointer, then as a template argument
- the `get_ptr` functions are not static; bizarre as it may look, we have an example of a traits class which is actually meant to be instantiated (but used anonymously)

```
double add0()
{
   return 6.28;
}

double add1(double x)
{
   return x+3.14;
}

double add2(double x, double y)
{
   return x+y;
}


int main()
{
   double x[5] = {1,2,3,4,5};

   base<double>* f[3] =
   {
      MXT_FUNCTION_CALL_PTR(add0),
      MXT_FUNCTION_CALL_PTR(add1),
      MXT_FUNCTION_CALL_PTR(add2)
   };

   for (int i=0; i<3; ++i)
      std::cout << f[i]->eval(x, 5);

   // intentionally leak...
}
```

The above example executes `add0(), add1(x[0]), add2(x[0], x[1])`, via calls to the same interface.

9.3.2. Conversion of members to functors

The very same technique seen in the previous section can transform pointers into functors.[155]
Ideally, we would like to write:

```
struct Person
{
   unsigned int age;
   double salary() const;
};
```

```
std::vector<Person> data;

// warning: pseudo-c++

std::sort(data.begin(), data.end(), by(Person::age));
std::sort(data.begin(), data.end(), by(Person::salary));
```

[155] The analogous STL structures instead merely *embed* a pointer in a functor.

Here's a rough tentative version: unfortunately the instantiation is truly too verbose to be useful.

```
template <typename from_t, typename to_t, to_t from_t::* POINTER>
struct data_member
{
   const to_t& operator()(const from_t& x) const
   {
      return x.*POINTER;
   }
};

template <typename from_t, typename to_t, to_t (from_t::*POINTER)() const>
struct property_member
{
   to_t operator()(const from_t& x) const
   {
      return (x.*POINTER)();
   }
};
```

```
struct TEST
{
   int A;
   int B() const { return -A; }
};

TEST data[3] = {2,1,3};

std::sort(data, data+3, by(data_member<TEST, int, &TEST::A>()));
std::sort(data, data+3, by(property_member<TEST, int, &TEST::B>()));
```

However it's not possible to write a generic class pointer as the only template parameter:

```
template <typename A, typename B, B A::*POINTER>
struct wrapper<POINTER>                                  // illegal: not c++
```

So we resort again to a nested class template:

```
template <typename from_t, typename to_t>
struct wrapper
{
   template <to_t from_t::*POINTER>                         // legal!
   struct dataptr_t
   {
      const to_t& operator()(const from_t& x) const
      {
         return x.*POINTER;
      }
   };

   template <to_t from_t::*POINTER>
      dataptr_t<POINTER> get() const
   {
      return dataptr_t<POINTER>();
   }
};
```

```
template <typename from_t, typename to_t>
wrapper<from_t, to_t> get_wrapper(to_t from_t::* pointer)
{
   return wrapper<from_t, to_t>();
}
```

We wrote a function which takes the pointer to perform the first deduction, and again we are going to supply the same pointer twice, one run-time (whose *value* is basically ignored, but whose *type* is used for deduction) and one compile-time:

```
#define MEMBER(PTR)    get_wrapper(PTR).get<PTR>()
```

- `get_wrapper` deduce their arguments automatically, so `get_wrapper(PTR)` will return a `wrapper<T1, T2>` with the correct types deduced from `PTR`.
- Then we ask this wrapper to instantiate its member function `get` again on `PTR`, and this returns the right object.

If `PTR` has type, say, `int TEST::*`, it will return a `dataptr_t<PTR>` However any other overload will do. Here's an extended version:

```
template <typename from_t, typename to_t>
struct wrapper
{
   template <to_t from_t::* POINTER>
   struct dataptr_t
   {
      // optional:
      // typedef from_t argument_type;

      const to_t& operator()(const from_t& x) const
      {
         return x.*POINTER;
      }
   };

   template <to_t (from_t::*POINTER)() const>
   struct propptr_t
   {
      // optional:
      // typedef from_t argument_type;

      to_t operator()(const from_t& x) const
      {
         return (x.*POINTER)();
      }
   };

   template <to_t from_t::* POINTER>
      dataptr_t<POINTER> get() const
   {
      return dataptr_t<POINTER>();
   }

   template <to_t (from_t::*POINTER)() const>
      propptr_t<POINTER> get() const
   {
      return propptr_t<POINTER>();
   }
};
```

```
template <typename from_t, typename to_t>
wrapper<from_t, to_t> get_wrapper(to_t from_t::* pointer)
{
   return wrapper<from_t, to_t>();
}

template <typename from_t, typename to_t>
wrapper<from_t, to_t> get_wrapper(to_t (from_t::*pointer)() const)
{
   return wrapper<from_t, to_t>();
}
```

```
#define mxt_create_accessor(PTR)    get_wrapper(PTR).get<PTR>()
```

```
struct TEST
{
   int A;
   int B() const { return -A; }
};

TEST data[3] = {2,1,3};

std::sort(data, data+3, by(mxt_create_accessor(&TEST::A)));
std::sort(data, data+3, by(mxt_create_accessor(&TEST::B)));
```

As usual, if the name of the class contains a comma (i.e. `std::map<int, float>`) you need to typedef it before calling the macro.

> The & is not strictly necessary; it's possible to redefine the macro as `get_wrapper(PTR).get<&PTR>()` so to invoke it on the plain qualified name.
>
> Unfortunately the macro as written, according to the Standard, does not work inside templates: an additional `template` keyword is necessary for the compiler to deduce correctly what `get` is, so the best option is to define a second macro named (say) `mxt_create_accessor_template`
>
> `get_wrapper(PTR).template get<&PTR>()`
>
> This version needs to be used whenever PTR depends on a template parameter that has impact on the line where the macro expands; vice versa, it is forbidden whenever PTR does not depend on anything else.[156]

9.4. Accumulation

An ***accumulator*** is a functor that performs a logical "pass" over a sequence of elements and is updated via `operator+=` or `operator+`. This is implemented in STL algorithm `std::accumulate`

```
template <typename iterator_t, typename accumulator_t>
accumulator_t accumulate(iterator_t b, iterator_t e, accumulator_t x)
{
   while (b != e)
      x = x + *(b++);

   return x;
}
```

If `x` is `value_type(0)`, this actually produces the sum over the range.

[156] Some compilers, including VC, won't notice the difference; however GCC does care.

Accumulators can be classified as ***online*** or ***offline***: offline objects may accumulate only once over a range, and no more values can be added; on the opposite, online objects can accumulate disjoint ranges (an ordinary sum is an online accumulation process, because the new total depends only on the previous total and the new values; an exact percentile would be an offline process, because the Pth-percentile over two disjoint ranges depends on *all* the values at once[157]).

The first step in a generalization is to accumulate `F(*i)`, not necessarily `*i`.[158]

```
template <typename T>
struct identity
{
   T operator()(T x) const { return x; }
};

template <typename iter_t, typename accumulator_t, typename accessor_t>
accumulator_t accumulate(iter_t b, iter_t e, accumulator_t x, accessor_t F)
{
   while (b != e)
      x = x + F(*(b++));

   return x;
}

template <typename iter_t, typename accumulator_t>
accumulator_t accumulate(iterator_t b, iterator_t e, accumulator_t x)
{
   return accumulate(b, e, x,
      identity<typename std::iterator_traits<iter_t>::reference>());
}
```

With TMP it's possible to build multi-layered accumulators on the fly:

- recognize a set of similar operations that will get a performance boost being performed simultaneously, rather than sequentially[159]
- define a reasonable syntax for instantiating an unnamed multiple accumulator
- define a reasonable syntax for extracting the results

9.4.1. A step-by-step implementation (*)

In the rest of the section, we will write a suitable function named `collect` that will make possible to write:

---

[157] There are online accumulators that *estimate* percentiles with good accuracy, though.

[158] The reader may wish to read again page 246.

[159] For example, the `maxmin` algorithm described on page 234 has a complexity 25% lower than computing `max` and `min` in two steps

```
// collect F(*i) for each i in the range
// and produce sum, gcd and max

std::accumulate(begin, end, collect(F)*SUM*GCD*MAX)
```

We take advantage of the fact that `std::accumulate` returns the accumulator to dump the desired results, either one or many at a time:

```
int data[7] = { ... };
int S = std::accumulate(data, data+7,
collect(identity<int>())*SUM).result(SUM);
```

```
int sum, gcd, max;
std::accumulate(...*SUM*GCD*MAX).result(SUM >> sum, GCD >> gcd, MAX >> max);
```

Let's restart from the beginning.
First, identify the elementary operations and assign a code to each:

```
enum
{
   op_void,    // null-operation
   op_gcd,
   op_max,
   op_min,
   op_sum
};
```

We will use again template rotation: the main object contains the list of operations, it executes the first, then rotates the list and dispatches execution; T is the accessor.

```
template <typename T, int O1 = op_void, int O2 = op_void,…, int On = op_void>
class accumulate_t
{
   typedef accumulate_t<T, O2, O3, ..., On > next_t;     // rotation

   static const int OP_COUNT = 1+next_t::OP_COUNT;

   scalar_t data_[OP_COUNT];

   static void apply(/* ... */)
   {
      // perform operation O1 and store result in data_[0]
      // then...

      next_t::apply(...);
   }
};
```

Then we implement the binary operations:

```
template <int N>
struct op_t;

template <>
struct op_t<op_void>
{
private:
   explicit op_t(int = 0) {}
};
```

```
template <>
struct op_t<op_sum>
{
   explicit op_t(int = 0) {}

   template <typename scalar_t>
      scalar_t operator()(const scalar_t a, const scalar_t b) const
   {
      return a+b;
   }
};
```

We create some global constant objects: the explicit constructor has exactly this purpose.

```
const op_t< op_gcd > GCD(0);
const op_t< op_sum > SUM(0);
const op_t< op_max > MAX(0);
const op_t< op_min > MIN(0);
```

Note that nobody can construct `op_t<op_void>`.
Since we are able to perform exactly 4 different operations, we put 4 as the limit of template parameters:

```
template
<
   typename accessor_t,
   int O1 = op_void, int O2 = op_void, int O3 = op_void, int O4 = op_void
>
class accumulate_t
{
   typedef typename accessor_t::value_type scalar_t;

   typedef accumulate_t<accessor_t, O2, O3, O4> next_t;

   template <typename T, int I1, int I2, int I3, int I4>
      friend class accumulate_t;

   static const int OP_COUNT = 1 + next_t::OP_COUNT;

   scalar_t data_[OP_COUNT];
   size_t count_;
   accessor_t accessor_;
```

Every object is constructed via an instance of the accessor

```
public:

   accumulate_t(const accessor_t& v = accessor_t())
      : accessor_(v), count_(0), data_()
   {
   }
```

We have an array of results named `data_`: the i-th operation will store its result in `data_[i]`.
The recursive computation part is indeed simple: there's a public `operator+=` which calls a private static member function:

```
   template <typename object_t>
      accumulate_t& operator+=(const object_t& t)
   {
      apply(data_, accessor_(t), count_);    // <-- static
      return *this;
   }
```

And a global `operator+`

```
template <typename accessor_t,int N1,int N2,int N3,int N4,typename scalar_t>
accumulate_t<accessor_t,N1,N2,N3,N4>
            operator+(accumulate_t<accessor_t,N1,N2,N3,N4> s, const scalar_t x)
{
   return s += x;
}
```

`accessor_(t)` yields the value to be accumulated over the memory cell `*data`: if `count` is 0, which means that the cell is “empty”, just write the value, otherwise invoke the first binary operation that merges the previous cell value and the new one; then advance the pointer to the next cell, and forward the call to `next_t`:

```
   static void apply(scalar_t* const data, const scalar_t x, size_t& count)
   {
      *data = (count>0) ? op_t<O1>()(*data, x) : x;
      next_t::apply(data+1, x, count);
   }
```

The recursion is stopped when all operations are `op_void`: at this very point, we update the counter.

```
template <typename accessor_t>
class accumulate_t <accessor_t, op_void, op_void, op_void, op_void>
{
   /* ... */

   static const int OP_COUNT = 0;

   static void apply(scalar_t* const, const scalar_t, size_t& count)
   {
      ++count;
   }
```

We need another static recursion to retrieve the result:

```
private:

   template <int N>
      static scalar_t get(const scalar_t* const data, op_t<N>)
   {
      return O1==N ? data[0] : next_t::get(data+1, op_t<N>());
   }

public:

   template <int N>
      scalar_t result(op_t<N>) const
   {
      return get(data_, op_t<N>());
   }
```

The recursion stopper is not expected to be invoked, however it's necessary because `next_t::get` is mentioned (and thus, fully compiled anyway): it will be executed only if one asks for `result(op_t<K>)` to an object of type `accumulate_t<K1...Kn>` and `K` is not in the list.
In this case, we can induce any suitable run-time error:

```
template <typename accessor_t>
class accumulate_t <accessor_t, op_void, op_void, op_void, op_void>
{
private:

   template <int N>
      static scalar_t get(const scalar_t* const, op_t<N>)
   {
      // throw std::runtime_error("invalid result request");
      return std::numeric_limits<scalar_t>::quiet_NaN();
   }

public :

   /* nothing here */
```

So eventually we are going to call `std::accumulate(begin, end, /* ... */ ).result(SUM)`, since `SUM` is a global constant of the right type.

Now that we partially coded how to compute and how to retrieve the result, we encode the accumulator factory; the usual idea is: we let the user build `accumulate_t<T>` (which is `accumulate_t<T, 0, 0, ... ,0>`) via an helper function, and then we chain this object to an `op_t` via a static push-front: chaining via `operator*` (binary multiplication) reads:

```
template <int N, int N1, ... int Nk>
accumulate_t<T, N, N1, N2,..,Nk-1>
   operator*(accumulate_t<T, N1,..,Nk-1, Nk>, op_t<N>)
```

This chaining operator will contain a static assertion, to ensure that the "dropped term" `Nk` is `op_void`.
Here's the global helper function:

```
template <typename accessor_t>
inline accumulate_t<accessor_t> collect(const accessor_t& v)
{
   return v;
}
```

Finally, we are going to list in parallel the whole class and the recursion-stopping specialization

```
template
<
  typename accessor_t,
  int O1 = op_void, int O2 = op_void,
  int O3 = op_void, int O4 = op_void
>
class accumulate_t
{
  typedef typename accessor_t::value_type scalar_t;

  template <typename T, int I1, int I2, int I3, int I4>
    friend class accumulate_t;

  typedef accumulate_t<accessor_t,O2,O3,O4,op_void> next_t;

  static const int OP_COUNT = 1+next_t::OP_COUNT;

  scalar_t data_[OP_COUNT];
  size_t count_;
  accessor_t accessor_;

  static void apply
  (scalar_t* const data, const scalar_t x, size_t& count)
  {
    *data = (count>0) ? op_t<O1>()(*data, x) : x;
    next_t::apply(data+1, x, count);
  }

template <int N>
  static scalar_t get(const scalar_t* const data, op_t<N>)
  {
  return O1==N ? data[0] : next_t::get(data+1, op_t<N>());
  }

public:

  accumulate_t(const accessor_t& v = accessor_t())
    : accessor_(v), count_(0), data_()
  {
  }

template <int N>
accumulate_t<accessor_t,N,O1,O2,O3>
    operator* (op_t<N>) const
  {
    MXT_ASSERT(O4 == op_void);
    return accessor_;
  }

  template <typename object_t>
    accumulate_t& operator+=(const object_t& t)
  {
    apply(data_, accessor_(t), count_);
    return *this;
  }

  template <int N>
    scalar_t result(op_t<N>) const
  {
    return get(data_, op_t<N>());
  }

  size_t size() const
  {
    return count_;
  }
};
```

```
template
<
  typename accessor_t
>
class accumulate_t<accessor_t,op_void,op_void,op_void,op_void>
{
  typedef typename accessor_t::value_type scalar_t;

  template <typename T, int I1, int I2, int I3, int I4>
    friend class accumulate_t;



  static const int OP_COUNT = 0;



  accessor_t accessor_;

  static void apply
  (scalar_t* const, const scalar_t, size_t& count)
  {
    ++count;
  }

template <int N>
  static scalar_t get(const scalar_t* const, op_t<N> )
  {
    assert(false);
    return 0;
  }

public:

  accumulate_t(const accessor_t& v = accessor_t())
    : accessor_(v)
  {
  }

  template <int N>
  accumulate_t<accessor_t, N>
    operator* (op_t<N>) const
  {

    return accessor_;
  }

  template <typename object_t>
    accumulate_t& operator+=(const object_t& t)
  {

    return *this;
  }

};
```

The last feature is the ability of retrieving more results at a time; this is extremely important, since it avoids storing the result of the accumulation.
Simply introduce an operator that binds a reference to each `op_t` (we pick `operator>>` since it resembles an arrow; another possible choice is `operator<=`, since <= can be seen as ←) and builds a reference wrapper of unique type; from this temporary, an overloaded `accumulator::result` will extract back both operands and perform the assignment.

```
RESULT1 r1;
RESULT2 r2;
accumulator.result(SUM >> r1, MAX >> r2);
```

```
template <typename scalar_t, int N>
struct op_result_t
{
   scalar_t& value;

   op_result_t(scalar_t& x)
      : value(x)
   {
   }
};

template <typename scalar_t, int N>
inline op_result_t<scalar_t, N> operator>> (const op_t<N>, scalar_t& x)
{
   return op_result_t<scalar_t, N>(x);
}
```

Then we add these methods to the general template: (the macro is for brevity only)

```
#define ARG(J)    const op_result_t<scalar_t, N##J> o##J
// ARG(1) expands to "const op_result_t<scalar_t, N1> o1"

   template <int N1>
      const accumulate_t& result(ARG(1)) const
   {
      o1.value = result(op_t<N1>());
      return *this;
   }

   template <int N1, int N2>
      const accumulate_t& result(ARG(1), ARG(2)) const
   {
      result(o2);
      return result(o1);
   }

   template <int N1, int N2, int N3>
      const accumulate_t& result(ARG(1), ARG(2), ARG(3)) const
   {
      result(o3);
      return result(o1, o2);
   }

   template <int N1, int N2, int N3, int N4>
      const accumulate_t& result(ARG(1), ARG(2), ARG(3), ARG(4)) const
   {
      result(o4);
      return result(o1, o2, o3);
   }

#undef ARG
```

Thus the expression `MAX >> x` silently returns `op_result_t<[[type of x]], op_max>(x)`. If x has not the same type of the accumulated results, it will not compile.

A couple of extra enhancements will save some typing: instead of many `result`, add just the first, and chain the subsequent calls via `operator()`.[160]

```
template <int N1>
   const accumulate_t& result(const op_result_t<scalar_t, N1> o1) const
{
   o1.value = result(op_t<N1>());
   return *this;
}

template <int N1>
   const accumulate_t& operator()(const op_result_t<scalar_t, N1> o1) const
{
   return result(o1);
}
```

So instead of:

```
int q_sum, q_gcd, q_max;
std::accumulate(...).result(SUM >> q_sum, GCD >> q_gcd, MAX >> q_max);
```

the new syntax is:

```
std::accumulate(...).result(SUM >> q_sum)(GCD >> q_gcd)(MAX >> q_max);
```

Or even

```
std::accumulate(...)(SUM >> q_sum)(GCD >> q_gcd)(MAX >> q_max);
```

Second, add an overload that returns the first result, for functions that accumulate a single quantity:

```
scalar_t result() const
{
   // MXT_ASSERT(O2 == op_void);
   return result(op_t<O1>());
}
```

```
// now .result(SUM) is equivalent to .result()
int S = std::accumulate(data, data+7, collect(...)*SUM).result();
```

9.5. Drivers

A well-written algorithm avoids unnecessary multiplication of code: to rewrite an existing algorithm for greater generality, we remove some "fixed" logic from it and plug it in again through a template parameter, usually a functor:

[160] More on this in paragraph 10.3

```
template <typename iterator_t>
void sort(iterator_t begin, iterator_t end)
{
   for (...)
   {
      // ...
      if (a<b)   // operator< is a perfect candidate for becoming a functor
      {
```

So we rewrite as:

```
template <typename iterator_t, typename less_t>
void sort(iterator_t begin, iterator_t end, less_t less)
{
   for (...)
   {
      // now we ask the functor to "plug" its code in the algorithm
      if (less(a,b))
      {
```

A ***driver*** is an object that can guide an algorithm along the way.
The main difference between a functor and a driver is that the former has a general-purpose function-like interface (at least, `operator()`), which is open to user customization; on the opposite, a driver is a low level object, with a verbose interface, and is not meant to be customized (except for its name, it might not even be documented, as if it were a tag type): the framework itself will provide a small fixed set of drivers.

Consider the following example: we want a `sq` function which optionally logs the result on `std::cerr`. Because we cannot enforce such a constraint if we receive a generic logger object, we switch to drivers, and we provide some:

```
struct dont_log_at_all
{
   bool may_I_log() const   { return false;   }
};

struct log_everything
{
   bool may_I_log() const   { return true; }
};

struct log_ask_once
{
   bool may_I_log() const
   {
      static bool RESULT = AskUsingMessageBox("Should I log?", MSG_YESNO);
      return RESULT;
   }
};
```

```
template <typename scalar_t, typename driver_t>
inline scalar_t sq(const scalar_t& x, driver_t driver)
{
   const scalar_t result = (x*x);
   if (driver.may_I_log())
      std::cerr << result << std::endl;
   return result;
}

template <typename scalar_t>
inline scalar_t sq(const scalar_t& x)
{
   return sq(x, dont_log_at_all());
}
```

Note that `driver_t::may_I_log()` contains neither code about squaring, nor about logging: it just takes a decision, driving the flow of the algorithm.

The big advantage of drivers is to reduce debugging time, since the main algorithm is a single function. Usually drivers have minimal runtime impact; however nothing prevents a driver to perform long and complex computations.

As a rule, we always invoke drivers through instances: an interface such as

```
template <typename driver_t>
void explore(maze_t& maze, driver_t driver)
{
   while (!driver.may_I_stop())
```

is more general than its stateless counterpart:[161]

```
template <typename driver_t>
void explore(maze_t& maze)
{
   while (driver_t::may_I_stop())
```

A driver is somehow analogous to the "public non-virtual / protected virtual" classic C++ idiom (cfr. page 318); the key similarity is that the structure of the algorithm is fixed; the user is expected to customize only specific parts, which run only when the infrastructure needs.[162]

9.6. Algors

An ***algor***, or algorithmic functor, is an object which embeds an algorithm, or simply an algorithm with state.

[161] Traits would be somehow equivalent to stateless drivers

[162] See also http://www.gotw.ca/publications/mill18.htm

The standard C++ library provides an `<algorithm>` header, which includes only functions; so it's natural to identify function and algorithms, but it need not be the case.
The algor object implements a simple function-like interface – typically, `operator()` – for the execution of the algorithm, but its state grants faster repeated executions with "similar input".

The simplest case where an algor is useful is buffered memory allocation: `std::stable_sort` may require the allocation of a temporary buffer, which is necessarily released when the function returns. Usually this is not an issue, since time spent in (a single) memory allocation is dominated by the execution of the algorithm itself; a small input will cause a small memory request, which is "fast" (operating systems tend to favor small allocations); a large input will cause a "slow" memory request, but this time will be unnoticed, since the algorithm will need much more time to run.
However there are situations where a single buffer would suffice for many requests: when stable-sorting many vectors of similar length, we can save allocation/deallocation time with an object:

```
template <typename T>
class stable_sort_algor
{
   buffer_type buffer_;

public:

   template <RandomAccessIterator>
   void operator()(RandomAccessIterator begin, RandomAccessIterator end)
   {
      // ensure that buffer_ is large enough
      // if not, reallocate
      // then perform the stable sort
   }

   ~stable_sort_algor()
   {
      // release buffer_
   }
};
```

To sum up, the simplest algor is just a sort of functor with state (in the last case, a temporary buffer), but algors may have a richer interface, that goes beyond functors.

As a rule, algors are not copied or assigned: they are either constructed and reused (say, in a loop), or as unnamed temporaries for a single execution, so we don't worry about efficiency, but only about safety: if `buffer_type` cannot be safely copied (say, it's a pointer), we explicitly disable all the dangerous member functions, making them private or public do-nothing operations; if `buffer_type` is a value type (e.g. `vector<T>`), we let the compiler generate safe, possibly inefficient, operators.

Another useful kind of algor is a *self-accumulator* that holds multiple results at once: there's no buffer involved (cfr. paragraph 9.4)

```
template <typename T>
class accumulator
{
   T max_;
   T min_;
   T sum_;
   // ...

public:

   accumulator()
      : sum_(0) // ...
   {
   }

   template <typename iterator_t>
   accumulator<T>& operator()(iterator_t begin, iterator_t end)
   {
      for (;begin != end; ++begin)
      {
         sum_ += *begin;
         // ...
      }
      return *this;
   }

   T max() const { return max_; }
   T min() const { return min_; }
   T sum() const { return sum_; }
   // ...
};
```

```
double data[] = {3,4,5 };

// single invocation
double SUM = accumulator<double>()(data, data+3).sum();

// multiple results are needed
accumulator<double> A;
A(data, data+3);
std::cout << "Range: " << A.max()-A.min();
```

An ***interactive algor*** has an interface that allows the caller to run the algorithm step by step; suppose for example we have to compute the square root, up to some precision:

```
template <typename scalar_t>
class interactive_square_root
{
   scalar_t x_;
   scalar_t y_;
   scalar_t error_;

public:

   interactive_square_root(scalar_t x)
      : x_(x)
   {
      iterate();
   }

   void iterate()
   {
      // precondition:
      // y_ is some kind of approximate solution for y²=x
      // error_ is |y²-x|

      // now compute a better approximation
   }

   scalar_t error() const
   {
      return error_;
   }

   operator scalar_t() const
   {
      return y_;
   }
};
```

It's the user who drives the algorithm:

```
interactive_square_root<double> ISR(3.14);
while (ISR.error()>0.00001)
   ISR.iterate();

double result = ISR;
```

An algor of this kind usually takes all its parameters from the constructor.

A common use-case is an algorithm that produces *a set of solutions*: after execution, a member function permits the user to "visit" all the solutions in some order. These algors might do all the work in the constructor:

```
template <typename string_t>
class search_a_substring
{
   const string_t& text_;
   std::vector<size_t> position_;

public:

   search_a_substring(const string_t& TEXT, const string_t& PATTERN)
      : text_(TEXT)
   {
      // search immediately every occurrence of PATTERN in TEXT
      // store all the positions in position_
   }

   bool no_match() const { return position_.empty(); }

   // the simplest visitation technique
   // is... exposing iterators

   typedef std::vector<size_t>::const_iterator position_iterator;

   position_iterator begin() const
   {
      return position_.begin();
   }

   position_iterator end() const
   {
      return position_.end();
   }
};
```

In case of substring matching, the iterator will likely visit the matches from the first to the last; in a numerical minimization problem, the solutions may be N points where the function has the minimum value found so far.

A more complex visitor-accepting interface could accept two *output* iterators, where the algor would write its solutions; as described in 7.1.6, we could build a "custom view" on the solutions according to the iterator `value_type`: for example, the minimization algorithm that would normally output X1..XN, will emit pairs (Xj, F(Xj)) if possible:

```
public:

template <typename out_t>
out_t visit(out_t beg, out_t end) const
{
   typedef typename std::iterator_traits<out_t>::value_type> val_t;

   int i=0;
   while (beg != end)
      *beg++ = build_result(i++, instance_of<val_t>());

   return beg;
}
```

```
private:

std::vector<double> X_;

template <typename T>
double build_result(int i, instance_of<T>) const
{
   return X_[i];
}

template <typename T>
pair<double, double> build_result(int i, instance_of< pair<T, T> >) const
{
   return make_pair(X_[i], F(X_[i]));
}
```

9.7. Forwarding and Reference wrappers

It's a common idiom for a class template to hold a member of a generic type, to which the class dispatches execution.

```
template <typename T>
class test
{
   T functor_;

public:

   typename T::value_type operator()(double x) const
   {
      return functor_(x);   // call forward
   }
};
```

Since the exact type of the member is not known, sometimes we have to implement several overloads; the class template will instantiate what's actually needed and ignore the remaining.

```
template <typename T>
class test
{
   T functor_;

public:

   /* we don't know how many arguments functor_ needs */

   template <typename T1>
   typename T::value_type operator()(T1 x) const
   {
      return functor_(x);        // call forwarding
   }

   template <typename T1, typename T2>
   typename T::value_type operator()(T1 x, T2 y) const
   {
      return functor_(x, y);   // call forwarding
   }

   // more...
```

Invoking the wrong overload (i.e. supplying too many or unsupported arguments) will cause a compiler error. However we see that arguments are forwarded by value, so we would like to modify the prototypes:

```
   template <typename T1>
   typename T::value_type operator()(const T1& x) const
   {
      return functor_(x);        // call forwarding
   }
```

But if `T` requires an argument by non-const reference, the code will not compile.

To understand the severity of the problem, consider a slightly different example, where we *construct* a member with an unspecified number of parameters.
The STL guidelines suggest writing a single constructor for class `test`, which takes (possibly) an already build object of type `T`:

```
   test(const T& data = T())
      : member_(data)
   {
   }
```

But this strategy is not always possible, in particular `T` might have an inaccessible copy constructor or it may be a non-const reference.
In fact, let's forget the STL style for a moment, and adapt the same idiom of `operator()` above.

```
template <typename T>
class bad_test
{
   T member_;

public:

   template <typename X1>
   bad_test(X1 arg1)
   : member_(arg1)
   {
   }

   template <typename X1, typename X2>
   bad_test(X1 arg1, X2 arg2)
   : member_(arg1, arg2)
   {
   }
};
```

As written above, `bad_test<T&>` compiles, but a subtle bug rises:[163]

```
int main(int argc, char* argv[])
{
   double x = 3.14;

   bad_test<double&> urgh(x);       // unfortunately, it compiles
   urgh.member_ = 6.28;             // bang!

   int i = 0;

   assert(x == 6.28);               // assertion failed!

   // ...
```

The constructor of `urgh` is instantiated on type `double`, not `double&`, so `urgh.member_` refers to a temporary location in the stack of its constructor (namely, the storage space taken by `arg1`), whose content is a temporary copy of `x`.

So we modify `bad_test` to forward arguments by const reference. At least, `good_test<double&>` will not compile (`const double&` cannot be converted to `double&`)

[163] We write the example as if all members were public.

```
template <typename T>
class good_test
{
   T member_;

public:

   template <typename X1>
   good_test(const X1& arg1)
   : member_(arg1)
   {
   }
};
```

However an additional wrapping layer can solve both problems:

```
template <typename T>
class reference_wrapper
{
   T& ref_;

public:

   explicit reference_wrapper(T& r)
      : ref_(r)
   {
   }

   operator T& () const
   {
      return ref_;
   }

   T* operator& () const
   {
      return &ref_;
   }
};

template <typename T>
inline reference_wrapper<T> by_ref(T& x)
{
   return reference_wrapper<T>(x);
}
```

```
   double x = 3.14;

   good_test<double> y0(x);   // ok: x is copied into y1.member_

   good_test<double&> y1(x); // compiler error!
   y1.member_ = 6.28;         // would be dangerous, but does not compile

   good_test<double&> y2(by_ref(x));

   y2.member_ = 6.28;         // ok, now x == 6.28
```

Using `by_ref`, `good_test<double&>` constructor is instantiated on argument `const reference_wrapper<double&>&`, which is then converted to `double&`.

> Once again, the argument forwarding problem is solved in C++0x with R-value references.

10. The opaque type principle

Template types can be too complex for the user, so we should either publish a convenient typedef, or allow using objects ignoring their type at all.

Plain C is full of opaque types.
In C a file stream is handled via a pointer to an unknown `FILE` structure, which resides in system memory (the C runtime pre-allocates a small number of these structures); more, to retrieve the current position within an open file, we call `fgetpos(FILE*, fpos_t)` passing the file pointer and another opaque type that acts as a bookmark. We can't know or modify the current position, but only restore it via a call to `fsetpos(FILE*, fpos_t)`.
From the user perspective, an instance of `fpos_t` is completely opaque: since only the name is known, the type has no interface, except default constructor, copy constructor and assignment.

The opaque type principle instead is the opposite case: opaqueness is related only to the *type name*, not to the interface; in other words, the object has an unspecified type and a known interface: it may be an iterator or a functor.
Being the type "difficult to write", we don't want to store the object, but we strongly prefer to use it immediately, on the creation site.

10.1. Polymorphic results

Suppose a function performs a computation that produces several results at a time. We can pack all of them in a polymorphic result and allow the user to select what's needed:
Let's take a crude example:

```
template <typename iterator_t >
[[???]] average(iterator_t beg, iterator_t end)
{
    typename std::iterator_traits<iterator_t>::value_type total = 0;
    total = std::accumulate(beg, end, total);
    size_t count = std::distance(beg, end);

    return total/count;
}
```

A fixed return type will destroy the partial results, which could be useful. So we delay the aggregation of the sub-items and change the code like:

```
template <typename T, typename I>
class opaque_average_result_t
{
   T total_;
   I count_;

public:

   opaque_average_result_t(T total, I count)
      : total_(total), count_(count)
   {
   }

   // default result is the average

   operator T () const
   {
      return total_/count_;
   }

   T get_total() const
   {
      return total_;
   }

   I get_count() const
   {
      return count_;
   }
};
```

```
template <typename iterator_t >
opaque_average_result_t<VALUE_TYPE, size_t> average(iterator_t beg,
iterator_t end)
{
   VALUE_TYPE total = 0;
   total = std::accumulate(beg, end, total);
   size_t count = std::distance(beg, end);

   return opaque_average_result_t<VALUE_TYPE, size_t>(total, count);
}
```

Now the client can use the original algorithm in many more ways:

```
std::vector<double> v;

double avg = average(v.begin(), v.end());
double sum = average(v.begin(), v.end()).get_total();
```

Since the return type is opaque, it's not convenient to store the result, but it's easy to pass it to a function template, if needed:[164]

```
<???> x = average(v.begin(), v.end());
```

[164] See also section 13.3

```
template <typename T>
void receive(T res, double& avg, double& sum)
{
   avg = res;
   sum = res.get_total();
}

double avg, sum;
receive(average(v.begin(), v.end()), avg, sum);
```

10.2. Classic Lambda expressions

Lambda expressions are opaque function objects created on the call site, combining some elementary pieces with meaningful operators; the resulting functor will later replay the operator sequence on its arguments: for example, given two suitable objects of type "lambda variables" X and Y, then (X+Y)*(X-Y) will be a functor that takes two arguments and returns their sum multiplied by their difference.

It's a good exercise to build a simplified implementation and understand the underlying template techniques. These have been proposed originally by Todd Veldhuizen in his seminal article "Expression Templates".

We will write code like this: `cos(X+2.0)` is an expression that returns a functor, whose `operator()` computes `cos(x+2.0)` given a double `x`.

```
lambda_reference<const double> X;

std::find_if(..., X<5.0 && X>3.14);
std::transform(..., cos(X+2.0));
```

```
lambda_reference<double> Y;

std::for_each(..., Y+=3.14);
```

```
lambda_reference<const double, 0> ARG1;
lambda_reference<const double, 1> ARG2;

std::sort(..., (ARG1<ARG2));
```

We will make the following assumptions, some will be removed later, and some will hopefully become clear in proceeding:

- For clarity, T will be a friendly scalar type, `double` or `float`, so all the operators are well-defined
- A lambda expression will receive at most K=4 arguments, *all* of the same type `T&`. In particular:
    - `lambda_reference<double>` and `lambda_reference<const double>` are different, the latter being a "lambda-const reference to double".

  - An expression must contain references of the same kind.
- In this first paragraph only, all constants shall have type T and we consider invalid syntax `X+2`, because `X` refers to `double` and 2 is an `int`; we shall write `X+2.0`
- Most TMP involved here has the explicit objective of making all functions look identical, so they will be easily generated with preprocessor macros, even when they are not be listed here.

10.2.1. Elementary lambda objects

First, we define an *empty* static interface, for later use: even if T is not used, the interface will propagate it everywhere.

```
template <typename true_t, typename T>
class lambda
{
protected:

   ~lambda()
   {
   }

public:

   const true_t& true_this() const
   {
      return static_cast<const true_t&>(*this);
   }
};
```

Any lambda object is a functor.
The first (trivial) object is a lambda-constant: a functor that returns its constant result, whatever the arguments, and since in particular it's a lambda expression, we derive from the interface:

```
template <typename T>
class lambda_const : public lambda<lambda_const<T>, T>
{
   typedef const T& R;

   T c_;

public:

   typedef T result_type;

   lambda_const(R c)
      : c_(c)
   {
   }

   result_type operator()(R  = T(), R  = T(), R  = T(), R  = T()) const
   {
      return c_;
   }
};
```

We remark that a lambda-constant can take 0 or more arguments, but it is a function object, so the invocation must use some form of `operator()`.

The second concept is a `lambda_reference<T, N>` is a functor that takes at least N arguments of type `T&` and returns the N-th. The choice of accepting `T&` as argument implies that `lambda_reference<T>` won't work on a literal:

```
lambda_reference<double> X1;
lambda_reference<const double> Y1;

X1(3.14);    // error: needs double&
Y1(3.14);    // ok: takes and returns const double&
```

The selection of a variable is not trivial: as usual, argument rotation is the preferred technique; furthermore, since a reference is cheap, we introduce *duplication of the arguments* in order to reduce the number of overloads: the last argument of `operator()` is "cloned" so to pass always four items.

```
template <typename T, size_t N = 0>
class lambda_reference: public lambda<lambda_reference<T, N>, T>
{
   static T& apply_k(static_value<size_t, 0>, T& x1, T&, T&, T&)
   {
      return x1;
   }

   template <size_t K>
   static T& apply_k(static_value<size_t, K>, T& x1, T& x2, T& x3, T& x4)
   {
      return apply_k(static_value<size_t, K-1>(), x2, x3, x4, x1);
   }

public:

   typedef T& result_type;

   result_type operator()(T& x1, T& x2, T& x3, T& x4) const
   {
      MXT_STATIC_ASSERT(N<4);
      return apply_k(static_value<size_t, N>(), x1, x2, x3, x4);
   }

   result_type operator()(T& x1, T& x2, T& x3) const
   {
      MXT_STATIC_ASSERT(N<3);
      return apply_k(static_value<size_t, N>(), x1, x2, x3, x3);
   }

   result_type operator()(T& x1, T& x2) const
   {
      MXT_STATIC_ASSERT(N<2);
      return apply_k(static_value<size_t, N>(), x1, x2, x2, x2);
   }

   result_type operator()(T& x1) const
   {
      MXT_STATIC_ASSERT(N<1);
      return apply_k(static_value<size_t, N>(), x1, x1, x1, x1);
   }
};
```

10.2.2. Lambda functions and operators

A unary function F applied to a lambda expression is a functor that returns F on the result of the lambda.[165]

Thanks to the static interface, the implementation can treat *any* lambda expression at once.

Also, `lambda<X, T>` can be stored in an object of type X (and the copy is cheap).

[165] In symbols, $(F(\lambda))(x) := F(\lambda(x))$, where x may be a tuple

```
template <typename F, typename X, typename T>
class lambda_unary : public lambda<lambda_unary<F,X,T>, T>
{
   X x_;
   F f_;

public:

   lambda_unary(const lambda<X,T>& that)
      : x_(that.true_this())
   {
   }

   typedef typename F::result_type result_type;

   result_type operator()() const
   {
      return f_(x_());
   }

   result_type operator()(T& x1) const
   {
      return f_(x_(x1));
   }

   result_type operator()(T& x1, T& x2) const
   {
      return f_(x_(x1, x2));
   }

   result_type operator()(T& x1, T& x2, T& x3) const
   {
      return f_(x_(x1, x2, x3));
   }

   // ...
```

The code above builds a functor `f_`, whose `operator()` is called, but we will need to plug-in also global/static member functions; thus a small adapter is needed:

```
template <typename T, T (*F)(T)>
struct unary_f_wrapper
{
   typedef T result_type;

   T operator()(const T& x) const { return F(x); }
};
```

Next, we collect all global functions in traits class:

```
template <typename T>
struct unary_f_library
{
   static T L_abs(T x) { return abs(x); }
   static T L_cos(T x) { return cos(x); }
   // ...
};
```

And eventually we start defining functions on lambda objects:

```
#define LAMBDA_ABS_TYPE      \
      lambda_unary<unary_f_wrapper<T, &unary_f_library<T>::L_abs>, X, T>

template <typename X, typename T>
LAMBDA_ABS_TYPE abs(const lambda<X, T>& x)
{
   return LAMBDA_ABS_TYPE(x);
}
```

```
#define LAMBDA_COS_TYPE      \
      lambda_unary<unary_f_wrapper<T, &unary_f_library<T>::L_cos>, X, T>

template <typename X, typename T>
LAMBDA_COS_TYPE cos(const lambda<X, T>& x)
{
   return LAMBDA_COS_TYPE(x);
}
```

```
...
```

This scheme applies also to unary operators, simply using a different functor.

```
template <typename T>
struct lambda_unary_minus
{
  typedef T result_type;
  result_type operator()(const T& x) const { return -x; }
};
```

```
#define LAMBDA_U_MINUS_TYPE      lambda_unary<lambda_unary_minus<T>, X, T>

template <typename X, typename T>
LAMBDA_U_MINUS_TYPE operator-(const lambda<X, T>& x)
{
   return LAMBDA_U_MINUS_TYPE(x);
}
```

The more features we add, the more complex become the return types, but these are completely hidden from the user.

A binary operation, say +, behaves similarly: `(lambda<X1,T> + lambda<X2,T>)` is a functor that distributes its arguments to both its summands.[166]
As above, there will be a specific object, namely `lambda_binary<X1, F, X2, T>`.

166 In symbols again, (λ1+λ2)(x) := λ1(x)+λ2(x), where x may be a tuple

Mixed binary operations, such as `lambda<X1,T> + T`, are a special case, handled with a promotion of `T` to `lambda_const<T>`.

```
template <typename X1, typename F, typename X2, typename T>
class lambda_binary : public lambda< lambda_binary<X1,F,X2,T>, T >
{
   X1 x1_;
   X2 x2_;
   F f_;

public:

   lambda_binary(const lambda<X1,T>& x1, const lambda<X2,T>& x2)
      : x1_(x1.true_this()), x2_(x2.true_this())
   {
   }

   typedef typename F::result_type result_type;

   result_type operator()() const
   {
      return f_(x1_(), x2_());
   }

   result_type operator()(T& x1) const
   {
      return f_(x1_(x1), x2_(x1));
   }

   result_type operator()(T& x1, T& x2) const
   {
      return f_(x1_(x1, x2), x2_(x1, x2));
   }

   result_type operator()(T& x1, T& x2, T& x3) const
   {
      return f_(x1_(x1, x2, x3), x2_(x1, x2, x3));
   }

   // ...
```

In this implementation, logical operators will not use short circuit: if T were `int`, the lambda object `X>0 && (1/X)<5` will crash on a division by zero, while the analogous C++ statement returns false.

Arithmetic operators like + can be written as `f_(x1_(...), x2_(...))` as above; but this is incorrect for `&&` and `||`, whose workflow is more complex:

```
b1 := x1_(...);
if (f_(b1, true) == f_(b1, false))
   return f_(b1, true);
else
   return f_(b1, x2_(...))
```

In this discussion, we treat logical operators as normal binary predicates, but we would actually need partial specializations of `lambda_binary` with a different function call operator.
We leave this as an exercise.

Now we define "concrete" binary functions:

```
template <typename T, T (*f)(T, T)>
struct binary_f_wrapper
{
   typedef T result_type;
   T operator()(const T& x, const T& y) const { return f(x,y); }
};
```

```
template <typename T>
struct binary_f_library
{
   static T L_atan2(T x, T y) { return atan2(x, y); }
   // ...
};
```

```
#define LAMBDA_ATAN2_T(X1, X2)   \
 lambda_binary<X1, binary_f_wrapper<T, &binary_f_library<T>::L_atan2>, X2, T>

template <typename X1, typename X2, typename T>
LAMBDA_ATAN2_T(X1, X2) atan2(const lambda<X1,T>& L, const lambda<X2,T>& R)
{
   return LAMBDA_ATAN2_T(X1, X2) (L, R);
}
```

```
template <typename X1, typename T>
LAMBDA_ATAN2_T(X1, lambda_const<T>) atan2(const lambda<X1,T>& L, const T& R)
{
   return atan2(L, lambda_const<T>(R));
}

template <typename T, typename X2>
LAMBDA_ATAN2_T(lambda_const<T>, X2) atan2(const T& L, const lambda<X2,T>& R)
{
   return atan2(lambda_const<T>(L), R);
}
```

Finally, we need another extension: there are three types of operators

- binary predicates, with signature `bool F(const T&, const T&)`
- binary operators, with signature `T F(const T&, const T&)`
- assignments, with signature `T& F(T&, const T&)`

The following code is the literal translation in C++

```
enum lambda_tag
{
   LAMBDA_LOGIC_TAG,
   LAMBDA_ASSIGNMENT_TAG,
   LAMBDA_OPERATOR_TAG
};


template <typename T, lambda_tag TAG>
struct lambda_result_traits;

template <typename T>
struct lambda_result_traits<T, LAMBDA_ASSIGNMENT_TAG>
{
   typedef T& result_type;
   typedef T& first_argument_type;
   typedef const T& second_argument_type;
};

template <typename T>
struct lambda_result_traits<T, LAMBDA_OPERATOR_TAG>
{
   typedef T result_type;
   typedef const T& first_argument_type;
   typedef const T& second_argument_type;
};

template <typename T>
struct lambda_result_traits<T, LAMBDA_LOGIC_TAG>
{
   typedef bool result_type;
   typedef const T& first_argument_type;
   typedef const T& second_argument_type;
};
```

So we can write

```
template <typename T>
struct lambda_less
{
   typedef lambda_result_traits<T, LAMBDA_LOGIC_TAG> traits_t;

   typedef typename traits_t::result_type result_type;
   typedef typename traits_t::first_argument_type arg1_t;
   typedef typename traits_t::second_argument_type arg2_t;

   result_type operator()(arg1_t x, arg2_t y) const
   {
      return x < y;
   }
};
```

```
template <typename T>
struct lambda_plus
{
   typedef lambda_result_traits<T, LAMBDA_OPERATOR_TAG> traits_t;

   typedef typename traits_t::result_type result_type;
   typedef typename traits_t::first_argument_type arg1_t;
   typedef typename traits_t::second_argument_type arg2_t;

   result_type operator()(arg1_t x, arg2_t y) const
   {
      return x + y;
   }
};
```

```
template <typename T>
struct lambda_plus_eq
{
   typedef lambda_result_traits<T, LAMBDA_ASSIGNMENT_TAG> traits_t;

   typedef typename traits_t::result_type result_type;
   typedef typename traits_t::first_argument_type arg1_t;
   typedef typename traits_t::second_argument_type arg2_t;

   result_type operator()(arg1_t x, arg2_t y) const
   {
      return x += y;
   }
};
```

These objects have minimal differences.

Logical and standard operators are identical to any other binary function, except the return type (compare with `atan2` above); here is the implementation of lambda's `operator<`

```
#define LAMBDA_L_T(X1,X2)       lambda_binary<X1, lambda_less<T>, X2, T>

template <typename X1, typename X2, typename T>
LAMBDA_L_T(X1,X2) operator<(const lambda<X1,T>& L, const lambda<X2,T>& R)
{
   return LAMBDA_L_T(X1, X2) (L, R);
}

template <typename X1, typename T>
LAMBDA_L_T(X1, lambda_const<T>) operator<(const lambda<X1,T>& L, const T& R)
{
   return L < lambda_const<T>(R);
}

template <typename T, typename X2>
LAMBDA_L_T(lambda_const<T>, X2) operator<(const T& L, const lambda<X2,T>& R)
{
   return lambda_const<T>(L) < R;
}
```

The assignment operators do not allow the third overload: it would correspond to a lambda expression such as (2.0 += X), which looks anyway suspicious:

```
#define LAMBDA_PE_T(X1,X2)     lambda_binary<X1, lambda_plus_eq<T>, X2, T>

template <typename X1, typename X2, typename T>
LAMBDA_PE_T(X1,X2) operator+=(const lambda<X1,T>& L, const lambda<X2,T>& R)
{
   return LAMBDA_PE_T(X1,X2) (L,R);
}

template <typename X1, typename T>
LAMBDA_PE_T(X1,lambda_const<T>) operator+=(const lambda<X1,T>& L, const T&R)
{
   return L += lambda_const<T>(R);
}
```

Here is a sample that uses all the above code:

```
   lambda_reference<double, 0> VX1;
   lambda_reference<double, 1> VX2;

   double data[] = {5,6,4,2,-1};
   std::sort(data, data+5, (VX1<VX2));

   std::for_each(data,data+5, VX1 += 3.14);
   std::transform(data,data+5, data, VX1 + 3.14);
   std::transform(data,data+5, data, 1.0 + VX1);

   std::for_each(data,data+5, VX1 += cos(VX1));
```

Here's a sample that deliberately produces an error, which is still human-readable:

```
   const double data[] = {5,6,4,2,-1};
   std::for_each(cdata, cdata+5, VX1 += 3.14);
```

```
algorithm(29) : error C2664: 'double &lambda_binary<X1,F,X2,T>::operator ()(T &) const' :
cannot convert parameter 1 from 'const double' to 'double &'
        with
        [
            X1=lambda_reference<double,0>,
            F=lambda_plus_eq<double>,
            X2=lambda_const<double>,
            T=double
        ]
        Conversion loses qualifiers

        .\test.cpp(447) : see reference to function template instantiation being compiled

        '_Fn1 std::for_each<const double*,lambda_binary<X1,F,X2,T>>(_InIt,_InIt,_Fn1)'

        with
        [
_Fn1=lambda_binary<lambda_reference<double,0x00>,lambda_plus_eq<double>,lambda_const<double>,double>,
            X1=lambda_reference<double,0>,
            F=lambda_plus_eq<double>,
            X2=lambda_const<double>,
            T=double,
            _InIt=const double *
        ]
```

We would expect the following code to work correctly, instead it does not compile; the error log may be long and noisy, but it all leads to `operator+`. The precise error has been isolated below:

```
double data[] = {5,6,4,2,-1};
const double cdata[] = {5,6,4,2,-1};

lambda_reference<const double> C1;

std::transform(cdata,cdata+5, data, C1 + 1.0);
```

```
error: 'lambda_binary<X1,lambda_plus<T>,lambda_const<T>,T> operator +(const lambda<true_t,T> &,const T
&)' :

template parameter 'T' is ambiguous
     could be 'double'
     or       'const double'
```

The issue above is equivalent to:

```
template <typename T>
struct A
{
};

template <typename T>
void F(A<T>, T)
{
}
```

```
A<const double> x;
double i=0;

F(x, i);    // error: ambiguous call.
            // deduce T=const double from x, but T=double from i
```

This is where type traits come in: we take the T parameter only from the lambda expression and let the type of the constant be dependent; more precisely all mixed operators with an argument of type `const T&` should be changed to accept `typename lambda_constant_arg<T>::type`.

```
template <typename T>
struct lambda_constant_arg
{
   typedef const T& type;
};

template <typename T>
struct lambda_constant_arg<const T>
{
   typedef const T& type;
};
```

The C++ Standard specifies that if a parameter can be deduced from one of the arguments, then it's deduced and then substituted in the remaining; if the result is feasible, then the deduction is accepted as valid, so in particular in a signature like:

```
template <typename T>
void F(A<T> x, typename lambda_constant_arg<T>::type i);
```

the only context where T is deducible is the type of x, so ambiguities cannot occur any more.
In particular it's now possible to add constants of any type convertible to T:

```
std::transform(cdata, cdata+5, data, C1 + 1);        // not necessary to write
+ 1.0
```

Note finally that these lambda expressions are not too rigorous with the number of arguments: the only explicit check occurs as a static assertion in lambda reference.[167]

```
lambda_reference<const double, 0> C1;
lambda_reference<const double, 1> C2;

double t1 = ((C1<C2)+(-C1))(3.14);                 // error: C2 requires 2 args
double t2 = ((C1<C2)+(-C1))(3.14, 6.28);           // ok
double t3 = ((C1<C2)+(-C1))(3.14, 6.28, 22/7);     // ok, last argument ignored
```

10.2.3. Refinements

Note that unary and binary operations do contain a copy of the functor representing the operation, but the functor is always default-constructed. We can add a wrapper that embeds any user functor in a lambda expression. Just modify the constructor as follows:

```
public:

   lambda_unary(const lambda<X,T>& that, F f = F())
      : x_(that.true_this()), f_(f)
   {
   }
```

We shall use this feature immediately to create a *functor* that takes a functor-on-T and returns a functor-on-lambda:

[167] This can be fixed, storing a static constant named "min_number_of_arguments" in every lambda implementation; atomic lambdas, such as `lambda_reference`, will define it directly and derived lambdas will take the maximum from their nested types; finally this constant may be used for static assertions. We leave this as an exercise.

```
MyFunctor F;
lambda_reference<double> X;

std::transform(data, data+n, data, lambda_wrap[F](3*X+14));   // = F(3*X+14)
```

lambda_wrap is a global instance of lambda_wrap_t<void>, whose operator[] absorbs a suitable user functor: the choice of [] instead of () gives extra visual clarity, since it avoids confusion with function arguments.

```
template <typename F = void>
class lambda_wrap_t
{
   F f_;

public:

   lambda_wrap_t(F f)
      : f_(f)
   {
   }

   template <typename X, typename T>
      lambda_unary<F, X, T> operator()(const lambda<X, T>& x) const
   {
      return lambda_unary<F, X, T>(x, f_);
   }
};
```

```
template <>
class lambda_wrap_t<void>
{
public:
   lambda_wrap_t(int = 0)
   {
   }

   template <typename F>
   lambda_wrap_t<F> operator[](F f) const
   {
      return f;
   }
};
```

```
const lambda_wrap_t<void> lambda_wrap = 0;
```

This is used as in:

```
struct MyF
{
   typedef double result_type;

   result_type operator()(const double& x) const
   {
      return 7*x - 2;
   }
};
```

```
std::for_each(begin, end, lambda_wrap[MyF()](V+2)); // will execute MyF(V+2)
```

The same technique can be extended even further to implement the ternary operator (which cannot be overloaded) and the hypothetical syntax could be:

```
if_[CONDITION].then_[X1].else_[X2]
```

The dot that links the statements together shows clearly that the return type of `if_[C]` is an object, whose member `then_` has another `operator[]`, etc.

10.2.4. Argument and result deduction

Loosely speaking, a composite lambda object G:=F(λ) takes an argument x and returns F(λ(x)); so the *argument type* of G is the argument type of λ and the *result type* of G is the result type of F.
Up to now, we avoided the problem of defining these types, because they were either fixed or explicitly given.

- The scalar type T in the lambda interface acts as the argument of its `operator()`; whenever a function is applied to `lambda<X,T>`, T is borrowed and plugged in the result, which is say `lambda<Y,T>`.
- The return type of lambda's `operator()` instead may vary, so it's published as `result_type`: for example, `lambda_unary<F,X,T>` takes `T& x` from the outside and returns whatever F gives back from the call F(X(x)); F may return a reference to T or bool.

In the process, however, silent casts from `bool` to `T` may occur.
The function object:

```
abs(C1<C2);
```

takes two arguments of type `double`, it feeds them to `less`, which in turn returns `bool`, but this is promoted again to `double` before entering `abs`.
In general, this is the desired behavior:

```
(C1<C2);            // returns bool
((C1<C2)+2);        // operator+ will promote "bool" to "double"
```

`operator&&` can be implemented as a clone of `operator<`, however && would take two T, not two bool; in simple cases this will just work, but in general we need more flexibility.

```
(C1<C2) && (C2>C1);

// operator&& will promote two bools to double, then return bool
```

We want to prescribe only the arguments of `lambda_reference`, and let every lambda object *borrow both arguments and results* correctly. `lambda_reference` is in fact the only user-visible object and its type parameter is sufficient to determine the whole functor.

At the same time, we will remove T from the lambda interface:

```
template <typename X>
class lambda
{
protected:
   ~lambda()
   {
   }

public:
   const X& true_this() const
   {
      return static_cast<const X&>(*this);
   }
};
```

```
template <typename T, size_t N = 0>
class lambda_reference : public lambda< lambda_reference<T, N> >
{
public:

   typedef T& result_type;
   typedef T& argument_type;

   result_type operator()(argument_type x1) const
   {
      MXT_STATIC_ASSERT(N<1);
      return apply_k(static_value<size_t, N>(), x1, x1, x1, x1);
   }

   // ...
```

We are going to replace the usage of T in every "wrapping" lambda class with a (meta)function of the `result_type` of the inner object:

```
template <typename F, typename X>
class lambda_unary : public lambda< lambda_unary<F,X> >
{
   X x_;
   F f_;

public:

   typedef typename F::result_type result_type;
   typedef typename X::argument_type argument_type;
```

However, while T is a plain type (maybe `const` qualified, but never a reference), `argument_type` will often be a reference. So we need a metafunction to remove any qualifier:

```
template <typename T>
struct plain
{
   typedef T type;
};

template <typename T>
struct plain<T&> : plain<T>
{
};

template <typename T>
struct plain<const T> : plain<T>
{
};
```

```
template <typename T>
class lambda_const : public lambda< lambda_const<T> >
{
   typedef typename plain<T>::type P;

   P c_;

public:

   typedef P result_type;
   typedef const P& argument_type;
```

The nasty issue lies in the binary operators, where we have two lambdas X1 and X2.
Whose `argument_type` should we borrow? It's easy to see that *both types* must be inspected, because some deduction must be performed.
For example, if X is a lambda non-const reference, it needs `T&`; a lambda constant needs `const T&`, and we may write both `1.0+X` and `X+1.0`, so we'll need a commutative metafunction "deduce":

```
template <typename X1, typename F, typename X2>
class lambda_binary : public lambda< lambda_binary<X1,F,X2> >
{
  X1 x1_;
  X2 x2_;
  F f_;

public:

  typedef typename F::result_type result_type;
  typedef typename
    deduce_arg<typename X1::argument_type, typename X2::argument_type>::type
    argument_type;
```

However, the problem of combining two arbitrary functionals is even deeper: first, the elimination of T makes all the return types more complex; for example now the `lambda_plus` object will have to take care of the addition not of two T, but of *any* two different results, coming from any different lambdas:

```
lambda_binary<X1, lambda_plus<T>, X2, T>                                    // before
```

```
lambda_binary<X1, lambda_plus<typename X1::result_type, typename X2::result_type>, X2>  // after
```

Furthermore, the *return type* of "a generic addition" is not known:[168]

```
template <typename T1, typename T2>
struct lambda_plus
{
   typedef const typename plain<T1>::type& arg1_t;      // not a problem
   typedef const typename plain<T2>::type& arg2_t;      // not a problem

   typedef [[???]] result_type;

   result_type operator()(arg1_t x, arg2_t y) const
   {
      return x + y;
   }
};
```

So we will need another metafunction "deduce result" that takes arg1_t and arg2_t and gives back a suitable type.
Luckily, here the issue is solvable by TMP techniques and under reasonable assumptions, because we have only few degrees of freedom: involved types are `T` (deduced from `lambda_reference`, and it must be unique in the whole template expression), `T&`, `const T&` and `bool`.

---

[168] On the opposite, assignment and logical operators have a deducible return type: the former returns its first argument (a non-const reference), the latter returns `bool`. The new keyword `decltype` of C++0x will get rid of all these assumptions and allow deducing this type automatically.

10.2.5. Deducing argument type

We now look for a metafunction F that deduces the common argument type; F should satisfy:

- symmetry: `F<T1,T2> := F<T2,T1>`
- the strongest requirement prevails: `F<T&, ...> = T&`
- `const T&` and `T` have the same behavior: `F<const T&, ...> = F<T, ...>`

Meta-arguments of F are argument types of other lambda objects:

```
F<typename X1::argument_type, typename X2::argument_type>
```

Eventually it suffices that F returns either `T&` or `const T&`: the simplest implementation is to reduce both arguments to references; if they have the same underlying type, we pick the strongest; otherwise the compiler will give an error:

```
template <typename T>
struct as_reference
{
   typedef const T& type;
};

template <typename T>
struct as_reference<T&>
{
   typedef T& type;
};

template <typename T>
struct as_reference<const T&> : as_reference<T>
{
};
```

```
template <typename T1, typename T2>
struct deduce_argument
: deduce_argument
  <
    typename as_reference<T1>::type,
    typename as_reference<T2>::type
  >
{
};

template <typename T>
struct deduce_argument<T&, T&>
{
   typedef T& type;
};

template <typename T>
struct deduce_argument<T&, const T&>
{
   typedef T& type;
};

template <typename T>
struct deduce_argument<const T&, T&>
{
   typedef T& type;
};
```

Observe that the specialization

```
template <typename T>
struct deduce_argument<T&, T&>
{
   typedef T& type;
};
```

will be used when T is a constant type.

10.2.6. Deducing result type

Deduction of the result is similar: the expected result of a function call is *never* a reference, so we start ensuring that at the call location no references are passed:

```
template <typename T1, typename T2>
struct lambda_plus
{
   typedef const typename plain<T1>::type& arg1_t;
   typedef const typename plain<T2>::type& arg2_t;

   typedef typename
      deduce_result<typename plain<T1>::type, typename plain<T2>::type>::type
      result_type;

   result_type operator()(arg1_t x, arg2_t y) const
   {
      return x + y;
   }
};
```

This time we need four specializations:

```
template <typename T1, typename T2>
struct deduce_result;
```

```
template <typename T>
struct deduce_result<T, bool>
{
   typedef T type;
};

template <typename T>
struct deduce_result<bool, T>
{
   typedef T type;
};

template <typename T>
struct deduce_result<T, T>
{
   typedef T type;
};

template <>
struct deduce_result<bool, bool>
{
   typedef bool type;
};
```

The last specialization is necessary, otherwise `<bool, bool>` would match *any* of the three (with T=`bool`), so it would be ambiguous.

10.2.7. Static cast

The limitations in result/argument deduction may lead to some inconsistency: while a classic addition `bool+bool` has type `int`, the addition of boolean lambda objects returns `bool`:

```
lambda_reference<const double, 0> C1;
lambda_reference<const double, 1> C2;

((C1<C2) + (C2<C1))(x, y);        // it returns bool
```

Both (C1<C2) and (C2<C1) have "function signature" `bool (const double&, const double&)` and so `lambda_plus` will be instantiated on `<bool, bool>`; by hypothesis, when arguments are equal, `deduce_result<X, X>` gives X.

The only way to solve similar issues is a lambda-cast operator; luckily, it's easy to reproduce the syntax of `static_cast`, using a non-deducible template parameter:

```
template <typename T1, typename T2>
struct lambda_cast_t
{
   typedef T2 result_type;

   result_type operator()(const T1& x) const
   {
      return x;
   }
};
```

```
#define LAMBDA_CAST_T(T,X)    \
    lambda_unary<lambda_cast_t<typename X::result_type, T>, X>

template <typename T, typename X>
LAMBDA_CAST_T(T,X) lambda_cast(const lambda<X>& x)
{
   return x;
}
```

```
(lambda_cast<double>(C1<C2)+lambda_cast<double>(C1<C2))(3.14, 6.28);
// now returns 2.0
```

10.2.8. Arrays

Todd Veldhuizen was one of the first to suggest in his articles the application of "template expressions" for fast operation on arrays that minimize the usage of temporaries.[169]

```
valarray<double> A1 = ...;
valarray<double> A2 = ...;

valarray<double> A3 = 7*A1-4*A2+1;
```

[169] We borrow on purpose the name `valarray`, to remark that these techniques fit `std::valarray`

Naive operators will in general produce more "copies" of the objects than necessary: the subexpression `7*A1` will return a temporary array, where each element is 7 times the corresponding entry in `A1`; `4*A2` will return another temporary, and so on.

Instead we can use a lambda-like expression:

```
template <typename X, typename T>
class valarray_static_interface
{
   // X is the true valarray and T is the scalar
   // ...

   public:

   // interface to get the i-th component

   T get(size_t i) const
   {
      return true_this().get(i);
   }

   size_t size() const
   {
      return true_this().size();
   }

   operator valarray<T>() const
   {
      valarray<T> result(size());
      for (size_t i=0; i<size(); ++i)
         result[i] = get(i);

      return result;
   }
};
```

The interface can be cast to a real `valarray`; this cast triggers the creation of *one* temporary object, which is filled componentwise (which is the most efficient way). The product `valarray<T> * T` returns a `valarray_binary_op< valarray<T>, std::multiplies<T>, scalar_wrapper<T>, T>`; this object contains a const reference to the original `valarray`.

```
template <typename VA1, typename F, typename VA2, typename T>
class valarray_binary_op
: public valarray_interface< valarray_binary_op<VA1,F,VA2,T> >
{
   const VA1& va1_;
   const VA2& va2_;
   F op_;

public:

   // ...

   T get(size_t i) const
   {
      return op_(va1_.get(i), va2_.get(i));
   }
```

The key optimization for a successful use of expression templates with complex objects, such as arrays, is a careful usage of const references:

```
const VA1& va1_;
const VA2& va2_;
```

A const reference is generally fine, since it binds to temporaries, but it will not prevent the referenced object from dying.
For example, `(A*7)+B` will produce one temporary (`A*7`), and another object that has a const reference to it and a const reference to `B`; since `A*7` is alive "just in that line of code", if one could store the expression and evaluate it later, it would crash the program.

We may actually want to use traits to determine a suitable storage type: if `VA1` is `valarray<T>`, then it's convenient to use `const VA1&`, if `VA1` is simply a scalar `const VA1` is safer.

To sum up, the line

```
valarray<double> A3 = A1*7;
```

will somehow trigger the componentwise evaluation of the template expression on the right, thanks to the cast operator in the interface, or - even better - a dedicated template constructor/assignment in `valarray<T>`.[170]
The cast operator however is not easy to remove: since `A1*7` is expected to be a `valarray`, it might even be used as a `valarray`, say writing `(A1*7)[3]` or even `(A1*7).resize(n)`; this implies that `valarray` and `valarray_interface` should be very similar, when feasible.

[170] In other words, a constructor that takes `const valarray_static_interface<X,T>&`. The details should follow easily and are left to the reader.

Another advantage of the static interface approach is that there might be several objects that can be faked as a `valarray`; as an equivalent of `lambda_const`, we can let a scalar `c` act as the array `[c, c, ..., c]`:

```
template <typename T>
class scalar_wrapper
: public valarray_interface< scalar_wrapper<T> >
{
   T c_;
   size_t size_;

public:

   scalar_wrapper(T c, size_t size)
      : c_(c), size_(size)
   {
   }

   T get(size_t i) const
   {
      return c_;
   }
```

10.3. Creative syntax

This section is fully devoted to exploiting template syntax tricks, such as operator overloads, to express concepts that differ from the standard meaning.

Some operators convey a natural associativity: the simplest examples are sequences connected with +, <<, `comma`

```
std:string s = "hello";
std:string r = s + ' ' + "world" + '!';

std::ofstrean o("hello.txt");
o << s << ' ' << "world" << '!';

int a = 1,2,3,4,5,6,7;
```

The user expects these operators to be able to form chains of arbitrary length. On the opposite, `operator[]` and `operator()` can sometimes have a similar meaning, but, as for pointers, the former should be used when the length of the chain is *fixed*:

```
array a;
a[2];                     // ok: the user expects a single subscript

matrix m;
m[2][3];                  // ok: the user expects a matrix to have 2 coordinates

SomeObject x;
x[2][3][1][4][5];         // bad style, here the meaning is obscure

Tensor<double,5> t;
t[2][3][1][4][5];         // good style
```

We can take advantage of these operators writing operators that take the first argument and return a similar object that can handle the remaining chain:

```
std::cout << a << b << c;
```

The above line has the form: `F(F(F(cout, a), b), c)` so `F(cout, a)` should return *something* for which there exists an overload of `F` that accepts also `b`, and so on; in the simplest case `F(cout, a)` returns `cout`.

10.3.1. Argument chains with () and []

Sometimes `operator()` is used to form chains, starting from a function object. Let's analyze some hypothetical code:

```
double f(int, double, char, const char*);
```

```
double r1 = bind_to(f)(argument<2>('p')) (37, 3.14, "hello");
//          ^^^^^^^^^^^^^^^^^^^^^^^^^^^^^^
// produces a new function:
//
// double f1(int a, double b, const char* c)
// { return f(a, b, 'p', c);

double r2 = bind_to(f)(argument<0>(17))(argument<2>('p')) (3.14, "hello");
//          ^^^^^^^^^^^^^^^^^^^^^^^^^^^^^^^^^^^^^^^^^^^^^^
// produces a new function:
// double f2(double b, const char* c)
// { return f(17, b, 'p', c);
```

Given that f is a function taking N arguments, we can guess the following facts:

- `bind_to(f)` returns an object with two different `operator()`
- the first form takes an expression, whose syntax is `argument<K>(x)` and returns a functor that fixes x as the K-th argument of f; this first form can be invoked repeatedly, to fix several arguments in the same statement
- the second `operator()` takes all the remaining arguments at a time and evaluates the function

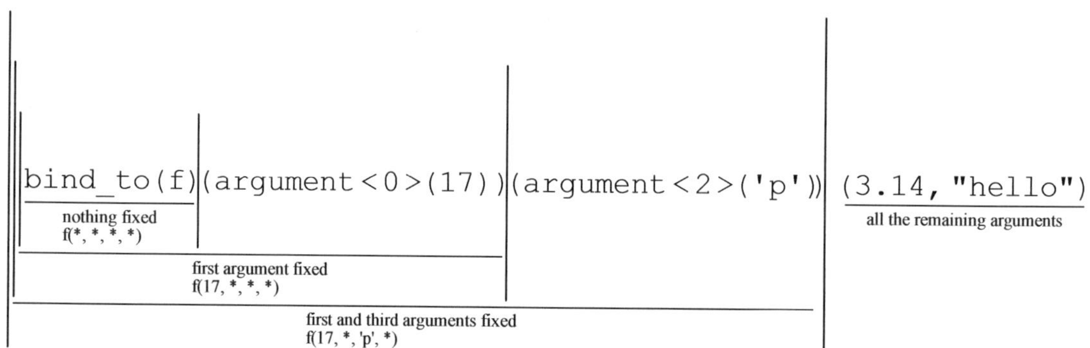

Another paradigmatic example is a function that needs several objects (usually functors or accessors, but there's no formal requirement), which we don't want to mix with the other arguments, because either:

- they are too many: `F(..., x1, x2, x3, x4...)`
- they cannot be sorted by "decreasing probability of having the default value changed" and the caller may have to put arbitrary values in unspecified positions: `F(..., X1 x1 = X1(), X2 x2 = X2()...)` may need to be invoked as `F(..., X1(), X2(), ..., x7, X8(), ...)`
- each object is associated with a distinct template parameter, say X1, X2... so a function call with two arguments swapped by mistake, will likely compile[171]

We shall invoke an algorithm that needs *three* objects: a less-comparator, a unary predicate and a logger:

```
template <typename iterator_t, typename less_t,
          typename pred_t, typename logger_t>
void MyFunc(iterator_t b, iterator_t e, less_t less, pred_t p, logger_t& out)
{
   std::sort(b, e, less);
   iterator_t i = std::find_if(b, e, p);
   if (i != e)
      out << *i;
}
```

However all these arguments would have a default type, namely `std::ostream` as logger (and `std::cout` as a default value for `out`) and the following two types:

[171] Cfr. "price" and "quality" in the knapsack examples in section 7.2.1

```
struct basic_comparator
{
   template <typename T1, typename T2>
   bool operator()(const T& lhs, const T& rhs) const { return lhs < rhs; }
};

struct accept_first
{
   template <typename T>
   bool operator()(const T&) const { return true; }
};
```

We often want to change *one* of those, maybe the last; however it's difficult to provide overloads, because arguments cannot be distinguished on their type:

```
template <typename iterator_t, typename less_t >
void MyFunc (iterator_t b, iterator_t e, less_t less)
```

```
template <typename iterator_t, typename logger_t>
void MyFunc (iterator_t b, iterator_t e, logger_t& out)
// error: same as above
```

So we use the ***argument pack*** technique: first we tag the arguments.

```
enum { LESS, UNARY_P, LOGGER };
```

```
template <size_t CODE, typename T = void>
struct argument
{
   T arg;

   argument(const T& that)
      : arg(that)
   {
   }
};

template <size_t CODE>
struct argument<CODE, void>
{
   argument(int = 0)
   {
   }

   template <typename T>
   argument<CODE, T> operator=(const T& that) const
   {
      return that;
   }

   argument<CODE, std::ostream&> operator=(std::ostream& that) const
   {
      return that;
   }
};
```

Then we provide named global constants:

```
const argument<LESS> comparator = 0;
const argument<UNARY_P> acceptance = 0;
const argument<LOGGER> logger = 0;
```

```
template <typename T1, typename T2, typename T3>
struct argument_pack
{
   T1 first;
   T2 second;
   T3 third;

   argument_pack(int = 0)
   {
   }

   argument_pack(T1 a1, T2 a2, T3 a3)
      : first(a1), second(a2), third(a3)
   {
   }
```

`argument_pack::operator[]` takes an `argument<N, T>` and replaces its N-th template argument with T:

```
template <typename T>
argument_pack<T, T2, T3> operator[](const argument<0, T>& x) const
{
   return argument_pack<T, T2, T3>(x.arg, second, third);
}

template <typename T>
argument_pack<T1, T, T3> operator[](const argument<1, T>& x) const
{
   return argument_pack<T1, T, T3>(first, x.arg, third);
}

template <typename T>
argument_pack<T1, T2, T> operator[](const argument<2, T>& x) const
{
   return argument_pack<T1, T2, T>(first, second, x.arg);
}
```

Finally we introduce a global constant named `where` and overload the original function twice (regardless of the actual number of parameters):

```
typedef argument_pack<basic_comparator, accept_first, std::ostream&> pack_t;

static const pack_t where(basic_comparator(), accept_first(), std::cout);
```

```
template <typename iterator_t, typename T1, typename T2, typename T3>
void MyFunc(iterator_t b, iterator_t e, const argument_pack<T1,T2,T3> a)
{
   return MyFunc(b, e, a.first, a.second, a.third);
}

template <typename iterator_t >
void MyFunc(iterator_t b, iterator_t e)
{
   return MyFunc(b, e, where);
}
```

So now it's possible to write:

```
MyFunc(v.begin(),v.end(),where[logger=clog]);
MyFunc(v.begin(),v.end(),where[logger=cerr][comparator=greater<int>()]);
```

`logger` is a constant of type `argument<2,void>`, which gets upgraded to `argument<2,std::ostream&>`; this instance replaces the third template parameter of `pack_t` with `std::ostream&` and the value of `pack_t::third` with a reference to `std::cerr`.

Observe that the code shown in this section is strongly tied to the specific function call, however complex functions that require argument packs are generally just a few per project.

10.4. The growing object concept

Let's start with an example. String sum has an expected cost of a memory reallocation:[172]

```
template <typename T>
std::string operator+(std::string s, const T& x)
{
   // estimate the length of x when converted to string;
   // ensure s.capacity() is large enough;
   // append a representation of x to the end of s;
   return s;
}
```

If there are multiple sums on the same line, evidently, the compiler knows the sequence of arguments:

[172] Note that `s` is passed by value: according to the NVRO (Named Value Return Optimization), if there is only one return statement and the result is a named variable, the compiler is usually able to elide the copy, directly constructing the result on the caller's stack.

```
std::string s = "hello";
std::string r = s + ' ' + "world!";

// repeated invocation of operator+ with arguments: char, const char*
// may cause multiple memory allocations
```

So we would like to:

- o collect all the arguments at once and sum their lengths.
- o execute a single memory allocation
- o traverse the sequence of arguments again and concatenate them

The ***growing object*** is a pattern that allows traversing a C++ expression before execution; the idea of the technique is to inject in the expression a proxy with special operators that "absorb" all the subsequent arguments.
The proxy is a temporary agglomerate object whose operators make it "grow" including references to their arguments; finally, when growth is complete, the object is able to process *all* arguments at once and transform into the desired result.

Thus in the above example, `s+' '` is not a string, but a proxy that contains a reference to `s` and a `char`; this object grows when `"world"` is added, so `s+' '+"world"` contains also a `const char*`.

Informally, a growing object is implemented as a pair containing the previous state of the object and some new tiny data (say, a reference); one of:

- o a class with two members: a reference to the previous growing object and a tiny object
- o a class with two members: a copy of the previous growing object and a tiny object
- o a class that derives from the previous growing object, with a tiny object as the only member

In pseudo-template notation, the three different models can be written:

```
template <…>
class G1<N>
{
    const G1<N-1>& prev_;
    T& data_;
};
```

```
template <…>
class G2<N>
{
    G2<N-1> prev_;
    T& data_;
};
```

```
template <...>
class G3<N> : public G3<N-1>
{
    T& data_;
};
```

The first is the fastest to build, because augmenting a temporary object G1 with new data involves no copy, but the lifetime of G1 is the shortest possible; the other types have similar complexity, since their construction involves copying Gj<N-1> anyway, but they slightly differ in the natural behavior.
The great advantage of G1 is that both constructors and destructors run exactly once and in order: instead, to create a G2<N>, we produce two copies of G2<N-1>, three copies of G2<N-2>... K+1 copies of G2<N-K>...
This is especially important because we may need G<N> to run some code *when the growth is complete* and the destructor of G<N> would be one of the options.
Any of these Gj contains references, so for example no growing object can be *thrown*.

Furthermore, there are some known recursive patterns in computing the result:

- ***Inward link***: G<N> either computes the result directly, or it delegates G<N-1>, passing information "inward"

```
private:

    result do_it_myself()
    {
        // ...
    }

    result do_it(arguments)
    {
        if (condition)
            return do_it_myself();
        else
            return prev_.do_it(arguments);
    }

public:

    result do_it()
    {
        return do_it(default);
    }
```

- ***Outward link***: G<N> asks recursively a result from G<N-1> and post-processes it.

```
    result do_it()
    {
        result temp = prev_.do_it();
        return modify(temp);
    }
```

- ***Direct access***: G<N> computes J and asks G<J> for a result; this pattern has a different implementation for inheritance-based growing objects.

```
template <…>
class G1<N>
{
    result do_it_myself(static_value<int, 0>)
    {
        // really do it
    }

    template <int K>
    result do_it_myself(static_value<int, K>)
    {
        return prev_.do_it_myself(static_value<int, K-1>());
    }

public:

    result do_it()
    {
        static const int J = [[...]];
        return do_it_myself(static_value<int, J>());
    }
};
```

```
template <…>
class G3<N> : G3<N-1>
{
    result do_it_myself()
    {
        // …
    }

public:

    result do_it()
    {
        static const int J = ...;
        return static_cast<growing<J>&>(*this).do_it_myself();
    }
};
```

10.4.1. String concatenation

We implement the first growing object with a sequence of ***agglomerates*** (see section 4.6.8).
Since objects involved in a single statement live at least until the end of the expression, we can think of an agglomeration of const references: the expression `(string+T1)+T2` should not return a string, but a structure containing references to the arguments (or copies, if they are small).[173]

```
template <typename T1, typename T2>
class agglomerate;

template <typename T>
agglomerate<string, const T&> operator+(const string&, const T&);174

template <typename T1, typename T2, typename T>
agglomerate< agglomerate<T1, T2>, const T&> >
    operator+(const agglomerate<T1, T2>, const T&);
```

[173] Cfr. paragraph 10.2.8
[174] The example is obviously fictitious, as we cannot really add the operator to `std::string`.

So the sum in our prototype example below would return `agglomerate< agglomerate<string, char>, const char*>`

```
std::string s = "hello";
std::string r = s + ' ' + "world!";
```

Eventually, all the work is done by a cast operator, which converts `agglomerate` to `string`:

- sum the lengths of `this->first` and `this->second` (`first` is another `agglomerate` or a string, so both have a `size()` function; `second` is a reference to the new argument)
- allocate a string of the right size
- append all the objects to the end of the string, knowing that internally no reallocation will occur.

Note that the agglomerates are built in reverse order, with respect to arguments, i.e. the object that executes the conversion holds the last argument, so it has to dump its `agglomerate` member *before* its `argument` member.

```
template <typename T, bool SMALL = (sizeof(T)<=sizeof(void*))>
struct storage_traits;

template <typename T>
struct storage_traits<T, true>
{
   typedef const T type;
};

template <typename T>
struct storage_traits<T, false>
{
   typedef const T& type;
};
```

```
// assume that T1 is string or another agglomerate
// and T2 is one of char, const char*, std::string

template <typename T1, typename T2>
class agglomerate
{
   T1 first;
   typename storage_traits<T2>::type second;

   void write(string& result) const
   {
      // member selection based on the type of 'first'
      write(result, &first);
   }

   template <typename T>
   void write(string& result, const T*) const
   {
      // if we get here, T is an agglomerate, so write recursively:
      // mind the order of functions

      first.write(result);
      result += this->second;
   }

   void write(string& result, const string*) const
   {
      // recursion terminator:
      // 'first' is a string, the head of the chain of arguments

      result = first;
   }

   size_t size()
   {
      return first.size() + estimate_length(this->second);
   }

   static size_t estimate_length(char)
   {
      return 1;
   }

   static size_t estimate_length(const char* const x)
   {
      return strlen(x);
   }

   static size_t estimate_length(const string& s)
   {
      return s.size();
   }

public:

   operator string() const
   {
      string result;
      result.reserve(size());
      write(result);
      return result;        // NVRO
   }
};
```

The first enhancement allows accumulating information in a *single pass* through the chain:

```
void write(string& result, size_t length = 0) const
{
   write(result, &first, length + estimate_length(this->second));
}

template <typename T>
void write(string& result, const T*, size_t length) const
{
   first.write(result, length);
   result += this->second;
}

void write(string& result, const string*, size_t length) const
{
   result.reserve(length);
   result = first;
}
```

```
operator string() const
{
   string result;
   write(result);
   return result;
}
```

```
std::string s = "hello";
std::string r = s + ' ' + "world!";
```

In classic C++, each call to `string::operator+` returns a different temporary object, which is simply copied, so our initial example produces two intermediate results, namely t1="hello " and t2="hello world!"; since each temporary involves a copy, this has quadratic complexity.

With C++0x language extensions, `std::string` is a moveable object; in other words, its operators will detect when an argument is a temporary object and secretly steal or reuse its resources; so the code above would actually call two very different sums, the first produces a temporary, the second detects the temporary and reuses its memory.
Conceptually, the implementation could look like:

```
std::string operator+(const std::string& s, char c)
{
   std::string result(s);
   return result += c;
}

std::string operator+(std::string&& tmp, const char* c)
{
   std::string result;
   result.swap(tmp);
   return result += c;
}
```

Or more simply:

```
std::string operator+(std::string s, char c)
{
   return s += c;
}

std::string operator+(std::string&& tmp, const char* c)
{
   return tmp += c;
}
```

In other words, C++0x string sum is identical to:

```
std::string s = "hello";

std::string r = s;
r += ' ';
r += "world!";
```

But a growing object performs even better, since it's equivalent to:

```
std::string s = "hello";

std::string r;
r.reserve(s.size()+1+strlen("world!"));
r += s;
r += ' ';
r += "world!";
```

So C++0x extensions alone will not achieve a better performance than a growing object.

10.4.2. Mutable growing objects

A growing object may be used to provide enhanced assertions:[175]

---

[175] See the article on assertions by Alexandrescu and Torjo (http://www.ddj.com/dept/cpp/184403745), which is also the source of the first sample in this paragraph

```
std::string s1, s2;
...
SMART_ASSERT(s1.empty() && s2.empty())(s1)(s2);
```

```
Assertion failed in matrix.cpp: 879412:
Expression: 's1.empty() && s2.empty()'
Values: s1 = "Wake up, Neo"
        s2 = "It's time to reload."
```

The code above may be implemented with a plain chainable `operator()`:

```
class console_assert
{
   std::ostream& out_;

   public:

      console_assert(const char*, std::ostream& out);

      console_assert& operator()(std::string& s) const
      {
         out_ << "Value = " << s << std::endl;
         return *this;
      }

      console_assert& operator()(int i) const;
      console_assert& operator()(double x) const;
      // ...
```

```
#define SMART_ASSERT(expr) \
      if (expr) {} else console_assert(#expr, std::cerr)
```

The line above starts an argument chain using `operator()`, and since it's not a growing object, *arguments must be used immediately*; but we could have a more intricate "lazy" approach:[176]

[176] For extra clarity, we omitted the information collection phase (e.g. estimation of the string length) from this example: in fact std::ostream does not need to be managed

```
template <typename T1, typename T2>
class console_assert
{
   const T1& ref_;
   const T2& next_;
   mutable bool run_;

 public:

   console_assert(const T1& r, const T2& n)
   : ref_(r), next_(n), run_(false)
   {}

   std::ostream& print() const
   {
      std::ostream& out = next_.print();
      out << "Value = " << ref_ << std::endl;
      run_ = true;
      return out;
   }

   template <typename X>
   console_assert<X, console_assert<T1, T2> > operator()(const X& x) const
   {
      return console_assert<X, console_assert<T1, T2> >(x, *this);
   }

   ~console_assert()
   {
      if (!run_)
         print();
   }
};
```

```
template < >
class console_assert<void, void>
{
  std::ostream& out_;

public:

  console_assert(const char* msg, std::ostream& out)
  : out_(out << "Assertion failed: " << msg << std::endl)
  {
  }

  std::ostream& print() const
  {
     return out_;
  }

  template <typename X>
  console_assert<X, console_assert<void, void> > operator()(const X& x) const
  {
     return console_assert<X, console_assert<void, void> >(x, *this);
  }
};
```

```
#define SMART_ASSERT(expr) \
     if (expr) {} else console_assert<void, void>(#expr, std::cerr)
```

The sample above shows that it's possible to modify the growing object from inside, stealing or passing resources through the members.
In particular, a step-by-step code expansion yields:

```
SMART_ASSERT(s1.empty() && s2.empty())(s1)(s2);
```

```
if (s1.empty() && s2.empty())
    {}
else
    console_assert<void, void>("s1.empty() && s2.empty()", std::cerr)(s1)(s2);
//  ^^^^^^^^^^^^^^^^^^^^^^^^^^^^^^^^^^^^^^^^^^^^^^^^^^^^^^^^^^^^^^^^^^^^^^^^^^^^^^^^
//  constructor of console_assert<void, void>
```

If assertion is false, three nested temporaries are created:

- T0: `console_assert<void,void>`
- T1: `console_assert<string, console_assert<void, void>>`
- T2: `console_assert<string, console_assert<string, console_assert<void, void>>>`
- `T2` is created and immediately destroyed: since `run_` is false, it invokes `print`
- `print` calls `next_.print`
  - `T0` passes its stream to `T1`
  - `T1` prints its message, sets `run_=true` and passes the stream up to `T2`
- `T2` prints its message and dies
- `T1` is destroyed, but since `run_` is true, it stays silent
- `T0` is destroyed

A specialization such as `console_assert<void,void>` is called the ***chain starter***.
Its interface might be significantly different from the general template.
The interface of the growing object usually does not depend on the number of arguments that were glued together.[177]

10.4.3. More growing objects

We generalize the pattern, implementing a generic agglomerate `chain<traits, C>`, where C is a type container; the only public constructor lies in the chain starter and the user can sum any `chain` and an argument.
For simplicity, the decision about how to store arguments in the chain (i.e. by copy or by reference) is given by a global policy:[178]

---

[177] This is not obvious at all: in the last example of paragraph 10.3, we considered an agglomerate, namely `bind_to(f)(argument)...(argument)`, whose syntax depends on the length of the chain: in fact, binding 1 argument of 4, yields a functor which takes 4-1=3 free arguments, and so on.
[178] This allows to present a simplified code; the reader can easily add a storage policy as a template template parameter

```
template <typename T>
struct storage_traits
{
   typedef const T& type;
};

template <typename T>
struct storage_traits<T*>
{
   typedef T* type;
};

template <typename T>
struct storage_traits<const T*>
{
   typedef const T* type;
};

template <>
struct storage_traits<char>
{
   typedef char type;
};
```

During the "agglomeration", a chain of length N+1 is generated by a chain of length N and a new argument: the new chain stores both and it combines some new piece of information (e.g. it sums the estimated length of the old chain with the expected length of the new argument).
Eventually, this piece of information is sent to a "target object", which then receives all the arguments in some order.
Since all these actions are parametric, we combine them in a traits class:

- `update` collects information from arguments, one at a time
- `dispatch` sends the cumulative information to the target object
- `transmit` sends actual arguments to the target object

```
struct chain_traits
{
   static const bool FORWARD = true;

   struct information_type
   {
      // ...
   };

   typedef information_type& reference;

   typedef ... target_type;

   template <typename ARGUMENT_T>
   static void update(const ARGUMENT_T&, information_type&);

   static void dispatch(target_type&, const information_type&);

   template <typename ARGUMENT_T>
   static void transmit(target_type&, const ARGUMENT_T&);
};
```

Update will be called automatically during object growth; dispatch and transmit will be called lazily if the chain is cast to or injected in a `target_type`.

First we implement the empty chain.
Analogous to the stream reference in paragraph 10.4.2 above, this class will store just the common information; additional layers of the growing object will refer to it using `traits::reference`.

```
template <typename traits_t, typename C = empty>
class chain;
```

```
template <typename traits_t>
class chain<traits_t, empty>
{
   template <typename ANY1, typename ANY2>
      friend class chain;

   typedef typename traits_t::information_type information_type;
   typedef typename traits_t::target_type target_type;

   information_type info_;

   void dump(target_type&) const
   {
   }

public:

   explicit chain(const information_type& i = information_type())
      : info_(i)
   {
   }

#define PLUS_T   \
   chain<traits_t, typename push_front<empty, T>::type>

   template <typename T>
   PLUS_T operator+(const T& x) const
   {
      return PLUS_T(x, *this);
   }

   const chain& operator >> (target_type& x) const
   {
      x = target_type();
      return *this;
   }

   operator target_type() const
   {
      return target_type();
   }
};
```

A nonempty chain instead contains:

- a data member of type `front<C>`, stored as a `storage_traits<local_t>::type`
- a chain of type `chain<pop_front<C>>`, *stored by const reference*: since C is nonempty, we can safely `pop_front` it.
- a reference to the information object; storage of `information_type` is traits-dependent: it may be a copy (when `traits_t::reference` and `traits_t::information_type` are the same), or a true reference.

The private constructor invoked by operator+ first copies the information carried by the tail chain, then it updates it with the new argument.

```
template <typename traits_t, typename C>
class chain
{
   template <typename ANY1, typename ANY2>
      friend class chain;

   typedef typename traits_t::target_type target_type;
   typedef typename front<C>::type local_t;
   typedef chain<traits_t, typename pop_front<C>::type> tail_t;

   typename storage_traits<local_t>::type obj_;
   typename traits_t::reference info_;
   const tail_t& tail_;

   void dump(target_type& x) const
   {
      tail_.dump(x);
      traits_t::transmit(x, obj_);
   }

   chain(const local_t& x, const tail_t& t)
      : obj_(x), tail_(t), info_(t.info_)
   {
      traits_t::update(x, info_);
   }

public:

   template <typename T>
   chain<traits_t,typename push_front<C,T>::type> operator+(const T& x) const
   {
      typedef chain<traits_t, typename push_front<C, T>::type> result_t;
      return result_t(x, *this);
   }

   const chain& operator >> (target_type& x) const
   {
      traits_t::dispatch(x, info_);
      dump(x);
      return *this;
   }

   operator target_type() const
   {
      target_type x;
      *this >> x;
      return x;
   }
};
```

The private `dump` member function is responsible for transmitting recursively all arguments to the target. Note that we can make the traversal parametric and reverse it with a simple boolean:

```
    void dump(target_type& x) const
    {
       if (traits_t::FORWARD)
       {
          tail_.dump(x);
          traits_t::transmit(x, obj_);
       }
       else
       {
          traits_t::transmit(x, obj_);
          tail_.dump(x);
       }
    }
```

Finally, we show an outline of the traits class for string concatenation:

```
struct string_chain_traits
{
   static const bool FORWARD = true;

   typedef size_t information_type;
   typedef size_t reference;

   typedef std::string target_type;

   template <typename ARGUMENT_T>
      static void update(const ARGUMENT_T& x, information_type& s)
   {
      s += estimate_length(x);
   }

   static void dispatch(target_type& x, const information_type s)
   {
      x.reserve(x.size()+s);
   }

   template <typename ARGUMENT_T>
      static void transmit(target_type& x, const ARGUMENT_T& y)
   {
      x += y;
   }
};
```

```
typedef chain<string_chain_traits> string_chain;
```

```
std::string q = "lo ";
std::string s = (string_chain() + "hel" + q + 'w' + "orld!");
```

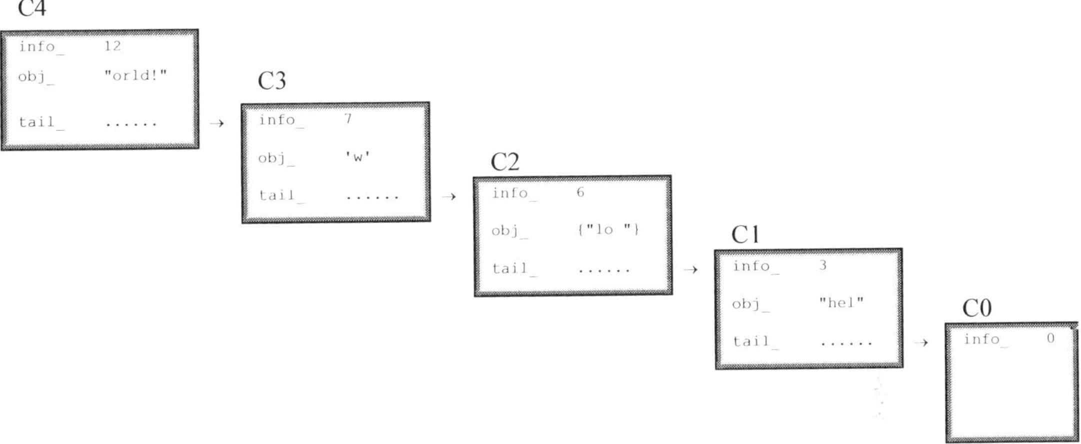

- Since we are not allowed to modify `std::string`, we have to start the chain explicitly with a default-constructed object;
- if we need some code to run only once, before a chain starts, we can put it in `information_type` constructor and begin the chain with `string_chain(argument)`
- the *storage policy* is a place where custom code may be transparently plugged-in to perform conversions: for example, to speed-up the int-to-string conversion, we could write:

```
template <>
struct storage_traits<int>
{
   class type
   {
      char data_[2+sizeof(int)*5/2];179

   public:

      type(const int i)
      {
         // perform the conversion here
         _itoa(i, data_, 10);
      }

      operator const char* () const
      {
         return data_;
      }
   };
};
```

10.4.4. Chain destruction

It may be possible to write custom code in the ***chain destructor***.
Since we have only one copy of each chain (they are linked by const references), and chain pieces are constructed in order from the first argument to the last, they will be destroyed in the reverse order, we have an opportunity to execute some finalization action at the end of the statement.

```
   ~chain()
   {
      traits_t::finalize(obj_, info_);
   }
```

```
std::string s;
std::string q = "lo ";
(string_chain() + "hel" + q + 'w' + "orld!") >> s;
```

Then the leftmost object will append "hello world!" to s with at most a single reallocation; finally, the destructors will run `finalize` in reverse order (i.e. from left to right).

If chains are stored by value, then the order of destruction is fixed (first the object, then its members), but there will be multiple copies of each sub-chain (namely, all the temporaries returned by operator+): evidently, if C1 holds a copy of C0 and C2

[179] If n is an integer of type `int_t`, the number of digits in base 10 for n is `ceil(log10(n+1))`. Assuming that a byte contains 8 bits and that `sizeof(int_t)` is even, the largest integer is `256^sizeof(int_t)-1`, and when we put this in place of n, we obtain a maximum number of `ceil(log10(256)*sizeof(int_t)) ~ (5/2)*sizeof(int_t)` digits; we add 1 for sign and 1 for the terminator.

holds a copy of C1, there are three copies of C0 and so, without some additional work, we will not know which sub-chain is being destroyed.

10.4.5. Variations of the growing object

If we have to add growing objects to a read-only class (as `std::string` should be), instead of inserting manually a chain starter, we can:

- replace the chain starter with a global function that processes the first argument (this is equivalent to promoting the empty chain's `operator+` to a function)
- switch to `operator()` for concatenation (this makes the bracket syntax uniform)

```
template <typename traits_t, typename T>
chain<traits_t, typename push_front<empty, T>::type> concatenate(const T& x)
{
   typedef chain<traits_t, typename push_front<empty, T>::type> result_t;
   return result_t(x, chain<traits_t>());
}
```

```
std::string s = concatenate("hello")(' ')("world");
```

Another variation involves the extraction of the result. Sometimes the cast operator is not desirable; we may decide to replace both = and + with the stream insertion syntax, so to write:

```
std::string s;
s << string_chain() << "hello" << ' ' << "world";
```

This is feasible, but it requires some trick to break the associativity, because the language rules will make the compiler execute:

```
(s << string_chain()) << "hello" << ' ' << "world";
^^^^^^^^^^^^^^^^^^^^
```

While we would prefer:

```
s << (string_chain() << "hello" << ' ' << "world");
     ^^^^^^^^^^^^^^^^^^^^^^^^^^^^^^^^^^^^^^^^^^^^^^
```

In the old approach the result was the last piece of information, now it's the first, so we have to modify chain and carry it around: we store a pointer to the result in the empty chain, so that it can be read only once; the unusual `operator<<` fills this pointer and then returns its *second* argument, not the first: this is the associativity-breaker.

We only sketch briefly the differences with the previous implementation:

```
template <typename traits_t, typename C = empty>
class chain;
```

```
template <typename traits_t>
class chain<traits_t, empty>
{
   // ...

   mutable target_type* result_;

public:

   // ...

   const chain& bind_to(target_type& x) const
   {
      result_ = &x;
      return *this;
   }

   target_type* release_target() const
   {
      target_type* const t = result_;
      result_ = 0;
      return t;
   }
};
```

```
template <typename traits_t>
const chain<traits_t>&
   operator<<(typename traits_t::target_type& x, const chain<traits_t>& c)
{
   return c.bind_to(&x);
}
```

```
template <typename traits_t, typename C>
class chain
{
 // ...

 target_type* release_target() const
 {
    return tail_.release_target();
 }

public:

 template <typename T>
 chain<traits_t, typename push_front<C,T>::type> operator<<(const T& x) const
 {
    typedef chain<traits_t, typename push_front<C, T>::type> result_t;
    return result_t(x, *this);
 }

 ~chain()
 {
    if (target_type* t = release_target())
       dump(*t);
 }
};
```

The last object in the chain will be destroyed first, and it will be the only one to succeed in `release_target`.

10.5. Streams

As introduced in the previous section, the stream insertion syntax is one of the most uniform, so it's visually clear, but it's flexible and open to customizations.

10.5.1. Custom Manipulators and Stream Insertion

We want to print a `bitstring` (see page 241) in the C++ way, via stream insertion. A `bitstring` implements many static interfaces at the same time.

```
class bitstring
:
   public pseudo_array<bitstring, bit_tag>,
   public pseudo_array<bitstring, nibble_tag>,
   public pseudo_array<bitstring, byte_tag>
{
```

How do we decide which of the interfaces should send its data to the stream? In other words, how can we elegantly select between bit-wise, byte-wise and nibble-wise printing?

Recall that a manipulator is an object which flows in the stream, takes the stream object and modifies its state:[180]

```
std::ostream& flush(std::ostream& o)
{
   // flush the stream, then...
   return o;
}

// a manipulator is a function pointer
// that takes and returns a stream by reference
typedef std::ostream& (*manip_t)(std::ostream&);

std::ostream& operator<<(std::ostream& o, manip_t manip)
{
   manip(o);
   return o;
}

std::cout << std::flush << "Hello World!";
```

Note that, while some objects modify permanently the state of the stream, in general the effect of a manipulator insertion is lost after the next insertion: in the above code, `cout` will need reflushing after the insertion of the string.

However nothing prevents the manipulator to return an entirely different stream: being part of a subexpression, the original stream is surely alive, so it can be wrapped in a shell that intercepts any further call to `operator<<`.

[180] Cfr. section 2.4.7 on manipulators.

```
class autoflush_t
{
   std::ostream& ref;

public:
   autoflush_t(std::ostream& r)
   : ref(r)
   {}

   template <typename T>
   autoflush_t& operator<<(const T& x)
   {
      ref << x << std::flush;
      return *this;
   }

   operator std::ostream& () const
   {
      return ref;
   }
};

autoflush_t* autoflush() { return 0; }

inline autoflush_t operator<<(std::ostream& out, autoflush_t* (*)())
{
   return autoflush_t(out);
}
```

```
std::cout << autoflush << "Hello" << ' ' << "World";
```

All insertions after `autoflush` are actually calls to `autoflush_t::operator<<`, not to `std::ostream`.
Note also that we generate a unique signature for the manipulator with the proxy itself.

A ***stream proxy*** need not be persistent; it may implement its own special insertion and a generic operator that "unwraps" the stream again if the next object is not what's expected.
Suppose we have a special formatter for `double`:

```
class proxy
{
   std::ostream& os_;

public:

   explicit proxy(std::ostream& os)
   : os_(os)
   {
   }

   std::ostream& operator<<(const double x) const
   {
      // do the actual work here
      // finally clear the effect of the manipulator, unwrapping the stream

      return os_;
   }

   // the default insertion simply reveals the enclosed stream

   template <typename T>
   std::ostream& operator<<(const T& x) const
   {
      return os_ << x;
   }
};
```

```
proxy* special_numeric() { return 0; }

inline proxy operator<<(std::ostream& os, proxy* (*)())
{
   return proxy(os);
}
```

```
std::cout
   << special_numeric << 3.14         // ok, will format a double
   << special_numeric << "hello";     // ok, the manipulator has no effect
```

If instead the template `operator<<` is omitted, then a double will be *required* after the manipulator.

To sum up, altering the return type of `operator<<` we can write manipulators that:

- have effect only on the next insertion, as long as an instance of `X` is inserted, otherwise they are ignored
- have effect only on the next insertion and require the insertion of X immediately after, otherwise there's a compiler error
- have effect on all the next insertions, until the end of the subexpression
- have effect on all the next insertions, until X is inserted:

```
   template <typename any_t>
   proxy_dumper& operator<<(const any_t& x) const
   {
      os_ << x;
      return *this;
   }
```

This is exactly the solution we need for `bitstring`: treating the static interface type tags as manipulators; insertion returns a template proxy that formats the next `bitstring` according to the (statically known) type tag, using a suitable function from the static interface itself.

```
template <typename digit_t>
class bistring_stream_proxy
{
   std::ostream& os_;

public:

   bistring_stream_proxy(std::ostream& os)
   : os_(os)
   {
   }

   std::ostream& operator<<(const pseudo_array<bitstring, digit_t>& b) const
   {
      b.dump(os_);
      return os_;
   }

   template <typename any_t>
      std::ostream& operator<<(const any_t& x) const
   {
      return os_ << x;
   }
};
```

```
inline bistring_stream_proxy<bit_t> operator<<(std::ostream& os, bit_t)
{
   return bistring_stream_proxy<bit_t>(os);
}

inline bistring_stream_proxy<octet_t> operator<<(std::ostream& os, octet_t)
{
   return bistring_stream_proxy<octet_t>(os);
}

inline bistring_stream_proxy<nibble_t> operator<<(std::ostream& os, nibble_t)
{
   return bistring_stream_proxy<nibble_t>(os);
}
```

10.5.2. Range insertion with a growing object

Another exercise is the insertion of a range into a stream: we need a custom item to start a chain

```
std::cout << range << begin << end;
```

The first proxy (returned by `std::cout << range`) takes an iterator and grows (see the previous section); the insertion of a second iterator of the same kind triggers the full dump:

```
template <typename iterator_t = void*>
class range_t
{
   std::ostream& ref_;
   iterator_t begin_;

public:

   explicit range_t(std::ostream& ref)
      : ref_(ref), begin_()
   {
   }

   range_t(range_t<> r, iterator_t i)
      : ref_(r.ref_), begin_(i)
   {
   }

   std::ostream& operator<<(iterator_t end)
   {
      while (begin_ != end)
         ref_ << *(begin_++);

      return ref_;
   }

   std::ostream& operator<<(size_t count)
   {
      while (count--)
         ref_ << *(begin_++);

      return ref_;
   }
};
```

```
range_t<>* range() { return 0; }

inline range_t<> operator<<(std::ostream& os, range<>* (*)())
{
   return range_t<>(os);
}

template <typename iterator_t>
inline range_t<iterator_t> operator<<(range_t<> r, iterator_t begin)
{
   return range_t<iterator_t>(r, begin);
}
```

The range proxy accepts a range represented either by `[begin...end)` or by `[begin, N)`; in theory it's possible to specialize even more:

```
template <typename iterator_t = void*>
class range_t
{
private:

   // ...

   void insert(iterator_t end, std::random_access_iterator_tag)
   {
      // faster algorithm here
   }

public:

   // ...

   std::ostream& operator<<(iterator_t end)
   {
      insert(end, typename iterator_traits<iterator_t>::iterator_category());
      return ref_;
   }
```

10.6. Comma chains

The comma operator is sometimes overloaded together with assignment to get some form of lazy/iterative initialization. This mimics the common C array initialization syntax:

```
int data[] = { 1,2,3 };

// equivalent to:
// data[0] = 1; data[1] = 2; data[2] = 3
```

Because of standard associativity rules, regardless of its meaning, an expression like

```
A = x, y, z;
```

is compiled as

```
(((A = x), y), z);
```

where each comma is actually a binary operator, so actually

```
((A.operator=(x)).operator,(y)).operator,(z)
```

Note the difference between this syntax and the ***growing object***: the latter associates all the items on the right side of assignment, left to right:

```
A = ((x+y)+z);
```

Here we have the opportunity to modify A iteratively, because the part of expression containing A is the first to be evaluated:

- define a proxy object `P<A>`, which contains a reference to `A`
- define `P<A>::operator,` so that it takes an argument `x`, it combines `A` and `x` and returns `*this` (i.e. the proxy itself)
- define `A::operator=(x)` as `return P<A>(*this),x`

Suppose we have a wrapper for a C array:

```
template <typename T, size_t N>
struct array
{
   scalar_t data[N];
};
```

Being a struct with public members, such an object can be initialized with the curly bracket syntax:

```
array<double, 4> a = { 1,2,3,4 };
```

However we cannot do the same on an already existing object:

```
array<double, 4> a = { 1,2,3,4 };

// ok, but now assign {5,6,7,8} to a…

const array<double, 4> b = { 5,6,7,8 };
a = b;

// is there anything better?
```

> C++0x extensions instead do allow generalized curly bracket initializations.
> However this feature is not yet available in popular compilers.
>
> Furthermore, in C++0x there is an `array` class in std namespace.

Let the assignment return a proxy with a special comma operator:

```
template <typename T, size_t N>
struct array
{
   T data[N];

private:

   template <size_t J>
   class array_initializer
   {
      array<T, N>* const pointer_;

      friend struct array<T, N>;

      template <size_t K>
      friend class array_initializer;

      array_initializer(array<T, N>* const p, const T& x)
         : pointer_(p)
      {
         MXT_ASSERT(J<N);
         pointer_->data[J] = x;
      }
```

The proxy, being the result of `operator=`, is logically affine to a reference, so it's quite natural to forbid copy and assignment declaring a member `const` (as in this case) or reference.
For convenience, the proxy is an inner class of array and its constructor is private; array itself and all proxies are friends.
Note that the constructor performs a (safe) assignment.

The proxy has a public comma operator that constructs another proxy, moving the index to the next position. Since the user expects the expression `A = x` to return a reference to A, we also add a conversion operator:

```
   class array_initializer
   {
      // ...

      public:

      array_initializer<J+1> operator, (const T& x)
      {
         return array_initializer<J+1>(pointer_, x);
      }

      operator array<T, N>& ()
      {
         return *pointer_;
      }

   }; // end of nested class
```

Finally, `array` assignment just constructs the first proxy:

```
public:

   array_initializer<0> operator=(const T& x)
   {
      return array_initializer<0>(this, x);
   }

};
```

Note that the fragment:

```
array<int, 4> A;
A = 15,25,35,45;
```

is roughly equivalent to:

```
((((A = 15),25),35),45);
```

where, as mentioned, each comma is an operator; this expression, after `array::operator=`, expands at compile time to:

```
(((array_initializer<0>(A, 15), 25), 35), 45);
```

The construction of `array_initializer<0>` sets `A[0]=15`, then `array_initializer` comma operator constructs another initializer that assigns `A[1]`, and so on.
To build a temporary `array_initializer<I>` we have to store a const pointer in a temporary on the stack, so the whole process is roughly equivalent to:

```
array<int, 4>* const P1 = &A;
P1->data[0] = 15;
array<int, 4>* const P2 = P1;
P2->data[1] = 25;
array<int, 4>* const P3 = P2;
P3->data[2] = 35;
array<int, 4>* const P4 = P3;
P4->data[3] = 45;
```

If the compiler is able to propagate the information that all assignments involve A, the code is totally equivalent to a hand-written initialization. All `const` modifiers are simply hints for the compiler to make its analysis easier.

Often comma chains exploit another language property: destruction of temporary proxy objects.
In general the problem can be formulated as: *how can a proxy know if it is the last one?*
In the previous example, we would like:

```
array<int, 4> A;
A = 15,25;                 // equivalent to {15,25,0,0}
```

But also

```
array<int, 4> A;
A = 15;                    // equivalent to {15,15,15,15} not to {15,0,0,0}
```

The expression compiles as `array_initializer<0>(&A, 15).operator,(25)`; this returns `array_initializer<1>(&A, 25)`.
The only way a proxy can transmit information to the next is via comma operator: the object can keep track of invocation and its destructor can execute the corresponding action:

```
template <size_t J>
class array_initializer
{
   array<T, N>* pointer_;        // <-- non-const

public:

   array_initializer(array<T, N>* const p, const T& x)
      : pointer_(p)
   {
      MXT_ASSERT(J<N);
      p->data[J] = x;
   }

   array_initializer<J+1> operator, (const T& x)
   {
      array<T, N>* const p = pointer_;
      pointer_ = 0;               // <-- prevent method re-execution
      return array_initializer<J+1>(p, x);
   }

   ~array_initializer()
   {
      // if operator, has not been invoked
      // then this is the last proxy in chain

      if (pointer_)
      {
         if (J == 0)
            std::fill_n(pointer_->data+1, N-1, pointer_->data[0]);
         else
            std::fill_n(pointer_->data+(J+1), N-(J+1), T());
      }
   }
};
```

Altering the semantics of destructors, in general, is risky: here, however, we assume that these objects should not be stored or duplicated, and the implementation enforces that (non-malicious) users cannot artificially prolong the life of these proxies.[181]

- Put the proxy is in a private section of `array`, so its name is inaccessible to the user.
- Declare all dangerous operators as non-const, so if a proxy is passed to a function by const reference, they cannot be invoked; a non-const reference must refer to a non-temporary variable, which is unlikely.
- Forbid copy construction.

While it is possible to perform an illegal operation, it *really* requires malicious code:

```
template <typename T>
T& tamper(const T& x)
{
    T& r = const_cast<T&>(x);
    r, 6.28;

    return r;
}
```

```
array<double, 10> A;
array<double, 10> B = tamper(A = 3.14);
```

- The argument of `tamper` is `const T&`, that can bind to any temporary, thus it defeats the name-hiding protection
- `const_cast` removes the const protection and makes the comma operator callable.
- `r.operator,(6.28)` as a side effect sets `r.pointer_ = 0`
- The returned reference is still alive when the compiler is going to construct B, but the conversion operator dereferences the null pointer.

Observe that a function like `tamper` looks harmless and may compile for every `T`.

10.7. Simulating an infix

Let's analyze the following fragment:

```
double pi = compute_PI();
assert(pi IS_ABOUT 3.14);
```

[181] Exception safety may be a dependent issue: if the destructor of a proxy performs non-trivial work, it could throw.

We will not solve the problem of comparing floats, but this paragraph will give an idea of simulating new infixes. If an expression contains operators of different priority, we can take control of the right part before we execute the left part (or vice versa): IS_ABOUT may be a macro that expands to:

```
assert(pi == SOMETHING() + 3.14);
```

SOMETHING::operator+ runs first, so we immediately capture 3.14; then a suitable operator== takes care of the left side.
Here's some code that will do:

```
template <typename float_t>
class about_t
{
   float_t value_;

public:

   about_t(const float_t value)
   : value_(value)
   {
   }

   bool operator==(const float_t x) const
   {
      const float_t delta = std::abs(value_ - x);
      return delta < std::numeric_limits<float_t>::epsilon();
   }
};
```

```
template <typename float_t>
inline bool operator==(const float_t x, const about_t<float_t> a)
{
   return a == x;
}
```

```
struct about_creator_t
{
   template <typename float_t>
   inline about_t<float_t> operator+(const float_t f) const
   {
      return about_t<float_t>(f);
   }
};
```

```
#define IS_ABOUT          == about_creator_t() +
```

Obviously, the role of + and == can be reversed, so to read the left hand side first. Note also that if all these objects belong to a namespace, the macro should qualify about_creator_t fully.

> The curious reader may wish to investigate the following algorithm, which is given without explanations:

Two numbers X and Y are given.

1) If X==Y return true
2) Check trivial cases, when one or both numbers are infinite or NAN and return accordingly
3) Pick epsilon from `std::numeric_limits`
4) Let D := |X-Y|
5) Let R = max(|X|,|Y|)
6) return R<epsilon OR D<(R*epsilon)

(a variant of the algorithm tests also D<epsilon)

#include <prerequisites>

#include <techniques>

#include <applications>

11. Refactoring

Templates can be considered a generalization of ordinary classes and functions. Often a pre-existing function or class is promoted to template, because of new software requirements; this will often save debugging time.

Be careful before adding template parameters that correspond to implementation details, because they are going to be part of the type, so objects that do not differ significantly may not be interoperable. Consider again the example from paragraph 2.4.9, a container that violates the rule above:

```
template <typename T, size_t INITIAL_CAPACITY = 0>
class special_vector;
```

It makes sense to have operators, say test equality, on any two `special_vector<double>`, regardless of their initial capacity.
In general, all member functions that are orthogonal to extra template parameters need either to be promoted to templates or to be moved to a base class.[182]
Two implementations are possible:

- `special_vector<T,N>::operator==` is a template function that takes `const special_vector<T,K>&` for any K;
- `special_vector<T,N>` inherits from a public `special_vector_base<T>`, with a protected destructor and `operator==(const special_vector_base<T>&)`.

The latter allows more flexibility: the base class should not be visible to users, but we can expose wrappers as smart pointers/references, to allow arbitrary collections of special vectors (having the same T), without risking accidental deletion.

[182] A similar debate was raised about STL allocators: the notion of "equality of two containers of the same kind" obviously requires the element sequences to be equal, but it's unclear whether this is also sufficient.

```
template <typename T>
class pointer_to_special_vector          // <-- visible to users
{
      special_vector_base<T>* ptr_;      // <-- hidden

public:

      pointer_to_special_vector(special_vector_base<T>* b = 0)
         : ptr_(b)
      {}

      special_vector_base<T>* operator->() const
      {   return ptr_; }
};
```

```
std::list< pointer_to_special_vector<double> > L;

special_vector<double, 10> S1;
special_vector<double, 20> S2;

L.push_back(&S1);
L.push_back(&S2);      // ok, even if S1 and S2 have different static type
```

11.1. Backward compatibility

A typical refactoring problem consists in modifying an existing routine, so that any caller is able to choose either the original behavior or a variation.
To begin with a rather trivial example, assume we want to (optionally) log the square of each number; so we modify our classic function template `sq`:

```
template <typename scalar_t>
inline scalar_t sq(const scalar_t& x)
{
   return x*x;
}
```

```
template <typename scalar_t, typename logger_t>
inline scalar_t sq(const scalar_t& x, logger_t logger)
{
   // ...
}
```

```
struct log_to_cout
{
   template <typename scalar_t>
   void operator()(scalar_t x, scalar_t xsq) const
   {
      std::cout << "the square of " << x << " is " << xsq;
   }
};
```

```
double x = sq(3.14);                    // not logged
double y = sq(6.28, log_to_cout());     // logged
```

The user will turn on the log passing a custom functor to the 2-argument version of `sq`: but there are different ways to implement the new function over the old one:

- ***Encapsulation***: make a call to `sq(scalar_t)` inside `sq(scalar_t, logger_t)`; this is the solution whose implementation risk is minimal.

```
template <typename scalar_t>
inline scalar_t sq(const scalar_t& x)
{
   return x*x;
}

template <typename scalar_t, typename logger_t>
inline scalar_t sq(const scalar_t& x, logger_t logger)
{
   const scalar_t result = sq(x);
   logger(x, result);
   return result;
}
```

- ***Interface adaptation***: transform `sq(scalar_t)` so to secretly call `sq(scalar_t, logger_t)` with a no-op logger; this is the most flexible solution.[183]

```
struct dont_log_at_all
{
   template <typename scalar_t>
   void operator()(scalar_t, scalar_t) const
   {
   }
}

template <typename scalar_t, typename logger_t>
inline scalar_t sq(const scalar_t& x, logger_t logger)
{
   const scalar_t result = x*x;
   logger(x, result);
   return result;
}

template <typename scalar_t>
inline scalar_t sq(const scalar_t& x)
{
   return sq(x, dont_log_at_all());
}
```

- ***Kernel macros***: when the core of the algorithm is extremely simple and needs to be shared between static and dynamic code.

```
#define MXT_M_SQ(x)    ((x)*(x))
```

[183] While encapsulation conveys to the user a "sense of overhead", interface adaptation suggests that the new `sq` is so much better and it can be used freely.

```
template <typename scalar_t>
inline scalar_t sq(const scalar_t& x)
{
   return MXT_M_SQ(x);
}
```

```
template <typename int_t, int_t VALUE>
struct static_sq
{
   static const int_t result = MXT_M_SQ(VALUE);
};
```

The use of kernel macros will be superseded by C++0x keyword `constexpr`. See the note on page 47.

The square/logging example is trivial, but code duplication is regrettably common; in many STL implementations, `std::sort` is written twice:

```
template <typename RandomAccessIter>
void sort(RandomAccessIter __first, RandomAccessIter __last);
```

```
template <class RandomAccessIter, typename Compare>
void sort(RandomAccessIter __first, RandomAccessIter __last, Compare less);
```

Using interface adaptation, the first version is a special case of the second:

```
struct weak_less_compare
{
   template <typename T1, typename T2>
   bool operator()(const T1& lhs, const T2& rhs) const
   {
      return lhs < rhs;
   }
};

template <typename RandomAccessIter>
void sort(RandomAccessIter __first, RandomAccessIter __last)
{
   return sort(__first, __last, weak_less_compare());
}
```

11.2. Refactoring Strategies

We'll consider an example problem and see some different techniques.

11.2.1. Refactoring with interfaces

A pre-existing `private_ptr` class holds in a `void*` the result of a `malloc`, and frees the memory block in the destructor:

```
class private_ptr
{
   void* mem_;

public:

   ~private_ptr()
   {
      free(mem_);
   }

   private_ptr()
      : mem_(0)
   {
   }

   explicit private_ptr(size_t size)
      : mem_(malloc(size))
   {
   }

   void* c_ptr()
   {
      return mem_;
   }
```

Now, we need to extend the class so that it can hold either a pointer to a `malloc` block, or to a `new` object of type T.
Since `private_ptr` is responsible for the allocation, we could just introduce a private interface with suitable virtual functions, create a single derived class - a template - and let `private_ptr` make the right calls:

```
class private_ptr_interface
{
public:
   virtual void* c_ptr() = 0;
   virtual ~private_ptr_interface() = 0;
};
```

```
template <typename T>
class private_ptr_object : public private_ptr_interface
{
   T member_;

public:

   private_ptr_object(const T& x)
      : member_(x)
   {
   }

   virtual void* c_ptr()
   {
      return &member_;
   }

   virtual ~private_ptr_object()
   {
   }
};
```

```
template < >
class private_ptr_object<void*> : public private_ptr_interface
{
   void* member_;

public:

   private_ptr_object(const void* x)
      : member_(x)
   {
   }

   virtual void* c_ptr()
   {
      return member_;
   }

   virtual ~private_ptr_object()
   {
      free(member_);
   }
};
```

```
class private_ptr
{
   private_ptr_interface* mem_;

public:

   ~private_ptr()
   {
      delete mem_;
   }

   private_ptr()
      : mem_(0)
   {
   }

   explicit private_ptr(size_t size)
      : mem_(new private_ptr_object<void*>(malloc(size)))
   {
   }

   template <typename T>
   explicit private_ptr(const T& x)
      : mem_(new private_ptr_object<T>(x))
   {
   }

   void* c_ptr()
   {
      return mem_->c_ptr();
   }
```

Note that virtual function calls are invisible outside `private_ptr`.

11.2.2. Refactoring with trampolines

The former approach uses two allocations to store a `void*`, one for the memory block and one for the auxiliary `private_ptr_object`. Trampolines can do better:

```
template <typename T>
struct private_ptr_traits
{
   static void del(void* ptr)
   {
      delete static_cast<T*>(ptr);
   }
};

template <typename T>
struct private_ptr_traits<T []>
{
   static void del(void* ptr)
   {
      delete [] static_cast<T*>(ptr);
   }
};

template < >
struct private_ptr_traits<void*>
{
   static void del(void* ptr)
   {
      free(ptr);
   }
};

template < >
struct private_ptr_traits<void>
{
   static void del(void*)
   {
   }
};
```

```
class private_ptr
{
   typedef   void* (*delete_t)(void*);

   delete_t del_;
   void* mem_;

public:

   ~private_ptr()
   {
      del_(mem_);
   }

   private_ptr()
      : mem_(0), del_(&private_ptr_traits<void>::del)
   {
   }

   explicit private_ptr(size_t size)
   {
      mem_ = malloc(size);
      del_ = &private_ptr_traits<void*>::del;
   }

   template <typename T>
   explicit private_ptr(const T& x)
   {
      mem_ = new T(x);
      del_ = &private_ptr_traits<T>::del;
   }

   template <typename T>
   explicit private_ptr(const T* x, size_t n)
   {
      mem_ = x;
      del_ = &private_ptr_traits<T []>::del;
   }

   void* c_ptr()
   {
      return mem_;
   }
```

11.2.3. Refactoring with accessors

Suppose we have algorithms that process a sequence of simple objects:

```
struct stock_price
{
   double price;
   time_t date;
};
```

```
template <typename iterator_t>
double computePriceIncrease(iterator_t begin, iterator_t end)
{
   return ((end-1)->price - begin->price)
         / std::difftime(begin->date, (end-1)->date) * (24*60*60);
}
```

Refactoring can be needed to allow processing data from two independent containers:

```
std::vector<double> prices;
std::vector<time_t> dates;

// now what?
```

We have several choices for the new algorithm I/O:

- assume that iterators point to `pair`, where `first` is `price` and `second` is `date` (in other words, write `end->first - begin->first`...): this in general a poor style choice, as discussed previously
- mention explicitly `begin->price` and `begin->date` (as above): the algorithm does not depend on the iterator, but the underlying type is constrained to the interface of `stock_price`.
- pass two disjoint ranges: the complexity of this solution may vary

```
template <typename iter1_t, typename iter2_t >
... (iter1_t price_b, iter1_t price_e, iter2_t date_b, iter2_t date_e)
{
   double p = *price_b;
   time_t t = *date_b;
```

- pass one range and two accessors:

```
template <typename I, typename price_t, typename date_t>
... (I begin, I end, price_t PRICE, date_t DATE)
{
   double p = PRICE(*begin);
   time_t t = DATE(*begin);
```

```
struct price_accessor
{
   double operator()(const stock_price& x) const
   {
      return x.price;
   }
};

struct date_accessor
{
   time_t operator()(const stock_price& x) const
   {
      return x.date;
   }
};

computePriceIncrease(begin, end, price_accessor(), date_accessor());
```

Note that we can trick accessors into looking elsewhere, for example in a member variable:

```
struct price_accessor_ex
{
   const std::vector<double>& v_;

   double operator()(const int x) const
   {
      return v_[x];
   }
};

struct date_accessor_ex
{
   const std::vector<time_t>& v_;

   time_t operator()(const int x) const
   {
      return v_[x];
   }
};
```

```
std::vector<double> prices;
std::vector<time_t> dates;

// ...

assert(prices.size() == dates.size());

std::vector<int> index(prices.size());
for (int i=0; i<prices.size(); ++i)
   index[i] = i;

price_accessor_ex PRICE = { prices };
date_accessor_ex DATE = { dates };

computePriceIncrease(index.begin(), index.end(), PRICE, DATE);
```

Accessors may carry around references to an external container, so they pick an element deduced from the actual argument; in some special cases, we can use pointers to avoid the creation of a container of indices: this approach however should be used with extreme care.

```
// warning: this code is not bulletproof

struct price_accessor_ex
{
   double operator()(const double& x) const
   {
      return x;
   }
};

struct date_accessor_ex
{
   const double* first_price_;
   size_t length_;
   const time_t* first_date_;

   time_t operator()(const double& x) const
   {
      if ((&x < first_price_) || (&x >= first_price_+length_))
         throw std::runtime_error("invalid reference");

      return first_date_[&x - first_price_];
   }
};
```

```
price_accessor_ex PRICE;
date_accessor_ex DATE = { &prices.front(), prices.size(), &dates.front() };

computePriceIncrease(prices.begin(), prices.end(), PRICE, DATE);
```

The algorithm takes a reference to a price and it deduces the corresponding date accordingly.

11.3. Placeholders

Every C++ object is able to execute some actions. Empty objects, such as `instance_of`, can execute meta-actions, such as declare their type and "bind" their type to a template parameter, or to a specific function overload.

Sometimes the job of TMP is to *prevent* work from being done, replacing an object with a similar empty objects, and an action with a corresponding meta-action.

We say that type P<T> is a ***placeholder for T*** if P<T> is a class whose public interface satisfies the same pre- and post-conditions as T, but has the least possible runtime cost: in the most favorable case, it does nothing at all.

11.3.1. Switch off

The switch off is an algorithm refactoring technique, which allows to selectively "turn off" some features, without rewriting or duplicating functions. The name comes from the paradigmatic situation where a function takes an object by reference, which is "triggered" during execution, and eventually returns an independent result, which is a by-product of the execution; the object may be a container that receives information during the execution, or a synchronization object.

```
void say_hello_world_in(std::ostream& out)
{
   out << "hello world";
}
```

```
double read_from_database(mutex& s)
{
   // acquire the mutex, return a value from the DB and release the mutex
}
```

A quick and elegant way to get a different result with minimal code rework is to supply a hollow object with a reduced interface and which, in particular, does not need any dynamic storage. Step by step:

- Rename original the function and promote the parameter to a template type:

```
template <typename T>
void basic_say_hello_world_in(T& o)
```

- Add an overload that restores the original behavior:

```
inline void say_hello_world_in(std::stream& o)
{
   return basic_say_hello_world_in(o);
}
```

- Finally, provide an object that "neutralizes" most of the effort:

```
struct null_ostream
{
   template <typename T>
   null_ostream& operator<<(const T&)
   {
      return *this;
   }
};
```

```
inline void say_hello_world_in()
{
   null_stream ns;
   basic_say_hello_world_in(ns);
}
```

The switch-off idiom requires exact knowledge of the (subset of the) interface of the object used in the main algorithm.

When designing a custom container, it may occasionally be useful to add an extra template parameter to enable a ***hollow-mode***: take the original class and promote it to a template:

```
class spinlock
{
  typedef void* ptr_t;
  typedef volatile ptr_t vptr_t;

public:
  spinlock(vptr_t*const);

  bool try_acquire();
  bool acquire();

  // ...
};
```

→

```
template <bool SWITCH_ON = true>
class spinlock;

template < >
class spinlock<true>
{
  typedef void* ptr_t;
  typedef volatile ptr_t vptr_t;

public:
  spinlock(vptr_t* const);

  bool try_acquire();
  bool acquire();

   // ...
};
```

```
template < >
class spinlock<false>
{
  // hollow implementation

  spinlock(void*)
  {}

  bool try_acquire()
  { return true; }

  bool acquire()
  { return true; }
```

Had the class been a template, we would just have added one more boolean parameter.

Of course, the crucial point of the duplication of the interface, is the set of cautious but meaningful default answers of the hollow class: provided that such a duplication is possible (see below for a counterexample), this also allows identifying the minimal interface for an object to be considered "valid". The interface of an object is defined by its usage.

Finally, we can restrict the program either to `spinlocks` (which may be "on" or "off")

```
template <typename ..., bool IS_LOCKING_REQURED>
void run_simulation(..., spinlock<IS_LOCKING_REQURED>& spin)
{
   if (spin.acquire())
   {
```

Or to objects of unspecified type, whose interface is implicitly assumed compatible with `spinlock`:

```
template <typename ..., typename lock_t>
void run_simulation(..., lock_t& lock)
{
    if (lock.acquire())
    {
```

Either choice is valid, but there are situations where one is preferred (see section 6.2 for more details).

Another application is ***twin reduction***: there are algorithms that manipulate either one or two items at a time, and execute the same actions simultaneously on both; to avoid duplication, we want a single implementation of the algorithm, which accepts one or two arguments.

Prototype examples are sorting two "synchronized" arrays, and matrix row reduction: this algorithm, due to Gauss, performs a sequence of elementary operations on a matrix M and brings it in diagonal (or triangular) form; if the same operations are applied in parallel on an identity matrix, it obtains also the inverse of M.[184]
So we write a general purpose function which *always takes two* matrices, of different static type, but treats them as identical:

```
template <typename matrix1_t, typename matrix2_t>
void row_reduction(matrix1_t& matr, matrix2_t& twin)
{
   /* ... */

         for (size_t k=i+1; k<ncols && pivot!=0; ++k)
         {
            matr(j, k) -= pivot*matr(i, k);
            twin(j, k) -= pivot*twin(i, k);
         }

   /* ... */

}
```

Assume that we already have a matrix class:[185]

[184] A non-mathematically inclined reader may wish to consider an analogous case: a software that executes a series of actions, and at the same time records a list of "undo" steps.
[185] We remark that frequently the interface of a data structure is remodeled for ease of algorithms. This lesson was one of the milestones of the STL design.

```
template <typename scalar_t>
class matrix
{
public:

   typedef scalar_t value_type;

   size_t rows() const;
   size_t cols() const;

   void swap_rows(const size_t i, const size_t j);

   value_type& operator()(size_t i, size_t j);
   value_type operator()(size_t i, size_t j) const;

};
```

It's not possible to extend it following the hollow-mode idiom, because there's no satisfactory default answer for functions returning a reference:[186]

```
template <typename scalar_t, bool NO_STORAGE = false>
class matrix;

template <typename scalar_t>
class matrix<scalar_t, false>
{
   /* put the usual implementation here */
};
```

```
template <typename scalar_t>
class matrix<scalar_t, true>
{
public:

   value_type& operator()(size_t i, size_t j)
   {
      return /* what? */
   }
```

So we drop entirely the reference and move down one level: we neutralize both the container and the contained object. The twin matrix is a container defined on a ***ghost scalar***, a class whose operators do nothing:

[186] As a rule, hollow containers own no memory; a reader could object that here we could put a single `scalar_t` data member, and reuse it for any pair of indices, but this strategy would consume a lot of CPU runtime, overwriting the same memory location for no purpose.

```
template <typename T>
struct ghost
{
   // all operators return *this

   ghost& operator-=(ghost)
   {
      return *this;
   }

   //…
};

template <typename T>
inline ghost operator*(T, ghost g)        { return g; }

template <typename T>
inline ghost operator*(ghost g, T)        { return g; }
```

```
template <typename scalar_t>
class matrix<scalar_t, true>
{
   size_t r_;
   size_t c_;

public:

   typedef ghost<scalar_t> value_type;

   size_t rows() const { return r_; }
   size_t cols() const { return c_; }

   void swap_rows(const size_t, const size_t) {}

   value_type operator()(size_t i, size_t j)
   {
      return value_type();
   }

   const value_type operator()(size_t i, size_t j) const
   {
      return value_type();
   }
};
```

`ghost<T>` shall be a stateless class such that every operation is a no-op: in particular, the line `twin(j, k) -= pivot*twin(i, k)` translates into a sequence of do-nothing function calls.

Some more detail on this point is needed.

11.3.2. The ghost

There's no truly satisfactory way to write ghost scalars; most implementations are semi-correct but they can be dangerous:

- o ghosts are likely to haunt our namespaces if they are not properly constrained; since their interface should support virtually all C++ operators, we will probably need to write some global operators, and we want to be sure these will appear only when necessary;

- o the main purpose of ghosts is to prevent work from being done: if G is a ghost, then G*3+7 should compile and do nothing; it's very easy to obtain an implementation that compiles, but erroneously does some work - say - casts G to 0;

A ghost should be a class template that mimics its template parameter T and it shall reside in a different namespace. We can assume for simplicity that T is a built-in numeric type, so we implement all possible operators.

```
template <typename T>
struct ghost
{
   ghost(T)   {}
   ghost()    {}
```

For coherence, comparison operators return a result compatible with the fact that `ghost` is monostate (i.e. all `ghosts` are equivalent), so `operator<` is always false and `operator==` is always true.

As a rule, most arithmetic operators can be defined with suitable macros: [187]

```
#define mxt_GHOST_ASSIGNMENT(OP)                                    \
      ghost& operator OP##= (const ghost) { return *this; }

#define mxt_GHOST_UNARY(OP)                                         \
      ghost operator OP() const { return *this; }

#define mxt_GHOST_INCREMENT(OP)                                     \
      ghost& operator OP () { return *this; }                       \
      const ghost operator OP (int) { return *this; }
```

```
template <typename T>
struct ghost
{
   ghost(const T&){}
   ghost()    {}

   mxt_GHOST_INCREMENT(++);    // defines pre- and post-increment
   mxt_GHOST_INCREMENT(--);

   mxt_GHOST_ASSIGNMENT(+);    // defines operator+=
   mxt_GHOST_ASSIGNMENT(-);
   // ...

   mxt_GHOST_UNARY(+);
   mxt_GHOST_UNARY(-);
```

[187] Mind the usage of token concatenation `##`: one would be tempted to write `operator ## OP` to join `operator` and `+` but this is illegal, because in C++ `operator` and `+` are two different tokens; vice versa `##` is required between `+` and `=` to generate `operator +=`, so we will write `operator OP ## =`

For the arithmetic/comparison operators, we need to investigate the possibilities:

- member operators with argument `ghost<T>`
- member operators with argument `T`
- `template <typename X>` member operators with argument `const X&`
- nonmember operators, such as

```
template <typename T>
ghost<T> operator+(ghost<T>, ghost<T>)          // variant #1
```

```
template <typename T>
ghost<T> operator+(T, ghost<T>)                 // variant #2
```

```
template <typename T1, typename T2>
<???> operator+(ghost<T1>, ghost<T2>)           // variant #3
```

```
template <typename T1, typename T2>
<???> operator+(T1, ghost<T2>)                  // variant #4
```

Each choice has some problems.

- Member operators will perform argument promotion on the right side, but ***template global operators*** require a perfect match for argument deduction[188]: with member operators `ghost<T>::operator+(ghost<T>) const`, any sum of the form `ghost<T> + X` will succeed whenever it's possible to build a temporary `ghost<T>` from `X` (since ghost constructor is not explicit), vice versa `X + ghost<T>` will not compile.
- The problem is mostly evident when `T` is a numeric type (say, `double`) and `X` is a literal zero: member `operator+` will take care of `ghost<double> + 0`, since 0 (int) → 0.0 (double) → `ghost<double>`, but `0 + ghost<double>` must be handled by a global operator, whose signature cannot be too strict, as 0 is not a double.
- This implies in our case that only variant #4 is feasible, because no other operator would match exactly `(int, ghost<double>)`.
- However, we want operators to match as many types as possible, but not more; while we should be able to write `int + ghost<double>`, we don't want to accept *anything*

[188] The user-defined constructor that converts `T` to `ghost<T>` is considered only after template argument deduction. Note that the constructor here is not even `explicit`. See [2], section B.2

```
ghost<double> g;

g + 0;              // should work
0 + g;              // should work

std::cout + g;      // should not work!
g + std::cout;      // should not work!
```

As a rule, the global operator should delegate the execution to a member function:

```
template <typename T1, typename T2>
inline ghost<T2> operator+ (T1 x, const ghost<T2> y)
{
   return y + x;
}
```

`y + x` is indeed a call to any member `operator+`, so we pass to the ghost's own interface the responsibility for accepting T1 as argument (the compiler will try all overloaded `operator+`).

A conversion operator is necessary to make assignments legal:

```
   operator T() const
   {
      return T();
   }
```

```
ghost<double> g = 3.14;
double x = g;        // error: cannot convert from ghost to double
```

Conversely, with the conversion operator and a bad implementation of operators, innocuous code will become suddenly ambiguous:

```
ghost<double> g;
g + 3.14;
```

For example, there may be an ambiguity between:

- promotion of 3.14 to `ghost<double>`, followed by `ghost<double>::operator+(ghost<double>)`
- conversion of `g` to double, followed by ordinary sum

Since both paths have equal rank, the compiler will give up.
In different situations, the conversion will be unexpectedly called:

```
ghost<double> g = 3.14;
double x = 3*g + 7;
```

should be translated by the compiler into the sequence

```
double x = (double)(operator*(3, g).operator+(ghost<double>(7)));
```

If the global `operator*` cannot be called for any reason (say, it expects `double,ghost<double>`, so it won't match), the code is still valid, but it silently executes something different:

```
double x = 3*(double)(g) + 7;
```

This costs two floating-point operations at runtime, so it defeats the ghost purpose.[189]

Summing up, the best implementation:

- ghost constructor is strongly typed, so it needs one argument convertible to T
- we need both member and non-member operators
    - member operators will accept any argument (i.e. any type X), and check X with a static assertion (using the constructor itself)
    - non-member operators will blindly delegate anything to member functions

We describe an implementation without making use of macros; anyway, functions generated by the same preprocessor directive have been grouped:

[189] Hint: always leave a breakpoint in the conversion operator...

```
#define mxt_GHOST_GUARD(x)        sizeof(ghost<T>(x))


template <typename T>
struct ghost
{
   ghost(const T&)    {}

   ghost()    {}

   operator T() const
   {
      return T();
   }

   ghost& operator ++ () { return *this; }
   const ghost operator ++ (int) { return *this; }

   ghost& operator -- () { return *this; }
   const ghost operator -- (int) { return *this; }


   template <typename X> ghost& operator += (const X& x)
   { mxt_GHOST_GUARD(x); return *this; }

   template <typename X> ghost& operator -= (const X& x)
   { mxt_GHOST_GUARD(x); return *this; }


   template <typename X> ghost operator + (const X& x) const
   { mxt_GHOST_GUARD(x); return *this; }

   template <typename X> ghost operator - (const X& x) const
   { mxt_GHOST_GUARD(x); return *this; }


   template <typename X> bool operator == (const X& x) const
   { mxt_GHOST_GUARD(x); return true; }

   template <typename X> bool operator != (const X& x) const
   { mxt_GHOST_GUARD(x); return false; }

   ghost operator +() const { return *this; }

   ghost operator -() const { return *this; }
};


template <typename T1, typename T2>
ghost<T2> operator + (const T1& x, const ghost<T2> y) { return y + x; }

template <typename T1, typename T2>
ghost<T2> operator - (const T1& x, const ghost<T2> y) { return -(y - x); }

template <typename T1, typename T2>
bool operator == (const T1& x, const ghost<T2> y) { return y == x; }

template <typename T1, typename T2>
bool operator != (const T1& x, const ghost<T2> y) { return y != x; }
```

12. Debugging Templates

As TMP code induces the compiler to perform calculations, it's virtually impossible to follow it step by step. However there are some techniques that help.
This chapter in fact contains a mix of pieces of advice and debugging strategies.

12.1. Identify types

Modern debuggers will always show the exact type of variables when the program is stopped.
Moreover, a lot of information about types is visible in the call stack, where (member) functions usually are displayed with their full list of template arguments.

However, we often need to inspect intermediate results and return types.
The following function helps:

```
template <typename T>
void identify(T, const char* msg = 0)
{
   std::cout << (msg ? msg : "") << typeid(T).name() << std::endl;
}
```

While debugging lambda expressions, we may want to check if the return type has been correctly deduced, so we add a small (public) data member:

```
template <typename X1, typename F, typename X2>
class lambda_binary : public lambda< lambda_binary<X1,F,X2> >
{
   // ...

   typedef typename
   deduce_argument
   <
      typename X1::argument_type,
      typename X2::argument_type
   >::type
   argument_type;

#ifdef MXT_DEBUG
   instance_of<result_type> RESULT_;
#endif
```

```
    result_type operator()(argument_type x1, argument_type x2) const
    {
       identify(RESULT_);
       return f_(x1_(x1, x2), x2_(x1, x2));
    }
```

In general, whenever a metafunction compiles but gives the wrong results, add members of type `instance_of` and `static_value` to inspect intermediate steps of the computation, then create *a local instance* of the metafunction on the stack.

```
template <size_t N>
struct fibonacci
{
   static const size_t value = fibonacci<N-1>::value + fibonacci<N-2>::value;

   static_value<size_t, value> value_;
   fibonacci<N-1> prev1_;
   fibonacci<N-2> prev2_;
};
```

```
int main()
{
   fibonacci<12> F;
```

Then look at F in the debugger: you can inspect the constants from their type.

12.1.1. Trapping types

Sometimes in large projects, an erroneous pattern is detected and we need to list all the code lines where this pattern is used. We can use templates to create *function traps* that do not compile, and inject them in the error pattern, so that the compiler log itself will point to all the lines we are looking for.
Suppose for a moment that we discover that a `std::string` is passed to `printf` and we suspect this happens several times in the project.

```
    std::string name = ...;
    printf("Hello %s", name);    // should be: name.c_str()
```

Brute-force iteration through all occurrences of `printf` would take too much time, so we add some trap code in some common included file:

```
template <typename T>
void validate(T)
{
}

void validate(std::string)
{
   static_assert(false, "don't pass string to printf");
}
```

```
template <typename T1>
void printf_trap(const char* s, T1 a)
{
   validate(a);
}

template <typename T1, typename T2>
void printf_trap(const char* s, T1 a, T2 b)
{
   validate(b);
   printf_trap(s, a);
}

template <typename T1, typename T2, typename T3>
void printf_trap(const char* s, T1 a, T2 b, T3 c)
{
   validate(c);
   printf_trap(s, a, b);
}

// ...
```

```
#define printf printf_trap
```

This trap code will cause a compiler error every time a string is passed to `printf`; A necessary condition is to be able to mention `std::string` (in validate), so the file above must include `<string>`. But if we are testing some user class, this may not be feasible (including project headers might cause loops), so just replace the explicit validation test with a generic SFINAE static assertion:

```
template <typename T>
void validate(T)
{
   static_assert(!is_class<T>::value, "don't pass classes to printf");
}
```

12.1.2. Incomplete types

Class templates may or may not require that T is a complete type.
This requirement is usually not explicit, and it depends on implementation details.

STL containers, such as vector, list and set, can be implemented so to accept incomplete types, because they allocate storage dynamically: a necessary and sufficient condition to decide if T may be incomplete is to put in a class a container of itself.

```
struct S1
{
   double x;
   std::vector<S1> v;
};

struct S2
{
   double x;
   std::list<S2> l;
};
```

In particular an *allocator* should not assume that T is complete, otherwise it might be incompatible with standard containers.

A static assertion is easily obtained taking the size of a type:

```
template <typename T>
struct must_be_complete
{
   static const size_t value = sizeof(T);
};
```

```
struct S3
{
   double x;
   must_be_complete<S3> m;
};
```

```
test.cpp: error C2027: use of undefined type 'S3'
```

This is used to implement *safe deletion*: a pointer to an incomplete type may be deleted, and this causes undefined behavior (in the best case, T's destructor won't be executed).

```
template <typename T>
void safe_delete(T* p)
{
     typedef T must_be_complete;
     sizeof(must_be_complete);
     delete x;
}
```

Determining if a template will get a complete type as argument may not be easy. Standard allocators have a `rebind` member that allows any `allocator<T>` to create `allocator<X>`, and different implementations will take advantage of the feature to construct their own private data structures: a container, say `std::list<T>`, may need `allocator< node<T> >` and *this* class may be incomplete.

```
template <typename T>
class allocator
{
   typedef T* pointer;

   template <typename other_t>
   struct rebind
   {
      typedef allocator<other_t> other;
   };
```

```
template <typename T, typename allocator_t>
struct list
{
   struct node;
   friend struct node;

   typedef
    typename allocator_t::template rebind<node>::other::pointer node_pointer;

   // the line above uses allocator<node> when node is still incomplete

   struct node
   {
      node(node_pointer ptr)
      {
      }
   };
```

To compile `node` constructor, `node_pointer` is needed; so the compiler looks at `allocator ::rebind<node>::other`, which is in fact `allocator<node>`.

Suppose now we have an efficient class that manages "atoms" of memory of fixed length N:

```
template <size_t N>
class atomic_pool;
```

To wrap it correctly in a generic allocator we cannot write simply:

```
template <typename T>
class pool_allocator
{
   static atomic_pool<sizeof(T)>& get_storage();
```

The presence of `sizeof(T)` at class level requires T to be complete.
Instead we switch to a lazy instantiation scheme with a template member function:

```
template <typename T>
class pool_allocator
{
   template <typename X>
   static atomic_pool<sizeof(X)>& get_storage()
   {
      static atomic_pool<sizeof(X)>& p = *new atomic_pool<sizeof(X)>;
      return p;
   }

   // ...

   void deallocate(pointer ptr, size_type)
   {
      get_storage<T>().release(ptr);
   }
```

Now, at class level `sizeof(T)` is never mentioned.

> As pointed out in paragraph 10.14 of [7], there's a difference between stack and heap allocation:
>
> ```
> static T& get()
> {
>    static T x;
>    return x;
> }
> ```
>
> and
>
> ```
> static T& get()
> {
>    static T& x = *new T;
>    return x;
> }
> ```
>
> The former will destroy x at some unspecified moment at the end of the program, while the latter never destroys x.
> So, if `T::~T()` releases a mutex, the first version is the right one; however if the destructor of another global object invokes `get()`, it might be that x has already been destroyed (a problem known as "static initialization order fiasco").

12.2. Integer computing

We quickly review some problems that static integer computations may cause.

12.2.1. Signed and unsigned types

Common issues may arise from the differences between T(-1), -T(1), T()-1, ~T() when T is an integer type.

- If T is unsigned and large, they are all identical.
- If T is signed, the first three are identical.

- o If T is unsigned and small, the second and the third expressions may give unexpected results.

Let's borrow a function from the implementation of `is_signed_integer` (cfr. section 5.3.2).

```
template <typename T>
static selector<(T(0) > T(-1))> decide_signed(static_value<T, 0>*);
```

Replace T(-1) with -T(1) and suddenly two regression tests fail: (which?)

```
bool t01 = (!is_signed_integer<unsigned char>::value);
bool t02 = (!is_signed_integer<unsigned int>::value);
bool t03 = (!is_signed_integer<unsigned long long>::value);
bool t04 = (!is_signed_integer<unsigned long>::value);
bool t05 = (!is_signed_integer<unsigned short>::value);

bool t11 = (is_signed_integer<char>::value);
bool t12 = (is_signed_integer<int>::value);
bool t13 = (is_signed_integer<long long>::value);
bool t14 = (is_signed_integer<long>::value);
bool t15 = (is_signed_integer<short>::value);
```

The reason for failure is that unary negation of small unsigned integers returns `int`, so `-T(1)` is `int` and the whole comparison is promoted to `int`, where `0 > -1` is true. To see this, execute:

```
unsigned short u = 1;
identify(-u);
```

12.2.2. References to numeric constants

As a rule, don't pass static constants to functions directly:

```
struct MyStruct
{
   static const int value = 314;
}

double myarray[MyStruct::value];
std::fill_n(myarray, MyStruct::value, 3.14);      // not recommended
```

If `fill_n` takes an argument by const reference, then the code above may fail *linking*, because a compiler could be taking the address of the constant, an operation that requires the constant to be redeclared in the .cpp file (as for any other static member), and in TMP this is never the case.

As a cheap workaround, build a temporary and initialize it with the constant:

```
std::fill_n(myarray, int(MyStruct::value), 3.14);      // usually ok
```

12.3. Common workarounds

12.3.1. Debugging SFINAE

A common "cut & paste" error is the addition of a useless non-deducible template parameter to a function: sometimes, the compiler will complain, but if the function is overloaded, the SFINAE principle will silently exclude it from overload resolution and this will generally lead to subtle errors:

```
   template <typename X, size_t N>
   static YES<[condition on X]> test(X*);

   static NO test(...);
```

In the fragment above, N cannot be deduced, thus the second test function will always be selected.

12.3.2. Trampolines

Compiler limitations may affect trampolines; in classic C++, local classes have some limitation (they cannot bind to template parameters). They may cause spurious compiler and linker errors:

```
template <typename T>
struct MyStruct
{
   template <typename X>
   void doSomething(const X& m)
   {
      struct local
      {
         static T* myFunc(const void* p)
         {
            // compilers may have problems here using X
         }
      };

      // going to call local::myFunc(&m);
```

The workaround is to move most of template code outside of the local class:

```
template <typename T>
struct MyStruct
{
   template <typename X>
   static T* myFunc(const X& m)
   {
      // do the work here
   }

   template <typename X>
   void doSomething(const X& m)
   {
      struct local
      {
         static T* myFunc(const void* p)
         {
            // put nothing here, just a cast
            return MyStruct<T>::myFunc(*static_cast<const X*>(p));
         }
      };

      // ...
```

12.3.3. Compiler bugs

Compiler bugs are rare, but occur, especially within template metaprogramming, and usually produce obscure diagnostics:

```
test2003.cpp(80) : error C2365: 'function-parameter' : redefinition; previous definition was a
'template parameter'
        test2003.cpp(80) : see declaration of 'function-parameter'
```

Compilers get confused by templates, when:

- they cannot deduce that an expression is a type
- they don't perform automatic conversion correctly, or in the right order, so they emit incorrect diagnostics
- some language keywords may not work correctly in a static context

Here is an example of this last statement: `sizeof` will usually complain if an expression is invalid; for example we cannot dereference a `double`:

```
   sizeof(**static_cast<double*>(0));
```

```
test.cpp: error: illegal indirection
```

The same compiler will instead accept the same code inside a template: oddly, SFINAE does not trigger and the compiler will run *the first* test (a function whose return type... does not exist).[190]

[190] `decltype` suffers from similar issues

```
template <size_t N>
struct dummy
{
};

template <typename X>
dummy<sizeof(**static_cast<X*>(0))>* test(X*)
{
   return 0;
}

char test(...)
{
   return 0;
}
```

```
double x;
test(&x);
```

The next example instead is due to implicit conversions:

```
double a[1];
double b[1];
double (&c)[1] = true ? a : b;
```

```
test.cpp: error: 'initializing' : cannot convert from 'double *' to 'double (&)[1]'
        A reference that is not to 'const' cannot be bound to a non-lvalue
```

Thus we see that the compiler is erroneously converting the array to pointer in the ternary operator.
Here it *might happen* that promoting the function to template, it just works:

```
template <typename T>
void f()
{
   T a;
   T b;
   T& c = true ? a : b;
}
```

```
f<double [1]>();
```

Ensuring *portability* is a non-trivial development effort: portability means "code that works"; standard conformance means "code that works, given a bug-free compiler".
In C++ there's no "reference compiler" that builds successfully if and only if the code is correct according to the Standard.[191]

[191] The closest entity is possibly the compiler from Greg Comeau, which is kindly made available online. See http://www.comeaucomputing.com/tryitout

On the opposite, there exist many proprietary extensions to the language, or simply some subtle nonstandard behavior, so that minor syntax errors will be silently ignored (such as `this->` or the use of `::template`), and even some ambiguities will be resolved (e.g. static casts of objects with multiple bases).

If code that looks correct does not compile, it may help to:

- simplify a complex type introducing extra typedefs, or vice versa.
- promote a function to template or vice versa
- if code is sufficiently portable, test a different compiler

13. C++0x

"I note that every C++0x feature has been implemented by someone somewhere"
Bjarne Stroustrup

We discuss only a minimal subset of C++0x features, whose "ease of implementation" for compiler vendors makes them unlikely to change or disappear. Unfortunately, major compilers do not offer yet a consistent set of features, but some of the forthcoming language features that have an impact on TMP are already being implemented, as they come almost for free: the new compilers just make some of their private information available interactively to the source code.

The simplest example is the metafunction `std::has_trivial_destructor<T>`, introduced by tr1.
It's not possible to detect if a type has a trivial destructor by language only: the default implementation, when there's no specific support, is: "false, unless T is a native type", but obviously the correct information is known by the compiler.
As a rule, metafunctions may return the wrong value, when "wrong" means "suboptimal": if a class destructor is known to be trivial, then the code will likely skip some unnecessary steps; a default assumption "no destructor is trivial" may be fine, it will slow the program, but it won't make it wrong.

13.1. type_traits

Some compilers already offer a complete set of metafunctions:

```
#include <type_traits>
```

This will bring some metafunctions in namespace `std` or `std::tr1` (depending on the compiler and the standard library). They are described in the freely downloadable "Draft Technical Report on C++ Library Extensions".[192]

In particular, some metafunctions that were described in this book are present in C++0x, with a different name:

[192] In a search engine, it can be found by filename: n1836.pdf

C++0x equivalent	This book
integral_constant	static_value
enable_if	only_if
conditional	typeif
is_convertible	has_conversion
...	...

13.2. Decltype

Similarly to `sizeof`, `decltype` resolves to the type of the C++ expression given in brackets, and we may put it wherever a type is required.

```
int a;
double b;

decltype(a+b) x = 0;        // x is double
```

The expression is not evaluated.

`decltype` can have a positive impact on SFINAE. The following metafunction detects correctly a `swap` member function, testing the expression `x.swap(x)`, where `x` is a non-constant reference to `X`.
Since `swap` usually returns `void`, we use pointer-to-decltype for types that pass the test, and a non-pointer class for the rest; then we cast this to yes/no as usual:

```
#define REF_TO_X    (*static_cast<X*>(0))

struct dummy {};

template <typename T>
struct has_swap
{
   template <typename X>
   static decltype(REF_TO_X.swap(REF_TO_X))* test(X*);

   static dummy test(...);


   template <typename X>
   static yes_type cast(X*);

   static no_type cast(dummy);


   static const bool value = sizeof( cast(test((T*)0)) )==sizeof(yes_type);
};
```

13.3. Auto

The keyword `auto` has a new meaning in C++0x, it is used to declare a local variable, which needs to be initialized immediately; the initialization object is used to deduce the actual type of the variable, exactly as it happens for template parameters:

```
auto i = 0;
```

The actual type of `i` is the same as the template deduced from the call `f(0)`, where `f` would be:

```
template <typename auto>
void f(auto i);
```

The left side of the expression need not be a value:

```
const auto& i = cos(0.0);
```

`auto` will resolve to `double`, because that's what would happen calling `g(cos(0.0))`, with

```
template <typename auto>
void g(const auto& i);
```

Remember that a generic template parameter will not match a reference:

```
int& get_ref();

template <typename T>
void f(T x);

f(get_ref());        // T = int, not reference-to-int
```

So in particular, `auto` will always resolve to a value type; this is a nice feature, because its intended use is to actually store results. On the opposite, `decltype` returns the exact static type of an expression, as defined:

```
int i = 0;
decltype(get_ref()) j = i;      // j is reference-to-int
```

13.4. Lambdas

Lambda expressions ("lambdas" in short) provide a concise way to create simple function objects.
It's not a new language feature, but rather a new syntax:

```
[](int i) { return i<7; }
```

```
[](double x, double y) { return x>y; }
```

Each line represents an *instance* of an object of type "functor" (called ***closure***) taking one or more arguments and returning `decltype(return statement)`; so we can pass this object to algorithms:

```
std::partition(begin, end, [](int i) { return i<7; });
```

```
std::sort(begin, end, [](double x, double y) { return x>y; });
```

This obviously is equivalent to the more verbose:

```
struct LessThan7
{
   bool operator()(int i) const
   {
      return i<7;
   }
};
```

```
std::partition(begin, end, LessThan7());
```

The brackets [] are called ***lambda introducers***, and they can be used to list local variables that we want "captured", which means added to the functor as members: in the example that follows, the closure gets a copy of N (the introducer [&N] would pass a reference).

```
int N = 7;

std::partition(begin, end, [N](int i) { return i<N; });
```

There are some more syntax details: if the body of a lambda is longer than a single statement, the return type must be explicitly specified after the argument list.

```
[](int i) -> bool { ... }
```

Closures can be stored using `auto`:

```
auto F = [](double x, double y) { return cos(x*y); }
```

The following example (due to Stephan T. Lavavej) shows that lambdas can interact with template parameters: here a lambda is used to perform the logical negation of an unspecified unary predicate.

```
template <typename T, typename Predicate>
void keep_if(vector<T>& v, Predicate pred)
{
    auto notpred = [&pred](const T& t) { return !pred(t); };

    v.erase(remove_if(v.begin(), v.end(), notpred), v.end());
}
```

13.5. Initializers

If a function has a long return type, then we may be forced to write it twice, both in the function signature and when building the result: this redundancy is likely to cause maintenance and refactoring problems.

```
      template <typename X>
      console_assert<X, console_assert<T1, T2> > operator()(const X& x) const
      {
         return console_assert<X, console_assert<T1, T2> >(x, *this);
      }
```

In classic TMP, this is avoided with non-explicit single-argument constructors:

```
template <...>
class console_assert
{
   public:
      console_assert(int = 0) {}
};
```

```
      template <typename X>
      console_assert<X, console_assert<T1, T2> > operator()(const X& x) const
      {
         return 0;    // much better!
      }
```

In C++0x, a new language feature called *braced-init-list* allows building an object using curly brackets and omitting the type name:

```
std::pair<const char*, double> f()
{
   return { "hello", 3.14 };
}
```

```
     template <typename X>
     console_assert<X, console_assert<T1, T2> > operator()(const X& x) const
     {
        return { x, *this };
     }
```

The compiler will match the items in the initializer list against the arguments of all constructors and pick the best, according to the overload resolution rules.

14. Exercises

In all the following problems, you can freely modify the single file where the template code resides, or add more files; the rest of the project is read-only.

14.1.1. Extension

A function template is given:

```
template <typename T>
void f(T x)
{
   printf("hello T");
}
```

- Add another overload that is to be called for every class that derives from BASE and prints “hello BASE-or-derived”.
- Ensure that your solution is robust: change the return type of `f` to `int` and see if your solution still holds
- Ensure that your solution is robust: add a plain function – say `int f(double x)` – in the same file and see if compilation fails
- Think of an alternative solution that minimizes the changes to existing code

14.1.2. Integer

The following code:

```
template <typename T>
uint32 f(T x) { … }
```

```
// …
printf("%x", f(a));
```

emitting a warning: return type of f is incompatible with %x.

- What kind of investigation would you perform?

14.1.3. Date format

Following paragraph 8.7.1, implement a constant generator with an even more natural syntax, such as:

```
   YYYYMMDD = dateformat<'Y','Y',Y','Y','M','M','D','D'>::value
```

Or

```
YYYYMMDD = dateformat<'Y','Y',Y','Y','/','M','M','/','D','D'>::value
```

14.1.4. Specialization

A template class is given:

```
template <typename T>
class X
{ /* very long implementation... */ };
```

Modify `X` so that precisely `X<double>` has an additional data member (say, `int`) and an extra member function, but perform minimal changes to existing code (so if the source file is under a version control software, the differences are self-explanatory).

14.1.5. is_prime<N>

As an exercise for debugging techniques, we present an example of a non-trivial metafunction `is_prime<N>::value`.
The reader is expected to be able to understand the code, at least in principle, even if some of the algorithm details are not known.

```
#define mxt_EXPLICIT_VALUE(CLASS, TPAR, VALUE)      \
template <> struct CLASS<TPAR> { static const size_t value = VALUE; }
```

```
template <size_t N>
struct wheel_prime;

mxt_EXPLICIT_VALUE(wheel_prime, 0,  7);
mxt_EXPLICIT_VALUE(wheel_prime, 1, 11);
mxt_EXPLICIT_VALUE(wheel_prime, 2, 13);
mxt_EXPLICIT_VALUE(wheel_prime, 3, 17);
mxt_EXPLICIT_VALUE(wheel_prime, 4, 19);
mxt_EXPLICIT_VALUE(wheel_prime, 5, 23);
mxt_EXPLICIT_VALUE(wheel_prime, 6, 29);
mxt_EXPLICIT_VALUE(wheel_prime, 7, 31);
```

```
template <size_t A>
struct nth_tentative_prime
{
   static const size_t value = 30*((A-3)/8) + wheel_prime<(A-3) % 8>::value;
};

mxt_EXPLICIT_VALUE(nth_tentative_prime, 0, 2);
mxt_EXPLICIT_VALUE(nth_tentative_prime, 1, 3);
mxt_EXPLICIT_VALUE(nth_tentative_prime, 2, 5);
```

```
template
<
   size_t A,
   size_t N,
   size_t K = nth_tentative_prime<N>::value,
   size_t M = (A % K)
>
struct is_prime_helper
{
   static const bool EXIT = (A < MXT_M_SQ(K));
   static const size_t next_A = (EXIT ? 0 : A);
   static const size_t next_N = (EXIT ? 1 : N+1);
};

template <size_t A, size_t N, size_t K>
struct is_prime_helper<A, N, K, 0>
{
   static const size_t next_A = 0;
   static const size_t next_N = 0;
};
```

```
template <size_t A, size_t N = 0>
struct is_prime
: is_prime<is_prime_helper<A, N>::next_A, is_prime_helper<A, N>::next_N>
{
};

template <> struct is_prime<0, 0> { static const bool value = false;  };
template <> struct is_prime<0, 1> { static const bool value = true;   };
template <> struct is_prime<1, 0> { static const bool value = true;   };
template <> struct is_prime<2, 0> { static const bool value = true;   };
```

15. Bibliography

[1] Alexandrescu A., "Modern C++ Design", Addison-Wesley
[2] Vandevoorde, D. and Josuttis, N., "C++ Templates: The Complete Guide", Addison-Wesley
[3] Abrahams D. and Gurtovoy A., "C++ Template Metaprogramming", Addison-Wesley
[4] Sutter H., "Exceptional C++ Style", Addison-Wesley
[5] Wilson, "Imperfect C++", Addison-Wesley
[6] Austern M., "Generic Programming and the STL", Addison-Wesley
[7] Cline M., "C++ FAQ (lite)", http://www.parashift.com
[8] Meyers S., "Effective STL"
[9] Coplien, J., "Curiously Recurring Template Patterns", C++ Report, February 1995, pp. 24-27.
[10] Stroustrup, B., "Design and Evolution of C++", Addison-Wesley, Reading, MA, 1993.
[11] Barton, J.J. and Nackman L.R., "Scientific and Engineering C++", Addison-Wesley, Reading, MA, 1994.
[12] Veldhuizen, T. "Expression Templates", C++ Report, June 1995, reprinted in http://oonumerics.org/blitz/papers/
[13] Veldhuizen, T., "Techniques for Scientific C++", Indiana University Computer Science Technical Report #542, Version 0.4, August 2000
[14] Myers N., "A New and Useful Template Technique: Traits", C++ Report, June 1995, http://www.cantrip.org/traits.html
[15] C++ 0x Final Committee Draft http://www.open-std.org/jtc1/sc22/wg21/docs/papers/2010/n3092.pdf
[16] Meucci, A. "Risk and Asset Allocation", Springer 2005

16. Table of contents